FEENIN

Duke University Press
Durham and London
2023

ALEXANDER GHEDI WEHELIYE

ENIN

R&B MUSIC AND THE MATERIALITY OF BLACKFEM VOICES AND TECHNOLOGY

CONTENTS

A playlist is available on the Spotify streaming service:
http://bit.ly/3ZhcOzg.

Good day in my mind, safe to take a step out
Get some air now, let your edge out
Too soon, I spoke, you be heavy in my mind
Can you get the heck out?
I need rest now, got me bummed out
You so, you so, you, baby, baby, babe
I've been on my empty mind shit
I try to keep from losin' the rest of me
I worry that I wasted the best of me on you, baby
You don't care
Said, not tryna be a nuisance, it's just urgent
Tryna make sense of loose change
—SZA, "Good Days" (2020)

GOOD DAYS

R&B Music and Critical Fabulation
in the Frequencies of the Now

December 26, 2020. Chicago, Illinois: The second wave (of what will turn out to be many) of high numbers of coronavirus infections, resultant hospitalizations, and deaths has overtaken most of the United States as well as many other parts of the globe. It also happens to be the day after the release of SZA's "Good Days," which I play on a continuous loop, streaming it on repeat without realizing until later that I'm already on my tenth listen of the day. Over the next few months, I will engage this song a few hundred more times. Though I obsessively lent my ears to Jazmine Sullivan's "Lost One" over the preceding six weeks, because I was happy about Sullivan's first publicly available recording after five years of radio silence and because the song gave shape to some of my feelings about the sudden death of a very close friend, there was something different about Solána Imani Rowe's (SZA's government name) latest release, with its soothingly foraging and baroque-sounding acoustic guitar loop, tender yet persistent drums, sampled seagull noises, intermittently undecipherable lyrics due to SZA's unique delivery, and extended outro with the following reiterated mantra: "Always in my mind, always in my mind, mind."[1] These lines succinctly encapsulated in the form of a gorgeous four-minute, thirty-nine-second R&B song the preceding nine months, during which life took place for many almost exclusively in their minds and on their screens, that is, if life occurred at all.

All these factors amalgamate into something akin to a vibe that might best be described as melancholic jubilance or euphoric melancholy. When combined with those parts of the song's words that are readily discernible and that address interiority, being in one's mind, the potential dangers of the outside, the end of the world, and particularly the repeated invocation of "I be on my empty mind shit," they combine to form a pandemic anthem.[2] A hymn that is not too thoughtlessly celebratory but that wistfully insists on good days both in the song's Now and in the hope for a (post)pandemic future. In this scenario, as in the "real world," the pandemic will most likely not end anytime soon, but many people's lives, both those that did and those that did not die, will have been incontrovertibly altered regardless.[3]

As intimate as it is capacious in lyrical content, sung intonation, and sonic architecture, "Good Days" is very of its—of this—of our—moment: unambiguously from and of the Now while at the same time amplifying the extensive history of R&B music's deft fusion of the personal and the political. Accordingly, SZA's lyrics pertain to a romantic relationship gone awry as much as they tackle through interior monologue the broader dimensions of life during the COVID-19 pandemic. In fact, the inarticulacy of parts of the "Good Days" lyrics, which results from SZA's unique style of vocalization, which has been dubbed by some disparagingly as "singing in italics," consti-

---

1 SZA, "Good Days," Top Dawg Entertainment, 2020, MP3, https://www.discogs.com/release/16639632-SZA-Good-Days. For a recounting of how the record was made by SZA's cowriters and producers, see Phillips, "'It's Just a Family Record.'"

2 I identified with these lines especially, because quarantine "brain fog" hit me full force in the late fall of 2020, just before "Good Days" was released. See, for instance, Grose, "Why Your Brain Feels Broken"; and Cushing, "Late-Stage Pandemic."

3 See Jordan, *Some of Us*.

tutes a part of what makes the song so special and able to give expression to the complicated life situation defined by the COVID pandemic, where death is even more lurkingly ever present than it is in a "normal" cisheteropatriarchal anti-Black world.[4] "Good Days" sounds newly emergent forms of heart/////break without forgetting the preexisting conditions that got us here. It carries forth the tradition of R&B music speaking obliquely, in hushed sotto voce tones, to the politics of its age, for instance, Aretha Franklin demanding R-E-S-P-E-C-T or Sam Cooke imparting that a change is going to come (see track 8.0 for more about this), while also conjuring what I've referred to elsewhere as the nonwordness of sound.[5] SZA's singing style takes on this extralinguistic dimension because Rowe frequently enunciates words in ways extremely counterintuitive to how they would be pronounced in everyday English-language speech, in either "standard" or "colloquial" idioms, and as a result exquisitely boosts their sonic materialities and aesthetic virtualities to realms beyond linguistic meaning. Hear, for instance, how Rowe sings the English-language word for female dogs on "Love Galore" (from *Ctrl*) in a manner that makes it sound like the title of that 1980s movie starring Bette Midler and Barbara Hershey—yes, the one with that song with the wind and the wings.[6] Here are the lyrics in question:

Skrrt, skrrt on b****es
I don't know these b****es
Dig dirt on b****es
Do it for fun
Don't take it personal baby
Love 'em all lately[7]

Not coincidentally, this also represents a moment where queerness slyly disrupts the traditionally heterosexual proceedings of most pop music with SZA admitting that she's dated a few ladies:

Luh-love to my ladies
I dated a few

4 Townsend, "SZA Sang in Italicized."
5 See Weheliye, *Phonographies*.
6 If one must listen to *that* song, it should at least be the original: Gladys Knight & the Pips, "Hero," on *Visions*, CBS Records, 1983, LP, https://www.discogs.com /release/1590822-Gladys-Knight-The-Pips-Visions.
7 SZA, "Love Galore," on *Ctrl*, Top Dawg Entertainment, 2017, MP3, https://www .discogs.com/release/10416609-SZA-Ctrl.

Given that I generally tend to not experience pop music lyrics as content transmissions but as textural frequencies of nonwordness, the queerness of these particular lyrics had to be pointed out to me by students in my fall 2017 The Politics of Black Popular Music course at Northwestern even though I'd listened to this song countless times. When I asked the class whether SZA had ever addressed her queerness in her music, three students recited these lyrics almost simultaneously. Though queer content in R&B has existed for years in the oeuvres of Me'Shell Ndegeocello, Rachid, Kehlani, Moses Sumney, THEESatisfaction, Serpentwithfeet, Janelle Monáe, Rahsaan Patterson, Syd, MNEK, Frank Ocean, Tevin Campbell, Wuhryn Dumas, Sylvester, Durand Bernarr, and Jackie Shane, among others, queer listeners are often still compelled to engage with the genre through the frequential wavelengths of what Treva Ellison calls a "Black Femme Praxis," which Ellison defines as "a lived politics of double-crossing, or making queer use of, racialized and gendered labor constructs and heteronormative nuclear familial relations."[8] In general, R&B lends itself to "making queer use of" because of its emphasis on the affective and domestic in interpersonal (mostly) heterosexual and normative relations.

Along with Frank Ocean, SZA has been instrumental in introducing new vocal and thematic languages into R&B music as well as into everyday observational styles of singing that move away from the church-derived melismatic dramatics that once defined the genre to embrace more introverted, restrained, observational, and conversational topics and modes of vocalizing/singing. The constitutive opacity of SZA's lyrics, sung delivery, and the overall sound of the instrumentation make "Good Days" perfect for conjuring the meeting point of low-level claustrophobic anxiety and reticent pleasure precipitated by the realities of a COVID world. The critique of vibe singing and R&B's increasing dissociation from Black churches as spaces of musical apprenticeship has for some positioned post-1970s R&B music as inauthentically Black, as unable to sonically illuminate Black folks' lifeworlds. Though the genre has surely undergone some fundamental shifts during this time, it remains *the* foundation for most other popular musical styles, ranging from Afrobeats to country and hip-hop, and I believe its discrediting is clearly due to the genre's perceived femininity beginning with the disco era and continuing with the ascendancy of hip-hop (see tracks 7.0 and 8.0 in this volume) as well as to the more universal devaluation of BlackFem critical and creative

8 Ellison, "Black Femme Praxis," 14.

labor.[9] Thus, while surely charting new territories within the genre, Rowe's and Ocean's oeuvres remain unmistakably Black and unambiguously R&B, very much bearing witness to and fabulating with Black life, theirs and ours.

This mistreatment of R&B, which is frequently tethered to the narrative form of the genre's putative decline, if not its altogether unceremonious death, has dominated scholarly and journalistic commentary on the genre; but there has also been some excellent scholarship that takes post-1970s R&B music seriously, by writers such as Daphne Brooks, Francesca Royster, Robert Patterson, Mark Anthony Neal, Elliott Powell, Simone White, Jason King, Treva Lindsey, Michael Awkward, Ayanna Dozier, Richard Iton, Brittnay Proctor, and Farah Jasmine Griffin.[10] With *Feenin* I aim to contribute to this ever-changing archive of conversations, which do not neglect the changes hip-hop has wrought on R&B music, and vice versa, at the same time as they still hear the genre as a viable and thriving venue for the continued expression of Black thought and life. Good day in my mind.

I have taken Deborah McDowell's *The Changing Same: Black Women's Literature, Criticism, and Theory* (1995) as a model for this volume; it has not

9 Analogously, Matthew Morrison shows how beginning in the nineteenth century what he calls "Blacksound" provides "a way of uncovering the political implications of embodying, making, and commercializing popular music in the United States, from its origins in blackface to the present." M. Morrison, "Race, Blacksound, and the (Re)Making of Musicological Discourse," 783.

10 The locus classicus for this narrativization of the decline of post-1970s R&B remains Nelson George's *The Death of Rhythm and Blues*.

I should further observe that because much of the journalistic and scholarly criticism of Black music is still produced by white writers, it remains imperative for me to contribute to the growing counterarchive represented by the following critics. See Brooks, "'All That You Can't Leave'"; Brooks, "'It's Not Right but It's Okay'"; Brooks, *Liner Notes for the Revolution*; Griffin, "When Malindy Sings"; Royster, *Sounding Like a No-No*; Iton, *In Search of the Black Fantastic*; White, *Dear Angel of Death*; Patterson, *Destructive Desires*; Lindsey, "If You Look in My Life"; Neal, *Black Ephemera*; Neal, *Songs in the Key of Black Life*; Neal, *Soul Babies*; Powell, "Addict(ive) Sex"; Powell, "Funking Our Way to Freedom"; Proctor, *Minnie Riperton's Come to My Garden*; Proctor, "'Shout It Out'"; J. King, "Any Love"; J. King, "Sound of Velvet Melting"; D. Smith, *Shine Bright*; Awkward, *Soul Covers*; and Dozier, *Janet Jackson's "The Velvet Rope."*

merely provided a template for content but also serves as my prototype for form, since it for the most part collects McDowell's previously published essays, interspersing them with a few retrospective and connective pieces.[11] The essays and conversations included in *Feenin* were produced over the past twenty years, and though prompted separately by different occasions and often by conversations with specific collaborators, interlocutors, and respondents, collectively the tracks also represent an intensive and ongoing documentation of my thinking with and about the fate of R&B music as a genre in the postsoul moment since the late 1970s. What has struck me over the years about *The Changing Same* is how resolutely McDowell's essays engage with the present of criticism even when the literary texts under discussion (Nella Larsen's *Passing*, Emma Dunham Kelley's *Four Girls at Cottage City*, or Toni Morrison's *Sula*, for instance) hail from earlier time periods. The temporalities of address, reception, and dialogue are rendered even more complex in this context, because many of the novels McDowell considers were not widely available until the 1980s. In fact, McDowell's brilliant essays about Larsen's (1929) and Kelley's (1895) novels were initially published as introductions to critical editions of these texts that made them accessible to larger audiences for the first time since their initial publication.[12] McDowell writes about and to the states of Black feminist criticism and theory in the Now of the essays and preserves those initial contexts for their compiling in the 1995 book.[13] The preservation of their previous format, however, does not imply that the essays do not shift in their potential significations, since they retain some of the "original" impulses yet also gain new layers of signification by being recontextualized via the interfacing with the other essays in *The Changing Same*. Similarly, I have chosen to largely leave the pieces in this volume intact to demonstrate, orchestrate, visualize, and choreograph methodologies of bearing witness to the Now via the frequencies of R&B music. It appears that we currently have at our disposal a much more robust

11 All but one of the essays included in McDowell's *The Changing Same* were first published between 1980 and 1989.

12 See Larsen, *"Quicksand" and "Passing"*; and E. Kelley, *Four Girls at Cottage City*.

13 Beyond the pathbreaking essay "New Directions for Black Feminist Criticism," which was first published in 1980 as a response to Barbara Smith's "Toward a Black Feminist Criticism" (1977), the direct conversation with the Now of criticism is most apparent in the final, previously unpublished chapter of McDowell's book, "Transferences: Black Feminist Discourse: The 'Practice' of 'Theory.'"

set of questions and approaches to Black life in the historical past than we do for Black existence as it unfolds in the present tense. Where to find the languages and parameters of the Now in Black studies?

One of the central debates in the recent history of critical Black studies has revolved around Saidiya Hartman's concept "critical fabulation," especially as it pertains to the enslaved within the context of the archive as violently fraught conundrum.[14] Critical fabulation becomes a necessary analytic/method, according to Hartman and others, because so few echoes of the enslaved remain in official archives. As Hartman writes, "The intention here isn't anything as miraculous as recovering the lives of the enslaved or redeeming the dead, but rather laboring to paint as full a picture of the lives of the captives as possible. This double gesture can be described as straining against the limits of the archive to write a cultural history of the captive, and, at the same time, enacting the impossibility of representing the lives of the captives precisely through the process of narration. The method guiding this writing practice is best described as critical fabulation."[15] Although critical fabulation as theoretical and methodological praxis germinates in the immense gaps in the archival vestiges of racial slavery, Hartman does not so much seek to suture these caesural lacerations as call attention to the violence of the lacunae in ways not possible through either a "detached" historiographic lens or the allegedly "freer" fictional imagination. It is important here to indubitably differentiate Hartman's work from the ways this concept/ methodology has been taken up by other scholars from either straight-up historiography or fiction, not because of any adherence to strict disciplinary protocols, but because critical fabulation genuinely represents an approach, a modality of thinking, that diverges from both. Black women novelists like Gayl Jones, Toni Morrison, Jewelle Gomez, Octavia Butler, Maryse Condé, and Shirley Anne Williams have explored and reimagined the violent interruptions in the archives of racial slavery in their fiction since the 1970s, and

14 Beyond the original salvo—Hartman's "Venus in Two Acts"—see, for instance, Haley, *No Mercy Here*; Haley, "Intimate Historical Practice"; McKittrick, "Mathematics Black Life"; Fuentes, *Dispossessed Lives*; Fuentes, "Genres of History and the Practice of Loss"; J. Johnson, *Wicked Flesh*; Nyong'o, *Afro-Fabulations*; Nyong'o, "Unburdening Representation"; Campt, *Black Gaze*; Smythe, "What Is to Be Done?"; Carby, *Imperial Intimacies*; Allen, *There's a Disco Ball*; Young, *Illegible Will*; Greene-Hayes, "'Queering' African American Religious History"; Valdés, "Afterlives of Arturo Alfonso Schomburg"; Edwards, "Taste of the Archive"; and T. King, *Black Shoals*.
15 Hartman, "Venus in Two Acts," 11.

even as these novels without a doubt overlap with contemporary feminist historiography of plantation slavery, there also exist, it must be said, some profound differences in terms what these modes of thought and practices of writing allow us to conjure and thematize. As Tavia Nyong'o maintains, "Critical fabulation is not a genre or a discourse but a mode by which both genre and discourse can be set into oscillating tension, through the upsetting of a key demand of representational mimesis: the demand that a representation be either true or false, either history or fiction."[16] Refusing to disentangle history from fiction in order to posit some ultimate form of transparent truth makes it possible for critical fabulation to cautiously emerge from the shadows to take its improper place as the ghost in the machines of fiction and historiography.

In another part of the essay, Hartman highlights how her critically fabulist narratives seek "to bridge the past and the present" at the same time as they "dramatize the production of nothing—empty rooms, and silence, and lives reduced to waste."[17] If critical fabulation serves to connect the past and the present, my questions are, What occurs in the absence of traditional archives, as fractured, nonexistent, entombing, and violent as they may be? What takes their place as the building blocks for critical fabulation for the Now? What are the "empty rooms, and silence, and lives reduced to waste" of the present? In her 2019 book *Wayward Lives, Beautiful Experiments: Intimate Histories of Social Upheaval*, Hartman has moved away from the period of de jure enslavement and extended her approach into the middle of the twentieth century, albeit without forgetting to carefully pinpoint the numerous ways the structures and affects of slavery are forcibly bequeathed to these subsequent historical epochs. Accordingly, it remains imperative for Black studies to not completely cede the study of the contemporary to the social sciences and their complicated—if not outright violent—relationship to Black life.[18]

In her expansive and sinuous analysis of Black studies' history until the mid-1990s, Hortense Spillers describes how the student protests of the late 1960s, which put pressure on administrations in mainstream US universities to admit more Black students and include Black studies in their curricula, led to two subsequent interrelated institutional phenomena:

16 Nyong'o, "Unburdening Representation," 77.
17 Hartman, "Venus in Two Acts," 4.
18 See Judy, "Untimely Intellectuals and the University"; and R. Kelley, *Yo' Mama's Disfunktional!*, esp. 15–42.

(1) an appointment in black studies, as some of the programs fashioned an Afrocentric/Africanist response to the traditional disciplines, heavily influenced by the American social science paradigms and their empiricist concept of 'reading,' or (2) an appointment in one of the traditional disciplines in the humanities or social sciences, with a complementary appointment in black studies. In some instances, the institutions pursued a mix of procedures, with the black studies protocol filled in by both disciplinary and extra-disciplinary appointments.[19]

What remains significant about this bifurcation is that the putative inter- or antidiscipline of Black studies outside of traditional sociology, history, literature, or political science departments was and still is heavily defined by US social scientific discourses and the empiricist valences that accompany, if not downright define, them. Of course, historiography, also usually in varieties characterized profoundly by empiricist "readings" at sight, has secured its permanent residency along with sociology as the defining critical modality of Black studies as it is practiced in Black studies programs and departments across the United States today. Though there exist exceptions, Black literary/cultural studies and Black critical theorizing mainly take place beyond the confines of African American/Africana/African diaspora/Black studies administrative units in the US university system, as does much of Black feminism as well as Black queer and trans studies. I'm dwelling on these institutional protocols because critical fabulation (and the debates it has engendered) represents a pivotal contemporary formulation of Black studies' critical edge not beholden to empiricist proprieties, neither sociological nor historiographical. Rather, critical fabulation offers conceptual and inventive pathways to theorizing the status of the historical within the context of Black studies—gracefully smudging its deeply entrenched empiricist sheen—and, as such, it epitomizes the creative reimagining of the complex interstitial entanglements betwixt and between historiography, literary studies, and critical theory in Black studies.

In this vein, I'm trying to ascertain what a critical fabulation of the present would feel, look, and sound like so as to make it speak to archives that cannot be

---

19 Spillers, "Crisis of the Negro Intellectual," 463. In addition to Spillers's important essay, see Wynter, "On How We Mistook the Map for the Territory." It bears mentioning that these two important critical theorizations of the Black studies project come from Black feminist literary scholars working outside Black studies departments. I thank Henry Washington Jr. for inviting me to think about these disciplinary questions in a more explicit fashion.

found in the strict historical past. Or, phrased in a different register, although all scholarly work has the potential to be creative and fabulative, where does nonempiricist Black studies scholarship that centers on or takes off from the contemporary/the Now/the current fit into the vital conversations around critical fabulation?[20] What is the conceptual status of the Now in Black studies? What particular methodological and conceptual apparatuses become de rigueur for imagining the contemporary as not merely always already there and present-at-hand? To be flagrantly candid, I am not looking to the contemporary as a ruse to indulge in shameless ahistorical presentism but am instead after something approximating the opaque density of synchronic and diachronic frequencies that thrust the present toward multiple concurrent—and at times diverging—presents (synchronic) as well as a plethora of possible pasts and yet-to-comes (diachronic) so as to approach the potential forceful fullness of the Now.[21] This method is less concerned with the periodization of the contemporary as such than with how to simultaneously think from *and* through the Now in all its complexities. As categorically muddled and difficult to disentangle as the synchronic and diachronic may be under any circumstance, my point is that they are differently ensnared when they concern primarily the present.

There's something to be said about being able to access the ambience and "vibes" of the historical eras one has lived through and having scholarly writing explicitly reflect these temporalities. A note of caution, though, since this neither means that everyone experiences the Now in the same ways (depending on many different factors such as gender, sexuality, or geopolitical location) nor implies that this Now is in any way straightforwardly accessible. Therefore, something along the lines of critical fabulation also becomes

20 On the potential inventiveness and creativity of scholarly work in the humanities, see Weheliye, *Phonographies*, especially "Outro: Thinking Sound/Sound Thinking (Slipping into the Breaks Remix)."

21 David Scott fruitfully poses the following questions about the temporal cum conceptual parameters of the contemporary: "So, how should we think the time of the contemporary? What kind of time is this? What experience of temporality marks it? Is the contemporary usefully thought of only as now-time, the shared or coexperienced present? What present is it that one can be copresent with? What is the duration of contemporariness? How do we know when one contemporary has been eclipsed by another?" Scott, "Untimely Experience of the Contemporary," viii. See also Scott, "Preface." For a consideration of the fleeting present represented by contemporary queer and trans archives, see moore, "DARK ROOM."

vital for ruminating with and writing about the present, since it gives shape to the leap that introduces invention into existence and the spark that enfleshes being.[22] How does inhabiting and being possessed by a zeitgeist, that conglomerate of "vibes" and atmosphere of a specific historical epoch, shape scholarly writing, whether it's explicitly addressed in the text or not? How can we unearth and amplify this zeitgeist, render it unfamiliar and make it usable for critical nonempiricist Black studies projects, especially for the varied frequencies of critical fabulation? McDowell's essays, for example, make no secret of tackling head-on the Now of criticism at the time of their writing and initial publication; nonetheless, this present becomes transformed once the essays are assembled in the 1995 volume with the additional material that retrospectively reflects on some of the pieces included in *The Changing Same.* Comparably, critical fabulation arose within the context of Hartman's research for *Lose Your Mother: A Journey along the Atlantic Slave Route* (2007), which is at least partially a "memoir" concerned with understanding the originary breach of racial Blackness, the rift between the African continent and its violently established diasporas from the purview of Now, as is so aptly encapsulated by the book's now well-known Hughesian aphorism: "I, too, am the afterlife of slavery."[23] While Hartman phrases the statement in the present tense ("I, too, am"), the overarching temporality establishes just how intensely the Now is constituted by entwined constellations of pasts assumed to not exist ("the afterlife of slavery"). So much so, in fact, that the past transfigures into the present, and vice versa.

I intend to inquire about "objects" of study and the ways we as scholars interact with them in the same movement as considering the leaps of imagination needed to produce any form of academic analysis, which means insisting on the *fabulation* part of *critical fabulation.* Is fabulation required only for the past, and, if not, how do we describe and imagine contemporary archives? How do the archives of the contemporary participate in the entombing of Black life? Are the records of the present just as violent, only differently so, as those concerned with the annals of the historical past? In the introduction to *Black Skin, White Masks,* Frantz Fanon unequivocally thematizes his compulsory situatedness in the temporal Now, fabulating about the repercussions thus:

> Every human problem must be considered from the stand point of time.
> Ideally, the present will always contribute to the building of the future.

22 See Wynter, "Unsettling the Coloniality"; and Fanon, *Wretched of the Earth.*
23 Hartman, *Lose Your Mother,* 6.

And this future is not the future of the cosmos but rather the future of my century, my country, my existence. . . . I belong irreducibly to my time. And it is for my own time that I should live. The future should be an edifice supported by living men. This structure is connected to the present to the extent that I consider the present in terms of something to be exceeded.[24]

Of course, the present cannot but transcend itself, because it cannot remain cordoned off from its neighboring pasts and virtual but no less real futures, and because it is haunted by alternate present tenses: there is no such thing as a singular Now or present tense. Might we also lovingly nudge Frantz toward the "future of the cosmos," because it, too, is nothing other than part of "my existence"? How do we critically engage the present without flattening it? As the conversations around critical fabulation highlight, the very spatial propinquity of the terms *Black* and *archive* on the page already points to a fracture, a wound, and a potential abyss that we will have a difficult time choreographing our movements around.[25] How do we summon the archives of contemporary Black life not as straightforward but as always already going over and above themselves temporally, conceptually, politically, and aesthetically? As a result, critical fabulation necessarily tunes into and crisscrosses the oscillation of different historical frequencies in the form of related irregularities that recur. In this context Tina Campt offers an "an understanding of frequency . . . as an unstable temporality which produces complex forms of repetition that, rather than reproducing or replicating what came before it, creates new beginnings instead."[26] Thus, perhaps then we can envisage history and the present as a series of nonsequential but overlapping frequencies that comprise the elementary particles for both related irregularities and "new beginnings."

For Daphne Brooks, writing about the frequently concealed histories of Black women's contribution to the production of and criticism about Black music, archives take on primarily two different configurations: "the documentary record preserved by institutional powerbrokers and the faded pages we might imagine stored in an elderly sister's trunk," which we might label as the official, institutionalized and the vernacular variants of accreted knowledge, respectively.[27] In ascertaining how "Black women musicians and critics

24 Fanon, *Black Skin, White Masks*, 14–15.
25 On the womb abyss gestated by racial slavery, see Glissant, *Poetics of Relation*.
26 Campt, *Black Gaze*, 81.
27 Brooks, *Liner Notes for the Revolution*, 4.

have had to negotiate in relation to their own artistic ambitions and to the problem of Black historical memory more broadly," Brooks takes an additional vital leap in stating, "Black women artists have played crucial roles as archives, as the innovators of performances and recordings that stood in for and as the memory of a people."[28] Thus, not only the torn concert tickets, brittle vinyl records with fading liner notes, stickers whose adhesiveness has long since evaporated, rusty button badges, ripped band T-shirts, disheveled copies of music magazines no longer in existence, or barely legible printed lyric sheets in the older sister's crate function as vernacular archives, but the artists themselves operate in several significant archival capacities as well. Rhythm and Blues music more broadly operates as a series of interlocking and historically mutable archives of different expressions of Black life and affect. In the universe of contemporary R&B, for instance, artists such as Mary J. Blige, Jazmine Sullivan, Me'Shell Ndegeocello, and Mariah Carey are explicit archivists of musical traditions in terms of their choices for cover versions (e.g., Blige's version of Rose Royce's "I'm Goin' Down," Ndegeocello's archive of 1980s R&B songs on her 2018 album *Ventriloquism*, or Carey's remake of Cherrelle's "Didn't Mean to Turn You On"), samples (e.g., Sullivan's sampling of "Jump to It" by Aretha Franklin on "Don't Make Me Wait"), references to other R&B singers and musicians (e.g., Carey's interpolation of Babyface's and Bobby Womack's vocal intonations on "We Belong Together"), which amplifies Brooks's insight about the wide array of archival manifestations for Black music and the important role of BlackFem R&B artists in maintaining them. These represent but a few examples of an expanded notion of the contemporary archive as they interface with R&B music and BlackFem performers/archivists.

For me Black popular music, especially R&B, has served as the primary archive of the Now, as my lane to remaining in the present while still amplifying aesthetic, political, and conceptual questions about Blackness, technology, history, humanity, community, diaspora, nationhood, and so on; the pieces in this book are both products of and testimonies to thinking with and about Black music since the 1980s. Pop music in general and R&B music in particular refuse detachment and "objectivity," often demanding an immediate response to get on the dance floor or remain in my seat at the club or party, to press either the skip or repeat button on my phone, or to turn up the volume on the car radio or rotate the proverbial dial to change the radio station in repugnance, in the process compelling me to show up more fully as

28 Brooks, *Liner Notes for the Revolution*, 4.

a listener, a critic, a scholar, a thinker, and a fan. If, as Keguro Macharia argues, "queers need fabulation. We need to imagine and theorize and practice strategies that make our beings possible. Against our training. For something else," R&B music sets in motion this process of fabulation for me, pushing me to strain toward something else, tenderly prodding me in the direction of further frequencies of the Now.[29] In addition, Ellison's "Black femme praxis," mentioned earlier, operates as a form of critical fabulation given that it unleashes those queer frequencies—vibrating in the key "that must traditionally remain inaudible and/or relegated to the domain of the nonexistent."[30]

Rhythm and Blues music represents the portal and archive incarnate through which to critically fabulate with some of Black life's intricately complex presents. Though the tracks and interludes in *Feenin* are principally about music, they also draw attention to the continued precarity of Black life and culture in late capitalism. Because in some cases, such as the centrality of Christianity in Black German music detailed in track 4.0 or the two-way pagers discussed in track 3.0, which have both completely disappeared from the horizon, these pieces also represent a series of testimonies of and to vanishing presents, or, rather, presents that have been rendered opaque by subsequent historical frequencies. In those instances, the fabulative dimension lies in the endeavor of conjuring particular historical eras and geographic contexts that we can no longer access in the same fashion. In other cases, for instance, the perceptible use of Auto-Tune or the incorporation of mobile phones in R&B music, the pieces in this volume bear witness to and fabulate with those spatiotemporal intervals in which the main deployments of these technologies had not stabilized or become unnoteworthy. Critical fabulation via the specific frequential intensities of the present transforms this domain via an encounter with the phantoms that lurk in the crevices of the Now—the *Geist* in *zeitgeist*—in the process thrusting it beyond itself, on the path toward the

29 Macharia, *Frottage*, 136.
30 Though I don't give it fuller attention here, Kara Keeling's notion of "looking after" as an affectively charged queer ethics of care is also apposite here: "The second way that *Looking for Langston* 'looks after' Hughes is colloquially and affectively; it generates Hughes's purported homosexuality and makes it recognizable in a time when it might be useful, thereby protecting or sheltering a homosexual desire it attributes to Hughes by making it meaningful for and within a collectivity that presently needs it and therefore affectionately 'looks after' or cares for it." Keeling, "Looking for M," 572.

new and unknown, but always welcoming that something else. For something else. I, too, am the future of the cosmos.

Rather than being arranged chronologically, the pieces in *Feenin* are loosely organized by theme, with track 1.0, "Engendering *Phonographies*: Sonic Technologies of Blackness," representing the broadest and perhaps most abstract consideration of Black music and technology. Though the track does center R&B music per se, there are plenty of references to specific recordings from the genre throughout, and certainly, many of its points are applicable to the music. Tracks 2.0 and 3.0 zoom in most patently on specific technological apparatuses (vocoders, talk boxes, cell phones, pagers, and the Auto-Tune software) while still pursuing broader questions about Blackness, technology, communication, humanity, and enfleshment. How do technologies become a part of the very historical *Stoff* of worlding?[31] What role does R&B music—and the Black singing voice more broadly—play in this worlding?

Almost all of track 2.0, "'Feenin': Posthuman Voices in R&B Music," was written in the spring of 2001, after I had presented a much shorter version at a symposium in the previous year. I consider "'Feenin'" my "freedom" essay, so to speak, produced after finishing my dissertation but before I began revising it into what would later become *Phonographies*. Despite—or maybe because of—"Feenin" being concerned with the machinic distortion of human vocalization, it is the first piece that felt like it was written in my writerly "voice," which was at least partially due to the fact that I was thinking with and writing about (then) contemporary R&B music in ways I had not done before. I then was able to take back what I had learned writing "'Feenin'" and apply those insights to the process of reworking my dissertation into *Phonographies*. Alondra Nelson, who edited the special issue of *Social Text* on the topic Afrofuturism in which "'Feenin'" was first published, was also the founder of the LISTSERV with the same name, and all the contributors to the special issue were active members of this LISTSERV. The LISTSERV was an amazing hub of conversations about Blackness, science, technology,

---

31 Sedgwick, *Between Men*, 6. For some recent considerations of Blackness and technology, see R. Benjamin, *Race after Technology*; Brock, *Distributed Blackness*; Gallon, "Making a Case"; Noble, *Algorithms of Oppression*; and Towns, *On Black Media Philosophy*.

and science fiction at the end of the 1990s and in the early 2000s, and those formative conversations there influenced the ideas in "'Feenin.'"

Clearly, I would not write "'Feenin'" in the same way today, given that the twenty years in the interim have taught me much, and my thinking and my intellectual, affective, aesthetic, political, pedagogical investments have shifted, but it is surprising how much it still reflects my present-day ideas about R&B music, Blackness, humanism, and technology. Gender and sexuality would most certainly take up more analytic space in this piece if written today, but many of the other pieces contained in *Feenin* do that work within the context of R&B music. Additionally, I mistakenly attributed vocoder use to Zapp's Roger Troutman, when, in fact, he used a talk box to roboticize his voice. Though I don't suppose this changes the larger point about the audible mechanization of the Black singing voice, I've adjusted this in the version included here. I was also not aware of the name of the Auto-Tune software, just its effects, which is why I described it as the *vocoder effect*. Neither were the journalists writing about turn-of-the-millennium R&B, or at least they did not mention this specific software at that point in history; I have amended that here as well.

Retrospectively "'Feenin'" chronicles and preserves the specific historical moment (and another vanishing former present) after Cher's producers had deployed Auto-Tune so conspicuously on her 1998 megahit "Believe" and before T-Pain and other rappers using Auto-Tune came to the forefront of popular music about ten years later, when Auto-Tune was used creatively primarily in R&B and teen pop but not in hip-hop.[32] A brief historical interval that gets downright forgotten in subsequent historicizations of Auto-Tune's pivotal role in the recent history of popular music, for instance, in the episode of 2021 Netflix series *This Is Pop* devoted to the rise of audible Auto-Tune use in pop music, which completely erases the years between 1998 and 2005.[33] An omission that is clearly indicative of how R&B and BlackFem performers are usually treated when it comes to musical and technological innovation. Ready to hand for all the plundering—and I do mean *all*—R&B music receives none of the accolades.

The earliest ideas for track 3.0, "Rhythms of Relation: Black Popular Music and Mobile Technologies," began their journey with materials cut from the

---

32 Cher, "Believe," Warner Records, 1998, CD, https://www.discogs.com/master /69286-Cher-Believe.

33 *This Is Pop*, Banger Films, CTV Television Network, 2021, https://www.imdb.com /title/tt14155414/?ref_=tt_mv_close.

published version of "'Feenin.'" The incorporation of mobile communication devices into R&B music seemed ancillary and nascent at best in 2001. Over the course of the next ten years (2001–11), however, these miniature computers qua cellular telephones had not only thoroughly suffused the lyrical and sonic universes of hip-hop and R&B but had become mainstays in many quotidian landscapes around the globe. This was when I revisited these questions to chart how mobile communication devices crested to the center of R&B music. By 2015, in the wake of the immense success of Drake's "Hotline Bling," Erykah Badu created a complete mixtape replete with eleven songs that either are cover versions or contain significant samples of R&B songs about telecommunications by such artists as New Edition, The Isley Brothers, Usher, and Uncle Jamm's Army. Though Badu does not include them in her history lesson, there also exists an elaborate archive of BlackFem R&B performers singing about telephones, for instance, Aretha Franklin's "Call Me" or Stephanie Mills's version of Prince's "How Come U Don't Call Me Anymore."[34] Badu gives us a history lesson in the form of sonic pageantry that accents the Now, since the mixtape as a whole serves to contextualize and respond to Drake's crooning about (missed) telephonic interaction, that is, why we instantly know that "it can only mean one thing if that hotline bling."[35] After several years have passed, I'm still not sure I understand why Drake deems "wearing less and goin' out more" as undesirable, though (insert shoulder shrug emoji here). Interlude 1, "Calling My Phone," surveys how these constellations play out in the early 2020s at the intersection of Black popular music and mobile technologies.

Track 4.0, "My Volk to Come: Specters of Peoplehood in Diaspora Discourse and Afro-German Popular Music," and track 5.0, "'White Brothers with No Soul': UnTuning the Historiography of Berlin Techno," focus on Germany's recent past and Black music's vexed place in it. "My Volk" makes an intervention into the then-central debate in critical Black studies about diaspora and its significance for Black populations in Europe, fusing it with a consideration of how religious discourses were being marshaled by Black German R&B musicians in the early part of this century. In this way, the musical part of this piece offers a continuation of my discussion in the last chapter

34 Erykah Badu, *But You Caint Use My Phone*, Motown Records, 2015, MP3, https://www.discogs.com/Erykah-Badu-But-You-Caint-Use-My-Phone/master/1057379.

35 Drake, "Hotline Bling," Cash Money Records, 2015, MP3, https://www.discogs.com/release/7312552-Drake-Hotline-Bling.

of *Phonographies* of how the German group Advanced Chemistry deployed hip-hop to present themselves as both Black and German. Highlighting the complexities of envisaging community, the theoretical and the musical halves of track 4.0 bring attention to the complexities of being Black and German, both in relation to other Black diasporic populations and within the context of the shifting administrative and ideological borders of the German nation-state. Undoubtedly, Blackness and Black music, whether R&B or techno, resolutely defy any such borders and distinctions given that Black folks are frequently imagined as existing outside of the nation-states in the western world, especially in Europe.

The localization qua making white—a reracination rather than a deracination—of techno in Berlin and many other places in Europe consisted of numerous active processes—rather than a single sleight of hand—in the early 1990s, and it went hand in hand with the extreme violence Black and other nonwhite communities experienced after the fall of the Berlin Wall in 1989 and German reunification a year later. These public forms of violence against Black and other nonwhite people in the years around reunification are now vigorously expunged from the celebratory historiographies of techno in Berlin and the founding of the "Berliner Republik." My own experiences as a teenager with the clubbing scene in West Berlin as well as the fundamental anti-Blackness of German society in the 1980s and early 1990s provided the spark here, since the retrospective considerations of techno in Berlin through oral histories and documentary films, which started appearing around 2010, rarely addressed the presence of Black music in the city before the advent of techno and seldom mentioned the violence against nonwhite people during that time. Both this violence and the presence of Black music in Berlin disrupt the celebratory narrative that techno music offered the common musical ground for the friction-less coming together of young (cishet white male) Germans in East and West after reunification. In fact, this fervent whitening of techno has worked so well that any form of oontz music (an onomatopoetic rendering of four-on-the-floor dance music) is now thoroughly associated with (European) whiteness in the United States, just as occurred previously with rock music. To take just one obvious example, it was not until 2020 that Haitian Canadian producer and DJ Kaytranada was the first Black artist to win a Grammy Award in the Best Dance/Electronic Album category. Interlude 2, "Don't Take It Away," pays tribute to the often-nameless BlackFem voices found in many forms of popular music, but especially in electronic dance music, where we find a long history of integrally using BlackFem singing voices without crediting the vocalists, whether it's through session work or sampling. This centrality of the disembodied BlackFem singing voice also amplifies the deep connections between R&B and electronic dance music, especially house and techno.

In the vein of track 5.0, track 6.0, "New Waves, Shifting Terrains: Prince's and David Bowie's Transatlantic Crossovers," looks back to the 1980s, albeit the earlier part of the decade, to the transatlantic postdisco moment that would a few years later lead to the creation of house music in Chicago and techno music in Detroit. In this epoch there was a spirited but clearly not unproblematic "exchange" between musical cultures in the United Kingdom (synthpop), continental Europe (Euro-disco), and the United States (R&B/funk) in which Europeans would emulate and appropriate Black US sounds—sometimes with the help of Black American musicians such as Luther Vandross, who sang for the Italian group Change—and, then, finally, Black US artists would reappropriate these sounds, now supposedly baptized in exclusively culturally alabastrine waters. Prince's 1980s career offers one very prominent example of precisely this tendency in how he and his collaborators made use of musical and visual tropes associated with white Europeanness, translating them to Black American musical and cultural idioms.

While all the pieces in *Feenin* focus at least partially on the BlackFem singing voice and highlight questions of gender, readers will detect a shift from some of the earlier pieces going into the remaining tracks in this volume in that there's much more of an emphasis on and theorization of BlackFem vocal articulations and the many ways these are both exalted and denigrated in the world of Man. Tracks 7.0 and 8.0 in particular address these questions in the most head-on manner. As discussed in track 8.0, *BlackFem* rather than *Black woman* or even *Black femme* resulted from desiring an alternative to these other gendered and sexuated categories, a term that is capacious enough to include a wide variety of femininities that traverse gender, sex, and sexuality.

Track 7.0, "'Sounding That Precarious Existence': On R&B Music, Technology, and Blackness," and track 8.0, "'Scream My Name Like a Protest': R&B Music as BlackFem Technology of Humanity in the Age of #Blacklivesmatter," return to questions of technology, albeit in a slightly different register than some of the earlier tracks, focusing mostly on the BlackFem singing voice as a technology, as a series of enfleshed forms of Black knowledge and archives. Additionally, the two pieces, but especially track 8.0, speculate about R&B's relationship to politics with a capital *P*, since the genre is now often positioned as completely lacking political vision. As the two tracks amplify, this is neither right nor OK, seeing that (a) current R&B artists have used their recordings and music videos to bring attention to Black Lives

Matter or the prison-industrial complex and (b) the private, the interpersonal, and the erotic are not outside the purview of the political. Interlude 3, "#BeyondDeepBrandyAlbumCuts," is a short interlude that contains a playlist of R&B and R&B-adjacent tracks, supplying a brief snapshot of a specific moment in R&B music history that erupted online around a series of tweets by Solange Knowles in 2013.

Track 9.0, "808s and Heartbreak," and track 10.0, "Wayward Shuddering, Beautiful Tremors (AGW's Quiet Storm Remix)," bring to the fore how the affects, sounds, sensations, and ideas associated with contemporary R&B can operate methodologically, as a way to critically fabulate about Black life in the Now, as a modality of holding on to and magnifying the present's "fierce urgency."[36] What murmurs and frequencies does an R&B analytic render audible that other approaches tend to shush? What does it sound like to inhabit the crossroads of love and pain? How can heartbreak function as a critical apparatus rather than only being felt and lived as exasperatingly damaging?

Taking heartbreak, one of the principal themes of R&B music, track 9.0 threads quotations from R&B songs about heartbreak throughout with the aim of enfleshing the supposedly abstract mechanic technology of the 808 drum machine through the conceptual lens of the generalized heartbreak of Black life. As a result, heartbreak does not function in the frequential key of individuated and privatized neoliberal affect but as a far-reaching condition of Black life in an anti-Black world that nevertheless acts on different groups and individuals gathered under in this umbrella unevenly. Take, for instance, Melvin Dixon's powerful summoning of heart////break during the height of the AIDS crisis in 1992:

> I come to you bearing witness to a broken heart; I come to you bearing witness to a broken body—but a witness to an unbroken spirit. Perhaps it is only to you that such witness can be brought and its jagged edges softened a bit and made meaningful. We are facing the loss of our entire generation. Lesbians lost to various cancers, gay men lost to AIDS. What kind of witness will You bear? What truthtelling are you brave enough to utter and endure the consequences of your unpopular message?[37]

Faced with the recent death of his longtime lover and several of his friends as well as his impending worldly demise from the complications of AIDS, Dixon

---

36 Hartman, *Wayward Lives, Beautiful Experiments,* 24.
37 Dixon, "I'll Be Somewhere Listening," 81.

accentuates the brokenness of his heart before the frailty of his physical body and the resilience of his spirit, showing a deeply communal, political, and most decidedly nonindividuated understanding of heart////break that exists in the same frequential universe as the manifold references to this condition that suffuse R&B music. Track 9.0 also summons specific instances from the history of R&B music (Marvin Gaye, R. Kelly, or Rihanna, for example) to explore and map different kinds of heartbreak. Making it possible for us to lend an ear to heartbreak as it appears in those lower frequencies where the hum of the bass is most certainly physically palpable but just barely audible, in the melismatic techniques of Aretha Franklin, Gladys Knight, and Whitney Houston, or in the more restrained vocal virtuosities of Roberta Flack, Aaliyah, or Deniece Williams, R&B music serves as an intensive archival reservoir of and provides the soundtrack to existing within the force field of the wide-ranging heart///////break of Black life. Interlude 4, "Songify Your Life," conjures the querulously heartbreaking crossroads of race, sexuality, and voice-alteration technologies through one specific example that endures as the "real-world" doppelgänger of several of the pieces included in *Feenin*.

"This world may end. Not you and I."

Track 10.0 takes Saidiya Hartman's *Wayward Lives, Beautiful Experiments: Intimate Histories of Social Upheaval* as a launchpad and was first presented in New York at a salon in early 2019 to celebrate the text's publication. Instead of offering a "reading" of or a conventional scholarly response to Hartman's text, this track, as the name states, takes the shape of a remix that emphasizes certain aspects surely present but not necessarily centered in *Wayward Lives*. It is a recombination of Hartman's sentences, words, and ideas, crossfading them with R&B lyrics so as to unearth the messy feelings, both negative and positive, behind the numbers, skewed gender ratios, archival intervals, and so many other "official" data pertaining to Black life.[38] Hartman narrates and fabulates with several fraught and triangulated erotic/romantic relationships in *Wayward Lives*, for instance, the love triangle between Hubert Harrison, Amy Ashwood, and Marcus Garvey; or Mary White Ovington's clandestine affair with John Milholland; or W. E. B. Du Bois's numerous extramarital

---

38 Heading source: Dionne Warwick, "Heartbreaker," Arista Records, 1982, LP, https://www.discogs.com/Dionne-Warwick-Heartbreaker/release/378860. On the data of Black life, especially at the turn of the twentieth century, see Womack, *Matter of Black Living*.

dalliances. As a continuation of how R&B songs of heartbreak are mobilized in track 9.0, I respond to and reimagine parts of *Wayward Lives* through the aural and philosophical lens of R&B music's vast discotheque of songs dealing with love triangles, those desired by everyone involved and—much more often—those illicit affairs that necessarily take place in the dusk of dawn or just purely after dusk in the shadows, the hallways, the hotel rooms, and the alleyways. Moreover, while derived from Du Bois's late nineteenth-century sociological and later autobiographical writings, *tremble* and *shudder* appear several times over the course of *Wayward Lives* and seem to "capture" the knotty intersection of fear, pleasure, disappointment, jubilation, and pain that the historical figures Hartman fabulates with and about experience and that contemporary R&B music has so gorgeously sounded out in greatest detail over the past thirty years.[39] An R&B method activates listening to the invisible but hearable space between *heart* and *break*: heart/////break in Hartman's written text.

Rhythm and blues music partakes in what Barbara Christian has celebrated as specifically Black modalities of theorizing, which customarily materialize "in forms quite different from the Western form of abstract logic. . . . My folk . . . have always been a race for theory though more in the form of the hieroglyph, a . . . figure which is both sensual and abstract, both beautiful and communicative," and thus offer some fertile topsoil for critical fabulation in frequencies of the Now.[40] As a genre with complex aesthetic and political parameters as well as with historical lineages and archival sedimentations, contemporary R&B sonically chronicles and theorizes the "beautiful and communicative" fluctuating contours that Black interior life, interpersonal relationships, and erotics take on under the protracted genocidal conditions of neoliberal racial capitalism:

What's the sound a broken heart makes?[41]

---

39 See Hartman's notes on Du Bois's use of *trembled* in *The Philadelphia Negro* and *shudder* in *Autobiography of W. E. B. Du Bois*. Hartman, *Wayward Lives*, 347, 375.

40 Christian, "Race for Theory," 52.

41 Shalamar, "Heartbreak," On *Heartbreak*, Solar Records, 1984, LP, https://www.discogs.com/Shalamar-Heartbreak/release/1431870.

ENGENDERING *PHONOGRAPHIES*

Sonic Technologies of Blackness

A Response to Tavia Nyong'o

I am extremely grateful to Tavia Nyong'o for his generous and elegant engagement with the central ideas of *Phonographies* and to Julian Henriques's *Sonic Bodies: Reggae Sound Systems, Performance Techniques, and Ways of Knowing* and to the editor of *Small Axe*, David Scott, for providing the forum

This track was first published in *Small Axe: A Caribbean Journal of Criticism* 18, no. 2 (44) (2014): 180–90; it is a response to Tavia Nyong'o, "Afro-Philo-Sonic Fictions: Black Sound Studies after the Millennium," *Small Axe: A Caribbean Journal of Criticism* 18, no. 2 (44) (2014): 173–79.

to participate in this conversation.[1] It is perhaps fitting, for someone like me, who tends to exhibit symptoms of intellectual nomadism, that I would be given the opportunity to reflect on *Phonographies* ten years after its writing.

In revisiting *Phonographies* on the eve of the publication of my second book, *Habeas Viscus: Racializing Assemblages, Biopolitics, and Black Feminist Theories of the Human*, the text seems both far removed from my later thinking with regard to the objects of analysis yet also proximate in terms of its conceptual underpinnings. *Habeas Viscus* concerns the relationship between Black studies, Black feminist theory, political violence, and alternate conceptions of humanity, elaborating the central place of Blackness in modernity from different angles than *Phonographies*. First, *Habeas Viscus* is not concerned with sound but with the visual, and, second, it focuses more squarely on the theoretical frameworks for analyzing how race shapes the very idea of what it means to be human. Though present in *Phonographies*, these ideas were not at the front and center in the same way as they are in *Habeas Viscus*, which is primarily about theoretical discourses and their attendant institutional politics. Although the two books seem dissimilar in their objects of study, they proffer parallel arguments about the significance of race and Blackness for the study of modernity. On the whole, *Habeas Viscus* insists on the importance of Black studies and Black feminist perspectives in the study of modern humanity. In what follows, I will address some of the insightful points raised by Nyong'o, using these as an occasion for a metameditation about *Phonographies'* place in my thinking and developments in Black studies. In particular, my comments will concentrate on the analytics of Blackness as it relates to Western modernity and decolonial critiques, the absence of Africa and African cultures from *Phonographies*, and the conceptual provenances of Black feminist approaches.

Heading sources: "Be Real Black for Me" is from Roberta Flack and Donny Hathaway, "Be Real Black for Me," Atlantic Records, 1971, single, https://www.discogs.com/Roberta-Flack-Donny-Hathaway-Youve-Lost-That-Lovin-Feelin-Be-Real-Black-For-Me/release/2236719; and "Look at Y'all Boys" is from Nicki Minaj, "Lookin A**," on Young Money, *Rise of an Empire*, Cash Money Records, 2014, MP3, https://www.discogs.com/Young-Money-Rise-Of-An-Empire/release/5742091.

1   In light of his passing, I was reminded that I thanked Stuart Hall along with a few others for being a teacher from afar in *Phonographies'* acknowledgments. I want to reiterate that sentiment here, since Hall's thinking and presence in the world have left indelible traces on everything I have written, and dedicate my part of this conversation to Hall, who made the ideal of the rigorous yet generous debate of ideas seem both necessary and effortless.

"Be Real Black for Me"

Nyong'o accurately states that despite many appeals for decolonial critiques, neither Henriques nor I are fearful of claiming western modernity from an Afro-diasporic vantage point; that we do not feel "compelled to indigenize" our "thought is noteworthy at the present moment, wherein calls for a decolonial aesthetics are frequently heard (if less frequently carried through)."[2] For me claiming, though not owning, the centrality of Blackness and Black cultures to the genesis of the West is as important as it is necessary for the particular decolonial critique developed within Black studies. As C. L. R. James and Hortense Spillers, among many others, have shown, to construe Blackness, Black studies, and Black feminism as local, ethnographic phenomena rather than as "the history of Western Civilization," or as a "vestibular moment" in the engendering of the West, feeds the very racialized coloniality we are trying to demolish.[3]

Given that Blackness is frequently thought to reside beyond the iron grip of the West and modern technologies, despite being a product of these forces, one significant way to dismantle the coloniality of being in Western modernity is to continually insist on just how fundamental Blackness, Black people, Black cultures are to this territory, albeit without falling prey to a politics of recognition, which merely adds window dressing to the systemic colonial territoriality of the modern West. This, however, cannot occur by removing the specificity of Black life, but by using the liminal yet integral spatiotemporal positioning of Blackness as a way to call into question modernity as such. The central concern of my writing has been to theorize how Blackness functions as an integral part of modern Western thought and life. That is, instead of imagining Afro-diasporic cultures as disconnected from the heart of modernity's whiteness, I demonstrate how Black cultures have contributed to the very creation and imagination of the modern, exploring the "facticity of Blackness," that is, how certain groups of humans became Black through a multitude of material and discursive powers. Blackness is an effect of Western modernity, though not reducible to a colonialist imposition on Black people. Following theorists such as Sylvia Wynter, Frantz Fanon, Stuart Hall, and Hortense Spillers, my writing calls attention to Blackness as an ontological formation that not only forms a part of the modern West but

2 Nyong'o, "Afro-Philo-Sonic Fictions," 174.
3 C. L. R. James, "Black Studies and the Contemporary Student," 397; and Spillers, "Idea of Black Culture," 25. See also Spillers, *Crisis of the Negro Intellectual.*

must be understood as constitutive of this domain; the emphasis on sound, technology, and Blackness in *Phonographies* represents one particular part of that larger intellectual project.

The Middle Passage, transatlantic racial slavery, the plantation system, and the gendered racial terror erected on them were not one-time events; they spanned almost five hundred years, from the early fifteenth century to well into the nineteenth century, and their reverberations can still be felt around us not only in the Americas but in many places around the globe, including continental Africa. Though the "proper" colonization of continental Africa did not extend over the same period, it must be seen as part of this continuum if we consider that the "Scramble for Africa" took place almost contemporaneously with the abolition of slavery in Brazil, thus extending this form of racial terror to the 1970s, when Portugal "ceded" its African colonies. The subjugation, expropriation, enslavement, rape, and killing of Black life continues under different guises in among other places the prison-industrial complex in the United States and the economic neocolonization of many African nations by the West.

Blackness as a category of analysis does not disappear Black bodies as much it highlights how Black subjects are positioned in relationship to this abstract force differently than other groups and are internally differentiated depending on gender, sexuality, class, phenotype, nationality, elocution, and so on. Understanding Blackness as an abstract force or assemblage also allows us to see how it can be abstracted from and appropriated by people not categorized as Black (e.g., the history of US popular music or Blackface minstrelsy). As a category of analysis, Blackness—just as whiteness—then, is not primarily about cataloging the existence of racial groups (map) but about addressing a spectrum of power along which all racial groups are unequally positioned (territory).[4] Put schematically, the closer the group is presumed to be to whiteness, the more power they possess, and the closer the group is thought to be to Blackness, the less power they have access to. In other words, the ontological territory of Blackness actualizes the mirage of the empirical existence of racial groups, which makes possible the categorization and hierarchization of different groups so that the unequal access to resources and power remains in place.

One of the many reasons that invocations of *diaspora* in Black studies since the 1990s remain inadequate for understanding the complexities of Blackness and Black life in the modern world is that they elide the map of specific

---

4 See Wynter, "On How We Mistook the Map."

African-descended populations around the world with the territory of Blackness that enables their legibility as identifiable Black communities.[5] Thus, the idea of diaspora in Black studies—in its rush to cook up a conceptual and nominal ointment to heal the constitutive ontological fracture of Blackness in western modernity—transmogrifies into a flight from the uneven territory of Blackness. Stuart Hall insists on this global perspective when writing about the idea of postcolonialism: "The term 'post-colonial' is not merely descriptive of 'this' society rather than 'that', or of 'then' and 'now.' It re-reads 'colonisation' as part of an essentially transnational and transcultural 'global' process—and it produces a decentred, diasporic or 'global' rewriting of earlier, nation-centered imperial grand narratives."[6] Correspondingly, critically examining Blackness facilitates the comprehensive reconfiguration of Western modernity as opposed to extending the ethnographic confinement of particular Black cultures. Nonetheless, the two strategies are far from mutually exclusive, and this is not an emigration from Black cultures but rather a comprehensive recalibration of their preordained place in the modern West. For accepting this destined place of primitive outsiders for those who are darker than blue would leave unspoiled the larger territory of modernity.

Through the ruptures of technology and sound, *Phonographies* offers one particular conceptual path in thinking together Blackness and what it means to be human in western modernity. Technology is construed as at once necessary to the dominance of West over the rest and antithetical to western being. Similarly, sound, speech, and music, while considered natural to the being of Man, threaten his self-perception as rationality and disembodiment incarnate, since these structures are sublated through the technology of writing.[7] It is important that although *Phonographies* includes discussions of musical artifacts in literature, film, and recorded sound, it is decidedly not a book about music, which is how it has been read by some critics, but instead is concerned with the nexus of Black culture, sound, and technology. If the text were a study of Black musical cultures (map), then the ontological dimensions (territory) that make possible the apperception of Black music

5   On the limitations of diaspora discourse in Black studies, see track 3.0 in this volume; and on Black studies and the ontological sphere of Blackness, see Weheliye, "Introduction."

6   Hall, "When Was 'the Post-colonial'?," 247.

7   Following Sylvia Wynter, I use *Man* to designate the modern, secular, white, heteromasculine, and western version of the human that differentiates full humans from not-quite-humans and nonhumans on the basis of biology and economics. See, for instance, Wynter, "Unsettling the Coloniality."

as an entity putatively distinct from western music would remain deafeningly inaudible. As Hortense Spillers notes, "Because it was set aside, Black culture could, by virtue of the very act of discrimination, become culture, insofar as, historically speaking, it was forced to turn its resources of spirit toward negation and critique."[8] Ergo, before exploring the specificities of Black culture, we do well to interrogate how it became *Black* and under which conditions certain acts carried out by Black people transmuted into *culture*. Not a text about Black music per se, *Phonographies* unearths the historical, conceptual, cultural, and technological grounds that sanction Black music's functioning as a foundation for modern consumer culture and a hub of identification for Black populations across the globe.

While several works have been published between 2005 and 2013 that analyze the intersections of sound, race, and technology (by Julian Henriques, Kara Keeling, Michael Hanson, Andreana Clay, Michael Veal, Daphne Brooks, Louis Chude-Sokei, Edwin Hill, Francesca Royster, Adam Banks, Tsitsi Jaji, Guthrie Ramsey, and Tavia Nyong'o, among others), and while some of the essays that appeared in special issues of *American Quarterly* and *Social Text* dedicated to sound highlight this particular relationship, I would be hesitant to say that a field such as "Black sound studies" exists.[9] For what unites these texts and those that Nyong'o mentions as laying the groundwork—"Paul Gilroy's *The Black Atlantic*, Fred Moten's *In the Break*, Kodwo Eshun's *More Brilliant Than the Sun* and Lindon Barrett's *Blackness and Value* (alongside now classic references such W. E. B. Du Bois's *The Souls of Black Folk* and Amiri Baraka's *Blues People*)"—is their absence from most genealogies and anthologies in the burgeoning subfield of sound studies.[10] I can also say with certainty that the vast majority of responses and reviews of *Phonographies* have been from Black studies rather than sound studies scholars, which is partially due to the racialized institutional structures that we labor under,

---

8 Spillers, "Idea of Black Culture," 26.
9 Banks, *Digital Griots*; Brooks, *Liner Notes for the Revolution*; Brooks, "'Sister, Can You Line It Out?'"; Jayna Brown, "Buzz and Rumble"; Chude-Sokei, "When Echoes Return"; Clay, "Like an Old Soul Record"; Hanson, "I'm a Brotha'"; Henriques, *Sonic Bodies*; Hill, *Black Soundscapes, White Stages*; Jaji, *Africa in Stereo*; M. Jones, *Muse Is Music*; Keeling, "Electric Feel"; Keeling and Kun, "Introduction"; Meintjes, *Sound of Africa!*; Nyong'o, "'I've Got You under My Skin'"; Nyong'o, "I Feel Love"; Ramsey, *Race Music*; Royster, *Sounding Like a No-No*; Stadler, "Politics of Recorded Sound"; and Veal, *Dub*.
10 Tavia Nyong'o, "Afro-Philo-Sonic Fictions," 174.

but also because I did not write the book with a sound studies audience in mind. Granted, this would have been impossible, because sound studies was barely a nascent idea during the writing of the book. Due to my training and politico-intellectual investments in Black studies, I situated my particular intervention within this context. Put more simply, I was not trying to understand modern sound via the detour of Black music but to magnify some of the ways Blackness—and thus modernity—is constituted by sound and technology.

The most extended critical conversation in *Phonographies* is with Paul Gilroy's *The Black Atlantic: Modernity and Double Consciousness*, which provided me with a different template for thinking together Black music and literature as well as for exploring how Black sounds from the United States and the Caribbean circulate among Black diasporas in western Europe. Despite my criticism of some of Gilroy's ideas in *Phonographies*, it cannot be understated just how much of a space Gilroy's text provided for the articulation of my own work. That is, I endeavored to expand the terrain diagrammed by Gilroy, especially those parts pertaining to the technological embodiment of Black musics, which remained marginal to *The Black Atlantic*. *Phonographies* also chronicles my search for writing styles that take on the technical specificity of academic English and mix it with other vernaculars, sounds, and sensations so as to amplify the objects of study and ideas under discussion from perspectives not possible in "academese." Given that standard US American English was the third language in which I acquired verbal fluency, *Phonographies* records my process of creatively grappling with a particular variant of written English so that—as the book shows, speech and text cannot be opposed—the prose could approximate the different idiomatic tongues that inspired me and that I had inhabited, if uneasily so. It helped that the struggle with and creative utilization of major languages, whether spoken, screamed, sung, written, ululated, whispered, or rapped, has been a hallmark of Black cultural production in and beyond the academy. Rest assured, though, I still shudder when reading some of those Germanic sentences.

#itiswhatitis

In some quarters, the response to *Phonographies* has progressed through an emphasis on the Black musical cultures discussed—and some that I didn't analyze, it must be said—and a concomitant oversight of its technological dimension, which, for me, is just as, if not more, important to the conceptual architecture of the book. It is impossible and undesirable to regulate how one's ideas are taken up once they circulate in the intellectual commons; I conceive of scholarly inquiry as a collective effort, so it has been gratifying to see what other scholars have done with the ideas in the book. However, this mode of reception simultaneously neglects and replicates precisely *Phonographies'* principal critique: we cannot conceive of Blackness and technology as opposed. If anything, the disavowal of technology proves my point that Blackness and technology are often still considered antithetical opponents in the ongoing war that is Western modernity. Or, to put it in more quotidian terms, it gets incredibly exhausting when you are repeatedly asked whether you explore jazz music as a genre or what you have to say about jazz after writing *Phonographies.*

#dontstartnonewontbenone
Africa is my descent, and here I'm not at home[11]

For me as a first-generation African and Black European in the US academy (I spent equal parts of my life in Somalia and Germany before moving to the United States), the relationship between the African continent and its multifarious diasporas, especially as it routed through musical cultures, is never far from my mind. In fact, early in the writing process, I carried with me a memory of a television news story that crystallized perfectly some of the concerns animating *Phonographies.* The report about the beginning stages of the civil war in Somalia (1991–2006) aired the summer of 1992 on the German television program *Weltspiegel.* It featured a Somali woman—adorned with a colorful hijab and a Kalashnikov draped over her shoulder—seated in the passenger seat of an army jeep driving through war-torn Mogadishu as she nodded her head to the beat of Salt-N-Pepa's then globe-conquering safe-sex anthem "Let's Talk About Sex," which was emanating from a small boom box.

This brief news report poignantly underscored the global circulation of different technologies: the jeep, the Kalashnikov, the boom box, and, in particular, the recorded planetary reverberations of African American music in the late twentieth century. I was also struck by the seemingly incongruent juxtaposition, which I'm sure contributed to why this particular scene was chosen by the producers of the television show, of the now-ubiquitous "veiled Muslim woman" in need of rescue by the armed forces of postmodern empire and Salt-N-Pepa's sexually explicit lyrics. Yet the Somali woman's and Salt-N-Pepa's diverging positions vis-à-vis Blackness complicate this scene,

11 D'Angelo, "Africa," on *Voodoo,* Virgin Records, 2000, CD, https://www.discogs.com /DAngelo-Voodoo/release/15906733.

showing that the Muslim world is usually not perceived as Black, and vice versa. In fact, most US news reports about Somalia around the time of the 1992 US "humanitarian" military intervention, Operation Restore Hope, conspicuously omitted that the country was predominantly Islamic. Conversely, Salt-N-Pepa, even if functioning here as the embodiment of western sexual libertarianism and imagined as the ultimate counterpart to the piety and chasteness of "the veiled Muslim woman," also unmistakably bear the burden of the hypersexualization of Black women in slavery and after.

Likewise, the scene echoed my own initial encounters with the sounds of Black America in 1970s Mogadishu, as Ella Fitzgerald and Ray Charles streamed from my parents' light-brown, faux-leather-encased portable turntable and as worn-out, imported Carl Douglas and Millie Jackson tapes emanated from my friends' mobile cassette players. Since my friends and I could hardly be accused of commanding the English language, we frequently "indigenized" the English lyrics by phonetically sounding out what we heard in Somali. So, besides sketching the broader social-historical and philosophical contours of how Black music in its various technological guises came to define western modernity, I tried to conjure this moment of creative catachresis in *Phonographies*: What structures of feeling do technologized Black sounds encode beyond lyrical content? In what ways have recording and reproduction devices, when not understood as inert conduits that immaterial sounds can transcend but as constituent forces of their affective materiality, shaped the politico-sonic lower frequencies of Black music?

Nyong'o writes, "Music is so central to traditional and modern African societies, African music is so inexhaustible . . . , that Africa could easily be nominated (although perhaps not without contention) as the sonic grounding, not only of modern Black music, but of modern music as such. But such a nomination of Africa as the origin for (Black) music would have to contend with the terms by which western epistemology calls itself to order by consigning to Africa all that is 'disordered' in the sonic, aural, oral, embodied, and ecstatic excesses of music."[12] I consciously bracketed, insofar as such a thing is possible, Africa, because I was interested in examining the global reach and technological dimensions of Black American music, especially within Black cultures in the Americas and Europe. On this front, Jemima Pierre offers a salient diagnosis about the absence of Africa in diaspora discourse and certain variants of Black studies: "The varied critiques of Afrocentrism, Black cultural

12 Nyong'o, "Afro-Philo-Sonic Fictions," 175.

nationalism, and the idea of cultural retentions within diaspora studies are what led to more than a decade of scholarship explicitly distancing itself from continental Africa."[13] Despite being in wholehearted agreement with Pierre's statement, I cannot help but wonder whether there's not more at work in this estrangement than the missing conceptual frameworks for making "Africa" a part of Black diasporic critical conversations. First, is this continental rift partially a result of the different institutional histories of Black studies and African studies in the mainstream US academy given their respective roots in, on the one hand, Third World internationalism and the late 1960s student movement and, on the other, initially colonial anthropology and later the Cold War creation of area studies? Second, how do we account for disciplinary training and expertise in an era of increased specialization? In other words, how do we integrate Africa as an idea and a reality into Black studies responsibly without the necessary scholarly immersion that would allow us to understand the specificity of different national contexts, cultures, languages, colonial histories, and so on? To be clear, I am not advocating buying into the corporate siloization of knowledge production in the mainstream US academy, which Black studies does not sit well with, so much as highlighting the institutional constraints that contribute to this rift. However, if texts such as Pierre's *The Predicament of Blackness* and Tsitsi Jaji's study *Africa in Stereo: Modernism, Music, and Pan-African Solidarity* are any indication, there is also a change afoot with regard to productively thinking together "diaspora" and "Africa."

Besides Louise Meintjes's book about the high-tech process of producing a musical studio recording in early 1990s South Africa mentioned by Nyong'o, Jaji's *Africa in Stereo* accomplishes some of the theoretical labor required to bridge the conceptual, temporal, and spatial gaps between "Africa" and "the diaspora" in Black studies. Jaji's dazzling book centers on how African American musics have been received and remixed in three African countries: Ghana, Senegal, and South Africa since the late nineteenth century in order to offer "a perspective on diaspora that includes and inscribes Africa as a constitutive locus rather than viewing it as a 'source' for diasporic populations and practices but not an active participant."[14] Instead of imagining Africa as a prelapsarian "natural resource" to be mined by diaspora Black folk at their neocolonial will in order to claim the continent as a homeland, Jaji pursues a different path: "When considering the cultural productions of the

13 Pierre, *Predicament of Blackness*, 211.
14 Jaji, *Africa in Stereo*, 6; see also Meintjes, *Sound of Africa!*

diaspora, Africa should be understood as a constitutive component of that diaspora, rather than as a point of origin now removed from the contemporary diaspora."[15] Consequently, African cultures become players in the construction of modern Blackness and Black cultures, ceasing to act as premodern fountains of authentic and antitechnological Black life.

I also appreciate that Jaji describes the centrality of African American culture to modern Blackness in Africa without acceding to the now-commonplace assertion in diaspora discourse that this position constitutes a hegemonic formation or an instance of cultural imperialism. Curiously, the critique of the predominance of African American culture within Black communities around the world often occurs through the centering of Black US culture. In other words, when critics consider Black populations outside the United States, they often show how these groupings articulate themselves as diasporic via conduits of interactions with African American politics, culture, and people, which they, in turn, identify as a hindrance and use as an occasion to reject the US variant of Blackness. However, this rejection can only occur if the analytics of Blackness remains ensconced in the realm of the empirical (map) as opposed to attempting to understand how western supremacy resolutely maintains Black subjects in the prison quarters of the non-quite-human or nonhuman.[16]

#Blackisan'Blackain't

"Look at Y'all Boys"

While I am thankful to Nyong'o for discerning the presence of gender and sexuality analyses in the book, and for his critical amplification of these ideas, *Phonographies* also exhibits some deficiencies on this front. Daphne Brooks has rightfully observed:

15 Jaji, *Africa in Stereo*, 7. For a different take on how the sonic conundrum that the diaspora versioning of Africa "would forever be threatened by not only the messy presence of an actual Africa, but even more so by literal Africans," see Louis Chude-Sokei's incisive and exacting discussion of South African roots reggae singer Lucky Dube in "When Echoes Return" (79).

16 See Weheliye, "My Volk to Come," track 4.0 in this volume. This is not say that we should not investigate differences between diasporic groups in, on the one hand, North America and, on the other hand, Africa, Asia, Europe, Latin America, and the Caribbean, but that this need not and should not be performed through the abjection of African American culture and politics.

Weheliye considers the ways that past critics have often "abandon[ed] the phone or the graph in phonograph" rather than "taking into account how sound suffuses New World Black writing" (39). I am suggesting here that we explore the ways that Hurston's use of sound in relation to her discursive ethnography demands that we theorize other forms of phonography, ones in which, for instance, embodied sonic performances directly engage with and complicate written texts. Likewise, we might think more about the ways that Zora's angular voice interrupts the phonographic projects of the literary "race men" (Du Bois and Ellison) who sit at the forefront of Weheliye's cogent study.[17]

In fact, in addition to not including any written texts by Black female, queer, or gender-nonconforming writers (early versions included analyses of Toni Morrison's *Jazz* and Paule Marshall's *Praisesong for the Widow*), *Phonographies* seriously lacks gendered analyses at the conceptual level, which, from my current perspective, appears as a greater methodological glitch. Even though I could attempt to retroactively market my readings of Du Bois's and Ellison's texts as genderqueering the African American literary canon, I will instead, say: yes, Brooks is correct in that *Phonographies'* textual gallery does feature an inordinate number of great men, albeit a bit more melanated (#*noshade*) than usual. Let me give you one example: gender is absent as an analytical category in my recounting of the history of Afro-German organizing in the final track of *Phonographies*. Why is this a problem, you may ask? Well, because not only does the narrative omit the integral role of Black German women, both queer and straight, in this history, but also, and more significantly, my consideration fails to take into account how many women-of-color feminisms have not understood gender as an isolatable—or even primary—category of analysis but have grappled with the complex relationality between different forms of subjugation and offered alternatives to these.[18] Because I was determined to render Afro-German history legible within the confines of a story about the maturing of *race consciousness*, I was unable to reflect on how taking gender into account would have allowed me to tell a different and more interesting story about how Black feminism stood at the point of origin in the context of the Afro-German political movement; how feminism was not added to a race-first undertaking.

17 Brooks, "'Sister, Can You Line It Out?,'" 623n13.
18 See, for instance, Ayim, Oguntoye, and Schultz, *Showing Our Colors*; Davies and Fido, *Out of the Kumbla*; Crenshaw, "Mapping the Margins"; Moraga and Anzaldúa, *This Bridge Called My Back*; and B. Smith, *Home Girls*.

Habeas Viscus addresses this issue head-on by centering Black feminism as a conceptual apparatus, and Hortense Spillers's and Sylvia Wynter's work in particular, in the investigation of what it means to be human in the modern world. Black feminism differs from white/Black masculinist discourses and white feminism, because the latter often aspire to abstraction from gendered and/or raced particularities—for example, white, straight men speak for all humanity, while Black, straight men speak for all Black folks, and white, straight women speak for all women. Black feminist inquiry, however, articulates its intervention from vantage points that accent the impossibility of transcending these particularities, instead enunciating its critique from perspectives that are constitutively racialized, gendered, and marked by sexualities.

Take, for instance, Nicole Waligora-Davis's monograph *Sanctuary: African Americans and Empire,* which beautifully charts how African Americans have inhabited a juridicopolitical no-man's-land situated at the juncture of native/foreigner, insider/outsider, and friend/enemy, which has allowed the US state apparatus to violently subjugate and/or completely abandon its Black citizens in a number of significant ways since the abolition of slavery. Waligora-Davis begins her study with the case of Rosa Lee Ingram (rather than Emmett Till or the Scottsboro Boys, for example), which brings to the fore how the sexual violence perpetrated against Black women such as Ingram and others is central to the subjugation of all Black people and the creation of Blackness—it is not simply an exceptional occurrence but an integral part of the whole system—and also how racial violence and racial difference are always gendered/sexualized for all Black subjects of a variety of genders and sexualities. In other words, though the lynching of Emmett Till was clearly gendered and sexualized, it is usually presented as primarily—and even exclusively—an act of racial violence.

So, Waligora-Davis's strategic situating of the Rosa Lee Ingram case at the beginning of her book—and the fact that she does not introduce the sexual harassment and threats of rape Ingram faced until after she has described the case in detail—does not displace the specificity of the sexual violence experienced by Black women in slavery and well after but rather shows how in "the cotton field and in the courtroom, race took center stage. The racially gendered asymmetries of power governing segregation did more than sanction the sexual harassment she endured: it permitted her injuries to be dismissed, her act of self-defense to be viewed as murder, and it diminished the weight of her testimony."[19] Waligora-Davis rhetorically restages how the

19 Waligora-Davis, *Sanctuary,* 7.

exclusive attention to race serves to absent the different forms of gendered sexual violence so central to the workings of Jim Crow. In the second step, Waligora-Davis highlights the interdependence—but not sameness—of the sexual violence experienced by Black women and men: "For more than fifty years (1900–52) '[n]o Louisiana-born white man had ever been executed for rape.' Meanwhile, Black males were being killed by the courts not for an actual crime, but for the 'intent to commit rape.'"[20] Bringing to light these continuities without erasing the uneven particularities therein is indicative of a specifically Black feminist perspective, which is missing from parts of *Phonographies* but forms the conceptual crux of *Habeas Viscus*.

Similarly, Beth Richie's *Arrested Justice: Black Women, Violence, and America's Prison Nation* convincingly and devastatingly demonstrates that we cannot understand the scope and depth of the prison-industrial complex without considering how its tentacles ensnare poor Black women, even though they do not represent the majority of those in cages. As a consequence, Richie's and Waligora-Davis's volumes stand as resplendent examples of feminist *and* Black perspectives, because they enact how these categories cannot be understood in isolation from one another, and how studies of Blackness need not be incompatible with analyses of gender. Or, in Hortense Spillers's inimitable phrasing:

> Though you can't talk about the era of sound in the U.S. without talking about blues and Black women. You can't talk about the eras of slavery in the Americas without talking about Black women, or Black men without Black women and how that changes the community—there is not a subject that you can speak about in the modern world where you will not have to talk about African women and new world African women. But no one wants to address them. . . . And I am saying, I am here now, and I am doing it now, and you are not going to ignore me. . . . I am here now, "Whatcha gonna do?"[21]

#whatchufinnadonow?

20 Waligora-Davis, *Sanctuary*, 9.
21 Spillers et al., "'Whatcha Gonna Do?,'" 308.

"FEENIN"

Posthuman Voices in R&B Music

Book titles tell the story. The original subtitle for *Uncle Tom's Cabin* was "The Man Who Was a Thing." In 1910 appeared a book by Mary White Ovington called *Half a Man*. Over one hundred years after the appearance of Stowe's book, *The Man Who Cried I Am*, by John A. Williams, was published. Quickskill thought of all the changes that would happen to make a "Thing" into an "I Am." Tons of paper. An Atlantic of blood. Repressed energy of anger that would form enough sun to light a solar system. A burnt-out Black hole. A cosmic slave hole. —ISHMAEL REED, *Flight to Canada* (1976)

If you listen close to the music, you'll find . . . my syste-systic humanistic sound to prove you, yeeaah. —ROGER TROUTMAN, in Zapp, "It Doesn't Really Matter," on *The New Zapp IV U* (1985)

This track takes up N. Katherine Hayles's challenge to seize this critical moment in order "to contest what the posthuman means . . . before the trains of thought it embodies have been laid down so firmly that it would take dynamite to change them," by closely examining her text *How We Became Posthuman: Virtual Bodies in Cybernetics, Literature, and Informatics*.[1] I do this because Hayles's volume provides the most elaborate history and theory of the posthuman, even while her framework embodies the "trains of thought" she herself queries. In other words, Hayles's own formulations are on the way to becoming hegemonic, at least in the discrepant disciplines in the humanities and social sciences that make up the postdiscipline of cultural studies. I begin with two contentions: the first concerns the literal and virtual whiteness of cybertheory.[2] The second establishes at the very least an aporetic relationship between New World Black cultures and the category of the "human." In addition, this track also seeks to realign the hegemony of visual media in academic considerations of virtuality by shifting the emphasis to the aural, allowing us to conjecture some of the manifold ways in which Black cultural production engages with informational technologies.[3]

This is followed by a discussion of the distinct status of the "human" in Afro-diasporic politico-cultural formations. Then my attention turns to the foremost theorist of a specifically Black posthumanity: the British music and cultural critic Kodwo Eshun.[4] Eshun's work provides an occasion to imagine alternative stagings of the human and posthuman found in the crosscurrents and discontinuities marking the history of African American music and the

This essay was first published in a special issue of *Social Text* on Afrofuturism, edited by Alondra Nelson, *Social Text* 71 (Summer 2002): 21–47. The title is from Jodeci, "Feenin," on *Diary of a Mad Band*, Uptown/MCA Records, 1993, LP, https://www.discogs.com/Jodeci-Diary-Of-A-Mad-Band/release/251832.

1   Hayles, *How We Became Posthuman*, 291 (hereafter cited parenthetically in the text).

2   If anthologies geared toward undergraduate syllabi are any indication, then *The Cybercultures Reader* seems typical in the field of cybertheory, as only three of the forty-eight articles included address racial difference. Bell and Kennedy, *Cybercultures Reader*.

3   This conflation of all things virtual with cyberspace and/or cyberpunk narratives can be found in the influential volume *Virtual Culture: Identity and Communication in Cybersociety*. While Steven Jones's introduction includes references to a variety of technologies such as telephones and VCRs, all the other essays in the collection are primarily concerned with computer-mediated communication. See S. Jones, *Virtual Culture*.

4   Eshun, *More Brilliant Than the Sun*.

informational technologies in which it has been embodied over the course of the twentieth century. To this end, my focus will be on the role of the vocoder and talk box, devices that render the human voice robotic, in R&B, since the audibly machinic Black voice amplifies the vexed interstices of race, sound, and technology. In contrast to other forms of Black popular music (jazz or hip-hop, for instance), R&B, especially post-1960s manifestations of this genre, has received little critical attention. I would like to amend this neglect by insisting on the genre's importance as a pivotal space for the co-articulation of Black subjectivity and information technologies. The interaction between the audibly mechanized and more traditionally melismatic and "soulful" voice in contemporary R&B indicates a different form of posthumanism than the one suggested by cybertheory, a posthumanism not mired in the residual effects of white liberal subjectivity, and a subjectivity located in the sonic arena rather than the ocular.

How We Were Never Human: Race and the (Post)Human

The "human" or "man," as a critical category within various permutations of western thought, has received its fair share of scrutiny, yet antihumanist thinking surely cannot be deemed a recent phenomenon.[5] In fact, most thinkers associated with poststructuralism in one way or another sought to construct modes of thinking that did not posit "the human" as its centrifugal logos. Reading Jacques Derrida's "The Ends of Man," Michel Foucault's *The Order of Things: An Archaeology of the Human Sciences*, or Louis Althusser's "Marxism and Humanism" now, one cannot help but notice their manifesto-like character in historicizing the western conception of "man" (Foucault); providing a more scientific, nonhumanist version of Marxism (Althusser); or attempting to think at the limits of "humanism" while being aware that this just reinscribes "man" (Derrida).[6] Going back further, we could say that the axial project of structuralism in its linguistic, anthropological, and literary varieties was to displace a holistic notion of the "human" by focusing on the

5 I use "Man" critically throughout to acknowledge the history of this term/concept within various western scientific, cultural, political, and economic discourses and do not seek to reinscribe the androcentrism it harbors.
6 Surely this represents a brief sketch at best; however, since my argument is not centered on these developments per se, a crude outline shall suffice. See Althusser, "Marxism and Humanism"; Derrida, "Ends of Man"; and Foucault, *Order of Things*.

various structural matrices that constitute "man." We can even locate these tendencies in the German philosophical traditions that inspired a number of poststructuralist projects, Friedrich Nietzsche and Martin Heidegger, in particular, or, for that matter, in the holy trinity of contemporary critical piety: Sigmund Freud, Karl Marx, and Ferdinand de Saussure. However, these thinkers are hardly regarded as posthumanist philosophers; instead, they are classified as "antihumanist." The term *posthuman* is most readily associated with theories of virtuality and cyberspace. In these emerging fields of inquiry, the "human" interfaces with a plethora of informational technologies in order to shed its clearly defined parameters and enter into the space and time of the posthuman. More often than not, these two positions vis-à-vis "the human" or "man" (antihumanist and posthuman) appear as distinct from rather than as part of, at the least, a similar intellectual trajectory.[7] While both these strands of thought seek to dispel the mythology of the self-same western subject in the mien of the universal "human," they largely fail to consider questions of race and colonialism, which limits not only their scope but also their analytical acuity.[8]

It is obviously nothing new to declare that cybertheory has little if anything to say about the intricate processes of racial formation, whether US based or within a more global framework. While gender and sexuality have been crucial to theorizations of both cyberspace and the posthuman, the absence of race is usually perfunctorily remarked and of little consequence to these analyses.[9] Critics such as Joe Lockard and Kali Tal have dealt with the

7. The anthology edited by Neal Badmington does an admirable job of combining poststructuralist theses concerning "man" by Foucault and Roland Barthes, among others, with writings that address the fusion of "humanity" and informational technologies, and an excerpt from Frantz Fanon's *The Wretched of the Earth*. See Badmington, *Readers in Cultural Criticism*. See also the essays compiled in Halberstam and Livingston, *Posthuman Bodies*.

8. Here I am calling for rigorous thinking together of these antihumanist philosophies and Afro-diasporic discourses about humanism, rather than the "application" of poststructuralist theories to slavery and colonialism. The fusion of these discourses is most forcefully articulated in the sizable oeuvres of Stuart Hall, Hortense Spillers, Gayatri Spivak, and Sylvia Wynter.

9. At the outset of her monograph, Hayles briefly mentions postcolonial and feminist critics who have scrutinized the liberal humanist subject (4). Although gender appears throughout her project, race does not form an integral aspect of Hayles's analysis. Similarly, in her volume on Antigone, Judith Butler invokes race in relation to the questions of kinship at the core of her argument. Citing Angela Davis, Orlando Patterson, and Carol Stack, in what seems little more

erasure of race from these studies, but their work remains ghettoized rather than integrated into the mainstream of cybertheory.[10] Hayles is no exception in this regard: while gender takes center stage in much of Hayles's discussion of these cultural and technological constellations, her analysis seems to be symptomatic of the field as a whole. Although it is not Hayles's project per se to interrogate race in relation to virtuality, the erasure of race severely limits how we conceive of the complex interplay between "humans" and informational technologies.

---

than a politically correct afterthought, Butler contends that racial slavery eradicated any traditional notions of kinship for Black subjects. Yet, at the close of the text, Butler turns to questions of "humanity," positing that kinship is the precondition of the human and that Antigone asks us to imagine "a new field of the human, . . . when gender is displaced, and kinship founders on its own founding laws." Here race drops out of the picture, subsumed by gender, and Butler's earlier arguments about race, kinship, and slavery remain a mere footnote. However, New World slavery did not merely abolish normative kinship structures but positioned Black subjects as nonhuman; as Butler herself acknowledges, one is the precondition of the other. I am belaboring this seemingly minute point because it seems indicative of not only Butler's otherwise admirable work but the majority of Anglo-American poststructuralist-inflected cultural studies, where questions of race are a sideshow at best, and gender, sexuality, and class are accorded near-universal status. See Butler, *Antigone's Claim*, 72–82. Étienne Balibar brings this point home when he poses the following rhetorical question in order to highlight the different ways racism and sexism are treated as generalizable critical categories: "What would have been the reactions if I had proposed to talk *about sexism as universalism or nationalism as universalism*? Most likely you would have said: O.K., we agree, we know that already, since the case has already been argued and we made up our minds concerning the limits or conditions within which such formulas can be used." Balibar, "Racism as Universalism," 192. For an illuminating argument concerning slavery and kinship, see Hortense Spillers's brilliant "Mama's Baby, Papa's Maybe: An American Grammar Book."

10 See Tal, "Unbearable Whiteness of Being"; Tal, "Duppies in the Machine"; and Lockard, "Virtual Whiteness and Narrative Diversity." The fact that both Lockard's and Tal's important interventions have thus far been accessible only online, and not as part of traditional academic anthologies or journals, only magnifies their marginalization within cybertheory. See also the essays collected in Kolko, Nakamura, and Rodman, *Race in Cyberspace*. Thomas Foster argues—somewhat haphazardly, I might add—that African American culture prefigures cybertheory, which suspends Black culture in a pretechnological bubble, instead of making it central to contemporary techno-informational ecologies. See Foster, "Souls of Cyber-Folk."

Hayles's general argument provides a trenchant scrutiny of "how information lost its body," that is, the manifold ways in which information is thought to transcend materiality, continuing the Cartesian tradition of placing mind over matter, only in this framework the content of techno-informational flows replaces the "human" mind (2).[11] Not only does this particular form of disembodiment extend the Cartesian mind/matter dichotomy, it also preserves the idea of the liberal subject, represented as *having* a body but not *being* a body (4). Hayles draws her definition of subjectivity from C. B. Macpherson's classic, *A Theory of Possessive Individualism*, wherein he delineates the liberal subject as "the proprietor of his own person, or capacities, owing nothing to society for them. . . . The human essence is freedom from the will of others, and freedom is the function of possession."[12] Summarizing Macpherson's take on Thomas Hobbes and John Locke, Hayles asserts that the liberal subject was thought to predate the market by virtue of wielding ownership over the self (the natural self), which resisted corruption by market forces and was taken to be the unalienable natural right of "man" (3). Still, as both Hayles and Macpherson note, this "human" is very much a product of the market and in no way anterior to its forces, especially in the United States, where citizenship and personhood were, and in some ways still are, predicated on property ownership, and, thus, "freedom is the function of possession."[13] Though careful to stress that the liberal version of selfhood is only that—one particular way of thinking about what it means to be "human"—and not wishing resuscitate this rendition of subjectivity, in the end Hayles unwillingly privileges this modality, for it serves as her sine qua non for human subjectivity. Put differently, Hayles needs the hegemonic western conception of humanity as a heuristic category against which to position her theory of posthumanism, in the process recapitulating the ways in which the western liberal theory of the "human," instantiated in the eighteenth century, came to represent "humanity" sui generis.

According to Hayles, the posthuman subject renders this conception of the "natural self" obsolete, since discrete boundaries and unmitigated agency

11 This provides only one of the three narratives of Hayles's consideration; the other two concern "how the cyborg was created as a technological artifact and cultural icon" and how "the human is giving way to a different construction called the posthuman" (2).

12 Macpherson, quoted in Hayles, *How We Became Posthuman*, 3.

13 For arguments concerning the interlocking vectors of whiteness and property in the US context, see Lipsitz, *Possessive Investment in Whiteness*; and Harris, "Whiteness as Property."

give way to an "amalgam . . . of heterogeneous components, a material-informational entity whose boundaries undergo continuous construction and reconstruction" (3). While I sympathize with Hayles's desire to redraft this hegemonic western version of personhood, her singular focus on this particular historical composite unnecessarily weighs down her project, since the posthuman frequently appears as little more than the white liberal subject in techno-informational disguise. Even when giving examples of paradigmatic posthumans, Hayles falls back on white masculinist constructions by citing the Six Million Dollar Man and RoboCop as avatars of the posthuman condition; at the very least, the category could have been expanded by including the Bionic Woman (or her contemporary version, who appeared in the aftermath of Hayles's book, the transracial and transspecies main character from the TV show *Dark Angel*). Similarly, in the readings of classical science fiction (Philip K. Dick) and cyberpunk narratives (William Gibson and Neal Stephenson) or in the redaction of the history of cybernetics, Hayles reinscribes white masculinity as the (human) point of origin from which to progress to a posthuman state. It seems that one has to be always already "free from the will of others" (or think that one is) in order to mutate into the fusion of heterogeneous agents comprising the posthuman state of being, thereby excluding all cultural and political formations in which the history of subjectivity is necessarily yoked to the will—and/or the whips and chains—of others.[14] Certainly, New World Black subjects cannot inhabit this version of selfhood in quite the same manner as the "white boys" of Hayles's canon due to slavery, colonialism, racism, and segregation, since these forces render the very idea that one could be "free from the will of others" null and void.[15]

Ironically, the specters of race and slavery haunt the margins of Hayles's argument through the use of Toni Morrison's novel *Beloved* at a strategic point in her discussion. Here is how she describes her project: "This book is a 'rememory' in the sense of Toni Morrison's *Beloved*: putting back together parts that have lost touch with one another and reaching out toward a complexity too unruly to fit into zeros and ones" (13). However, Hayles neglects to explore the implications of Morrison's text, especially in regard to notions of humanity

14 Furthermore, Hayles seems to endorse the crass Cartesianism she finds deplorable in cybernetics when she writes, in a sentence that reads like a paraphrase of René Descartes's famous *cogito, ergo sum* formula, "People become posthuman because they think they are posthuman" (6).

15 While the designation "white boys" might sound flippant, I think it provides an apt description of the white techno-geek tradition Hayles draws on to construct her argument.

as they are refracted through the history of slavery. Morrison's novel highlights both the absence and the construction of what we now associate with the liberal humanist subject, depicting the dehumanizing effects of slavery on particular Black subjects and their struggle to reconstruct their fractured bodies and subjectivities in slavery's aftermath. But the novel also insists that there can be no uncomplicated embrace of liberal humanist subject positions by Black people after slavery. The literal dehumanization of Black people through chattel slavery as well as by the legal, political, anthropological, scientific, economic, and cultural forces supporting and enforcing this system, afforded Black subjects no easy passage to the sign of the human. To phrase this conundrum in the spirit of Morrison's narrative, once your animal characteristics have been measured against human ones in the pages of the plantation ledger, desiring the particular image of humanity on the other side of this very ledger seems, to put it mildly, futile. Or as Saidiya Hartman describes the transition from "subhuman" to "human": "The transubstantiation of the captive into the volitional subject, chattel into proprietor, and the circumscribed body of Blackness into the disembodied and abstract universal seems improbable, if not impossible."[16] Consequently, the human has had a very different meaning in Black culture and politics than it has enjoyed in mainstream America.

Because theories of posthumanity are so closely associated with theorizations of cyberspace, computer-mediated communication often appears to be the precondition for becoming posthuman. Even though critics such as Friedrich Kittler, Lisa Gitelman, Sadie Plant, and Steven Connor have cast a wider historical and conceptual net by analyzing film, the phonograph, the telephone, and the radio as informational technologies, these works largely assume the disciplinary guise of media theory and/or history and not cybertheory.[17] Moreover, cybertheory frequently positions computer-mediated communication as the be-all and end-all of virtuality and informational technologies.[18] To be sure, *How We Became Posthuman* skillfully fuses

16 Hartman, *Scenes of Subjection*, 123.
17 Connor, "Modern Auditory I"; Gitelman, *Scripts, Grooves, and Writing Machines*; Kittler, *Discourse Networks, 1800/1900*; Kittler, *Gramophone, Film, Typewriter*; and Plant, *Zeroes and Ones*.
18 One of the more egregious manifestations of this techno-myopia lurks in the pages of Paul Levinson's "natural history" of information technologies. He writes, "The phonograph and motion pictures of course also figure in this recent natural history, but in this rendition they play supporting rather than leading roles. . . . [T]he pace of invention came so quick in the nineteenth and twentieth century that I have focused on only those media whose presence

the scientific and literary discourses of the posthuman, yet save for canonical science fiction and contemporary cyberpunk, the traditional cultural topoi of cybertheory, the book examines little outside of the world of cybernetics. Incorporating other informational media, such as sound technologies, counteracts the marginalization of race rather than rehashing the whiteness, masculinity, and disembodiment of cybernetics and informatics.[19] In one of the first anthologies specifically concerned with racialized subjects and technology, the editors introduce the volume with the following cogent observation: "*Technicolor* presents a full spectrum of stories about how people of color produce, transform, appropriate, and consume technologies in their everyday lives. In order to locate these stories, we found it necessary to use a broader understanding of technology and to include not only those thought to create revolutions (e.g., information technologies) but also those with which people come in contact in their daily lives. For when we limit discussions about technology simply to computer hardware and software, we see only a 'digital divide' that leaves people of color behind."[20]

For my own purposes, these alternate configurations are most readily found in the histories of sound technologies and their interaction with

---

was clearly decisive in shaping our world prior to computers." Levinson, *Soft Edge*, xii. In addition to construing "computers" as the teleological end point into which all other information technologies flow, this quote begs a basic question concerning empirical evidence. If sound recording and cinema were/are not instrumental in "shaping our world," I'm not sure any other media would qualify. In fact, these two cultural technologies seem to be more influential in mediating past and current lifeworlds than any other media, especially in nonwestern contexts, where "computers" are still a rarity.

19 Hayles's critique and theory only "work" because she positions her own insights against the retrograde impulses of cybernetics and informatics as opposed to writing about more contemporary discourses that already incorporate notions of informational embodiment. Just to name one of the most obvious examples, Donna Haraway's hugely influential "A Cyborg Manifesto: Science, Technology, and Socialist Feminism in the 1980's," far from renouncing embodiment, is almost singularly concerned with questions of technology as they connect with the corporeal. Moreover, in contrast to Hayles, Haraway also makes race central to her interpretive endeavor.

20 Hines, Nelson, and Tu, "Introduction," 5. This sentiment echoes Samuel Delany's differentiation between "the white boxes of computer technology" and "the Black boxes of modern street technology," in which the former appear as much more technological than the latter. According to Delany, this hierarchical division is often racially color coded. Delany, in Dery, "Black to the Future," 192.

twentieth-century Black cultural practices. These counterhistories do not adhere to the effacing of embodiment Hayles exposes in cybernetics and informatics; they gesture toward a more complex interaction between embodiment and disembodiment, the human and the posthuman.

At the outset of *How We Became Posthuman*, Hayles envisions being posthuman as intrinsically tied to the ocular provenances of the computer screen: "As you gaze at the flickering signifiers scrolling down the computer screens, no matter what identification you assign to the embodied entities that you cannot see, you have already become posthuman" (xiv). This does not represent a significant departure from most cybertheory, which focuses almost singularly on the scopic; however, Hayles endeavors to compensate for this omission by including the sonic technology of tape recording in her conceptualization of the sign of the human as it is embodied by and in informational technologies. In a reading of William Burroughs's 1962 novel, *The Ticket That Exploded*, Hayles argues that the relationship between electronic voices and the body via the tape-recording mechanisms in this text are "harbingers of the posthuman body," which are fully realized informational technological environments. Tape recording, Hayles suggests, as opposed to the radio and the phonograph, harbored more interactive features by virtue of "permitting erasure and rewriting" (208). The phonograph, on the other hand, "functioned primarily as a technology of inscription, reproducing sound through a rigid disk that allowed neither the interactive spontaneity of telephone nor the ephemerality of radio" (208). Hayles recognizes that the technology of the phonograph dislodged the coupling of voice and presence by splitting sounds from the sources that produced them. But if we survey the cultural history of sound recording and reproduction, especially in its early stages as an office instrument and a technology that enabled erasure and rewriting as much as tape recording, we can surmise that a host of cultural practices around the phonograph rendered this technology no less interactive and ephemeral than either the telephone or radio.[21] In fact, the phonograph became an instrument of "rigid inscription" only because it so acutely unsettled prevalent notions of the voice, presence, and the "nature" of writing. Race was also a crucial factor in the late nineteenth-century debates around the phonograph, since the racial identity of musical performers was no longer visually verifiable due to the sound/source split. Because the technology of the phonograph did not allow easy access to racial categorization,

21 On this point, see Morton, *Off the Record*, 13–19.

among other things, various visual and cultural factors were introduced to fix the identity of vocal performers.[22]

If we follow Hayles's notion of the posthuman as an embodied virtuality, then recording and reproducing human voices certainly falls into the force field of the posthuman. Because technologically mediated human voices were considered nonhuman due to their mechanical embodiment, various cultural mechanisms had to be instantiated in order to reinscribe humanness and presence; early discourses on the phonograph testify to this embodied virtuality, picturing the voice emanating from the phonograph as nonhuman and ghostly.[23] This tension between the nonhuman and the human, presence and absence, reaches its pinnacle in the traffic between Black popular music and the various recording and reproduction technologies it has been transmitted through over the course of the twentieth century. From the onset of the mass production and distribution of recorded sound in the 1920s, Black popular music functioned as the embodiment of the virtual voice. Instead of merely producing a disembodied virtuality avant la lettre, the phonograph harbors an always-embodied virtuality, particularly in relation to Black voices. Paradoxically, Black voices are materially disembodied by the phonograph and other sound technologies, while Black subjects are inscribed as the epitome of embodiment through a multitude of US cultural discourses.

The Souls of Black Folks

Afro-diasporic thinking has not evinced the same sort of distrust and/or outright rejection of "man" in its universalist, postenlightenment guise as western antihumanist or posthumanist philosophies.[24] Instead, Black humanist

---

22 See Gitelman, *Scripts, Grooves, and Writing Machines*, 121–39.

23 The ghostliness of the voice emanating from the phonograph was also highlighted in scenes depicting "primitive" peoples' ascription of magical powers to this machinery, which they most often encountered as an instrument of western ethnography. Michael Taussig writes, "Here every effort is made to represent mimeticizing technology as magical, and the question must be repeated—because the phonographic *mis en scene* is surprisingly common in twentieth-century descriptions of 'primitive' peoples—as to why westerners are so fascinated by Others' fascination with this apparatus." Taussig, *Mimesis and Alterity*, 199.

24 Du Bois, *Souls of Black Folk*. Clearly this text represents one of the originating moments in twentieth-century African American intellectual history for

discourses emphasize the historicity and mutability of the "human" itself, gesturing toward different, catachrestic, conceptualizations of this category.[25] However, wielding this particular and historically contingent classification should not be read, as is often the case, as a mere uncritical reiteration, as if there were such a thing, of humanist discourses. Black discourses have consistently laid claim to "humanity" in multifarious ways, starting with Phyllis Wheatley's poetry at the end of the eighteenth century and continuing throughout the nineteenth century, as exemplified by the works of David Walker, Maria Stewart, Martin Delany, and Anna Julia Cooper. While invocations of humanism in the twentieth century surely stem from different motivations than those historically preceding them, these ideas are elaborated by such thinkers as W. E. B. Du Bois, Alain Locke, Jessie Fauset, Richard Wright, Zora Neale Hurston, Aimé Césaire, James Baldwin, Ralph Ellison, Frantz Fanon, Audre Lorde, and Édouard Glissant, to name a few. Far from renouncing "humanity," these intellectuals have all focused on this category. Clearly, this emphasis on "humanity" results from the histories of slavery and colonialism and the racial, gender, and sexual violence ensuing from these forces. Indeed, as Ishmael Reed's epigraph to this track conveys, the "middle passages" of Black culture to and in the New World are not marked so much by "humanity" as by an acute lack thereof, a "Black hole" of humanity, so to speak. Since Black subjects were deemed the radical obverse of enlightened and rational "man," various Black discourses have sought to appropriate this category. In the words of Frantz Fanon: "We must turn over a new leaf, we must work out new concepts, and try to set afoot a new man."[26] This new "man" is the subject of Ishmael Reed's "cosmic slave hole," where "humanity" neither begins nor ends with the white masculine liberal subject. Thus, any consideration of antihumanism and/or the posthuman should contemplate the status of humanity from the vantage point of this "cosmic slave hole."

Afro-Caribbean theorist Sylvia Wynter's attempt to recast the human sciences in relation to a new conception of "man" provides contexts in which to think the "human" that not only bridge the ever-widening gap between the cognitive life sciences and humanities but also incorporate the colonial

the twinning of music/voice and the soul of Black America. For an extended meditation on this issue, see Weheliye, "In the Mix."

25 On catachresis, see Spivak, *Outside in the Teaching Machine*, 137, 161–62, and passim; and Derrida, "White Mythology."

26 Fanon, *Wretched of the Earth*, 316.

and racialist histories of the "human."[27] Tracing the longue durée of western modernity, Wynter maintains that the religious conception of the self gave way to two modes of secularized subjectivity, first, the Cartesian "Rational Man" and then, beginning "at the end of the eighteenth century,... Man as a selected being and natural organism ... as the universal human, 'man as man.'"[28] In the discursive and material universe of "biological idealism," the second of Wynter's modes of secularized being, Black subjects served as limit cases by which "man" could define himself as the universal "human."[29] Here "man" appears as "man" via disidentification and abjection, wherein whiteness connotes the full humanity gleaned only in relation to the lack of humanity in Blackness. Moreover, "the Black population groups of the New World [acted] as the embodied bearers of Ontological lack to the secular model of being, Man, as the conceptual Other."[30] Because New World Black subjects were denied access to the position of humanity for so long, "humanity" refuses to signify any ontological primacy within Afro-diasporic discourses. In Black culture this category becomes a designation that shows its finitudes and exclusions very clearly, thereby denaturalizing the "human" as a universal formation while at the same time laying claim to

27 Wynter's articles are numerous; for my purposes here, I have chosen to consult the following three: "Beyond the Word of Man: Glissant and the New Discourse of the Antilles"; "On Disenchanting Discourse: 'Minority' Literary Criticism and Beyond"; and "Columbus, the Ocean Blue, and Fables That Stir the Mind: To Reinvent the Study of Letters." For a succinct introduction to Wynter's project in the context of Afro-Caribbean philosophy, see Henry, *Caliban's Reason*, 117–43. Wynter characterizes her disciplinary strategy as situated at the interstices of the humanities and cognitive sciences as "a science of the human, which takes as its objects of inquiry the correlation between our rhetorico-discursively instituted systems of meaning and the neurochemical signaling field that they orchestrate and which can therefore isolate and identify the rules of functioning of the meaning-neural dynamics which govern our behaviors, instituting us as specific modes of that hybrid logos/bios mode of existence: the human." Wynter, "Beyond the Word of Man," 646.
28 Wynter, "Beyond the Word of Man," 645. At a different point in the article, Wynter explains the "selected" in that quote: "The human as an evolutionarily selected natural organism now differed from other forms of organic life only by the fact that it created 'culture'" (640).
29 Wynter, "On Disenchanting Discourse," 436.
30 Wynter, "Beyond the Word of Man," 641. Wynter also lists the native, woman, worker, mad, and unfit as further ontological others; however, she insists that the designation "nigger" holds a particularly volatile position in the "Man as Man" configuration (642).

it. Put differently, at the moment in which Black people enter into humanity, this very idea loses its ontological thrust because its limitations are rendered abundantly clear. Black humanism disenchants "Man as Man," bringing "into being different modes of the *human*" because it deploys the very formulation of "man" as catachresis.[31] Both poststructuralist antihumanism and later debates about the posthuman might do well to incorporate these ontological others into their theories in order to better situate and analyze the porous perimeters of the "human."

Black humanism has found one of its most persistent articulations in the vexed discursive entanglements around Black people's souls over the course of the past 150 years, most markedly in relation to Black popular music. In *Blackness and Value: Seeing Double,* Lindon Barrett maintains that the Black voice functions as a figure of value within African American culture, particularly as it is contrasted with the lack of value ascribed to Blackness in American mainstream culture. In a complex argument, Barrett distinguishes the *singing voice* from the *signing voice* of Euro-American alphabetical literacy, writing that the singing voice "provides a primary means by which African Americans may exchange an expended, valueless self in the New World for a productive, recognized self."[32] The *signing voice*, by contrast, represents the literacy of the white Enlightenment subject discussed above.[33] As in Hayles's

31 Wynter, "On Disenchanting Discourse," 466.
32 Barrett, *Blackness and Value,* 57. Although I endorse Barrett's astute and useful differentiation between the *signing voice* and the *singing voice,* at times it runs the risk of configuring the Black singing voice as always already embodied rather than as a series of strategies and/or techniques of corporeality. Moreover, emphasizing the "ludic corporeality" of the Black singing voice also veers too close to positioning certain Black voices, Black female voices in particular, as more "authentically Black" than others. In this way, Barrett might find himself in cahoots—which I'm fairly certain is not his intention—with critics who deem Aretha Franklin's style "Blacker" than, let's say, Diana Ross's or Jessye Norman's. I would suggest the term *sanging* as more apt and nonontologizing, in line with Barrett's thinking, because it brings to the fore questions of technique and skill in addition to those factors outlined above.
33 In his discussion of Enlightenment notions of literacy and "humanity," Barrett conjures the same passage from Macpherson as Hayles. Barrett, *Blackness and Value,* 69. In addition, Barrett forcefully argues against the notion of alphabetical literacy as a guarantor of freedom in the annals of eighteenth- and nineteenth-century African American literature, a position central to the formation of contemporary African American literary studies, and previously exposed by Black feminist critics such as Valerie Smith (75).

account of western thinking, the *signing voice* signals full humanity, white-ness, and disembodiment, whereas the *singing voice* metonymically enacts Blackness, embodiment, and subhumanity. For Barrett the corporeality, or "sly alterity," as he terms it, furnishes the Black singing voice's most destabiliz-ing feature.[34] He writes, "The African American singing voice emphasizes—rather than merely glances at—the spatial, material, dative, or enunciative action of voice. Singing voices undo voice as speech per se. By highlighting the enunciative or vocative aspect and moment of voice, singing voices mark the absence that allows iteration and repetition. They imprint above all the pure sonorous audibility of voice, and not a seeming absolute proximity to fixed meaning and identity."[35]

In this sense, the Black *singing voice* suggests a rather different access to the category of "humanity" than the *signing voice*, and in the process under-mines the validity of the liberal subject as the sign for the "human," providing a fully embodied version thereof. Thus, Black subjectivity appears as the an-tithesis to the enlightenment subject by virtue of not only having a body but being the body—within enlightenment discourses Blackness is the body and nothing else. But what happens once the Black voice becomes disembodied, severed from its source, recontextualized, and appropriated? All these things occurred when the first collections of transcribed spirituals became readily available for public consumption during the Civil War and continued with the recording and reproduction through various media of the Black voice in the twentieth century.

Far from being transmitted "in [a] startlingly authentic form," as Barrett will have it, the Black singing voice, decoupled from its human source and placed in the context of spiritual collections and, subsequently, phonograph records, insinuates a much more overdetermined and unwieldy constella-tion within both Black and mainstream American cultural discourses.[36] As both Ronald Radano and Jon Cruz have shown, spirituals, once transcribed and compiled, served both white and Black abolitionist purposes as embodi-ments of Black humanity.[37] Moreover, according to Cruz, "white moral and cultural entrepreneurs found [Negro spirituals] to be their *preferred* cultural expression by Blacks."[38] Black sacred, and later secular, music took on two

---

34 Barrett, *Blackness and Value*, 58.
35 Barrett, *Blackness and Value*, 84.
36 Barrett, *Blackness and Value*, 86.
37 See Cruz, *Culture on the Margins*; and Radano, "Denoting Difference."
38 Cruz, *Culture on the Margins*, 4.

simultaneous functions: proving Black peoples' soul and standing in for the soul of all US culture, keeping the racially particular and national universal in constant tension. Thus, spirituals ushered in a long history of white appropriations of Black music, ranging from the "slumming" patrons of the Cotton Club to Norman Mailer's "white negroes" to 1990s hip-hop "whiggers" to the digital Blackface of the 2010s and 2020s.[39] All of this goes to show that while the Black singing voice harbors moments of value, as suggested in Barrett's scheme, it can hardly be construed as a purely authentic force, particularly once delocalized and offered up for national and/or international consumption. The "soul," and by extension the "humanity," of Black subjects, therefore, is often imbricated in white mainstream culture, customarily reflecting an awareness of this very entanglement.[40]

Taking the negative ontological placement of Black subjects in western modernity as his point of departure, Kodwo Eshun constructs an argument that posits a specifically Black constellation of the posthuman, in which New World Black subjects have privileged access to the posthuman because they were denied the status of human for so long.[41] Eshun belongs to a growing number of critics who explore the intersections of Black cultural production, technology, and science fiction, collected under the rubric Afrofuturism, including Greg Tate, Sheree Thomas, Mark Dery, Carol Cooper, Nalo Hopkinson, Paul D. Miller (DJ Spooky), and the many contributors to the Afrofuturism website and LISTSERV. Eshun's 1998 volume *More Brilliant Than the Sun: Adventures in Sonic Fiction* represents the most extensive manifesto of this movement, tracing different forms of alienness and posthumanity through various genres of post–World War II Black popular music, including jazz, funk, hip-hop, techno, and jungle, as well as providing a dazzling account of the technicity of Black music.[42] Eshun claims that the

39 On digital Blackface, see Jackson, *White Negroes.*

40 Here I am only listing the most obvious cases, although there are numerous other scenarios, especially ones outside the United States that involve non–African Americans utilizing Black popular music.

41 The following discussion of Eshun draws on my review essay of his book. See Weheliye, "Keepin' It (Un)Real."

42 The LISTSERV, http://groups.yahoo.com/group/afrofuturism (accessed January 12, 2003, no longer available). The website's address is http://www.afrofuturism .net. Sheree Thomas's edited anthology *Dark Matter: A Century of Speculative Fiction from the African Diaspora* contains mostly fictional pieces but also includes some essays about Black science fiction by such authors as Samuel Delany, Walter Mosley, and Octavia Butler. See also Diedrichsen, *Loving the Alien.* One might also

sign of the human harbors a negative significance, if any, in Afrofuturist musical configurations. In these genres, he argues, shifting forms of nonhuman otherworldliness replace the human as the central characteristic of Black subjectivity:

> The idea of slavery as an alien abduction means that we've all been living in an alien-nation since the 18th century. The mutation of African male and female slaves in the 18th century into what became negro, and into an entire series of humans that were designed in America. That whole process, the key behind it all is that in America none of these humans were *designated* human. It's in the music that you get this sense that most African-Americans *owe nothing to the status of the human*. There is this sense of the human as being a really pointless and treacherous category.[43]

As a result of the dehumanizing forces of slavery, in Eshun's frame of reference, certain Black popular musics stage Black subjectivity, bypassing the modality of the human in the process of moving from the subhuman to the posthuman. According to Eshun, Black posthumanism stands in stark contrast to the strong humanist strand found in a host of Black cultural styles, ranging from the majority of African American literature to the history of soul and the blues. Eshun describes these two modes of thinking as Afro-diasporic futurism and the humanist futureshock absorbers of mainstream Black culture. Eshun's important work unearths some of the radical strands of Black music, which refuse to uncritically embrace the western conception of "the human," are largely instrumental, and therefore do not rely on the Black voice as a figure of value.

In Eshun's argument, these allegedly Black humanist discourses continually appeal to humanity, at the same time positing the "human" as their Platonic ideal: "Like Brussels sprouts, humanism is good for you, nourishing, nurturing, soulwarming—and from Phyllis Wheatley to R. Kelly, present-day R&B is a perpetual fight for human status, a yearning for human rights, a struggle for inclusion within the human species."[44] While both of these schools of Afro-diasporic cultural discourses (Afrodiasporic futurism and humanist

consult John Akomfrah's film *The Last Angel of History*, which puts into practice the musical and literary provenances of Afrofuturism by way of both fictional narrative and documentary means.

43 Eshun, *More Brilliant Than the Sun*, 192–93 (emphases mine).

44. Eshun, *More Brilliant Than the Sun*, 006.

futureshock absorbers) surely exist, they are not quite as categorically antagonistic as Eshun imagines them to be.[45] If we consider the history of Black American popular music, we can see both forces, the humanist and posthumanist, at work. From nineteenth-century spirituals through the blues, jazz, soul, hip-hop, and techno, the human and the posthuman are in constant dynamic tension. It is precisely because slavery rendered the category of the human suspect that the reputedly humanist postslavery Black cultural productions cannot and do not attribute the same meaning to humanity as white American discourses. These inscriptions of humanity in Black culture provide particular performances of the human—singularities, if you will, that always incorporate their own multiplicities—as opposed to mere uncritical echoes of the white liberal humanist subject.[46] Eshun, in his move to polemicize against Black humanism, takes the performance of the human in Black literature and music at face value, leaving behind its most radical gesture of marking the boundaries and limitations of the human itself.[47]

Hypersoul

Even though numerous cultural discourses have done their best to authenticate and naturalize the soul of Black popular music, the musical practices themselves frequently defy these authenticating mechanisms by embracing new technologies, hybridities, and self-consciousness about the performative aspects of soul.[48] Beginning with the blues queens of the 1920s, Bessie Smith

45 Eshun himself recognizes that the opposition between Afrofuturism and Black humanism is far from absolute, but he insists on constantly invoking the split as a heuristic device throughout the text: "At Century's End, the Futurhythmachine has 2 opposing tendencies, 2 synthetic drives: the Soulful and the Postsoul. But then all music is made of both tendencies running simultaneously at all levels, so you can't merely oppose a humanist R&B with a posthuman Techno." Eshun, *More Brilliant Than the Sun*, 006.

46 This is a reference to Jean-Luc Nancy's conception of "being with" in which singularities such as the "I" or the "event" always harbor multiplicities rather than standing on their own. Nancy, *Being Singular Plural*.

47 On this point, see Donna Haraway's discussion of Sojourner Truth's appropriation of "humanity," which "holds the promise of a never settled universal." Haraway, "Ecce Homo," 92.

48 These discourses are continually entangled in contemporary cultural productions, as is apparent in the 1999 Pepsi commercial featuring that annoying curly-haired little girl channeling the voice of Aretha Franklin. The success of this advertisement, in which a white child moves her body in a manner *similar*

and Ma Rainey; followed by Motown, Philly sounds, and disco of the 1960s and 1970s; and continuing with contemporary hip-hop and R&B, so-called humanist musical practices display complex engagements with soul. In order to provide more specific examples of how the definitions of the human and posthuman might shift if we look and listen beyond the topical and analytical borders of cybertheory and Eshun's Afrofuturist figurations, I will now turn my attention to contemporary examples of Black popular music's engagement with informational technologies. I am most interested in the status of the recorded voice in contemporary mainstream R&B, because this genre, pace Eshun, does not so much absorb the "futureshock" of Afrofuturism but reconstructs the Black voice in relation to information technologies.

While singers remain central to the creation of Black music, they do so only in conjunction with the overall sonic architecture, especially in the turn away from the lead singer as the exclusive artist to more producer-driven and collaborative musical productions. This has its scattered origins in musics designated by terms such as the Motown or Philly sounds rather than the naming of oeuvres in relation to particular singers. Most Motown artists, for example, collaborated with Holland-Dozier-Holland; Norman Whitfield shaped the sonic provenances of the Temptations' early 1970s work; and Kenny Gamble and Leon Huff were instrumental in constructing the sound of the O'Jays and other artists on the Philly International label, which ensured that the technological mediation and creation of soul became part and parcel of the musical performance.

Currently, the most prominent R&B producers, such as Missy Elliott, Sean "Puffy" Combs, Timbaland, Rodney Jerkins (Darkchild), or the Neptunes, have become omnipresent on the vocal tracks of R&B and music videos for the songs they produce. Jerkins routinely announces his songs as Darkchild "products"; on Destiny's Child's "Say My Name," for example, he states "Darkchild 99" in the opening sequence of the track.[49] Oftentimes producers

---

to that of Aretha but is able to replicate Aretha's voice precisely—through the wonders of sound recording and reproduction—confirms that the tension between these discourses of soul still occupies center stage in American cultural productions.

49 Destiny's Child, "Say My Name," SONY Music, 1999, CD single, https://www .discogs.com/release/535616-Destinys-Child-Say-My-Name. Not only does Jerkins proclaim his musical "property," but his voice also forms a crucial component in the call-and-response part later in the song. In general, numerous R&B songs are identified with the producers, not primarily the performers; and most high-profile R&B and hip-hop producers also record and perform

provide guest raps, and the artists themselves acknowledge their production wizards in the lyrics, providing something akin to aural signatures.[50] On Ginuwine's "Same Ol' G," Timbaland half-sings and raps with the performer, constantly sonically inscribing his own name so that the line between performer and producer vanishes into thin musical air.[51] The human voice has signaled presence, fullness, and the coherence of the subject not only in western philosophical discourses but also in popular music and popular music criticism.[52] Other genres of popular music attempt to erase their technological mediation and embodiment, remaining mired in the myth of what Theodore Gracyk terms "recording realism," which insists on the authenticity, integrity, and naturalness of the recorded performance.[53] But no recorded performances, not even live recordings, are "real" or even representations of reality thereof; rather, they are virtual productions created through interactions of musicians and listeners with recording and reproduction technologies. By embracing new technologies such as remixing, scratching, and sampling, Black popular music producers and performers persistently emphasize the virtuality of any form of recorded music. Acknowledging the effects of these technologies on these musical practices, Black popular musical genres make their own virtuality central to the musical texts. Instead of pulling the strings in the background, that is, being disembodied, these producers, who plug the performers into the technological apparatus, take front and center stage with the artists. This creates a composite identity, a machine

---

in their own right. Jerkins makes his presence felt vocally on the tracks he has produced for Brandy, Toni Braxton, and Whitney Houston as well.

50 These aural signatures should be distinguished from "the sound" associated with particular producers since they do not unabashedly and unmistakably imprint the name and subjectivity of the producer. Rather, the producer's "sound" leaves room for the performer's vocal signature, which in these cases becomes secondary to the producer's aural presence.

51 Ginuwine, "Same Ol' G," Blackground/SONY Music, 1999, CD single, https://www.discogs.com/release/2917694-Ginuwine-Same-Ol-G.

52 See, for instance, John Corbett's point about the supposed "expressiveness" and "coherence" of the lead voice in pop music, which he distinguishes from the "harmonic bed" of the background vocals. Corbett, *Extended Play*, 64. See also Philip Brian Harper's pertinent observations about lead and background vocals as they are refracted through racial identity in *Are We Not Men? Masculine Anxiety and the Problem of African American Identity* (177–84).

53 See Gracyk, *Rhythm and Noise*, 53.

suspended between performer and producer that sounds the smooth flow between humans and machines.[54]

Since the early 1990s, R&B has undergone significant changes due to its symbiotic relationship with hip-hop, most clearly audible in the numerous guest rappers on R&B records.[55] While guest raps appeared in R&B as early as Melle Mel's stint on Chaka Khan's 1984 Prince cover version, "I Feel for You," or Rakim's on Jody Watley's "Friends" in 1989, these collaborations increased exponentially in the following decade; now the majority of mainstream R&B records feature some presence by rappers.[56] Hip-hop aesthetics have also exerted an enormous influence on the instrumental and studio production techniques and have altered the singing styles of modern R&B.[57]

54 An issue of *Vibe* magazine, the most successful mainstream hip-hop and R&B monthly, features a special section on producers. Craig Seymour introduces the section: "Maybe it dates back to Dr. Dre's smokin' *The Chronic*. Or perhaps it began when self-enamored Sean 'Puffy' Combs started giving himself shout-outs on the records he produced. . . . But whatever the catalyst, the effect is clear. Somewhere along the knotted and often intertwining time lines of Hip-Hop and R&B, the producers of songs became as important—if not more so—than the artists they produced." Seymour, "Producers," 123. I would locate the "origin" of this trend in modern R&B a little earlier, in Janet Jackson's work with Jimmy Jam and Terry Lewis. The duo, who have worked with Jackson collaboratively on all her albums since 1986's *Control*, appeared in several of the videos for singles from that record, adding a visual presence to their already sonically inscribed one.

55 I am using *symbiosis* in the manner suggested by Keith Ansell Pearson, where hitherto separate life-forms and/or technologies contaminate each other to form a new, albeit unstable, entity that is integral to both biological and technological "development" rather than auxiliary. See Pearson, *Viroid Life*, 132–34.

56 Chaka Khan, "I Feel for You," Warner Brothers Records, 1984, single, https://www.discogs.com/release/517013-Chaka-Khan-I-Feel-For-You; and Jody Watley, featuring Eric B. & Rakim, "Friends," MCA Records, 1989, single, https://www.discogs.com/master/131097-Jody-Watley-With-Eric-B-Rakim-Friends. The prime example of this development is SWV's very underrated final album, *Release Some Tension*, on which eight of the twelve tracks sport raps either by producers (Sean "Puffy" Combs and Missy Elliott) or rappers (Redman and Lil' Kim). SWV, *Release Some Tension*, RCA/BMG Records, 1997, CD, https://www.discogs.com/master/78404-SWV-Release-Some-Tension.

57 Although I focus on the impact of hip-hop on R&B, this relationship should not be construed as a one-way street, especially since hip-hop's immense popularity would not be thinkable without the infusion of R&B. In the early 1990s, hip-hop

As R&B producers began to utilize samples of rhythm tracks from old recordings, in much the same way that hip-hop records do, singers, in turn, adjusted their vocal styles to the rhythm of the sample rather than the melody. Mary J. Blige and her producers pioneered this trend: her first two albums made elaborate use of samples, and Blige's vocals followed suit; she refers to it as singing over beats as opposed to crooning traditional songs. Suspended between the mellifluous R&B phrasing and the rhythmic intonations of rapping, Blige's vocal style has been widely emulated.[58] In some sense, then, this focus on rhythmic dimensions of vocalization moves the R&B singing voice closer to the stereotypically mechanical, since the machinic is often associated with rigid rhythmic structures and not the "human" expansiveness of

---

producers, especially those from the West Coast like Dr. Dre, started to incorporate melodies into their heretofore primarily rhythmically oriented tracks. Also, in much the same way that R&B records by Jody Watley, Mary J. Blige, and Mariah Carey started featuring guest raps, hip-hop cuts routinely employ R&B singers to sing choruses and hooks. Most hip-hop hits since the mid-1990s, by Jay-Z, Lil' Kim, Nelly, Bone Thugs-n-Harmony, and Ja Rule, for instance, would not be possible without sung rather than rapped choruses. Kelefa Sanneh, in an article about the "rebirth" of R&B, only measures how this genre has been impacted and revitalized by hip-hop but falls short of ascertaining the reciprocal consequences of this symbiosis. See Sanneh, "Responding to Rap, R&B Is Reborn," 30–37. Mariah Carey's 1997 single with Bone Thugs-n-Harmony, "Breakdown," and Ja Rule's collaboration with Lil' Mo serve as good examples of this trend, where Rule's and Bone Thugs-n-Harmony's rapping/vocalizing seamlessly blend into Lil' Mo's and Carey's sung vocal parts, blurring any steadfast distinctions between rapping and singing, a blend which becomes dominant in hip-hop after 2010. See track 8.0 for a more sustained discussion of the intertwining of hip-hop and R&B vocalizing. Mariah Carey, featuring Bone Thugs-n-Harmony, "Breakdown," Columbia Records, 1997, CD single, https://www.discogs.com/Mariah -Carey-Featuring-Bone-Thugs-N-Harmony-Breakdown/master/138726; and Ja Rule, featuring Lil' Mo and Vita, "Put It on Me," Murder Inc./Def Jam Records, 2000, CD single, https://www.discogs.com/master/104665-Ja-Rule-Featuring-Lil -Mo-Vita-Put-It-On-Me.

58   This is not to argue that melody disappeared from the R&B landscape, or that rhythm did not form an indispensable component of earlier permutations of R&B, but that the emphasis shifted radically toward the rhythm. Mary J. Blige, *What's the 411?*, Uptown/MCA Records, 1992, CD, https://www.discogs.com/release /242752-Mary-J-Blige-Whats-The-411; and *My Life*, Uptown/MCA Records, 1994, CD, https://www.discogs.com/release/1824443-Mary-J-Blige-My-Life. Both Missy Elliott and Lauryn Hill smoothly navigate back and forth between singing and rapping in their work.

melody and harmony.[59] As the 1990s progressed, producers such as Missy Elliott and Timbaland, Rodney Jerkins (Darkchild), and She'kspere Briggs increasingly created their "own" adventurous studio sounds instead of relying on prerecorded beats, still emphasizing rhythm first and foremost. The lyrical content of R&B has also undergone major shifts, especially when compared to the late 1960s and early 1970s, stressing designer clothes, expensive cars, and hypersexuality, among other things.[60] This leads Bat to coin a new term for modern R&B: "*Hypersoul* is marked on all levels by antagonism towards soul values. Soul's religious and spiritual undercurrent is often pushed aside in favour of brazen aspirational materialism (AKA the 'playa' culture). Many tracks flaunt an obsession with hi-tech consumer gadgetry, especially mobile phones. This aspirational materialism has inspired some critics to resurrect/revitalise Marxist concepts of 'commodity fetishism' and 'false consciousness.'"[61]

As opposed to most other critics of contemporary R&B, Bat attempts to take the genre on its own terms, conjecturing its reconceptualization of older notions of "soul." Both the rhythmic singing and the increased attention to material goods render R&B machinic, rather than traditionally "soulful" or "human." Thus, contemporary R&B suggests a mechanized desire at the cusp of the human and posthuman. Furthermore, R&B's engagement with various

59 The difference between the clipped angularity of rhythmic singing and the effusive, mellifluous intonation of traditional R&B can best be heard on Destiny's Child's "Say My Name," where the rhythmic verses stand in unequivocal contrast to the ballad-like chorus. The main reason for this transmogrification, I would venture, is the increased amount of syncopation and other more adventurous rhythmic arrangements on contemporary R&B records, which summon the voice to take on a more mechanical character.

60 Paul Gilroy has addressed these shifts, bemoaning the disappearance of freedom as a form of transcendence in R&B. In this way, Gilroy is not all that far from most critical writings about R&B that read more like nostalgic eulogies rather than intellectual engagements with current manifestations of the genre. See R. Green and Guillory, "Question of a 'Soulful Style'"; Gilroy, "Analogues of Mourning"; and Gilroy, *Against Race*. Other critics who lament the demise of soul in contemporary R&B, if they write about the post-1960s at all, include Nelson George (*Death of Rhythm and Blues*), Gerri Hirshey (*Nowhere to Run*), and Brian Ward (*Just My Soul Responding*). Although Michael Hanchard does not write about the sonic provenances of R&B, he does take in the changes in genre without the same value judgments as the other critics. See Hanchard, "Jody." In general, the critical literature on R&B is rather scant, particularly when compared to such young genres as hip-hop or electronic dance music.

61 Bat, "What Is Hypersoul?"

technologies in both its production and its lyrics provides several avenues to configuring human beings so that they can be seamlessly articulated with (intelligent) machines, as Hayles suggests (3). In the final section, I will briefly gloss the general role of informational technologies in Black popular music and then focus on the use of vocoders, talk boxes, and Auto-Tune to better ascertain the specificity of the human-machine interaction in R&B.

Desiring-Machines in Black Popular Music

To say that communications and other technologies are leading actors on the stage of R&B since the 1990s would amount to no less than an understatement of gargantuan proportions; lyrically, hardly a track exists that does not mention cellular phones, beepers, two-way pagers, answering machines, various surveillance gadgets, email messages, and or the internet, stressing the interdependence of contemporary interpersonal communication and informational technologies. As a result, these technologies appear both as Brechtian "A-effects" and as sonic "cinema verité" that depict the "reality" of late twentieth-century and early twenty-first-century technologically mediated lifeworlds.[62] On "Beep Me 911," for instance, Missy Elliott and 702 ask an unnamed lover to beep or call them on the cell phone if they still love them, the 911 functioning here as an indicator of both urgency and monumental desire.[63] Destiny's Child admonish an unwanted admirer, a "Bug-A-Boo," to stop beeping their pagers, leaving them telephone messages, and sending them emails; if this techno-informational terrorism continues, they threaten to "block the caller's number," have "MCI cut the phone poles," "throw their pager out the window," and "have AOL make their email stop."[64] In a different vein, the members of Blaque describe their sexual superiority by insisting that their "love goes boom like an 808," a drum machine used on countless hip-hop, house, and techno recordings that does not mimic "human" capacities but is celebrated for its sonic and rhythmic deepness. Blaque's sexual braggadocio transforms them into "love machines" who can only describe the ve-

---

62 I owe the cinema verité reference to Ira Livingston.

63 Missy Misdemeanor Elliot, featuring 702, "Beep Me 911," Elektra Records, 1997, CD single, https://www.discogs.com/master/49367-Missy-Misdemeanor-Elliott-Featuring-702-And-Magoo-Beep-Me-911.

64 Destiny's Child, "Bug-A-Boo," on *The Writing's on the Wall*. SONY Music, 1999, CD, https://www.discogs.com/release/2863169-Destinys-Child-The-Writings-On-The-Wall.

locity of their lovemaking via the machinic, thus rendering the TR-808 drum machine more "human" than the human subjects themselves.[65] The prominence of these technological artifacts in R&B indicates the enculturation (the ways in which technological artifacts are incorporated into the quotidian) of informational technologies in cultural practices that diverge from Hayles's restricted scientific and literary archive and Eshun's alien otherworlds.[66]

This penchant for the machinic in R&B can also be found in the genre's use of cellular telephones both as a voice-distortion mechanism and as part of the sonic tapestry. Not only does Ginuwine and Aaliyah's duet "Final Warning" lyrically revolve around phone numbers and cell phones, but their staged lover's quarrel is continually interspersed by the sounds of a ringing cellular telephone.[67] This ringing, rather than functioning merely as sonic similitude, forms an integral element of the rhythmic dimension of this already complexly syncopated track. The ringing of the cell phone on this recording, however, is an exception rather than the rule. Generally, cellular phones entered the pantheon of R&B and hip-hop—the informational technological gadget de rigueur in these genres—both as a textual topic and, perhaps more important, as a voice-distortion device. Nowhere is this clearer than on rap super group The Firm's "Phone Tap."[68] Chronicling the Federal Bureau of Investigation (FBI) surveillance of the imaginary gangster personas the rappers

---

65 Blaque, "808," Columbia Records, 1999, CD single, http://www.discogs.com/Blaque -808/release/539643.
   The TR-808 is a drum machine produced by Roland. For another discussion of this song, see Track 9.0 in this volume. As Tricia Rose explains, "The Roland TR-808 is a rap drum machine of choice for its 'fat sonic boom,' because of the way it processes bass frequencies." Rose, *Black Noise*, 75. Rose cites several hip-hop producers who describe "the boom" of the TR-808 as its capacity for detuning and thereby distorting the bass sounds to make them more intense. For further elaboration of the significance of the TR-808 for Black music, see Track 9.0. in this volume.

66 The role of information technologies in R&B magnifies their position as "social technologies," "which sustain culture and produce or reproduce culture. Each spawn[ing], in turn, a little 'culture' of its own." Du Gay et al., *Doing Cultural Studies*, 23.

67 Ginuwine and Aaliyah, "Final Warning," on *100% Ginuwine*, Blackground/ SONY Music, 1999, CD, https://www.discogs.com/release/227125-Ginuwine-100 -Ginuwine.

68 The Firm, "Phone Tap," on *Nas Escobar, Foxy Brown, AZ, and Nature Present The Firm: The Album*, Aftermath/Interscope Records, 1997, CD, https://www.discogs .com/release/24998164-The-Firm-The-Album.

adopted for this project, the track features a slow beat and a Mexican-style acoustic guitar reminiscent of western film soundtracks. The rappers deliver their lyrics through a muffled microphone approximating voices on a cell phone, which achieves a haunting effect that aestheticizes surveillance practices by incorporating them into the musical text as much as it criticizes their utter infiltration of contemporary social and political formations. Most other uses of the "cell phone effect" are more benign, but still noteworthy, in that they have realigned notions of voice and soul within the contemporary Black popular musical landscape. In the late 1990s and early 2000s, almost all mainstream R&B productions featured parts of the lead or background vocal performance sounding as if they were called in over a cell phone as opposed to produced in a state-of-the-art recording studio.[69] This use of the cell phone became so ubiquitous that in an article in the *Village Voice*, Scott Woods feels compelled to classify all female pop R&B performers as "Cell-Phone Girls."[70]

69 Destiny's Child, Joe, TLC, Aaliyah, Janet Jackson, 702, Jamelia, Kandi, Mýa, Craig David, and Missy Elliott all used this cell phone effect on turn-of-the-millennium recordings, as have teen pop acts NSYNC, Britney Spears, and The Backstreet Boys.

70 Woods, "Will You Scrub Me Tomorrow." Woods focuses mainly on pop R&B artists; however, these technological tendencies can also be found in the more traditional strand of R&B, usually designated as "neoclassical soul," which summons the golden age of soul music. Maxwell, for instance, uses a voice-distortion device on "Submerge," and at the end of D'Angelo's *Voodoo*, blips of all the preceding tracks are played backward so as to remind us that we are indeed listening to a technologically mediated recording. Hear Maxwell, "Submerge," on *Embrya*, Columbia/SONY Music, 1998, CD, https://www.discogs.com/release/1900233-Maxwell-Embrya; and D'Angelo, *Voodoo*, Virgin Records, 2000, CD, https://www.discogs.com/DAngelo-Voodoo/release/15906733. In contemporary parlance this golden age stretches from the late 1960s to the mid-1970s and should more accurately be called the age of auteur R&B. This historical moment is usually invoked through the work of Isaac Hayes, Marvin Gaye, Curtis Mayfield, and Stevie Wonder, all of whom wrote and produced their own material, bridging the divide between the conventional interpersonal content of R&B and more politically oriented lyrics. Yet these artists also made extensive use of then newly available studio technologies. In fact, these performers would not have been able to become auteurs—write their own music, play most of the instruments, and record it themselves—without the aid of synthesizers and multitrack recording. Some of the practitioners of "neoclassical soul" or "neosoul" include Maxwell, Lauryn Hill, D'Angelo, Macy Gray, and Erykah Badu. All of these performers style themselves as all-around artists with a social conscience rather than as mere singers.

The cell phone effect marks the performers' recorded voices as technologically embodied. Instead of trying to downplay the technological mediation of the recording, the cell phone effect does away with any notion of the self-same presence of the voice, imbuing, as Simon Reynolds points out, the production of the voice in contemporary R&B with a strong sense of "anti-naturalism."[71] Reynolds's argument regards the overall treatment of the voice in R&B, but the cell phone effect holds a particular prominence in this scheme as an "index of technological audibility."[72] As Jeremy Gilbert and Ewan Pearson explain, in most popular musical genres technology is frowned on, creating a hierarchy of what counts as technological:

> In relation to their degree of historical familiarity and the immediate context in which they are operated, some items are considered *more* technological in status than others. In this scheme, a drum machine is more technological than a drum. . . . Such considerations are founded on an order of the real within which aesthetic preferences are transformed into ontological distinctions. . . . Such distinctions almost always proceed by rendering the technological components utilized in their favored forms invisible as technologies—they are more "real" or "natural," absorbed wholly into those that play them as expressive extensions of the performing body.[73]

71 Reynolds holds that R&B producers employ "anti-naturalistic studio techniques, . . . digitally processing vocals to make them sound even more mellifluous and diabetically ultra-sweet." Reynolds, "Feminine Pressure." The main thrust of this article concerns the sonic permutations of the British genre known as 2-step garage or UK garage, which often combines US-style R&B and house with the speed and syncopation of jungle. The vocally oriented spectrum of UK garage pushes the uttered sensibilities of US R&B to its provisional conclusion by dissecting sampled and/or sung vocal parts, radically recombining them in relation to the rhythm as opposed to the melody. Adopting a term by Bat, Reynolds calls this messing up of the vocals "vocal science"). For an introduction to this particular strand of UK garage, hear Artful Dodger's mix CD *Rewind—The Sound of UK Garage*, London/Sire Records, 2001, https://www.discogs.com/release/112146-The-Artful-Dodger-Rewind-The-Sound-Of-UK-Garage.

72 This phrase comes from Jeremy Gilbert and Ewan Pearson. I have changed the wording somewhat—they use "index of visibility"—but only in the spirit of their ideas concerning the interdependence of music and technology. See Gilbert and Pearson, *Discographies*, 112.

73 Gilbert and Pearson, *Discographies*, 112.

The "cell phone effect" resists such principles of the "real," choosing instead to stage voice-distortion devices as both technological *and* expressive "extensions of the performing body." More important, the "cell phone effect" fails to define technological mediation and "realism" as warring opponents; instead, R&B construes these factors as thoroughly entangled.

The technological demarcation of the voice in contemporary R&B also appears in the revival of the vocoder and talk box. Au courant in the early 1980s, these speech-synthesizing devices can also be heard on a spate of late 1990s and early 2000s pop and dance music recordings.[74] First used in popular music by such artists as Kraftwerk and Herbie Hancock, the vocoder's use exploded in the early 1980s, particularly in the electro genre, and is in many ways a sonic index of the early 1980s zeitgeist. The vocoder and talk box might best be thought of as "low technologies," to use Gilbert and Pearson's phrase, which achieve analog-sounding effects via digital means.[75] The

74 Cher's ultra-ubiquitous "Believe" (Warner Records, 1998) and Madonna's "Music" (Maverick/Sire Records, 2000) made extensive use of the "vocoder effect" via Auto-Tune. In Cher's case, much of the success of the biggest hit of her thirty-year career was attributed to Auto-Tune. Janet Jackson, Kandi, 3LW, Dream, and NSYNC, among others, have all produced tracks that utilize this effect. Vocoder tracks in the various genres that make up the category of electronic music are too numerous to name here. I will only single out French duo Daft Punk, whose album *Discovery* (Virgin Records, 2001) is an apotheosis of the vocoder, featuring virtually no tracks that do not use this device. The British outfit Super_Collider not only technologically distort their voices on all the cuts of their album *Head On* (Loaded Records, 1999) but also named themselves after a "SmallTalk-like programming language for the Apple Macintosh, designed especially for creating and manipulating sounds." See G. Morrison, "Vocoders and Vocoder-Derivatives with *SuperCollider.*" Some electronic musicians such as IB or Console use voice-generating software that emulates "human" speech instead of processing "human" voices and credit these on their CDs. For instance, IB attributes the vocals to several of the tracks on his album *Pop Artificielle* (Shadow Records, 2000) to the *raw* software.

75 Gilbert and Pearson, *Discographies*, 122–28. The cover of Herbie Hancock's 1978 album, *Sunlight* (CBS Records, 1978), includes a special note on his VSM 201 Sennheiser vocoder, explaining that "the voices you hear are entirely synthesized." Kraftwerk's many uses of the vocoder can be heard on their greatest-hits CD, *The Mix* (Elektra/Warner Brothers Records, 1991). For a general overview of electro classics, consult the compilations *Street Jams: Electric Funk, Parts 1 and 2* (Rhino Records, 1992). *Encyclopedia Britannica* defines *vocoders* in the following fashion: "In essence, they are electrical analogues of the human vocal tract. Appropriately arranged electric circuits produce

use of this sonic technology forms a part of a tendency to valorize older and obsolete machinery of musical production because it sounds "warmer" and more "human," which is ironic given that vocoders make the human voice sound robotic, in a now seemingly quaint c-3po way. Because the vocoder and talk box carry undertones of nostalgia for a more "technologically innocent" era (the 1980s), they lend an aura of increased "humanity" and "soulfulness" to the singer's voice. Current invocations of the mechanized voice in Black popular music render them less technological than the cell phone effect, for instance, since they sound like a historical relic. Kodwo Eshun puts a more menacing spin on the effects of the vocoder on the human voice: "The vocoder turns the voice into a synthesizer. . . . It synthesizes the voice into a voltage, into an electrophonic charge that gets directly onto your nerves, . . .

---

a voicelike tone, a modulator of the harmonic components of this fundamental tone, and a hissing-noise generator to produce the sibilant and other unvoiced consonant sounds." See "Synthetic Production of Speech Sounds," Britannica .com, https://www.britannica.com/topic/speech-language/Synthetic-production -of-speech-sounds (accessed February 27, 2023).

As an idea, synthesizing human voices can be traced back as far as the late eighteenth century, when Austrian phonetician Wolfgang von Kempelen constructed a device that mechanically approximated the human vocal apparatus. See Lastra, *Sound Technology and the American Cinema*, 16–60; and "Wolfgang von Kempelen's and Subsequent Speaking Machines." Twentieth-century speech synthesis took a big leap in 1939 when Homer Dudley, a research physicist at Bell Laboratories, developed two devices, voder and vocoder, that analyzed and synthesized human speech by electronic means. Later these contraptions were further developed and linked to computer technology; it was not until the late 1960s and 1970s, however, that they found their way into the musical productions of experimental artists such as Wendy Carlos and popular musicians like Kraftwerk. See Dudley, "Homer Dudley's Speech Synthesizer"; "Multimedia Communications *Research Laboratory*"; and "Vocoder." Friedrich Kittler describes the history of the vocoder somewhat differently than the sources cited above, ascribing its origins to Alan Turing and Claude Shannon's work for Bell Laboratories and the British Secret Service during World War II. In Kittler's scheme, the vocoder was designed as "a wonder weapon that would make the transatlantic telephone conversations between Churchill and Roosevelt safe from interception by Canaris and the German Abwehr." Kittler, *Gramophone, Film, Typewriter*, 49. Although this does not necessarily contradict the other histories, I remain suspicious of Kittler's account, at least as the only one, since he generally exhibits a proclivity for locating the origins of all informational media in what used to be called *the military-industrial complex*, and none of the other sources mention this particular fact.

petrifying the voice into a robotik current, and antagonistically nonhuman voice of doom."[76] Although Eshun briefly alludes to Zapp's work, discussed below, he mainly focuses on the electro genre, where the vocoderized human voice was employed somewhat differently than in R&B.[77] I would now like to analyze several specific instances of vocoder, talk box, and Auto-Tune use in R&B, tracing the shift from analog to digital, and its ramifications for questions of soul and virtual embodiment.

Zapp were a late 1970s and early 1980s group, associated with George Clinton in their infancy, that later made a name for themselves by virtue of their heavily mechanized funk and extensive talk-box use. In fact, Zapp "embody" the talk box and the mechanized Black singing voice like no other musical group, at least in Black popular music, since the group's idiosyncrasy was the prominence of this device on all their recordings. In retrospect, Zapp are largely known through samples of their funk oeuvre, with their most widely recognized tracks, "More Bounce to the Ounce" and "Dancefloor," appearing on a number of hip-hop tracks. Prominent 1980s hip-hop group EPMD, for instance, built their career on sampling bits and pieces of Zapp basslines, rhythms, and vocals; Zapp's leader, Roger Troutman, even lent his mechanized voice to Tupac Shakur's 1996 megahit "California Love."[78] However, Zapp also left their mark on R&B with their two luscious but now somewhat dated-sounding talk-box ballads, "Computer Love" and "I Want to Be Your Man."[79] These two ballads exert a subtler influence than the hip-hop

76 Eshun, *More Brilliant Than the Sun*, 080. Along the same lines, at a different point in the text Eshun contends that in the early 1980s, African American techno musicians adopted the rigidity of synthesizers and "white" new wave singing styles in order to recast themselves as "brothers from another planet" (177–78).

77 Roger Troutman, Zapp's lead singer, whose previous group went by the moniker Roger & The Human Body, used a talk box to mechanize his voice.

78 Commencing with EPMD's first hit, "You Gots to Chill," in 1986, this development continued through most of the duo's recorded output, wherein most of their albums contain one or more tracks that obviously sample Zapp. EPMD, "You Gots to Chill," Fresh Records, 1986, single, https://www.discogs.com/release/2174132 -EPMD-You-Gots-To-Chill.

79 Zapp, "Computer Love," Warner Brothers Records, 1985, single, https://www .discogs.com/release/1263885-Zapp-Computer-Love; and Zapp and Roger, "I Want to Be Your Man," on *Zapp and Roger: All the Greatest Hits*, Reprise Records, 1993, CD, https://www.discogs.com/release/179036-Zapp-Roger-All -The-Greatest-Hits. Tricia Rose briefly glosses the difference between Zapp's talk-box use on these two ballads and its deployment by producer Dr. Dre on

samples discussed above but provide inspiration for the reemergence of the vocoder and talk box in R&B through the audible use of Auto-Tune software.

In contrast to most other tracks in the Zapp canon, "Computer Love" features not only the talk-box voice of Roger Troutman but also the "human voices" of The Gap Band's Charlie Wilson and Zapp's longtime background singer Shirley Murdock, who enjoyed a brief solo career in the 1980s.[80] "Computer Love" commences with a very deep talk-box vociferation of "computer love," followed by what sounds like simulated scratching and a talk-boxed voice in a much higher key intoning "computerized."[81] Then we hear the higher machinic voice articulating the title in conjunction with Charlie Wilson, creating a dialogue between the two in which the "human" succeeds the "machinic." Once the verse commences, Wilson's and Murdock's voices overlap (although Wilson dominates) until the lyrics make explicit references to informational technologies, such as "could it be your face I see on my computer screen" and "thanks to my technology," which are bolstered by the talk box in the background, leading to a crescendo in which all three voices grow higher, in both pitch and loudness. The chorus consists mainly of Troutman's mechanized singing of "Shoo-be-do-bop shoo-do-bop I wanna love you / shoo-be-do-bop computer love," reinforced by the "feminine" *sanging* of "I wanna love you baabeee."[82] The second verse follows the same trajectory as

---

the Tupac track "California Love," which featured Roger Troutman's talk-box presence. About "I Want to Be Your Man," she writes, "Troutman is using the vocoder on top of what some might consider to be pre-high-tech narratives of 'whole' 'unmediated' human relationships." Conversely, Dr. Dre uses "the vocoder (and sampling equipment more generally) to narrate mediated and fractured relationships." Rose, "Sound Effects," 147.

80 Kelly Price covered Murdock's biggest solo hit, "As We Lay," with some success in 2000.

81 Scratching consists of DJs moving vinyl records back and forth on one of the two turntables (that constitute the basic DJing setup) to create a scratching sound that corresponds with the rhythm of the record sounding on the other record player.

82 *Sanging*, as opposed to just *singing*, emphasizes the highly performative and "emotional" vocal styles of Black musical genres such as gospel or soul that underscore the physicality of "human" voice production. The distinction is crucial here, because the affective labor is carried out by the female voice in one of the only instances where Murdock's vocal apparatus does not merely serve to prop up the masculine and machinic voices but sounds by itself. This affective excess of the Black female voice can also be heard in a crucial moment of "I Want to Be Your Man," the other well-known Zapp talk-box ballad,

the first until the talk box interrupts Wilson and Murdock to proclaim, "I want to keep you up tonight / you are such a sweet delight," which gives way to an additional female solo performance telling us that she "will cherish the memory of this night." After another chorus the song eschews "meaning" by simply repeating "computer love" or "digital love" for sonic effect rather than narrative closure; the feminine presence also evaporates from the sonic text.[83] While the title indexes Kraftwerk's earlier cut of the same name, the two aural formulations' sonic similarity is scant. Although both share a slow tempo, Kraftwerk exploit their stereotypically Germanic voices to excavate the nonhuman and mechanical dimension of their "computer love," as opposed to Zapp, who wield both the audibly technologized and human voices to unearth the "humanity" of their machinic affections.[84] The Zapp track achieves this feat by drawing on the traditions of melismatic R&B singing and creating a three-way conversation, albeit an unequal one, among the male, female, and machinic utterances on the vocal track of the song. Overall, the lyrics of the tune fail to provide a clear picture of this computer love, so overbearing that it can only be expressed through the combined forces of female, male, and machinic voices. Although "a special girl" appears briefly

---

where the male voice sings "words can never say how I feel." This crisis in linguistic meaning making is followed by a talk-boxed "it's too intense," heightening the way in which desire disrupts the flow of language. Finally, we hear the female voice, in her only solo performance on this track, cooing "oohooo ohooo oooooh," in effect eschewing linguistic meaning altogether. Thus, the female voice represents the nonlingual sonorousness needed to carry out the affective labor that both the male and machinic voices cannot. The female voice becomes the channel for the sonic representation of unmitigated desire.

83 The remainder of the lyrics consist of the following:

   (digital love) digital love
   (computer love) computer love

   . . . .

   (digital love) digital love
   (a beautiful love) beautiful love
   (digital love) digital love
   (digital love) digital love
   it's a beautiful digital beautiful, beautiful love

   you are my computer love.

84 Kraftwerk, "Computer Love," on *The Mix*. I use terms such as *human, machinic, masculine*, and *feminine* not as indicators of ontological absolutes but as signifiers inscribed within a particular musical and cultural matrix.

in the words, mostly the repeated incantations of "computer love" are isolated, decoupled from merely serving as the conduit for anthropomorphic desire. If read/heard solely within the tradition of R&B love songs, "Computer Love" utilizes the talk box to intensify the longing of the male subject, and even though this current is surely prominent here, the track also suggests desire for the machine itself by deferring a conclusive or coherent identification of its target. Thus, we might say by way of Gilles Deleuze and Félix Guattari that "Computer Love" sonically formulates the following dictum: "Desire and its object are one and the same thing: the machine as a machine of a machine. Desire is a machine, and the object of desire another machine connected to it."[85]

Where Zapp employ the talk box as a forceful and poignant "index of technological audibility," thematizing technology conspicuously in their lyrics so that this technology bears an obvious mimetic relevance to the textual signification of the track, 702's "You Don't Know," emblematic of late 1990s mechanized voice-distortion techniques in R&B, which are achieved through the audible use of pitch-correction software such as Auto-Tune and Melodyne, fails to offer any definitive correlation between the technologically altered voice and the textual content of the song.[86] The easy and techno-determinist explanation for this development lies in the large-scale shift from analog to digital technologies in musical (re)production during the fourteen years separating the two recordings, enabling producers to add "the vocoder effect" without the singers having to physically sing into a vocoder or talk box, transforming vocals into a portion of the many "zeroes and ones" that constitute the totality of a digitally produced sound recording.[87] "You Don't Know" comes from the female trio's eponymous 1999 album and encapsulates the sonic provenances of millennial R&B succinctly. Beginning with the obligatory shout-out to the producers of the song, the Swedish duo Soulshock and Karlin, the midtempo cut deploys the cell phone effect throughout and melds musical syncopation with the rhythmic singing so popular in contemporary R&B. The "vocoder effect," achieved here through the Auto-Tune software, weaves in and out of the sung verses, in both the main and background vocals, without any decisive connection to the signification of

85 Deleuze and Guattari, *Anti-Oedipus*, 26.
86 702, "You Don't Know," Motown Records, 1999, CD single, https://www.discogs .com/release/1258668-702-You-Dont-Know.
87 The "vocoder effect," in contradistinction to the vocoder and talk box as material entities, is indicative of the wider popular music landscape where most recordings apply this effect in similar ways.

the lyrics. Some of the lyrics heard through the Auto-Tune effect during the first half of the track include

So why won't you tell me
Why you mean so much to me?
. . . .
Now whata girl gotta do
To make you see
. . . .
"I want your love"
. . . .
"Let me down, down (down)."

A portion of these lines is repeated in different parts of the recording but not characterized by the Auto-Tune effect, only adding to the indeterminate significance of this technique. During the final two minutes, the auto-tuned voice rears its sonic head only once, supporting the central voice as it declares, "Just don't know." As a whole, the "vocoder effect" via Auto-Tune alters the function of the vocoder and talk box, even if the former shares a parasitical relationship with the latter, by dispersing the machinic across the musical text rather than giving it an integral and system-maintaining role. Auto-Tune "deterritorializes" the vocoder and talk box, becoming one production among many to process the "human" voice in contemporary Black popular music. Ironically, the use of Auto-Tune in Black popular music amplifies the human provenances of the voice, highlighting its virtual embodiment, because it conjures a previous, and allegedly more innocent, period in popular music, bolstering the "soulfulness" of the human voice. Here the "human" and "machinic" become mere electric effects that conjoin the human voice and (intelligent) machines.[88]

Surely desire serves as the central topos for all R&B, even if it is desire for material objects rather than human subjects; nevertheless, it is always desire that has no "real" destiny. The vocoder, talk box, and auto-tuned "vocoder effect" are literalizations of Deleuze and Guattari's "desiring-machines" in that they excavate the productive and machinic provenances of desire not chained

88 See Deleuze and Guattari, *Thousand Plateaus*. Here is how Deleuze and Guattari imagine sonic deterritorialization: "It seems that when sound deterritorializes, it becomes more and more refined; it becomes more specialized and autonomous. . . . When sound deterritorializes, it tends to dissolve, to let itself be steered by other components" (347).

by lack found in all R&B.[89] This productive force has no object, because the performance of desire in R&B is always one-sided, invariably a rumination by a desiring subject (the R&B singer) and not the desired subject or object. In addition, R&B desire is always already a desire of the second order; the performance of desire rather than desire as such.[90] Instead, the R&B desiring-machine "does not lack anything; it does not lack its object. It is, rather, the *subject* that is missing in desire, or that desire lacks a fixed subject."[91] In the move from the vocoder to Auto-Tune, the centrality of the human voice dissipates throughout the desiring-machine that is R&B. Moreover, other clearly technological treatments of the voice, such as the "cell-phone effect," the presence of producers in the musical texts, and thematization of informational technologies in the lyrics, aggregate to form the R&B desiring-machine. The audibly technologized voice highlights the machinic dimension of the R&B desiring-machine by synthesizing all the other parts into a "sound machine, which molecularizes and atomizes, ionizes sound matter."[92] Deleuze and Guattari continue this trajectory by claiming that "the synthesizer makes audible the sound process itself, the production of that process, and puts it in contact with still other elements beyond sound matter."[93] The presence of speech-synthesizing devices in R&B intensifies the technological mediation of the recorded voice per se ("the sound process itself"), since it dodges the naturalism associated with the human voice in so many other popular music genres. In circumventing this naturalism, R&B imagines interpersonal relations and informational technologies as mutually constitutive rather than antithetical foils.

The title of this track, "Feenin," comes from a pre-Auto-Tune 1993 track by the R&B group Jodeci, who were among the forerunners of hip-hop-inspired Black pop.[94] "Feenin" deploys a vocoder to transmit only the word *feenin* in its chorus; the rest of the track is sung in a traditional, read "human," R&B

89 This is a reference to Deleuze and Guattari's anti-Freudian conception of desire that is not framed by a primary lack in the subject but functions as a productive force that brings the subject into being and fuels the social-machine. See Deleuze and Guattari, *Anti-Oedipus*, 1–50.

90 Here I am not suggesting that desire can ever be formulated without being mediated by a host of material and discursive forces but that this particular machination of desire incorporates its own performativity.

91 Deleuze and Guattari, *Anti-Oedipus*, 26.

92 Deleuze and Guattari, *Thousand Plateaus*, 343.

93 Deleuze and Guattari, *Thousand Plateaus*, 343.

94 Jodeci, "Feenin," on *Diary of a Mad Band*, Uptown/MCA Records, 1993, CD, https://www.discogs.com/Jodeci-Diary-Of-A-Mad-Band/release/251832.

singing style. The term *feenin* derives from *fiend*, as in *drug fiend*, and Jodeci use it to signify their all-encompassing desire. The lyrics suggest an unequivocal link between the desire for a human love object and the "feenin" of a junkie, in lines like the following:

> All the chronic [marijuana] in the world couldn't even mess with you
> You're the ultimate high
>
> . . . .
>
> Girl it's worse than drugs
> Cause I'm an addict of you
>
> . . . .
>
> Surely girl, without a doubt
> You know you got me strung out.

Thus, desire, in this scenario, refuses to signify any traditional humanist provenances, instead appearing in the guise of a self-generating addiction-machine. Moreover, the shift from vocoder/talk box to auto-tuned "vocoder effect" is clearly audible on K-Ci and Jo Jo's 2001 single "Crazy" when compared with the earlier recording of these two former members of Jodeci.[95] Where "Feenin" wields the vocoder to emphasize one particular aspect of the lyrics, "Crazy" weaves Auto-Tune in and out of the musical text throughout without any particular correlation between form and content, recapitulating the difference between Zapp's and 702's mechanized enunciations. Thus, the term *feenin*, as it is sung by a Black vocoderized voice, might be more apt vis-à-vis contemporary R&B than *desire*, since it pushes desire to the extreme. In this extreme, either the human subject stands in for a mind-altering substance (locating desire for a love object in the realm of neurochemical reactions) or desire is yoked to nonhuman "objects" such as cars and designer clothes (moving desire from the realm of the ideal to the crassly material). This *feenin* dissolves the parameters of the coherent subject in such radical ways that human all-too-human desire can only be represented in the guise of the machinic, and the human is thus inextricably intertwined with various informational technologies. Taken together, these factors recast the R&B "desiring-machine" as a "feenin-machine," which explosively sounds the passage from *soul* to *hypersoul*.

95 K-Ci and Jo, "Crazy," MCA Records, 2001, CD single, https://www.discogs.com/release/6157721-K-Ci-JoJo-Crazy.

The virtual embodied in contemporary R&B follows neither the orbit of those that usually populate the annals of cybertheory nor Eshun's Afrofuturist ruminations; rather, R&B desiring- and feenin-machines reticulate the human voice with intelligent machines without assuming that "information has lost its body" or that any version of Black posthumanism must take on an alien form. Because, for reasons I have outlined above, Black cultural practices do not have the illusion of disembodiment, they stage *the body* of information and technology as opposed to the lack thereof. Where Eshun zeroes in on the antihumanist cultures of Afrofuturism, Hayles discusses the history of cybernetics and informatics, as well as classical science fiction and cyberpunk narratives. Eshun provides a singular account of nonhumanist Black popular music as it explosively interfaces with sound technologies, but in doing so he fails to take in the ramifications of these discourses in genres that do not explicitly announce themselves as Afrofuturist, such as R&B. Hayles's conclusions seem indicative of numerous studies of virtuality and/or cyberspace, where race is heard in a minor key, and computer-mediated communication is the sole melody of the song we know all too well: the virtual. I hope to have shown that any theory of posthumanism would benefit from making race central to its trajectory and not ancillary as well as from venturing beyond purely visual notions of subjectivity. At the very least, this would diversify the purview of this newly burgeoning line of inquiry, while rendering this field more interesting and less myopic. We could do far worse than turn the critical dial on our radio to those lower frequencies, where the sounds of Black popular music, in the immortal talk-boxed words of Zapp, are "still bubbalistic, realistic, supalistic / whatever is right for you / you can find it all on your radio."[96]

While both Hayles and Eshun seek to venture beyond the category of the human personified by the white liberal humanist subject in order to advance versions of the posthuman, I think the historical and contemporary practices of the seemingly humanist strands of Black popular music and their relation to informational technologies not only expand these two notions of the posthuman but are at the forefront of coarticulating the "human" with informational technologies. These segments of mainstream Black popular music, particularly in regard to the status of recorded voices and the representations of soul and subjectivity they harbor, provide different circuits to and

96 Zapp, "Radio People," on *The New Zapp IV U*, Warner Brothers Records, 1985, LP, https://www.discogs.com/release/224328-Zapp-The-New-Zapp-IV-U.

through the (post)human. Instead of dispensing with the humanist subject altogether, these musical formations reframe it to include the subjectivity of those who have had no simple access to its western, post-enlightenment formulation, suggesting subjectivities embodied and disembodied, human and posthuman. My final claim is modest, but hopefully no less consequential: in proclaiming the historical moment of the posthuman, we might do well to imagine "other humanities" and not just discard this category wholly, as Eshun does, or equate humanity with the white liberal subject, as in Hayles.[97] This way, we might actually begin to ameliorate the provinciality of "humanity" in its various western guises as opposed to simply rehashing the same old stories ad infinitum.

97 I am borrowing the phrase *other humanities* from the title of Lisa Lowe's talk delivered at the Humanities Institute, SUNY Stony Brook, March 2000.

RHYTHMS OF RELATION

Black Popular Music and Mobile Technologies

Track 3.0 of *Feenin* focuses on the singular performances of the interface between (Black) subjectivity and informational technologies in popular music, asking how these performances impact definitions of the technological. To this end, after a brief examination of those aspects of mobile technologies that gesture beyond disembodied communication, I turn my attention to the multifarious manifestations of techno-informational gadgets (especially cellular/mobile telephones) in R&B from 2000 to 2010, in both content and form, a genre acutely concerned with the conjuring of interiority, emotion,

Track 3.0 was first published in *Oxford Handbook of Mobile Music Studies*, edited by Sumanth Gopinath and Jason Stanyek (New York: Oxford University Press, 2014), 361–79.

and affect.[1] The genre's emphasis on these aspects provides an occasion to analyze how technology thoroughly permeates spheres that are thought to represent the hallmarks of humanist hallucinations of humanity. I outline the extensive and intensive interdependence of contemporary Black popular music and mobile technologies in order to ascertain how these sonic formations refract communication and embodiment and ask how this impacts ruling definitions of the technological. The first group of musical examples surveyed consists of recordings released between 1999 and 2001, while the second set appeared between 2009 and 2010. Since ten years is almost an eternity in the constantly changing universes of popular music and mobile technologies, analyzing the sonic archives from two different historical moments allows me to stress the general codependence of mobiles and music without silencing the breaks that separate these "epochs." Finally, I will also gloss a visual example that stages overlooked dimensions of mobile technologies so as to amplify the rhythmic flow between the scopic and the sonic. The artifacts in question boost the singular corporeal sensations of informational technologies without resorting to a naturalization of these machines. In other words, Black musical formations relish the synthetic artificiality of cell phones and other mobile gadgets as much as making these a vital component of the performed body. They achieve this by transforming the sounds of mobile telephones into rhythmic patterns vital to their musical texts, which make audible how humans and mobile machines form a relational continuum.

I frequently return to Samuel Delany's constructive differentiation between "the white boxes of computer technology" and "the black boxes of modern street technology," because it highlights the racialized core of the very definition of technology.[2] Although things have changed somewhat—Delany made this statement in 1994—due to the proliferation of mobile devices (laptops, netbooks, smartphones, portable music players with web capabilities, tablet computers, etc.) and the move away from "white boxes" as the de facto model for personal computing, Delany's pithy distinction still holds, both in its general implications and in the racialized provenances of this split. As several studies have shown, most youth of color in the United States log on to the internet from mobile devices or public personal computer terminals and thus still only have access to the "the black boxes of mod-

1 On the complexities and im/possibilities of Black affect, see T. Palmer, "'What Feels More Than Feeling?'"
2 Delany, interviewed in Dery, "Black to the Future," 192.

ern street technology."[3] Moreover, Black and Latinx youth have been early adopters of "street technologies," especially portable music players such as the boom box and Walkman. The culture of using boom boxes and other portable music devices to occupy public space continues in "sodcasting": "the public playing of trebly MP3s off mobile phones on British public transport—mostly buses, mostly in London, mostly by teenagers, often non-white teenagers."[4] Generally, the pioneering use of mobile "black boxes" such as pagers and boom boxes in nonmainstream cultures does not figure into the histories of cellular telephones, MP3 players, or internet-enabled mobile devices, showing how the inclusion or exclusion of particular machines determines how technology is defined.[5]

Much of the early critical literature about cellular telephones tends to focus on how radically this technology has altered communicative patterns at the node of public and private through its mobility and on how people use cell phones to distinguish themselves from others or project images of themselves as hip teenagers or successful businesspeople in a Veblenesque or Bourdieuesque fashion. Communications studies scholars James Katz and Mark Aakhus, for instance, propose a theory of "Apparatgeist" that encapsulates the particular historical instantiation of cell phones as well as other social technologies; they write, "We coin the neologism Apparatgeist to suggest the spirit of the machine that influences both the designs of the technology as well as the initial and subsequent significance accorded to them by users, non-users and anti-users."[6] This approach is useful for locating the significance of technologies in the interstices between the apparatus and a variety of attendant practices, rather than accenting one at the cost of the other. Writing more specifically about the cell phone, Katz and Aakhus argue that the machine's Apparatgeist follows the logic of "perpetual contact" that

3   Black Digerati, "I Use My T-Mobile Sidekick to Get Online"; Brustein, "Mobile Web Use"; Contreras, "Young Latinos, Blacks Answer Call"; Lang, "Young Blacks and Latinos Are Labeled"; Schiffer, *Portable Radio in American Life*; Watkins, *Young and the Digital*; and Wortham, "Mobile Internet Use Shrinks Digital Divide."

4   Hancox, "On the Buses"; see also Marshall, "Mobile Music and Treble Culture."

5   Araujo, "History of Pagers and Beepers"; Heckman, "'Do You Know the Importance?'"; and Schiffer, *Portable Radio in American Life*. These "facts" should not be construed as providing sociological evidence for the musical examples I will discuss later; instead, they contextualize the pivotal place of mobile technologies and sound in Black culture.

6   Katz and Aakhus, *Perpetual Contact*, 307.

combines mobile communication, private talk, and public performance. Still, the notion of perpetual contact leaves intact the largely communicative and content-centered bias in many theories of information technologies. While those aspects clearly remain important in any considerations of technology, too often the tactile or haptic dimensions of these machines remain muted. How can we think about cell phones as communicative devices without losing sight and sound of their ringtones, vibrate modes, visual displays, touch screens, keypads, and so on, as well as the feel and color of the material the machines are made of?

Many critics have noted how mobile communication reduces the nonlinguistic aspects of the communicative performance between the two or more speakers given that they appear to each other only as disembodied voices and/or snippets of text (email, SMS, and mobile chat, for example), including Leopoldina Fortunati, who asserts, "Mediated communication lowers the quality of communicative performance, as far as to deprive it of the support by non-verbal language, proxemics, kinesics, etc."[7] Nevertheless, these forms of interaction also buttress the non-face-to-face tête-à-tête, for instance, through the different environments (temporal, geographic, social, etc.) the speakers inhabit and the various textures (sonic, haptic, visual, olfactory, etc.) of the mobile devices. Accordingly, body-to-body communication does not vanish in mobile communication but (re)materializes in both the participants' respective location and in the apparatus itself.[8] Put simply, mobile devices are bodies too, even if they exist chiefly in relation to and in symbiosis with humans. Given the ubiquity of mobile devices in the western world and across the globe, it would behoove us to not merely conceptualize them as disembodied tools that facilitate pure communication but also devise languages that allow for the analysis of the "fuzzy" and textural dimensions of mobile communication and the different apparatuses in which it is bodied forth.[9]

7 Fortunati, "Mobile Phone," 517. See also Urry, *Mobilities*, 177.
8 Fortunati, "Is Body-to-Body Communication Still the Prototype?"
9 According to the ICT (information and communication technologies) Development Index, there were four billion mobile subscriptions worldwide in 2010 (61 percent penetration rate) while there existed 1.3 billion landlines (19 percent penetration rate). Given that these numbers only include subscriptions and exclude various modes of mobile sharing that are prevalent in the poorer parts of the globe, the overall penetration rate is likely higher. See International Telecommunication Union, *Measuring the Information Society*. On mobile sharing, see, for instance, Steenson and Donner, "Beyond the Personal and Private."

For my purposes, contemporary Black popular music presents not only sonic redactions of techno-ecologies but, more important, their transposition into the realms of sensation via rhythm. These musical formations stage the "rush" of itinerant information technologies, what Anna Everett has referred to as "digital plentitude."[10] Instead of merely focusing on the communicational dimensions of these machines, contemporary R&B unearths the aspects of technology above, beyond, and between the transmission of zeros and ones, highlighting, for instance, a body registering a pager set to vibrate mode. Brian Massumi elucidates the different modalities through which humans experience the world, differentiating *perception*, "[which refers] to object oriented experience," from *sensation*, "[which refers to] 'the perception of perception,' or self-referential experience. Sensation pertains to the stoppage- and stasis-tending dimension of reality. . . . Sensation pertains to the dimension of passage, or the continuity of immediate experience. . . . Perception is segmenting and capable of precision; sensation is unfolding and constitutively vague."[11] Conveying sensation is crucial, for it locates the import of technologies not merely in the contents they transmit or their sociopolitical significance but also in the textural provenances of these machines, which are a considerable part of their allure and utility while oftentimes eluding the grip of critical discourse. In this regard, the sonic represents an ideal venue for hearing and being affected by "the constitutive vagueness" of information technologies due to its nonlinguistic qualities such as timbre and rhythm that resonate throughout the body. Whereas scholarly discussions tend to focus on the perception of mobile technologies, (Black) popular music intensifies their sensation: the textural relay and relation between human bodies and machines.

I will now make a few points about the generic parameters of R&B, particularly its overdetermined relationship to hip-hop. Although post- or hypersoul manifestations of R&B have imported certain masculinist tendencies from hip-hop, it still remains a "feminine" genre.[12] While hip-hop routinely trades in Black "masculine" exterior braggadocio in its obsessions with guns, hypersexuality, and conspicuous consumption, R&B might be said to stage a more "feminine" version of the (Black) subject that traffics in love and sex stories without hip-hop's hardened outer shield. I am not, however, suggesting any strict correlation between biology and the performative body,

10 Everett, "Digitextuality and Click Theory," 14.
11 Massumi, *Parables for the Virtual*, 258–59n11.
12 Bat, "What Is Hypersoul?"

although R&B is the only musical category in which Black female performers dominate; I merely wish to register some broad discursive markers.[13] Modern R&B is also the popular musical field most concerned with interpersonal relationships, and while it is considered a particularly "Black" genre due to the racial identity of most of its performers, obvious sociopolitical overtones remain a rarity. For every "I'm Black and Proud," there are numerous invocations of "Will You Satisfy?," "Turn Off the Lights," or "Where Is the Love?" Even in some of the more politically inspired soul of the 1960s and 1970s, explicit political messages appear in a rather oblique fashion, hence song titles like "A Change Is Going to Come," "Respect," and "People Get Ready." This tendency to circumvent the strictly political and the genre's "femininity" might explain the absence of any sustained critical discourse about R&B (particularly when contrasted with the sizable archive of hip-hop criticism) or discussions that do not reduce the genre to the musical manifestation of the civil rights movement. In this way, R&B figures in scholarly debates primarily through its manifest (political) content, echoing the functionalist Cartesianism found in so many considerations of technology.[14]

When not fettered to the benchmark of political content, R&B emerges as the deterritorialization of hip-hop, especially in the genre's differently tuned configuration of the Black (female) voice. In the wake of hip-hop, singing appears as "softer" and less assertive than rapping, which has now become the standard against which Black musical expressivity is measured, hence the statements by many rappers, who claim that they feature R&B singers to sing hooks on their records to "appeal to the ladies." While contemporary hip-hop is engulfed by and has in some sense been superseded by R&B in popularity, its femininity is often kept at bay by masculinist retrenchment. Because R&B centers on a variety of interpersonal intimacies, it creates a complex rhythmic arrangement for the sensation of human-machine enmeshments.

13 These tendencies have shifted somewhat in the past fifteen years with the growing popularity of rappers (Kanye West and Drake, for instance) who do not conform to hip-hop's masculinist template.

14 See Ward, *Just My Soul Responding*; and C. Werner, *Change Is Gonna Come*. The problem here is not R&B's inherently apolitical nature but the fact that critics value the genre if the lyrics "transcend" the interpersonal and putatively private domain by espousing recognizably political themes, which rehashes the long-standing gendered qualities of the public/private divide. For a general consideration of the public/private split and gender, see Elshtain, *Public Man, Private Woman*.

Communications and other technologies have been a steady presence on R&B recordings as lyrical topics and as structural components for some time. Since the early 2000s, lyrically, nary a hit song exists without the mention of cellular phones, beepers, two-way pagers, iPhones, BlackBerrys, Samsung Galaxies, answering machines, various surveillance gadgets, email messages, the internet, Twitter, Instagram, or the like, stressing the interdependence of contemporary interpersonal communication and informational technologies.[15] This penchant for machines in R&B can also be found in the genre's use of cellular telephones both as a voice-alteration apparatus and as part of the sonic tapestry. In fact, the uses of the "cell phone effect" have recalibrated conceptions of the voice and soul within the contemporary popular musical landscape. In the late 1990s, a plethora of mainstream R&B productions featured parts of the lead or background vocal performance sounding as if they were called in over a cell phone as opposed to produced in a state-of-the-art recording studio.[16] The increased prominence of these technological artifacts in R&B indicates the enculturation of informational technologies in practices that are customarily relegated to the dominion of the non- and/or pretechnological, as well as amplifying some neglected attributes of modern techno-informational flows.

Instead of trying to downplay the technological mediation of the recording, the cell phone effect does away with any notion of the selfsame presence of the voice. Jeremy Gilbert and Ewan Pearson explain that in the majority

15 Here is a partial list of contemporary songs (1995–2010) that devote a significant part of their lyrics and sounds to mobile technologies: R. Kelly, "3-Way Call," "Remote Control," and "Text Me"; Soulja Boy, "Kiss Me Thru the Phone"; Ludacris, "Sexting"; Christina Milian, "Call Me, Beep Me! (The Kim Possible Song)"; Hi-Town DJs, "Ding-A-Ling"; Jackie Boyz, "Callin' Me"; The Firm, "Phone Tap"; Field Mob, "Stop Callin"; Vybz Kartel, "Video Recorder" and "U Nuh Have a Phone (Hello Moto U)"; Three 6 Mafia, "2 Way Freak"; J-Luv, "Telefon Liebe"; Romeo, "Romeo Dunn"; Beyoncé and Lady Gaga, "Video Phone"; Trina, "Phone Sexx"; The Game, "Camera Phone"; Ciara, "Pick Up the Phone"; Adina Howard, "Phone Sex"; Next, "Phone Sex"; Rayvon, "2-Way"; Teairra Marí, "Phone Booth"; Lil' Romeo, "2 Way"; Destiny's Child, "Bug-A-Boo"; Sammie, "Twitter Freak"; and Big Boi, "Ringtone." The following songs contain references to previous communications technologies: Skyy, "Call Me"; Blondie, "Call Me"; Missy Elliott, "Beep Me 911"; De La Soul, "Ring, Ring, Ring"; ABBA, "Ring Ring"; Jodeci, "My Phone"; and A Tribe Called Quest, "Skypager."

16 See Woods, "Will You Scrub Me Tomorrow." See "'Feenin'," track 2.0 in this volume.

of popular musical practices, newer technologies are considered artificial and inartistic, creating a hierarchy of what counts as technological: "Some items are considered *more* technological in status than others. In this scheme, a drum machine is more technological than a drum. . . . Such considerations are founded on an order of the real within which aesthetic preferences are transformed into ontological distinctions. . . . Such distinctions almost always proceed by rendering the technological components utilized in their favored forms invisible as technologies—they are more 'real' or 'natural', absorbed wholly into those that play them as expressive extensions of the performing body."[17] The cell phone effect resists such principles of the "real," choosing instead to stage voice-processing devices as both technological *and* expressive "extensions of the performing body." More important, the cell phone effect makes audible the sensation of hearing the human voice distributed across the digits of binary code. In addition, cell phones appear not as cumbersome synthetic obstructions of "authentic" and "natural" human speech at either end, but as integral to postmillennial interpersonal communication, while also rhythmifying their acoustic properties. The mobile "Black boxes" of street technology break through the sound barrier between humans and machines; their mobility allows for a relational engagement with the technological.

R&B features numerous lyric incantations of cell phone use qua social interaction, often positioning this ubiquitous feature of early twenty-first-century lifeworlds as the embodiment of interpersonal relations. On her 2000 track "Hey Kandi," Kandi, one of the only prominent female R&B songwriters and producers, responsible for such hits as Destiny's Child's "Bills, Bills, Bills" and TLC's "No Scrubs," deploys a variety of voice-processing maneuvers to almost baroque extremes.[18] "Hey Kandi" is structured around a cell phone heart-to-heart between the artist and a friend concerning Kandi's new beau. All the background vocals are sung and/or spoken through the phone, we often hear a dial tone, and the track makes ample usage of the popular Auto-Tune voice-alteration software.[19] Here the cell phone func-

17 Gilbert and Pearson, *Discographies*, 112.
18 Kandi, "Hey Kandi," on *Hey Kandi*, Columbia Records, 2000, CD, http://www .discogs.com/Kandi-Hey-Kandi/release/1486224.
19 Auto-Tune software was initially designed to correct the pitch of a singer's voice in the recording process; it was, however, taken up primarily by popular musicians as a voice-distortion mechanism that rendered the human voice robotic. This altered use of auto-tuning, which has now become the defining feature of the software for the majority of pop music audiences, was initially popularized by its prominence in R&B at the end of the 1990s. See Tyrangiel,

tions as the conduit for interpersonal communication as well as aiding the creation of intimacy. This particular track also renders audible quite a few sounds associated with cell phones (the voice at the other end of the "line," busy/free signal, and ringing), producing a technological intimacy that arises from both the content and mode of transmission.

Aaron Soul's "Ring, Ring, Ring" (2001), which echoes the previous recordings that bear similar names by ABBA and De La Soul, begins with a shout-out to "one to one Ericsson" and then tells a sad story about the hurtful words he uttered to his girlfriend "when [they] were last face-to-face," leading to the couple's subsequent estrangement.[20] By the time we get to the chorus, Soul's cell phone has transmogrified into a prime indicator of his amorous woes: "Ring, ring, ring, my cell phone's not ringing," and apparently his girlfriend's "cell phone keeps ringing," because the caller ID feature on her phone allows her to ignore his persistent calls. What strikes the ear here is that Soul's voice almost shape-shifts into a cell phone through the incessant chanting of "ring, ring, ring," in what initially sounds like a musical figuration of onomatopoeia.

Nevertheless, the repetition of *ring* fails to dissolve into a mimetic ocean since it sounds nothing like the real-world ringing of a cell phone. Instead, the track imagines a sonico-linguistic modality of hearing mobile technologies that traverse the fields of desire and are embodied in the recorded human voice. Later in the song, Soul tells us that he wishes his mobile would sing, thus affecting a reversal in which the singer transforms into a cell phone, and the machine takes on the singer's attributes. Rather than accurately reproducing cell phone sounds, Aaron Soul channels and seems possessed by its ringtones. The song brings to mind Sadie Plant's comments regarding the cell phone's significant realignment of contemporary acoustic bionetworks: "The warbles, beeps and tunes of the mobile have become so common that their calls have begun to constitute a new kind of electronic bird song, changing the soundtrack of cities and altering the background noise in regions as varied as the forests of Finland and the deserts of Dubai. [In fact,] many urban songbirds have become adept at impersonating mobile tones and melodies."[21] Perhaps we can think of Aaron Soul's sonic redaction of his cell phone as the

---

"Auto-Tune." See track 2.0 in this volume for an extended consideration of early audible Auto-Tune use in R&B music.

20 Aaron Soul, *Ring, Ring, Ring*, Def Soul, 2001, CD, https://www.discogs.com/release/2290917-Aaron-Soul-Ring-Ring-Ring.
21 Plant, *On the Mobile*, 29.

emergence of a different sort of urban songbird, one that codes humans and machines not as separate entities but both as components of a constitutive relation, which performs the technicity of the human via rhythm and the humanity of machines through vocalization.

On "Call Me" (2000), Soul's compatriot Jamelia tells a different story.[22] Accompanied by the ringing of a cell phone and the sounds of an ultramodern clavichord, Jamelia instructs her own man and, by extension, all other men, "Don't forget to call your boo tonight, baby is waiting for your call." This track differs most manifestly from "Ring, Ring, Ring" by weaving cell phone ringtones into its rhythmic fabric, albeit only during its final minutes. Rather than hearing these tones as similitude, I want to ask, How might we understand the effects of their rhythmic recurrence within the confines of Black musical formations? These musical examples equate verbal communication with mobile technologies by merging the supposedly deeply personal with technological gadgets. In this way, the technological appears not so much in the Nokias and Ericssons as it does in the spaces between the apparatus and social practices, what Édouard Glissant calls "a poetics of relation."[23] In these songs mobile phones are so much more than mere facilitators for the intricacies of intimate affairs; they serve as sonic indices of desire and as machines of longing.

Ginuwine's "2 Way" (2001) revolves around the two-way pager, which, as opposed to regular pagers (only numeric and one-way), allows its users to exchange text messages.[24] When this song was released ten years ago, two-way pagers and similar devices were widespread in the United States, while cell phone text messaging was already hugely popular in Europe and the rest of the world.[25] The track begins with the ringtones of a pager, which give way to

22 Jamelia, "Call Me," Rhythm Series, 2000, CD single, http://www.discogs.com /Jamelia-Call-Me/release/1108420.

23 Glissant, *Poetics of Relation*.

24 Ginuwine, "2 Way," on *The Life*, Sony Music, 2001, CD, http://www.discogs.com /Ginuwine-The-Life/master/258621. Two-way pagers were in vogue popular communication devices when Ginuwine's song was released in 2001.They have since been replaced by text messaging on mobile phones. See Wikipedia, s.v. "Pager," last updated November 21, 2022, 18:15 (UTC), http://en.wikipedia.org/wiki/Pager (accessed July 12, 2010).

25 On the history of text messaging, see Goggin, *Cell Phone Culture*, 65–88. There are a variety of reasons for the initial slow adoption of text messages in the United States; however, US mobile subscribers have sent and received

a cascade of strings and Ginuwine's introductory speech and is followed by the chorus:

> It's a two-way street, it a two-way door
> It's a two-way life (Pick it up and two way me)
> It's a two-way sky it's a two-way tel
> It's a two-way life, pick it up girl and hit me.

This passage is striking because it references the pager only implicitly, choosing instead to signify on the interpersonal connotations of the *two-way* moniker. Ginuwine equates the give and take of an intimate relationship with the machine's reciprocal attributes so as to sound the constitutive technicity of "human communication." As the song continues, Ginuwine offers a cornucopia of sensations through the aural lens of the two-way pager:

> The Auditory
> Now I got mine on loud
> if you get at me I'll hear you

> The Visual
> If it's dark light it up, put 'em up. Put 'em up
> If it's closed, flip it up
> in the club, beam me up"

> The Haptic
> I got mine on vibe, so if you get me
> I'll feel you
> I'll call you back real quick
> no lie better yet, I'll just reply.

While communication surely represents one of the main functions of the two-way pager, Ginuwine's track is more interested in exploring the "constitutively vague" dimensions of this machine. In this context, sound performs the sensation of communicational technologies by virtue of its a-signifying signifying properties; those aspects of the sonic that exceed linguistic content but nonetheless engender strong tactile and aural responses.

All the recordings I have discussed thus far were released at the dawn of the millennium when ringtones were primarily monophonic and could easily

---

more written messages than voice calls for the last fifteen years. See Reardon, "Americans Text More Than They Talk."

be differentiated from music.[26] While early mobile ringtones consisted of a particular sequence of tones and did not differ significantly from the functional sounds of a ringing landline, around 2004 mobile phone ringtones later largely became MP3 clips (usually around fifteen seconds in duration) of existing musical recordings. Besides featuring only parts of songs, these clips attain ringtone character by virtue of their repetition, which blurred the line between their utility as sonic indicators of incoming calls and musical consumption. Moreover, just as the previous examples musicalize functional ringtones via rhythmification, using excerpts of songs as ringtones embeds them in a different rhythmic context.[27] In fact, the incorporation of monophonic or polyphonic ringtones into popular musical recordings is largely a historical relic given the almost complete disappearance of these types of ringtones specifically designed to alert users to incoming calls, which were in 2004 replaced with ringtone sounds culled from musical recordings. For, in order to achieve the same effects as Jamelia, Ginuwine, or Kandi, later artists would have to interpolate, repeat, and rhythmify other pieces of music, which would be akin to the practice of sampling and require a completely different set of musical and legal practices. Before 2004, consumers used the functional ringtones that were preinstalled on their mobile; in 2014 users either acquired bits and pieces of preexisting songs or created ringtones from their own MP3 collection.[28] Despite the virtually total move to using digital audio

26 Sumanth Gopinath describes different mobile ringtones thus: "The commodification of the ringtone has occurred in several stages. These stages provide the outline of a model for ringtone development, whereby functional tones become: 1) monophonic ringtones or simple melodies; 2) polyphonic tones (midi synthesizer music); and, 3) digital sound files (True Tones or other company–specific formats, and ultimately mp3 files)." Gopinath, "Ringtones," 6. In the earlier period around 2000, ringtones were primarily monophonic and were slowly being replaced by polyphonic ringers; now digital sound files have all but eclipsed the other two forms. Nonetheless, nonmusical sounds (beeps, chirps, and so on) are still prevalent in signaling incoming text messages, Twitter alerts, instant messages, emails, calendar reminders, and so on.

27 Goggin, *Global Mobile Media*, 55–79; Gopinath, "Ringtones"; and Licoppe, "Mobile Phone's Ring."

28 Due to the increasing demand for these recordings, *Billboard Magazine* introduced its "Hot RingTones" chart, which first tracked the sales of polyphonic ringtones, in the November 6, 2004, issue. The "Hot RingMasters" chart that tabulated the sales for all ringtone species superseded this chart in December 2006. See "Ringmasters Chart Debuts." Even though ringtones based on popular hits still represented a significant portion of digital musical sales in

recordings as indicators of incoming voice calls between 2004 and 2010 and the absence of actual ringing sounds, these sonic marks still carried the name and operated as ringtones. The pendulum seems to have swung back completely, seeing that in 2022 ringtones have almost completely disappeared from the aural and social landscape of the United States, and if they do become audible, they do so in the form of functional cell phone presets. Due to the decline in ringtone sales around 2010, some alternative modes of interanimation between mobile devices and popular music initially flourished: the immensely popular app by musician T-Pain that allows everyone to emulate the musician's trademark auto-tuned voice, or the purchase of songs for the massively popular rhythmic iPhone game Tap Revenge, for instance.[29]

More generally, with the advent of Apple's iPhone and similar devices, mobile phones and portable music players are no longer separate physical entities but housed in the same gadget. Recorded music and mobiles enjoy an unprecedented symbiotic relationship in terms of content and at the hardware level. So much so, in fact, that on May 10, 2022, Apple announced that it would stop manufacturing the iPod touch, the last of its iPods still in existence (the first iPod was launched in 2001). There was no need for them any longer, because all their functionality has been incorporated into Apple's other devices, such as iPhones and iPads.[30] Furthermore, mobile devices have become the embodiment of "convergence culture," since they now also include calendars, alarm clocks, notebooks, compasses, e-readers, still and video cameras, voice recorders, flashlights, calculators, navigation devices, answering machines, and video players.[31]

In another instance of the continual blending of popular music and mobile technologies, hip-hop superstar Drake proclaimed early in his rap career that he could write his rhymes only on his BlackBerry mobile device, now, of

---

the United States in 2011, it had at that point become quite easy to produce ringtones from digital music files in iTunes or smartphone apps such as Ringdroid. See Bull, *Sound Moves*; and May and Hearn, "Mobile Phone as Media."

29 The I Am T-Pain iPhone app sold 300,000 in its first three weeks of release and continued to average 10,000 downloads per day for the year after its 2009 release. The Tap Revenge game requires players to tap a series of colored balls in accordance with the rhythm of a particular song. By 2010, Tap Revenge had sold more than five million tracks through its in-game music store. See Dredge, "5m Song Sales Milestone for Tap Revenge Games"; and L. Johnson, "Sorry Jay-Z Auto Tune Isn't Dead."

30 Mickle, "Farewell to the iPod."

31 See Goggin, *Cell Phone Culture*, 143–211; and H. Jenkins, *Convergence Culture*.

course, a historical relic. In a 2010 MTV documentary, Drake's producer describes the artist's process thus: "All Drake's raps for eternity have been written inside of a BlackBerry. I've had dummy BlackBerrys around that I just pull out for him to write on, like if he needs one . . . that don't actually even work!" This is how Drake portrays how he works: "I can't write my raps on paper. The BlackBerry keys—my thumbs were made for touching them."[32] The documentary then cuts to a shot of Drake in the sound booth of a recording studio, reading his raps from a BlackBerry. It bears noting that of all the functions contained in such a device, Drake singles out the haptic sensation of the keyboard in the portrayal of his compositional process. Since the early 2000s's ringtones and mobile technologies have become an essential part of composing, recording, distributing, and commodifying contemporary popular music: all musical recordings can potentially be used or sold as ringtones; all ringtones can possibly become songs, but only some of them are used in this way.

In addition, the financial success of ringtones led to the creation of a (almost universally derided) subgenre of hip-hop dubbed *ringtone rap* in the early to mid-2000s. Recordings by artists such as Soulja Boy, Mims, and Dem Franchize Boyz that fall into the purview of ringtone rap were generally written/produced (catchy short singsong hooks, tinny beats, nonsensical rhymes) so as to sound best when heard through cell phone speakers and therefore sell as many ringtones as possible.[33] Hence, ringtone rap reverses the absorption of monophonic ringtones into popular music that occurred around 2000 by transmogrifying songs into extended ringtones. Although Trey Songz's "LOL :-)" (2009) is sung rather than rapped, it features two prominent Southern rappers, Soulja Boy and Gucci Mane, and bears the sonic hallmarks of the subgenre, sounding like a crunk version of the children's song "Frère Jacques."[34] The lyrics further compound the interweaving of popular music and mobile technologies:

> Cruisin' in that Benz around the city (round tha city Yup!)
> Then I felt my phone buzz, I know that she like thugs
> . . . .
> Then she sent a text that had read, "baby, I'm at home"

32 Ziegbe, "Drake Reveals Songwriting Process"; see also Mack and Warren, *Drake*.

33 Moody, "Rappers Aim for Ringtones."

34 Trey Songz, "LOL :-)," Atlantic Recording Corporation, 2009, CD single, http://www.discogs.com/Trey-Songz-lol—The-Remixes/release/2044187.

Then she sent another one that said she's all alone
So I texted her a smiley face and said, "let's do the grown"
She said, "lol boy you crazy, come on" . . .
Sent that lil' face with the tongue 'cause I'm nasty
I'm on my way (way), girl I can't wait (wait)
Twitter me a picture, lemme see that okay.

Songz's song narrates his mobile interaction with a female love/lust object via text messaging, which is why his phone does not ring but buzzes.[35] In response to her initial written missive, Songz sends an SMS that contains a "smiley face" emoticon, and later he includes another emoticon, a face with its tongue sticking out—":-P"—which is usually used to indicate playful defiance. Here it presumably works as an indicator of Songz's willingness to engage in cunnilingus ("'cause I'm nasty").[36] The smiley face, like other emoticons, is a pictogram, which can be formed either by combining punctuation marks [:-)] so that they visually approximate the shape of a smiling face or by using a graphic image (☺). The emoticon's power of signification does not rely on the sound of the graphic marks; it is solely based on the iconic shape of its signifiers. In this way, pictograms operate in diametric opposition to logograms (*u = you, 2nite = tonight*, etc.), which depend entirely on the sound of the letters and numbers.[37] Instead of substituting a short series of punctuation marks or an image for two words for the sake of brevity, the smiley face symbolizes a particular sentiment (happiness). Conversely, this pictogram enters the phonetic record as a linguistic approximation of an image (smiley face) and not a description of a sentiment; otherwise, Songz would sing the words *happy* or *happiness* instead of *smiley face*. Songz's rendition of the smiley face—translating the emoticon to words and ensconcing

---

35 Even when musical ringtones were primarily used for voice calls, incoming text messages, emails, and instant messages were and frequently continue to be signaled by a buzz, a beep, or other "nonmusical" noises.

36 Wikipedia defines *emoticon* as "a textual expression representing the face of a writer's mood or facial expression. Emoticons are often used to alert a responder to the tenor or temper of a statement, and can change and improve interpretation of plain text." Wikipedia, s.v. "Emoticon," http://en.wikipedia.org/wiki /Emoticon (accessed July 12, 2010). In instant messaging, email, and text messaging, images such as these ☹☺ are used rather than punctuation marks. For instance, whenever I typed the title of Songz's song while writing this track, MS Word autocorrected the punctuation marks to look like this ☺.

37 Crystal, *Txtng*, 37–62.

this alphabetic amalgam in his rhythmically stylized vocalization—extends the sign's reach into the realm of the sonic, albeit only insofar as it refers back to the graphic image of a smiley face.

The chorus of "LOL :-)" introduces another composite that hails from the land of electronically mediated communication:

> Shawty just text me, say she wanna sex me (LOL smiley face, LOL
>   smiley face)
> Shawty sent a Twit pic saying come and get this (LOL smiley face, LOL
>   smiley face).

One of the most common abbreviations used in internet and mobile written communication, LOL (or its adjacent expressions, ROFL and LMAO) also represents one of the few instances in which initialisms from this jurisdiction have successfully crossed over to spoken English.[38] As with the smiley face, the LOL (initially a contraction of three words: *laughing out loud*) makes the jump from written to spoken language not by simply restoring the acronym to its original three-word glory but by giving voice to the letters: *L O L*. Thus, the invocations of LOL and the smiley face, both of which were initially used to append affect to written communication, achieve their effects in the context of the song, because they have already transitioned from electronic script/image to oral communication. They have become a part of conversational spoken English as noticeable symbols of and for (mobile) electronic communication. In addition, the backing track—expressly designed to sound like a simulacrum of an even then historical monophonic ringtone—as well

38 The abbreviations ROFL (rolling on the floor laughing), TTYL (talk to you later), LMAO (laughing my ass off), and OMG (oh my god) have also made the jump to spoken English. See Crystal, *Language and the Internet*; Tagliamonte and Denis, "Linguistic Ruin?"; and Ulaby, "OMG." In addition, LOL plays a crucial role in the codification of a sociolect (*lolspeak* or *kitty pidgin*) particular to the internet phenomenon Lolcats, which combines images of cats with witty captions. See Dash, "Cats Can Has Grammar." In her discussion of "cyberpunctuation," Jennifer Brody shows how emoticons are mobilized in contemporary cinema, which suggests another modality for the cultural logics I have been outlining here. See Brody, *Punctuation*. Finally, the transposition of LOL into face-to-face communication has a precedent in the "air quotes" (using one's fingers to make quotation marks in the air during conversation) that are now synonymous with the "ironic 1990s." Beers, "Irony Is Dead! Long Live Irony!" Although air quotes are not spoken per se, they are written characters that are at present used to punctuate verbal communication with affect (irony).

as the singing and repetition further accents the sonorous dimensions of these traditionally silent signs/phrases. Rhythm, which is defined by recurring patterns of sound, sets in motion a conversion of the expressive signification that has accrued to "LOL" and "smiley face." Accordingly, "LOL" and "smiley face" cease connoting humor and happiness; they are now phonic signifiers for the rhythmic relationality of mobile technologies.

In a slightly different vein, Monica's "Blackberry" (2010) track begins with a nonmusical sonic indicator for an incoming text message and goes on to narrate the singer's powers of electronic detection (her willingness to check his phone and her ability to crack the device's lock code).[39] These powers impart warnings to Monica's boyfriend, whom she accuses of infidelity ("Who you sneakin' wit 'cause I already got the code to ya phone"), and the "other woman" ("Get yo hands off my man / Girl you already know"). Monica's beau conducts his affairs on a BlackBerry smartphone (now largely defunct), which was launched in 1999 as a two-way pager, took on its smartphone capabilities in 2002 (email, web browsing, SMS, etc.), and owed its success primarily to its outstanding emailing capabilities.[40] At the outset BlackBerrys were pitted against similar devices produced by Motorola: BlackBerrys were used by elite personalities such as Bill Gates or Al Gore while Motorola pagers were allied with rappers and sports figures, Jay-Z and Shaquille O'Neal, for instance.[41] Rapper Jay-Z's immensely popular "I Just Wanna Love U (Give It 2 Me)" (2000) includes the following lines: "Only way to roll, Jigga and two ladies / I'm too cold, Motorola, two way page me, c'mon," which cemented the gadget's place in the popular imagination.[42] According to Howard Rheingold, "Hip-hop culture, streetwise and fashion-conscious fans of rap music, favor Motorola's two-way pagers, while young stockbrokers, suits, and geeks in the information technology industry favor the BlackBerry wireless

39 Monica, "Blackberry," bonus track on *Still Standing*, J Records, 2010, CD, http://www.discogs.com/Monica-Still-Standing/release/2279141.
40 Barack Obama's avowed dependency on his BlackBerry and the public discourse about Obama's relationship with this device epitomize the apex of BlackBerry's cultural omnipresence in the United States during the early 2000s. See Clifford, "For BlackBerry, Obama's Devotion Is Priceless"; and Hauser, *Obama's BlackBerry*.
41 Century, "World Divided."
42 Jay-Z, "I Just Wanna Love U (Give It 2 Me)," Roc-A-Fella Records, 2000, CD single, http://www.discogs.com/Jay-Z-I-Just-Wanna-Love-U-Give-It-2-Me/release/781701.

pagers from Research in Motion."[43] BlackBerrys were initially associated almost exclusively with white-collar work, the corporate world, masculinity, and whiteness. Motorola two-way pagers (and subsequent devices such as the Sidekick), by contrast, signaled leisure, sexuality, youth, femininity, Blackness, and so on, thus rescripting the Black/white boxes of technology partition for the era of ubiquitous mobile communication and computing.[44]

As a consequence of the widespread dissemination of smartphones in the years following the release of the iPhone in 2007, the BlackBerry traveled beyond its early professional stomping ground, yet it still registered in the cultural imagination around 2010 primarily as a professional and masculine tool. All these factors contribute to how Monica mobilizes the BlackBerry, since the device stands in for her male love object as well as his infidelity. On the one hand, this provides a reference to the pivotal role of the BlackBerry in the 2009 public spectacle of Tiger Woods's extramarital affairs: Monica, like Woods's wife, will uncover his dalliances by monitoring his mobile phone.[45] On the other hand, the BlackBerry, as a signifier for the business world and masculinity, magnifies the lover's transgression, since he is using the device to conduct personal and illicit communication. Monica's "untrustworthy boo" does not appear in the song; he is personified by the repurposed Black-Berry and the singer's affective relationship with the machine.

Akin to Aaron Soul's "ring, ring, ring" chant, the word BlackBerry materializes in this song in such an interrupted, rhythmic, and digitally altered way that it barely registers any relation to the linguistic unit that it is based on:

43 Rheingold, *Smart Mobs*, 23.
44 Sage, "Study: BlackBerry Adds 15 Hours to Work Week." The Sidekick (introduced in 2002) was the precursor to smartphones, featuring an LCD screen, a full QWERTY keyboard, email, instant messaging, and web capacity. The gadget entered the annals of popular culture in 2005 when a group of hackers appropriated the private information from Paris Hilton's Sidekick and posted it on the web.
45 In the aftermath of Woods's much-publicized text-message conversations with his mistresses, there existed an iPhone app (TigerMail: Tigers Don't Always Leave Tracks) that promised to erase the traces of potentially incriminating notes once they have been received. As Gerard Goggin shows, mobile technologies have acquired cultural meaning in part by being associated with the uncovering and making public of illicit celebrity romances (Prince Charles's taped phone conversations with Camilla or the text messages found on Paris Hilton's stolen Motorola Sidekick). Goggin, *Cell Phone Culture*, 126–40.

I'm the one that
Checks (checks),
Check the (chicks)
Black (Black) ber (ber) ry (ry)
Yep that's me
I'm the one
That checks his phone
When he falls asleep
Early in the morn
You better have a call, go to your phone, ring leave it on with the
    Black (Black) ber (ber) ry (ry).

You-you-you
Betta have a co-co-code
In yo phone
And lemme alone
With ya Black-ber-er-er-ry

In fact, if the song were not named "Blackberry," the listeners would probably not be able to decipher the signification of the word through the Auto-
Tune haze, and, accordingly, it signifies chiefly in the domain of sensation.
While the verses concentrate on the intricacies of intimate relationships as
refracted through mobile technologies, the scat-like singing and auto-tuning
of "Blackberry" in the chorus locate it beyond the grasp of wordness and
meaning. The chorus is the only part of "Blackberry" in which Monica intonates in this scat-like fashion (emphasizing rhythm and sonority rather
than melody or meaning), and her voice appears audibly digitally altered,
providing a stark contrast to the naturalistic and melismatic grain of the
singer's voice throughout the rest of the track. Thus, Monica's particular staging of the word BlackBerry relies on its cultural meanings (mobile
device and attendant practices) at the same time as it recodes this linguistic unit as a sonic emoticon. The way Monica vocalizes BlackBerry in the
chorus supplements the song's narrative with nonlinguistic affect. Monica's
"Blackberry" takes a different path than Trey Songz's "LOL :-)" to the aural
rendering of emoticons: Songz takes written electronic signs, sounding them
out through song while fully retaining their sociolinguistic signification;
Monica, however, transforms a word into a sonic affective sign that almost
leaves behind linguistic meaning altogether. In both cases R&B allows for
the rhythmic ensnaring of machines and emotions, because the genre
possesses an expansive repertoire—in lyrical content, available styles of

"emotive" singing, and musical gestalt—for the sonic transaction of inter-personal affairs.

I will now turn to the British TV series *Metrosexuality* (1999) to draw attention to the rhythmic representation of mobile technologies in a chiefly ocular medium.[46] In *Metrosexuality* much of the social interaction between the characters takes place on mobile and sedentary telephones, and phone conversations constitute at least half of the screen time. In the very first scene after the opening credits, we are introduced to teenager Kwame, who is desperately trying to reunite his divorced fathers, Max and Jordan. Before Kwame makes a visual entrance on the screen, we witness a fast-paced montage of the telephone call Kwame places on his mobile. Rather than showing Kwame dialing his father Max's number, however, the screen is taken up by a series of accelerated-motion images featuring city streets and buildings that are soundtracked by swishing sounds and accelerated recordings of mobile dial and ringing tones. Moreover, the camera angles are frequently irregular, which only adds to the perplexity engendered by these shots, especially since these shots also function as an introduction to *Metrosexuality*. The expedited noises and visual montage come to an abrupt halt with the tone of Max's mobile as he answers Kwame's call while sitting in a hair salon. Then the editing crosscuts between Kwame's position on the streets of Notting Hill (the lettering on-screen reads, "In the heart of Notting Hill . . .") and Max's location at the salon as up-tempo dance music plays in the background. In this part of the sequence, the camera circles restlessly around Kwame as he moves around and speaks to his father, while a stable camera frames a medium close-up of Max's face.

Once the phone conversation between the two has ended, we cut to a close-up of Kwame's hands as he dials Papa Jordan's number, which is followed by another fast-motion montage that depicts the rapid travel of information over cellular networks via the rhythmic editing of image and sound. Jordan takes Kwame's call on a gray cordless phone while working in a recording studio with midtempo bass-heavy music emanating from the studio speakers. In his conversations with his fathers, Kwame tells both that the other parent has failed to pick him up from soccer practice; as a result, Max and Jordan arrive at Kwame's location at the same time, while Kwame

46 Beadle-Blair, *Metrosexuality*. For an extended consideration of mobile music players in the cinematic construction of urban space, see Weheliye, *Phonographies*, 123–44.

and his two best friends watch them interact at a distance. Sadly, Max and Jordan do not reconcile as Kwame had hoped in devising this elaborate ruse. In Jordan's portion of this tripartite interaction, the diegetic music, the telephone, and Jordan's clothing provide a muted contrast (monochrome, largely gray clothing, enclosed space, only the bass of the music is audible, etc.) to the brash, colorful, and buoyant sounds and colors that structure the shots featuring Kwame (canary-yellow hip-hop outfit, electric-blue cellular phone, lots of movement, etc.) and Max (red mobile phone, blond dreadlocks, red flowery outfit, etc.). There are many instances like this over the course of the show's narrative that imagine how aural information traverses space via the deployment of highly accelerated and rapidly intercut images accompanied by swishing and ringing noises to accentuate the velocity of the montage. Here velocity registers as the intensification of sensation, because the viewer is forced to bear witness to the duration of its escalation. The collages of the telephone calls in *Metrosexuality* punctuate the triangulated visual and sonic flow between the different locales/characters, channeling the rush of mobile communication in ways that are specific to the medium of television; they also set in motion a rhythmic "poetics of relation" at the juncture of mobile devices and humans.

Nicola Green's treatment of rhythm accents the different temporal structures of mobile technology use, distinguishing between three modalities of mobile rhythm: "the rhythms of mobile use; the rhythms of integrating mobile use into everyday life; and the rhythms of relation between use in everyday life and institutional social change."[47] The examples discussed in this track add another rhythmic layer to the relational complexities of mobile time by initially removing mobile technologies from everyday life. Wrested from the vagaries of the quotidian and interfaced with pop songs or televisual narratives, these machines have radically different functions, moving, to put it in schematic terms, from practical use to aesthetic sensation. Surely, both of these aspects already commingle before their musicalization, and in this way, it is a shift not in kind but in degree and intensity that amplifies those rhythmic dimensions beside and below routine information transmission. Moreover, once they have entered into rhythmic relations with other matters and forces, the textural facets of mobile technologies reenter the annals of everyday life, becoming integral to these devices' allure and functionality. According to Gilles Deleuze, "Rhythm . . . is more profound than vision,

47 N. Green, "On the Move," 285.

hearing, etc. . . . What is ultimate is thus the relation between sensation and rhythm, which places in each sensation the levels and domains through which it passes. . . . Sensation is not qualitative and qualified, but has only an intensive reality, which no longer determines within itself representative elements, but allotropic variations."[48] The instances of mobile rhythm analyzed above produce the polymorphic variations mentioned by Deleuze in their emphasis on the diverse rhythms of the technological and the human, hinting at an embodied relational theory of mobile technologies that accents their communicative *and* aesthetic facets.

As a conceptual tool and a mode of apprehending the world, "rhythm" mobilizes "the processes of bringing-into-relation" that are fundamental to any social formation and/or object but are habitually neglected in favor of their stagnant counterparts.[49] Still, these models of rhythm (and Glissant's notion of relation) do not simply replace the metronomic beat of the inert and unchanging with sheer flux; instead, they dwell in the uneven territory at the junction of mobile use, everyday life, institutional social change, and aesthetics. Indeed, rhythm names and transacts the dialectical liaison of these at times opposing forces, making them constitutive of the objects or practices they envelop. Therefore, rhythm produces the multifaceted processes through which mobile technologies (along with a host of other technologies and rituals) come into being as consuming textural, sonic, and haptic relations; in Henri Lefebvre's phrasing: "To grasp a rhythm it is necessary to have been *grasped* by it."[50] Taken together, the cell phone rings; the pager sounds; Drake's BlackBerry authorship; ringtone rap; and the repeated sung vociferations of *ring, ring, ring, call me, 2-way, LOL, smiley face*, and BlackBerry; as well as the optico-sonic overflow of *Metrosexuality*, boost the mobile sensations of communication technologies through the conduit of rhythm. The aforementioned rhythmifications might appear auxiliary, but they tap into facets central to the existence and utility of mobile technologies that do not register on the metronomic radar of many critical dialects. If, as John Urry remarks, "humans are sensuous, corporeal, technologically extended and

48 Deleuze, *Francis Bacon*, 37–39. I am not advocating the privileging of rhythm as a sign of Afro-diasporic alterity, as occurs frequently, but attempting to make its formal properties usable for a conceptualization of mobile technologies. For a critical genealogy of how rhythm came to be heard as an enactment of radical Black difference, see Radano, *Lying Up a Nation*, especially chapter 5.
49 Glissant, *Poetics of Relation*, 95.
50 Lefebvre, *Rhythmanalysis*, 27.

mobile beings," then cellular telephones, because they are highly mobile and facilitate interpersonal contact, operate as prime indicators of what it means to be human at this point in history.[51] The sonic incorporation of mobile technologies into popular music extends and remixes these machines' anthropomorphic bass line and, as a result, embodies the rhythmic relation of all technologies.

51 Urry, *Mobilities*, 51.

I was reminded again of how centrally telephones and mobile devices still feature in many R&B and hip-hop releases on a sunny day in the spring of 2021. Through the open windows in my apartment, I could hear a car on the street blasting a song I didn't immediately recognize. Because the beat was catchy, I summoned the Shazam app on my phone to reveal its identity. Even though this app is a marvel of modern technology, Shazam sometimes fails when confronted with distance and distorted bass-heavy and moving car speakers. Fortunately, in this case the trusty sonic detection software did not disappoint, and once the app had concluded its digital alchemy, I went to stream the track and could not get past the following line from what turned out to be Polo G's " Rapstar": "Only b***h I give a conversation to is Siri." How does such a statement become possible and intelligible in a number-one hit on the Billboard charts in 2021?[1] Siri is an artificially intelligent voice-activated assistant that has been an integral part of iPhones since 2011. Until 2021 the US version of the software had a default "white female voice" immediately recognizable to many people (Amazon's Alexa, Google Assistant, and Microsoft's Cortana deploy similar voices). Even though the idea of Siri as feminine has been part and parcel of the virtual assistant's cultural footprint since its initial popularization, the affective personification of Siri in this particular fashion depends on just how deeply mobile communication devices have become intertwined with the *Stoff* of everyday life, communication, and interpersonal relationships in the western world and beyond.

Alternately, take Lil Tjay and 6LACK's "Calling My Phone," another big hit from the spring of 2021, in which the performers melancholically bemoan a former lover continuing to contact them long after the romantic or sexual relationship has ended.[2] The song's postchorus, discernibly distinct from the

1   Polo G, "Rapstar," Columbia Records, 2021, MP3, https://www.discogs.com/Polo-G -Rapstar/release/18220837.
2   Lil Tjay, featuring 6LACK, "Calling My Phone," Columbia Records, 2021, MP3, https://www.discogs.com/Lil-Tjay-Ft-6LACK-Calling-My-Phone/release/17601781.

other two rapping/singing voices on the track, associated with Lil Tjay and 6LACK, consists of a sped-up and pitched-up vocal sample on a loop chanting "can't get you off my mind now" and seemingly conjures the persistent female counterpart who keeps calling Lil Tjay's and 6LACK's phones. Even though the incantation of "can't get you off my mind now" is an integral part of the song (to my ears it's the most memorable part of the track, even more so than the actual chorus), who this voice belongs to is not divulged in the song, in the music video, or even in the song credits on streaming services.[3] In addition, despite featuring women dancers and actors, in the music video the camera cuts to an old-school analog answering machine on a table in an empty room during the postchorus instead of having the women featured in the video mime the lyrics. The answering machine remains a nagging presence in the video, just as the chipmunk-style postchorus does in the song, but what endures as simultaneously beautiful and frustratingly hazy is whether the sped-up vocals approximate the phone as such, the obsessive replaying of a digital voicemail, or the now former—and presumed female—love object. I say *frustrating*, because despite all the different avenues for alternate imaginaries facilitated by this mechanized voice and "Calling My Phone" in general (for example, the song's verses could very plausibly be interpreted as the two male performers, Lil Tjay and 6LACK, addressing each other and not an imaginary ex-girlfriend), the overall vibe journeys down well-trodden and resolutely cisheterosexist pathways, in much the same register as Polo G's invocation of Siri. What frequencies would critically fabulating with and about this song through Treva Ellison's "Black femme praxis" amplify?[4] Would it facilitate interpreting the song's verses as the two male performers, Lil Tjay and 6LACK, addressing each other and not an imaginary ex-girlfriend? Would this fabulation make it possible to hear the feminized voice as purely machinic, as a software plugin and not a human person? In the end I'm left with a question: Is it still a homosocial triangle if the affectively charged and exchanged "object" appears seemingly "technological"—though undoubtedly feminized—rather than "human"?

---

3 According to several internet chat rooms, the loop is based on a sample from the software plugin Arcade, produced by the Output company.
4 Ellison, "Black Femme Praxis."

MY VOLK TO COME

Specters of Peoplehood in Diaspora Discourse
and Afro-German Popular Music

The exoticization of Western thought [must result from the examination of] this thought itself
from the landscape or perspective of the *blues* people—and therefore from the perspective, not
of the-people-as-*Volk*, but as in the *popular* aspect of the [1960s Black liberation] movements,
of the people as the movements of people who are logically excluded . . . from our present order.
—SYLVIA WYNTER, "On How We Mistook the Map for the Territory and Re-imprisoned Ourselves in Our Unbearable Wrongness of Being, of Désêtre" (2006)

The prominence of diaspora discourse in Black studies has supplanted the
emphasis on African American identity that defined the field for some time
with the interrogation of US Black life within and against the context of other

diasporic groups. The nominal passage from Black studies to African American studies, and now diaspora studies, sets some of the groundwork for querying the conceptual underpinnings of these developments. Replacing the designation Black with African American signals foremost a turn away from a primarily political category toward an identitarian marker of cultural and/or ethnic specificity, while diaspora suggests a concurrent deemphasizing of specificities in the embrace of transnational frames of reference and also a return of said particularities via the comparison of Black populations that differ in nationality. The turn to the diaspora concept in the history of Black studies frequently positions the nation as a dialectical stepping stone toward a supranational sphere that appears as more desirable than its national shadow. Still, these discourses often replicate and reify the very nation form they are seeking to escape in their comparison of different national literatures, cultures, languages, and so on.

The appeal and success of diaspora as a concept within critical discourse lies in its reframing of rigid national precincts. Instead of focusing on the bounded historical continuity of the nation-state, diaspora offers pathways that retrace layerings of difference in the aftermath of colonialism and slavery as well as the effects of other forms of migration and displacement. Thus, diaspora enables the desedimentation of the nation from the "interior," by taking into account groups that fail to comply with the reigning definition of the people as a cohesive political subject due to sharing one culture, one race, one language, one religion, and so on, and from the "exterior," by drawing attention to the movements that cannot be contained by the nation's administrative and ideological borders.

We might sum up diaspora's promise as that of a virtual technology of collectivity, or at least as a formation that highlights its virtuality in more acute ways than the nation. Of course, nations are also virtual, but their virtuality tends to be actualized in sovereign territories and the states that rule over and through them. Diasporas, in contrast, generally do not follow the same patterns of actualization as the nation, although they are forced to exist within and between nation-states. The severing of collectivity from territory and the state marks diaspora's virtuality and the concept's radical potential vis-à-vis the theorization of Black cultures. But this decoupling also represents a danger, since cultural and/or ethnic peoplehood frequently emerge as defining traits of community when the state and its concomitant geographic terrain have taken a leave of absence.

While many commentators have censured the intermural sameness smuggled in through the back door in the idea of a seamless continuity between various African-descended populations around the globe, these critiques of-tentimes assume stable, if not coherent, diasporic populations. Thus, despite the thoroughgoing problematization of the homeland conundrum, what remains largely uninterrogated thus far is the particular shape of Black collectivity within diasporic groups. There exists a basic assumption in much of diaspora discourse that diasporic groups are indeed communities and that these communities, if not better than national ones, are at least more open; otherwise, the very invocation of the *D*-word would be moot.

Some statements from the burgeoning field of Black European studies have shifted the emphasis from conceptualizing the African diaspora as a semihomogeneous field to portraying it as a malleable space marked above all by difference. Although this modification is in many ways laudable, the insistence on difference as the defining attribute of diaspora leaves the door open for the hushed entry of peoplehood as the principal mode of articulating not the African diaspora tout court, as in prior conceptions of this field, but specific national diasporas. Following the groundwork laid by Paul Gilroy, the subsequent work of Jacqueline Nassy Brown concerned with the Black British diaspora in Liverpool, Tina Campt's writings on Afro-Germans during the Third Reich, and Brent Edwards's analysis of the history of the term/concept of *diaspora* in Black cultural contexts all focus on interdiasporic diversity rather than arguing for or assuming a common thread that magically unites various African-descended groupings around the world.[1] Campt writes of the oftentimes unequal "intercultural address" that marks the dialogue between diasporic groups, Brown ruminates on the "margins of the African Diaspora," and Edwards highlights the necessary but impossible linguistic and cultural translation in transnational Afro-diasporic conversations. All three authors have done much to draw our attention to the multiple vectors of interdiasporic differentiation and the specificities of Black groupings beyond the United States. Yet, in their, albeit differently pitched, insistence on the variable multiplicity of Black life, these authors still maintain the discrepancy between African Americans and other diasporic formations as *the* measuring device to calibrate the radical differences between individual diasporas defined by national or linguistic borders.

First published in *Black Europe and the African Diaspora*, edited by Darlene Clark Hine, Trica Danielle Keaton, and Stephen Small (Urbana: University of Illinois Press, 2009).

1 Jacqueline Brown, "Black Liverpool"; Campt, *Other Germans*; and Edwards, "Uses of Diaspora."

Brown, Campt, and Edwards are careful to distance themselves from previous progressivist narratives that construe Black European and other diasporas as nascent versions of the African American "community." Yet, by only taking in the divergences between this arrangement and British, French, and German configurations, these authors tend to reinscribe African America as the model for the African diaspora, perhaps not its Platonic ideal but a category through which European diasporas are qualified and circumscribed, nonetheless. Brown, for instance, in invoking "the margins of 'the African Diaspora,'" asks, "When does the unrelenting presence of Black America actually become oppressive, even as it inspires?"[2] Similarly, in his discussion of Léopold Sédar Senghor's notion of *décalage*, Edwards accents the "changing core of difference" found "among African Americans and Africans," describing décalage as "the received biases that refuse to pass over when one crosses the water."[3] Finally, Campt, who draws heavily on the previous two critics, suggests, "'Intercultural address' . . . encourages us to reflect on the status of Black America in relation to other Black populations in the process of articulating their own experiences and constructing alternative forms of Black identity and community."[4] Despite my agreement with much of these analyses, the pesky question remains as to why Black America appears as the

---

2 Jacqueline Brown, "Black Liverpool," 297. In the subsequent and revised book version of this essay Brown comes to an analogous conclusion: "We might begin by inquiring into the way particular Black communities outside the United States are affected by the global dominance of American culture. Britain is surely more inundated with things American than the reverse." Jacqueline Brown, *Dropping Anchor, Setting Sail*, 41. While this statement surely carries some validity, the presence of (African) American cultural artifacts in the global domain is not tantamount to political, cultural, or economic hegemony per se. In addition, this discussion is partially a response to an emergent consensus—among both US and European scholars of the African diaspora—at several conferences about an "African American hegemony" vis-à-vis other Black populations. Frequently, the long histories of Black studies in the United States—and the lack thereof outside the United States—and the global circulation of African American cultural artifacts are summoned to stand in as the grounds for said hegemony. Even though I'm not disputing these two points, I would strongly caution against the invocation of hegemony for the reasons I mention above, as well as the underfunded and embattled status of many US Black studies departments and the mass impoverishment, criminalization, and incarceration of so many people of African descent in the United States.
3 Edwards, "Uses of Diaspora," 65.
4 Campt, *Other Germans*, 207.

solitary point of comparison, especially given that all three critics explicitly reject African American "vanguardism" (Edwards), "cultural imperialism" (Brown), and "hegemony" (Campt). Thus, European diasporas materialize as differently constituted only by virtue of their analytic localization in the comparative context of Black America.

This is especially evident in the utilization of "margins" (Brown) and the descriptor "alternative" (Campt) to describe non–African American diasporic populations. The perspective from which Black Europeans appear at the "margins of Diaspora" or as "alternative forms of Black identity and community" runs counter to the political organizing and critical theorizing of Afro-European diasporas, particularly since these are generally more concerned with their marginalization within the nation-states in which they dwell, as opposed to their supposed radical divergence from US models of racial identity and community. Consequently, we should pause to query the conceptual work done by invoking terms/concepts such as *hegemony, imperialism, vanguardism, margins,* and *alternative.* If the task of diaspora discourse has been to aerate the putatively dominant position of African America within the African diaspora, then we need to ask why the scent of center and periphery still lingers so heavily in the comparative framework of Black European studies.

Furthermore, by so determinedly stressing the disparities between these different nationally located communities, these inquiries run the risk of interpellating individual African diasporas, whether in Europe, the United States, or the Caribbean, as primordially constituted beacons of racial kinship. Instead of a transnational ethnic notion of peoplehood that unites all African-descended subjects around the globe, national boundaries, or linguistic differences that often help define the national ones, become the ultimate indicators of differentiation. In this process, national borders and/or linguistic differences are in danger of entering the discursive record as ontological absolutes rather than as structures and institutions that have served again and again to relegate Black subjects to the status of the western modernity's nonhuman other.

My point is that the turn away from envisioning the African diaspora as a transcendental racial bond to a series of radical differences can unwillingly lead to the importation of what Étienne Balibar calls the "nation form" into diaspora discourse. Balibar describes the process by which collectivities are transformed into "the people" in the following fashion: "Social formations . . . [are] represented in the past or in the future *as if* they formed a natural community, possessing of itself an identity of origins, culture and interests which transcends individuals and social conditions."[5] This "natural community" also constitutes a spectral grammar of diaspora discourse. Given that people-hood represents the foremost mode of imagining, (re)producing, and legislating community, and thus of managing inequality in the intertwined histories of capitalism and the nation-state, peoplehood sneaks in as the de facto actualization of diasporas in the national context, especially when we avoid specifying how Black collectivity might be codified in the absence of this category.

Witness, for instance, the following statement by Anne Adams about the post-1980s history of Afro-German culture, which spells out what often remains tacit in writings about diaspora. In this passage Afro-Germans paradoxically emerge as a Volk as a result of being incorporated into the folk of the African diaspora: "African diaspora as condition *resolves* any 'contradiction' or 'oxymoron' in 'Afro-German;' African diaspora as process *resolves* the DuBoisian 'twoness' in the souls of Afro-German Black Folk/*Volk*."[6] The Volk appears here in terms of both the particularities of being Afro-German and the sublatory muscle of the African diaspora. This notion of community or peoplehood is precisely what diaspora discourse set out to avoid and reformulate by dislocating the nexus of people and territory.

In contrast to other critics, who see the category of the people as a unitary body politic, Giorgio Agamben locates a fundamental breach within this domain: "Any interpretation of the political meaning of the term *people* ought to start from the peculiar fact that in modern European languages this term always indicates also the poor, the underprivileged, and the excluded. The same term names the constitutive political subject as well as the class that is excluded—de facto, if not de jure—from politics."[7] Still, diaspora discourse

---

5 Balibar, "Nation Form," 96.
6 Adams, "Souls of Black Volk," 230–31.
7 Agamben, *Means without End*, 29. Michael Hardt and Antonio Negri have pitted the concept of the people against that of the multitude. The former stands for a traditional notion of a unified and closed collectivity, where the latter signifies immanent openness. See Hardt and Negri, *Multitude*, xiv, 99, 242–43. Ernesto Laclau, by contrast, places "the people" at the center of politics. Noting a similar fracture within "the people" as Agamben, he distinguishes between *populus* as "the body of all citizens" and *plebs* as " the underprivileged." Laclau asserts that this category becomes political when "a *plebs* claims to be the only legitimate *populus*—that is, a partiality which wants to function as the totality of the community." Laclau, *On Populist Reason*, 81.

at times conflates the unitary political subject with the excluded. While this does not occur at the level of the nation per se, it does so in terms of individual national diasporas by virtue of stressing their radical particularities and mutual cultural and linguistic incompatibilities; as a result, diaspora discourse reproduces the nation form by staging individual African diasporas in the idiom of peoplehood as cohesive culturo-political formations.[8] Agamben continues his ruminations by noting the particularities of the German designation *Volk* vis-à-vis the duality of the people: "We ought to understand the lucid fury with which the German *Volk*—representative par excellence of the people as integral body politic—tried to eliminate the Jews forever as precisely the internecine struggle that divides *People* and *people*. With the final solution . . . Nazism tried obscurely and in vain to free the Western political stage from this intolerable shadow so as to produce finally the German Volk as the people able to heal the original biopolitical fracture."[9] Since the German word *Volk* simply designates "people" in the English-language sense and does not necessarily evoke Nazism in the same way as the term *völkisch*, a distinction should be made between *das* Volk, which signifies the people as an undifferentiated mass of humans, including the oppressed, and *ein* Volk as a specific and supposedly homogeneous ethnic, cultural, and/or linguistic group. This contrast corresponds roughly with Agamben's distinction between *the people* with a capital *P* and those with a lowercase *p*. Hence, the biopolitical project of Nazism was to transform *das* Volk into *ein* ethnically pure Volk.

Given the history of the term *Volk*, it seems surprising that Adams would invoke it so lightly and link to *the folk*, which is both another name for *the people* with a lowercase *p* and the group abjected by the very idea of the Volk as it was defined and practiced during the Third Reich. Since African dias-

8   In her discussion of Edwards's work, Michelle Stephens makes a comparable point about the recurrence of difference as the central figure of diaspora in contemporary criticism when she states, "What I might be asking here, then, is whether or not a project of diaspora such as Edwards defines it, and the projects of black internationalism as West Indian radicals have chosen to define them over the course of the twentieth century, may be moving in fundamentally different directions: one toward the reification of difference and a form of disarticulation that actually maintains, theoretically, the borders between black nationalities, the other toward alternative unities and articulations that threaten to erupt and confront those of empire, that radicalize notions of blackness by revealing the limits of nationality." Stephens, "Disarticulating Black Internationalisms," 105.

9   Agamben, *Means without End*, 34.

poras generally tend to populate "the intolerable shadow," to use Agamben's phrase, within different nation-states, whether as prisoners in the United States or as victims of racial violence in contemporary Germany, Belgium, Austria, and Russia, diaspora discourse should claim and utilize this banishment rather than attempting to heal western modernity's constitutive biopolitical fracture by knowingly or inadvertently rendering the folk as *ein* Volk. I will now turn my attention to contemporary Afro-German musical practices in order to show how, in a similar vein to diaspora discourse, these sonic formations, as hard as they try, cannot move away from imagining collectivity through the form of peoplehood; I return to diaspora discourse in the closing section.

BrotherVolk

The early 2000s saw the materialization of two divergent yet intertwined forces within Afro-German popular music. On the one hand, Black musicians have shown an increasing politicization. The most prominent examples of this trend are two not-for-profit hip-hop projects, Brothers Keepers and Sisters Keepers, that consist of a large group of well-known Afro-German hip-hop, R&B, and reggae artists and were formed in 2001 to protest neo-Nazi terror and to publicly perform a collective Black presence in Germany. On the other hand, there was a proliferation of Afro-German R&B by artists such as Joy Denalane, Vanessa Mason, Chima, Bintia, Mic, Nadja Benaissa, J-Luv, Glashaus, and Xavier Naidoo that does not construe German Blackness in terms of the identitarian narratives often found in hip-hop or seek recognizably political goals, as in the case of Brothers and Sisters Keepers. I will focus on these two musical formations in the early 2000s in order to analyze how they ostensibly imagine Black collectivity differently but in the final instance fall back on community as primordial kinship: peoplehood surfaces again and again as the chief modality of inventing racial and/or religious collectivity.

The will to peoplehood is clearly exhibited in Brothers Keepers' grainy black-and-white video for their hit "Adriano (Letzte Warnung)" (Adriano [Final warning]), which shows the collective of Afro-German rappers and lead singer Xavier Naidoo traversing public spaces in Berlin. Both the lyrics of the song and the demeanor of the men stage the Afro-German Volk as a physical and symbolic threat to the German nation-as-Volk.[10] Naidoo

10 Brothers Keepers, "Adriano (Letzte Warnung)," YouTube video, accessed January 12, 2023, https://www.youtube.com/watch?v=NwEpVMwrF-g.

sings the following lines in the chorus, which highlight both the unity of the Brothers and their warlike posture vis-à-vis the mainstream German Volk:

> This is something like a final warning
> Because our counterattack has been in planning for a long time
> . . . .
> We'll finally stop your brown shit.
> . . . .
> We offer clenched fists and not open hands.
> Your downfall forever,
> And what we'll hear are your sobbing and moaning. [11]

Fortified by the militaristic lyrics, the images of the men forming an Afro-German phalanx as they move through Berlin are intercut with iconic figurations of neo-Nazi violence against which the masculine unity of Brothers Keepers serves as a bulwark. While a few women are featured in the final shots of this video, female musicians are completely absent, drawing attention to the constitutive (BlackFem) outside of this mode of racial unity. When Brothers Keepers were asked in interviews about the visible and audible absence of women from this group, the organizers responded that all the eligible female performers were either pregnant or on maternity leave.[12] Though women are needed to both literally and figuratively reproduce the Afro-German Volk, they remain absent from the Afro-German Volk envisioned by the Brothers, and they do not pose a threat to the whiteness of the German nation. In other words, Afro-German women are not needed to fight neo-Nazi violence but to bear children and to play the role of the consoling counterpart to Brothers Keepers' aggressive stance.

Sisters Keepers' song and video "Liebe und Verstand" (Love and understanding), which was released months after "Adriano" and was not nearly as successful in terms of sales and video airplay, bears this out in its can't-we-all-get-along vibe.[13] As opposed to "Adriano," which features a sung chorus

---

11 Brothers Keepers, "Adriano (Letzte Warnung)," Nitty Gritty Music, Warner Brothers, 2001, CD single, https://www.discogs.com/release/504374-Brothers-Keepers-Adriano-Letzte-Warnung. In this context, the color brown is a reference to Nazism or neo-Nazism and derives from the color of the SA uniforms worn during the Third Reich. Unless noted otherwise, all translations from German are mine.

12 Bax and Aikins, "Wir sind stolz, Deutsche zu sein."

13 Sisters Keepers, "Liebe und Verstand," Nitty Gritty Music, Warner Brothers, 2001, CD single.

interspersed with rapped verses, "Liebe und Verstand" is almost exclusively sung, and the lyrics are much more conciliatory. Whereas the Brothers refuse to shake hands, offering clenched fists instead, the Sisters ask of their audience, "Come on, give us your hand, we can change things with love and understanding." The video is shot in sumptuous color, imaging a harmonious Germany virtually devoid of white people. Even the Sisters' ostensibly "female" space in the guise of a Black Germany is framed by a male viewpoint, plus several of the Brothers Keepers have cameos in the video.[14] In fact, before the female performers come into view in the video, we hear a snippet of "Adriano" on a car radio and see a close-up of Brothers Keepers member Tyron Ricketts. Then rapper Meli appears—who in her other public appearances favors the hip-hop female masculinity look, which consists of heavy Timberland boots, baggy jeans, and cornrows—sporting a flowing haircut, full makeup, and tight-fitting clothing that partially reveals her stomach. In order to be a member of Sisters Keepers, Meli is forced to visually conform to hegemonic codes of femininity. While Sisters Keepers are excluded from the Afro-German Volk interpellated by the Brothers Keepers video, they also do not constitute their own Volk: Brothers Keepers' previous success and overbearing presence in the video give birth to and authorize this "female" version of Afro-Germanness.[15] By relegating female performers and feminism to the margins, or rather to the delivery room, Brothers Keepers runs counter to the very strong presence of women and feminism in the history of Afro-German political organizing.[16]

14 Sisters Keepers, "Liebe und Verstand," YouTube video, accessed January 12, 2023, https://www.youtube.com/watch?v=9eglBxGzWJM.

15 In her discussion of the gender politics of Afro-German hip-hop, including Brothers and Sisters Keepers, Fatima El-Tayeb points out that the masculinist tendencies of these two groups should be seen in relation, and perhaps also in reaction, to the defining role of women and feminist discourse within the history of Afro-German critical theorizing. See El-Tayeb, "'If You Cannot Pronounce My Name.'"

16 Nicola Lauré al-Samarai has observed that Black German theorizing is fairly unique, since feminism has been the defining force of Afro-German discourse over since the 1980s, which has resulted in a brand of feminism that does not take gender as its sole category of analysis but focuses on race in its complex intermingling with gendered subjectivity. See Lauré al-Samarai, "History, Theory, Experience." This becomes especially pertinent when contrasted to the rapid institutionalization of gender studies as the only form of minority discourse in the German university system. According to Eske Wollrad, by positing gender as the metacategory (i.e., white women) of analysis, the German variant

Apocalypse Now

In contrast to Brothers and Sisters Keepers, late 1990s and early 2000s German R&B does not feature explicit sociopolitical messages about racial identity, projecting instead a version of the collective that is not based on a racialized notion of peoplehood. In the following I will focus on Xavier Naidoo and Glashaus, whose lyrics prominently feature pan-religious themes that combine Christianity, Islam, and Rastafarianism, providing a utopian model for life and political change in ways that secular politics seemingly cannot offer. Xavier Naidoo's 1998 first album, *Nicht von dieser Welt* (Not of this world), remains one of the all-time bestselling German-language albums, and Naidoo is one of the most well-known and successful popular musicians in Germany since the 1990s.[17] Naidoo's arrival on the German music scene was remarkable not only because of his stratospheric rise to fame as a hyphenated German but also due to his overly melismatic singing style and devout lyrics; Naidoo takes the homonymic resonances between *Xavier* and *savior* very seriously. His lyrics are steeped in the Old Testament, oftentimes vis-à-vis the coming, or rather already-in-place, apocalypse. Glashaus consists of chanteuse Cassandra Steen, producer and rapper Moses Pelham, and pianist/producer Martin Haas. The latter two also form Pelham Power Productions (3P) and were responsible for the sonic architecture of Naidoo's first album. Although comparable in some respects to Naidoo, especially in the biblical librettos and the German-language singing, Glashaus's sound largely lacks the pathos and pomp so central to the aesthetic of *Nicht von dieser Welt*, replacing it with a minimalist aural tapestry, which better suits Steen's restrained intonation. What unites these two projects, besides the same team of producers, is the creation of a uniquely (Afro-)German form of R&B, a genre hitherto absent from this musical landscape.[18]

---

of gender studies institutes yet another way to displace discussions of race in the German context and erase the multifarious contributions of German women of color to feminist theorizing. See Wollrad, *Weißsein im Widerspruch*.

17 Xavier Naidoo, *Nicht von dieser Welt*, Pelham Power Productions, 1998, CD, https://www.discogs.com/release/529138-Xavier-Naidoo-Nicht-Von-Dieser-Welt.

18 Another version of German R&B, known as r'n'besk, has developed in the early 2000s. Performed by Turkish Germans, r'n'besk combines German-language R&B singing, hip-hop beats, and melodic elements, both in the instrumentation and in the vocal phrasing from the Turkish and Arabic genre arabesque. R'n'besk's most visible figure, Muhabbet, who has had several top-twenty hits in Germany, cites Xavier Naidoo as his main influence.

The forms of R&B performed by Xavier Naidoo and Glashaus espouse minoritarian instantiations of being Black and German, since neither Naidoo nor Steen addresses their Afro-German identity in their lyrics. But both are members of the Brothers Keepers collective so that their politicized racial identities infiltrate their musical output, even if not expressly figured in the text. Naidoo and Glashaus draw on and reformulate Afro-diasporic musical traditions (spirituals, gospel, hip-hop, soul, and reggae) that have used spirituality, especially Christianity and Rastafarianism, both as ways to imagine worlds beyond the immediate and as culturo-political modes of worldly resistance against racism and oppression. Even so, there exists no precedent for these artists' sonoric piousness in modern Germany, since spirituality had not been a component of German popular music; the only forms of religious music hitherto available were explicitly tied to the church. In fact, Naidoo, who rejects organized forms of religion, is both credited with and maligned, especially among young people, for introducing religion to contemporary German popular culture. While open proclamations and discussions of faith were largely anathema in German public discourse, they are now (grudgingly) accepted.[19]

One of the striking aspects of Naidoo's and Glashaus's religious imaginary is the turn away from the state as a guarantor of social justice, or even as the primary location of the political. Instead, a supranational and cross-denominational spiritual community of like-minded people replaces an immediately racialized collectivity as it might be recognized by the state. This circumvention of state power appears very clearly in the lyrics for Naidoo's "Seine Strassen" (His streets), where he sings the following lines:

> You're throwing parties on the streets approved by the wrong
>   authority.
> I hope you're all done with your foolishness.
> Are you ready for the final dance?
>
> . . . .
>
> His streets from the mountains to the sea.[20]

Naidoo believes that this combat between the worldly and the spiritual can be won only by the higher powers; the government is misguided in its attempt to legislate His streets. Naidoo stages his censure of the worldly fools

---

19   See Braun, "Oh Herr, Alles wird Dein!"; and Winkler, "Deutscher Pop entdeckt religiöse Inhalte."

20   Xavier Naidoo, "Seine Strassen," 3P (Sony BMG), 2000, CD single, https://www .discogs.com/release/2169657-Xavier-Naidoo-Seine-Strassen.

via the state's usurpation of powers proper only to the Lord, since the urban party locales are part of His dominion, one that extends from the mountains to the sea. The lyrics continue:

His lanes, because the Lord is leading his army
and your badly constructed trails
hinder the arrival of his throne-chariot.

Drawing on the Old Testament Book of Ezekiel, Naidoo envisions the metaphysically deficient trails hindering both the march of the Lord's army and the entrance of his throne-chariot.[21] The juxtaposition of His streets and profane paths illustrates Naidoo's resolve to completely negate the secular world. Naidoo is not after a peaceful coexistence of religious and secular forces, because God's higher authority both supersedes and displaces the political rule of the state; instead, he calls for a complete reversal of the current situation in which politics is firmly rooted in the spiritual domain.[22]

This antistatist stance also appears in the music video for this song, where we see Naidoo and his producer at the time, Moses Pelham, on a night drive toward one of Germany's borders. The clip illustrates the chasm between the spiritual and the secular already so prominent in the lyrics through an extreme close-up of the two men's German passports on the dashboard of their Porsche. The passport functions as an important signifier of citizenship for people of color in Germany, because they are positioned as de facto non-German by the national imaginary and therefore frequently have to prove their belonging by showing their identification papers. In their classic 1992 track "Fremd im eigenen Land" (Stranger in my own country), pioneering German hip-hop group Advanced Chemistry use the passport as a political tool for claiming and occupying public space.[23] In addition, this form of official identification makes a brief appearance at the end of Sisters Keepers' video "Liebe und Verstand." In

21 The book of Ezekiel, especially the prophet's vision of a fiery chariot in the sky, has exerted a marked influence on Jewish and Christian mysticism, modern UFO mythology, and the founding narratives of the Nation of Islam.

22 In an interview included in *God Is a DJ*, a collection of conversations with musicians about their relationship to religion and spirituality, Naidoo explicitly uses the term "Gottes-Volk" (God's people) to describe his vision of community, and he also makes clear that his vision of salvation is squarely located in the here and now and not in the afterlife. See Schröder, *God Is a DJ*, 122.

23 Advanced Chemistry, *Fremd im eigenen Land*, MZEE Records, 1992, CD single, https://www.discogs.com/release/1080189-Advanced-Chemistry-Fremd-Im-Eigenen-Land. For a more extensive treatment of the symbolic function of

an ironic reversal of the balance of power, one of the few white people featured in the video is forced to present his passport, as legal proof of his Germanness, to two Black German police officers. For Naidoo and Pelham, however, any form of identification issued by the state represents a barrier to full membership in the kingdom of God. The passports on the dashboard symbolize the hubris of the state in legislating national boundaries. There should only be "His streets," and all subjects who are a part of his flock should have equal access to these roads. Although these images, especially when contrasted with the lyrics, represent a fairly forceful critique of the restrictive immigration policies that are such a core feature of the modern nation-state, they still dwell in the domain of peoplehood, only here God administers belonging and membership rather than state institutions. The people as-Volk remains an absent presence here in the decisive rift between the blind dupes on the street, who only see the territory mapped by the state, and God's flock, which exceeds both the nation-state's territorial grasp and its legislation of peoplehood via citizenship.

While Naidoo at least brings to the fore the tension between the spiritual and the secular, Glashaus generally eschews secular politics altogether. Several of their records feature a number of songs with religious content, but often not overtly so; the paeans to peace and redemption could also reference a worldly love object. The group's second album, *Jah Sound System*, however, concretizes the group's otherwise hazy devout agenda.[24] Conjuring the Rastafarian name for God, derived from Jehovah (Jah), the title of the record already positions the group as God's sonic messenger by alternatingly emphasizing Armageddon and utopian divine salvation: they are, after all, Jah's sound system. Unlike the rest of Glashaus's oeuvre, which features mainly piano-heavy ballads, this album also includes several up-tempo tracks with hip-hop beats and ominous interludes spoken by Moses Pelham.

Pelham makes many more vocal appearances on this album than on the rest of the group's oeuvre, which insinuates that the more explicit politico-religious content needs to be accompanied by a masculine voice that counteracts the seeming femininity of R&B as a musical genre, especially when contrasted with hip-hop. Steen frequently sings about peace and love, whereas Pelham warns us about the impending Judgment Day in the here and now. This is

---

the passport for Advanced Chemistry and nonwhite Germans in general, see Weheliye, *Phonographies*, 145–97.

24 Glashaus, *Glashaus II (Jah Sound System)*, 3P, Mercury-Universal, 2002, CD, https://www.discogs.com/release/845834-Glashaus-Glashaus-II-Jah-Sound -System.

further underlined by the fact that the "male" voice performs the traditionally aggressive and masculine tasks, while the "female" voice provides solace, both lyrically and sonically. In the song "NAL (Nix als Liebe y'all" [Nuttin but love y'all]), for instance, Steen dreams of a higher spot enshrined only by love:[25]

> I saw that there was no place for retaliation and vengeance
> in this glorious (herrliche) thing.
> Hate did not exist
> blood did not flow there
> and there were no tears.
> I saw it when my eyes closed
> . . . .
> Who of us here doesn't want to go there.
> Then tell me why aren't we just like that.[26]

Steen projects a utopian scenario that also serves as a political injunction to actualize her dream of a superior realm by emulating this place of infinite love. Conversely, Pelham recites the following biblical verses in the spoken "Prelude zu Bald" (Prelude to now):[27]

> And ye shall hear of wars and rumors of wars: see that ye be not troubled: for all *these things* must come to pass, but the end is not yet. For nation (in German: ein Volk gegen ein Volk) shall rise against nation, and kingdom against kingdom: and there shall be famines, and pestilences, and earthquakes, in diverse places. All these *are* the beginning of sorrows. (Matthew 24:6–8)

The contrast to Steen's loving vociferations could not be any starker in their invocations of a coming holy war. However, some fissures in the lyrical and

25 Here the sample of a Buddhist monk reading from the Dhammapada that opens Glashaus's track "Erhalte meine Liebe" is also pertinent: "For in this world, hate never yet has dispelled hate. Only love dispels hate. This law is ancient and will last forever." Glashaus, "Erhalte meine Liebe," on *Drei*, Pelham Power Productions, 2005, CD, https://www.discogs.com/release/845825-Glashaus-Drei. In an interview I conducted with Moses Pelham, he cites this statement as closely echoing his own philosophy. See Weheliye, "'Ich will mich nicht ausgrenzen.'"

26 2016. Glashaus, "NAL," on *Glashaus II (Jah Sound System)*, 3P, Mercury-Universal, 2002, CD. The German word *herrlich* contains an explicit reference to the Almighty, as in *der Herr*.

27 Glashaus, "Prelude zu Bald," on *Glashaus II (Jah Sound System)*, 3P, Mercury-Universal, 2002, CD.

musical text counteract these traditionally "masculine" and "feminine" vocal performances by disassociating this process from the gendered body. The gendering of the male and female voices is recast in the German language recitation of a well-known spiritual poem, "Footprints in the Sand," where Pelham shows some humility (not something Pelham does very often in his music or public persona) by putting himself in the role of a child carried by the Lord in times of need:[28]

> "Lord, you said once I decided to follow you,
> You'd walk with me all the way.
> But I noticed that during the saddest and most troublesome times of
>   my life,
> there was only one set of footprints.
> I don't understand why, when I needed You the most, You would leave
>   me."
>
> He whispered, "My precious child, I love you and will never leave you
> Never, ever, during your trials and testings.
> When you saw only one set of footprints,
> It was then that I carried you."[29]

Steen leaves behind demure womanhood when she exhibits a more confrontational posture vis-à-vis the audience, for instance, singing of a "Jetzt" (now) in which she chastises the worldly herd for failing to decipher God's coded messages:

> These secret messages are supposed to reach you. Their worldly author doesn't get them, because he only writes what the powers want. They are supposed to encourage you to finally get up, it could happen in a few seconds.[30]

28 Glashaus, "Spuren im Sand," on *Glashaus II (Jah Sound System)*, 3P, Mercury-Universal, 2002, CD.

29 The quotation is from the English-language poem, which forms the basis of Glashaus's German spoken-word interlude. The poem has no singular author, and several writers have claimed ownership of these words. However, the poem circulates freely among various Christian and other monotheistic populations online. See "Footprints (poem)," Wikipedia, https://en.wikipedia.org/wiki/Footprints_(poem) (accessed January 18, 2023).

30 Here Walter Benjamin's notion of a "Jetztzeit/nowtime" serves as a pertinent echo, in terms of both Glashaus's messianic desire and their insistence on both apocalypse and redemption as categories of the present

Still, just as with Pelham's humbleness, Steen's hostile vociferations are only authorized by the Lord's otherworldly power, which renders the two positions closer than they initially seem. Consequently, the dispersal of the gender roles needs to be heard in a different light, since the powers inherent in Steen's and Pelham's voices are literally drawn from another world. Moreover, this gendering is further complicated by the fact that Pelham wrote all the lyrics for Glashaus's first two albums, even those sung by Steen.

Put differently, in Glashaus's universe, Armageddon and salvation are two sides of the same coin, as the former is the precondition for the latter. Accordingly, the differing gendered voices meld into a placeless totality that erases the material world to supplant it with a smooth holy realm of existence. And on this plane Pelham's and Steen's gendered positions do not register in the same way as they do in the secular sphere; on this plane both will not only be subject to a higher power but also, and more important, be one with God. In Glashaus's cosmology, then, this religious utopia denotes a genderless space of minoritization, where dyads such as woman/man or Black/white seemingly become irrelevant. Since worldly identities no longer play a constitutive role in the drama of collectivity, there appears to be no pressing need for the people-as-Volk. Thus, the combination of R&B and an ecumenical religious discourse aids Naidoo and Glashaus in creating a different mode of collectivity, one that ostensibly avoids the masculinist and identitarian traps of Brothers and Sisters Keepers.

Nonetheless, the quotes from Matthew explicitly draw on the language of the Volk by pitting one group against another as well as by taking this clash as the launch of a catastrophic temporality. In addition, the Volk surfaces in an offbeat way as the central trope of the Glashaus song "Eine Hymne für mein Volk" (An anthem for my people).[31] In this song the group suggests that the community envisioned by these sacred discourses does not so much interpellate a formation already in existence but a people to come that accentuates the positive, productive, creative, and provisional aspects of spiritual Volk building. The song's chorus proceeds:

---

and not the future. Benjamin writes, "The nowtime, which, as a model of messianic time, comprises the entire history of mankind in an enormous condensation, coincides exactly with *the* place the history of humanity occupies in the universe." W. Benjamin, "Über den Begriff der Geschichte," 1972, 703.

31 Glashaus, "Eine Hymne für mein Volk," on *Glashaus II (Jah Sound System)*, 3P, Mercury-Universal, 2002, CD, https://www.discogs.com/release/845834-Glashaus -Glashaus-II-Jah-Sound-System.

This song is an anthem
for my Volk that doesn't yet exist
but my Volk now has a voice
and is now united in this song.

Glashaus's song sounds a future people not yet actualized that nevertheless comprises a unified voice within the confines of this musical work. The paradoxical nature of this Volk is accentuated further by a series of oxymorons in the verse that describe its manifold properties; Glashaus has no problem dwelling in the realm of paradox:

We are mighty speakers
and don't say a word
We are acrimonious adversaries
and immediately love each other.

Accordingly, this Volk represents everything and nothing. The Volk can contain multitudes precisely because it has no actual existence, which is to say that futurity represents its defining trait insofar as this people remains perennially lodged in the domain of the "to come."

The lines from the chorus cited above are not a literal translation, since the German adverb *so* (in "mein Volk, das es so noch nicht gibt"), which forms a crucial part of Glashaus's formulation, cannot be easily rendered in English. Hence, a more literal translation would read thus: "My Volk that does not yet exist that way (or in this particular manifestation)." It would seem that the Volk already exists, just not in the way Glashaus desires. In order to secure its futurity, then, Glashaus's Volk has to figure as a continuation of a previous formation rather than a new sighting. As with the verses from Matthew in "Prelude zu Bald," the article used in conjunction with Volk specifies the contours of this community. Instead of "ein Volk," as in "Prelude," here Glashaus insists on "*mein* Volk," which couples *ein* Volk (*People* with a capital *P*) with belonging and ownership. The possessive pronoun *mein* both stages the Volk as homogeneous and intimates a strong sense of predetermined inclusion, because Steen vocalizes her connection to a group that has yet to make an appearance on the empirical corner: the Volk is not present thus far, but Steen's belonging to it is a given. For this automatic integration into an invented religious community is exactly what unites all the opposing forces Glashaus ascribes to this Volk and creates the gender- and raceless sphere of existence. In other words, the Volk's futurity is established in the face of an a priori membership, a chosenness, anchoring it in the primordial swamps of peoplehood we know all too well, which severely curtails the utopian dimensions of this cosmology. In the Glasshouse the fluids happen to be of the holy variety, but in other quagmires they are populated by culture, race, language, and so on.

Despite the impulse to think and perform collectivity not along strict identitarian lines, as with Brothers and Sisters Keepers, the religious dimensions do not shield Glashaus and Xavier Naidoo from being entrapped by peoplehood, since they posit a previous and seemingly natural connection as the unifying trait of community. These attempts to refashion collectivity as a future people resist the seeming naturalness that flows from peoplehood for a variety of complicated historical, epistemological, and cultural reasons. Instead of waiting for my Volk to come, perhaps, then, the time has come to let my people go. On the whole, the strong desire to envisage collectivity beyond peoplehood and the simultaneous failure to do so in early 2000s Afro-German popular music and diaspora discourse underlines the nagging pervasiveness of this category and the pressing need for some alternatives.

The People

As opposed to constructing Black Germans as ein Volk via their connection to the African diaspora, poet and theorist May Ayim contends that Afro-German subjectivity unearths the radical possibility found in the interstitial abyss of "die Zwischenwelt als Chance" (the in-between world as potential), which echoes W. E. B. Du Bois's thinking of double consciousness not only as a cumbersome hindrance to full subjectivity but also, and more important, as the gift of Black people to the world. Ayim writes, "In those instances in which Afro-Germans do not accept the externally imposed ostensible contradiction between being both African and German, a self-awareness can emerge that does not necessitate this particular limitation."[32] According to Ayim, Afro-Germans cannot form ein Volk precisely because they inhabit both German and Black worlds, which belies the mutually exclusive logic of western racial formation and launches modalities of being and belonging not reducible to mere amalgamation. Following Ayim's footsteps, we need to formulate and imagine nonempirical and visionary versions of Blackness and/as collectivity. This undertaking seems especially imperative in light of diaspora studies' institutional ascent to a catchall clearinghouse for various (minority) discourses, which, paradoxically, not only turns down the volume on colonialism and slavery but, in the context of Black studies, blunts the radicality of Blackness's working within and against

32 Opitz (Ayim), "Aufbruch," in Oguntoye, Opitz, and Schultz, *Farbe bekennen*, 141.

western modernity. For what gets lost in the traces of peoplehood qua unified political subject that trail the idea of diaspora, whether explicitly articulated or not, is precisely Du Bois's doubleness or Ayim's in-between world of Blackness. By deserting these important nonempirical and visionary formulations of Blackness and/as collectivity, we abjure the promise to undo the Afro and the Euro and concomitantly ruin their very conditions of possibility.

In order to impair these foundations, Blackness should not be defined as primarily empirical, as occurs so frequently in diaspora discourse by virtue of comparatively enumerating the minute differences between African Americans and other Afro-diasporic constellations. Situating Blackness and Black subjects in the jurisdiction of the epiphenomenal simply continues the work of white western hegemony, which invented and continues to circumscribe Blackness as its nonhuman other. Once we take into account how Blackness figures and materializes ontologically, we can practice a politics of being, which, rather than succumbing to the brutal facticity of Blackness, introduces invention into existence, as Sylvia Wynter states, in the footsteps of Frantz Fanon. She writes, "The struggle of our new millennium will be one between the ongoing imperative of securing the well-being of our present ethnoclass (i.e. Western bourgeois) conception of the human, Man, which overrepresents itself as if it were the human itself, and that of securing the well-being, and therefore the full cognitive and behavioral autonomy of the human species itself/ourselves."[33] This is a battle to supplant the modern instantiation of the human as synonymous with the objective existence of white Western Man and his various damned counterparts, especially Black subjects, offering in its stead new styles of human subjectivity and community that are no longer based on the glaring rift between the folk as the nonhuman other and ein Volk as the most extreme version of the immaculately homogeneous political subject.

Coda

Glashaus's "Eine Hymne für mein Volk" ends with a sample of James Brown's civil rights anthem "Soul Power" that repeats the phrase *power to the people*; in fact, Brown's voice is the last thing we hear. The recurring loop of "power to the people" fades into Brown chanting "soul power." This particular sample, which stands at the crossroads of people and soul power and might be said to conjure the blues people, puts Glashaus and their Volk-to-come

33 Wynter, "Unsettling the Coloniality of Being," 260.

in an Afro-diasporic lineage of political struggle motored among other things by religious impulses, particularly the civil rights movement. Not only does this establish a precedent for Glashaus's messianic quest for social justice, as does the use of the spiritual domain to make decidedly worldly demands in spirituals, gospel, and reggae, but it also disrupts the notion of peoplehood promulgated by the earlier lyrics in its addition of *das* Volk (people power, soul power) as a sanctuary of the excluded and oppressed to the collective mix of "mein Volk, das es so noch nicht gibt." Thus, Glashaus juxtaposes *mein* Volk and *das* Volk, rather than endeavoring to heal the fracture that segregates them, sounding for us listeners the Zwischenwelt below and beside these categories.[34] Glashaus dwells in the glasshouse, the interspatial location in which Cassandra Steen's restrained voice blurs the line between singing and everyday speech, where Moses Pelham's lyrics as sung by Steen veer from biblical grandiosity to pithy and at times devastating everyday observations. This (non)place has no walls, just so that it can radically transform the grand piano from *the* sign for western classical music and its concomitant projection of bourgeois individualism into a rhythmic, melodic, and textural instrument in the service of a Black musical idiom, while the engineering and production emphasize expansive space and melodic restraint so as to remind us that we have traveled beyond the borders of traditional architectural structures. Glashaus's sound, which manages to perform fragility and robustness in chorus and verse, constructs a contemporary version of the Kunstlied, albeit syncopated by R&B singing, hip-hop beats, and cinemascope sonic spaces that gesture toward other universes in which "to live in a glasshouse is a revolutionary virtue par excellence."[35] This cosmos, rather than being populated by *ein* Volk or a consortium of different Völker, shelters weary travelers May Ayim, Walter Benjamin, Octavia Butler, and W. E. B. Du Bois on their long journey "daheim unterwegs."

34 Similarly, Fred Moten cites a statement by Duke Ellington that beautifully blends *my* people and *the* people so that the very distinction between them becomes moot: "Oh but I have such strong influence by the music of the people—*the people*! That's a better word, *the* people rather than *my* people, because *the* people *are* my people." Ellington, quoted in Moten, *In the Break*, 261n2.

35 W. Benjamin, "Der Surrealismus," 299. The German term *Lied* as used in the English language refers to the works of classical and romantic composers such as Franz Schubert, Robert Schumann, and Johannes Brahms that also made extensive use of the piano as the counterpoint to the human voice. In German *Lied* refers to any musical work with a song structure, and the genre referenced here is known as the *Kunstlied* (art song).

TRACK 5.0

"WHITE BROTHERS WITH NO SOUL"

UnTuning the Historiography of Berlin Techno

Interview with Annie Goh

As Berlin's burgeoning electronic music scene becomes ever more a point of international focus, with numerous books and articles being written on its clubs, music, and parties every year, the politics of these structures often get neglected. Within the CTM: Festival for Adventurous Music and Art 2015 theme, "Un Tune," the dissonances as well as consonances of these stories are being explored: both inclusion and exclusion play out in systems of sonic affect such as the dance floor. Building on his extensive work on race, music, technology, and critical theory, CTM discourse program cocurator Annie Goh interviewed Professor Alexander Ghedi Weheliye on the racial politics of Berlin techno, and how its story is being narrated. This interview took place via Skype in December 2014.

ANNIE GOH: Thanks for taking the time for this interview, Alex. In the spate of books such as Felix Denk and Sven von Thülen's *Der Klang der Familie*, marking the twentieth anniversary of German reunification, the story of the birth of Berlin techno is told following the fall of the wall in 1989.[1] This narrative tells of the jubilance of a reunified Germany, the masses of empty spaces, huge social change and upheaval, and the heady parties and clubs that emerged out of this. Denk and Thülen narrate this as an "oral history," with interviews with various protagonists—DJs, promoters, club owners, partygoers, and the like. This is quite typical of the way this period is usually described—both as a story of German reunification and of the birth of Berlin techno, an upheaval of previous hierarchies and radical openness within the arena of the dance floor. How does this version of history compare to your own version?

ALEXANDER WEHELIYE: First of all, I wouldn't say it is just my version of history. It is also the version of history that many, I and other nonwhite Germans, have experienced. I see the narrativization of the reunification and the birth of Berlin techno and the Berlin Republic as part of a much longer tradition of thinking about Germany and Germanness. Throughout the post–World War II period, Germany had to reconstruct itself in many different ways and imagine itself as untainted by its Nazi past. One way it did that was by performing a kind of multicultural openness, however, only as long as that multiculturalism was located outside of Germany. That is one part of the larger discursive structure.

The reunification is typically imagined in mainstream histories as a seamless blending together of East and West, which leaves out the virulent racism and violence during this period, especially against nonwhite bodies. Although called *xenophobia* rather than *racism*, it didn't matter whether they were German or not so long as they were not white. Thus, it seems very limited to imagine the history of Berlin techno only as this coming together of what I refer to as "the white brothers with no soul," particularly since the early 1990s pogroms are still largely omitted from the German and international collective memory of the reunification period.

The other thing for me, at a basic experiential level that really made me take notice, was that these histories not only are recounting the emergence of Berlin techno per se but are also constructing a very particular story about musical cultures in West Berlin during the 1980s before the advent of techno.

This interview was first published in slightly different form on the CTM Festival website in 2015. https://www.ctm-festival.de/magazine/white-brothers-with-no -soul (accessed January 20, 2023).

1 See Denk and Thülen, *Klang der Familie*.

What generally gets left out are the not very elaborate but nevertheless very present Black music cultures in GI discos and other clubs that played Black music in West Berlin before the fall of the wall. In these narratives there is definitely a move to disassociate Berlin techno from Black musical influences. I'm not simply saying, "This is the appropriation of Black music," which it is, of course, but also asking, "What different histories of Berlin techno and of Germany would we get if we actually opened this up a little bit and looked at other dance music cultures and other forms of clubbing?" For me, it isn't an either-or question but a matter of highlighting that there existed other forms of clubbing and musical cultures, which are once again being written out of history. This ensures that Berlin techno, Germany, and Germanness are continually being imagined as white.

ANNIE GOH: At your presentations ("'White Brothers with No Soul': Wie der Berliner Techno weiß wurde," given at Berlin Music Days [BerMuDa], on November 7, 2013; and "Soundtrack ohne Soul? Germanozentrismus und Techno-Historiographie," presented at the Techno Studies conference held at Universität der Künste in Berlin, on December 6, 2014), you showed slides of the racist attacks against asylum homes (such as in Rostock and Hoyerswerda) juxtaposed with a jubilant image of the first Love Parade. During the celebrations around twenty-five years of the fall of the wall in Berlin, for example, things like that obviously get ignored.

ALEXANDER WEHELIYE: Yes, once again there is a tendency to only look at these racist attacks as weird exceptions and as mere violent by-products of the reunification. As I have written in other places, the mainstream political parties did not distance themselves from these pogroms. I recall at the time there were posters everywhere with the statement "The boat is full," implying that Germany could not take in any more asylum seekers because the resources needed to go to the German people in the East.

These assaults also created an environment of danger for German people of color like myself, given the real climate of discursive and physical violence in which we "other Germans" had to be excised from the body politic. This way Germany would be reunited without the presence of "troublesome" nonwhite others. Though the extreme violence was deemed "wrong," the anger of the perpetrators was presented as a "reasonable" fear of the "foreign" other. The attacks against people of color were not confined to East Germany, even if West German politicians held only East German impoverished youths accountable for these racist attacks. This was how I and many other nonwhite Germans perceived the reunification period after the first few weeks of the party were over.[2]

ANNIE GOH: In your talks you showed a clip of Tanith, from the documentary *We Call It Techno* (2008), describing how techno parties differed from other discos, such as [those at] the GI clubs in West Berlin, saying, "We were white brothers with no soul." Can you explain why you found that comment, which was said in a fairly flippant and throwaway style, so significant?

ALEXANDER WEHELIYE: Tanith has semipublicly (in a private Berlin techno chatroom) argued that this comment has been taken out of context. To me, though flippant and perhaps ironic, it also encapsulates a lot of the problems I see in the historiography and celebration of Berlin techno. Tanith says that there was house music—which was much more clearly Black because it was funky and had more soulful vocals—but that he and other white Berlin DJs wanted to go a harder route—one that didn't have anything to do with Blackness and Black music. It is clear that is what happened in the course of a few years, despite the fact that what would later become techno was initially brought to West Berlin within the context of clubs and radio shows that played Black music.

Originally there wasn't this separation between the "white brothers with no soul" and the "Black brothers and sisters with soul." My argument is that in order for Berlin techno to be imagined as something specific to Berlin and to Germany, it had to separate itself from Blackness, whether imagined or real. German public and academic discourse deny the existence of race. The moment that people of color bring up the question of race, they are put in the position of being too sensitive or of being racist themselves. So, what I found significant about that clip is that Tanith's statement really puts the racial dimension of Berlin techno out there in a way that is not common in Germany.

ANNIE GOH: Could you describe on the level of sounds the whiteness or becoming-white of Berlin techno—which key characteristics of the musics and sounds of electronic dance music do you identify with this, and where do you place these within a larger context? What was being accepted into the sonic language of techno, and what was being excluded?

2 See Weheliye, *Phonographies*, ch. 5.

ALEXANDER WEHELIYE: I think the interesting thing is that initially it didn't happen so much sonically. There weren't that many techno productions from Berlin itself. A lot sounded much more house-y, pop-like and soulful than one would think. It was only around 1992-ish that these kinds of Berlin productions emerged that had a lot less swing, a lot less funk, where it was much more about a steady, metronomic beat and a very stereotypically Teutonic or Germanic sound. Take the playlist by DJ Rok featuring those tracks popular at the Tresor club in the early 1990s—back then the most well-known techno club in reunified Berlin—which also appears appended to the *Klang der Familie* book. Many of the included tracks are by Black producers from Detroit and Chicago while several feature vocals, underscoring how fleeting the line between house and techno was then. Basic Channel/Maurizio, for instance, originally pressed their records in Detroit, because they wanted to be perceived as coming from Detroit or at least to be associated with it. Underground Resistance incorporated different kinds of sounds into the language of techno, harder and much more industrial, which appealed to people in Berlin. Furthermore, there existed also Belgian techno, which was much harder, much faster, and much less about syncopation than the early Detroit techno recordings.

The early 1990s veneration of Underground Resistance (UR)—who are, in contrast to earlier Detroit techno producers, explicitly political and put themselves in a lineage of Black nationalism and Black freedom struggles—in Berlin was based on their politicization of primarily instrumental music, and it also fed into an independent punk-rock ethos that was prevalent in the city at the time. The reception of UR in Berlin also suggested that Blackness and Black music could be enthusiastically celebrated, so long as it didn't involve Black Germans; it took place under the auspices that Blackness was foreign to Germany. Nevertheless, of course UR was hugely important.

There was a tendency early on in Berlin as well as in Cologne and other places to say that techno might have been "invented" in Detroit but now "we've made it our own and no longer need to look to other places." In the early 1990s, some involved in Berlin techno even used a different spelling, Tekkno, to distinguish themselves from Detroit. The other thing that also happened is that the more melodic, feminine, queer, and Black sounds associated with techno and electronic dance music went into the genre of Eurodance, which is very clearly separated from Berlin techno because the latter was an underground, independent, hard-core phenomenon.

In my talks I found it important to link these two things because they are so similar, perhaps not culturally similar, as Eurodance numbers by Snap! or

Real McCoy were produced for the pop charts and not necessarily for clubs, but nevertheless they used a lot of the same production techniques as the early techno productions. Originally there was a lot more overlap among techno, house, and Eurodance. It was important to me to bring these two strands together, as in Eurodance you see a lot of Black German performers—it was acceptable and even necessary for the success of that genre and not in Berlin techno, which distanced itself from Blackness. For instance, white Berlin producer Olaf "O-Jay" Jeglitza hired Black Germans Patricia Peterson and Shampro to front his group, MC Sar & the Real McCoy, even though he himself had performed the male vocal parts on the records. That is, he perceived the performers' visual Blackness as transcending the "inauthenticity" associated with his white German body performing in a Black musical genre.

I've experienced a lot of pushback from people on the continuum between Eurodance and techno during the early 1990s, because it collapses the social capital associated with the distinction between the mainstream (Eurodance/Kirmestechno) and underground (Berlin techno), but it is really about gendered, racialized, classed, and sexualized hierarchies of taste that allow the "white brothers with no soul" to claim they are the only keepers of the true techno grail.

ANNIE GOH: So, what changed around 1992 that brought about the transformation from more openness toward soulful, house-y, funkier sounds, to the harder industrial sound?

ALEXANDER WEHELIYE: I think there was an effort to claim techno as something that was Berlin's own in that process, which was also part of a new German nationalism: a nationalism that could not be articulated before the reunification. However, there weren't statements along the lines of "We are white men from Berlin who are no longer influenced by Black music." It was a proclamation not of "Germanness," as that was still taboo, but of a "Lokalpatriotismus"—so a patriotism of Berlin as opposed to Germany. Nevertheless, this was not a Lokalpatriotismus that embraced the city's multicultural communities given that its Germanness and whiteness remained unspoken. People in Berlin took very circuitous routes and invested a lot of energy in fabricating what they perceived to be more German or European (i.e., less Black) versions of electronic dance music, as can be seen, for instance, in this debate in *Spex Magazine* from 1992. While the Germanness and whiteness of techno may seem natural, in hindsight, the historical record shows that it was anything but that.[3]

3 See Niemczyk and Zabel, "Freie Abfahrt für freie Bürger."

ANNIE GOH: In Denk and Thülen's book, the Detroit connection plays a big role. The story of Detroit techno DJs and producers making hard, industrial-sounding militant techno but not finding the right audience until Dimitri Hegemann brought Underground Resistance over to Tresor, is a familiar one to most techno fans. When reading this story, it is easy to get the impression of a kind of well-functioning multiculturalism—Black DJs playing to largely white audiences. How do you read this part of Berlin's techno history, which clearly acknowledges Black techno artists and their influence?

ALEXANDER WEHELIYE: Yes, of course, because Underground Resistance were so popular in Berlin, they absolve white Germans of having to think about the racial politics of Berlin techno. Underground Resistance were the exception to the rule, and their reception in Berlin proceeded through a type of alternative exoticism such as Boney M. in the 1970s, who articulated this "Fernweh," a German-produced and German-sounding group who at the same time embodied a desire for something exotic and faraway. Underground Resistance were the underground version of that, they were from Detroit, and even though they were from a context of Black music, they conceived themselves in a similar way to people in Berlin. The underground ethos has not been a central part of Black popular music, which is usually very aspirational, so not about occupying dingy basements, but more typically embodying "the good life" in the form of financial success or designer clothes. Underground Resistance did not take this path, which aided their popularity in Berlin. I see it as very convenient; because UR were so political, because they were unabashedly Black politically, it was an easy exception to the rule. Their sounds were much harder and much more confrontational, with releases like "Sonic Destroyer" or *The Riot EP*. These have very particular meanings within Black freedom struggles, but that isn't necessarily how they were read and received in Berlin.

ANNIE GOH: How much was the success of UR in Berlin due to the absence of vocals or sparing use of vocals?

ALEXANDER WEHELIYE: The UR records that were successful in Berlin were not vocal recordings. The UR discography, however, is evenly split between the tracky, industrial recordings, on the one hand, and vocal, oftentimes gospel-inspired house tracks, on the other. For UR those things existed side by side, and that wasn't a problem, but that wasn't necessarily what the folks in Berlin took their inspiration from. In Berlin the popular UR releases (*The Riot*

EP, "Sonic Destroyer," "Panic," and so on) emphasized the former at the expense of the latter, which were perceived as both "Blacker" and more "feminine."

ANNIE GOH: So, apart from the sounds of UR and how they influenced Berlin techno, in your argument you want to draw attention to the other bits that get ignored . . .

ALEXANDER WEHELIYE: There were also early 1990s Berlin clubs that were hugely successful but didn't play techno per se. You had WMF, which primarily played house music, or 90 Grad, which played R&B and house but featured afterhours techno parties. Then you had Delicious Donuts, which featured what was then called *acid* or *nu jazz*. Jazzanova, the fairly well-known Berlin group with Black vocalists, came out of that. A bit later, you had clubs like Toaster, which helped popularize jungle in Berlin, a musical genre that can be seen as the Black British reclamation of techno in the aftermath of the genre's European whitewashing. These other currents were always there, but they are usually not integrated into the mainstream histories of Berlin techno.

ANNIE GOH: Kraftwerk also play an interesting role in all of this—not only being explicitly named as an influence by the Detroit techno pioneers but also embodying futuristic and machinic themes that get heavily played out in Berlin techno. Although they have a sort of "neutral" identity, it is basically one that is white, male, and heterosexual as a kind of default subjectivity. This is also something that plays out heavily in contemporary Berlin techno. How do Kraftwerk figure into this complex transatlantic web of musical influences?

ALEXANDER WEHELIYE: Anglo-American histories of electronic music lionize Kraftwerk's imagined heteromasculine and Germanic whiteness at the expense of the feminized/queered/Black genres they drew inspiration from: disco and R&B. While German histories of (Berlin) techno music do not glorify Kraftwerk as much, they establish Germanic whiteness by discounting the influence of the same genres (disco, Italo, hip-hop, and R&B) and club spaces for the creation of Berlin as the techno capital of the world. For instance, inspired by the success of "Trans-Europe Express" on US Black radio and in clubs, Kraftwerk hired Leanard "Colonel Disco" Jackson, an African American mixing engineer, who had already worked with Rose Royce and Undisputed Truth and would later work with Dynasty and Lakeside to mix their 1978 album *Die Mensch-Maschine*. The point being that Kraftwerk would not be accorded such high relevance in the history of electronic dance music without their popularization by Afrika Bambaataa, who sampled them, and the first generation of Detroit techno producers, who frequently cited them as a major influence. Still, Juan Atkins, Kevin Saunderson, and Derrick May mention George Clinton's use of sonic technologies just as frequently as Kraftwerk, but Clinton and the many other Black musicians that made innovative use of these machines cannot inhabit the domain of technological mastery, and thus appear as individual masculine geniuses, because they are not white brothers, or fathers as in the case of Kraftwerk.[4]

ANNIE GOH: You also mentioned the solidarity that some German activist groups showed with the Black Panther Party in the 1970s, but that this stood in contradiction to the lack of sympathy or support they showed for Black or migrant rights in their locality. Can you talk about this a bit more and explain why you think this was so?

ALEXANDER WEHELIYE: There were different so-called solidarity committees for the Black Panthers, especially for Angela Davis (who had lived in Germany in the 1960s) when she was imprisoned. You can also look at the history of the Red Army Faction (RAF), and how they thought of themselves as being colonial subjects. They saw themselves not only as in solidarity with the colonized cultures around the world but also as waging an anticolonial struggle against the German state. All those things were under the auspices of struggles taking place someplace else, since this white German solidarity did not apply to Black people or other ethnic groups in Germany—Turkish, Yugoslav, and Greek factory workers, for instance. Usually, the solidarity was with those folks of color not located in Germany, and who thus didn't threaten the idea that Germanness equals whiteness.

Similarly, in the early 1990s, there was a group of leftist artists and writers who were more open to popular culture and had a more cultural studies rather than a strict Marxist-Leninist approach ("Poplinke"). They created a group called the Wohlfahrtsausschüsse, who traveled throughout eastern Germany and tried to articulate a standpoint against the new German nationalism in the wake of the racist attacks during the reunification period.

4   For an exploration of how white German house and techno producers engaged and appropriated Blackness and Black sounds in the early 2000s, see Anthony Cokes's *Mikrohaus, or the Black Atlantic?*

They organized several conferences and also published an anthology called *Etwas Besseres als die Nation* (Something better than the nation).[5] What was really striking to me both then and in retrospect was, yes, that the group did include an extremely select few German people of color, but overall what was missing from this debate were existing organizations by and for Germans of color, for instance, African or Afro-German organizations, such as Initiative Schwarze Menschen in Deutschland and ADEFRA e.v.—Schwarze Frauen in Deutschland, and other political organizations. This created a largely white German leftist discourse about the violence against nonwhite bodies, but the voices of Germans of color were essentially excluded. Though this has changed a bit since, the tendency to speak about nonwhite Germans but not with them is still alive and well. This, in turn, reinforces the notion that non-whiteness must always be foreign in the German context; that there are no people of color here or that they, with a few selected exceptions, are not capable of speaking for themselves.

ANNIE GOH: In several techno documentaries, Berlin techno is portrayed as a very open and heterogeneous scene, in which all are welcome and usual prejudices are swept aside. Techno is often presented as politically "progressive." But the statistics brought out by female:pressure in 2013 (and updated in 2015, 2017, and 2020) show the gender bias of the techno scene, which can be extended to a racial bias too, as you have shown in your work.[6] In your opinion how does techno manage to keep up this profile of "progressiveness" in the face of such blatant exclusion?

ALEXANDER WEHELIYE: One of the reasons it is important to me to make these points is that it is still really relevant to the way Germany conceives of itself. The discursive and institutional grounds, the conditions of possibility, are already there, forming a mirage of openness. International perceptions of Germany have really greatly changed in past years, now that being German is no longer so tainted by Nazism, as it was twenty years ago. At least partially, this is due to Germany having a self-understanding as being really open, which it is to a certain extent. On the other hand, there is a deep-seated unwillingness to actually look at itself as a not exclusively white nation, which is not only a problem of a few neo-Nazis or the PEGIDA (Patriotic

---

5 Wohlfahrtsausschüsse, *Etwas besseres als die Nation.*
6 The female:pressure FACTS survey Goh references can be found here: https://femalepressure.wordpress.com/ (accessed January 20, 2023).

Europeans against the Islamization of the West) folks but also affects the white German liberal and leftist spheres. In fact, it seems much more pernicious in these contexts because of the systematic denial of everyday institutional racism.

The terms have changed slightly since the German colonial period, but nevertheless it often has the same feel for me: there is a public discourse about being open and taking so and so many asylum seekers every year, but there is a fundamental disconnect about the communities and folks who have lived here for generations and are still talked about as foreigners that can't be integrated because they refuse to comply with traditional, white notions of German culture. This has been happening for the past fifty years at least. The situation is different for Russian and Polish Germans who have been integrated, but it hasn't happened for Afro-Germans, Asian Germans, Arab Germans, and Turkish Germans, that is, those who are visibly different from white Germans.

The historiography of Berlin techno really benefits from precisely the idea of Germany as a newly loosened-up bastion of Teutonic whiteness. I've described this elsewhere as how Germany has had to constantly create a kind of "Unschuld" for itself, an innocence, by distancing itself from responsibility for anything that is not related to the Jewish community, which is now conveniently not very present within Germany. And, of course, the Holocaust did not only affect the Jewish community. These are tendencies that arc through German history and historiography. Partially this is due to the fact that large-scale German colonialism "only" lasted from the Berlin Conference to the end of World War I, which means it is something that can be continually disavowed in order to not "untune" the harmonic scaffolding of German collective memory.

My favorite example of this was a 2006 reality show on a private TV channel called *Wie die Wilden—Deutsche im Busch*, which translates as *Like Savages—Germans in the Bush*. They sent white Germans to Togo and Namibia, both former German colonies, among other places, to peoples perceived to be "uncivilized." I couldn't really believe this was happening in 2006. This was repeated in 2013 when another cable channel aired *Wild Girls—Auf High Heels durch Afrika* (Wild girls—across Africa on high heels), also set in the former German colony Namibia, which was aired around the time that debates about German recognition of the genocide against Herero and Nama peoples were being held publicly. I thought: How did this concept make it through all the different stages of TV production? Though some groups wrote protest letters, I was astounded both by how deep the white

German disavowal of colonialism and its afterlives runs and that this actually went through the ranks without anyone saying, "Maybe this isn't such a great idea?" (laughs).

Another contemporary example of this dis-remembering could be found during the 2014 World Cup, which represents one of the major ways western Europe has symbolically performed racial diversity since the early 2000s, the most prominent example being the French national team during the 2006 World Cup. The 2010 German World Cup team was heralded as the embodiment of German multiculturalism. In the 2014 World Cup, there were six Black German players on the US national team. It took me a while to figure out, as they are not often called Black Germans in the German or the US press, underscoring the disavowal of nonwhite Germans both at home and abroad.

It later emerged that many of these Black Germans were not given the chance to play for the national team, so Jürgen Klinsmann, the trainer for the US team, imported them to play for the American team. They could do so because they were Black and they had dual US/German citizenship, although most of these players had not lived in the United States and some barely spoke English. In addition, there wasn't much interest to have them play on the German team. In other words, these processes of externalization are quite subtle, since there isn't a sign saying, "We don't allow Black German players" or "There's only room for one, and the position has been filled by Jérôme Boateng" (laughs), but I think that to have folks who are very clearly German yet obviously not white make up half of its national soccer team would threaten the self-understanding of Germany and how the world views Germany. Lukas Podolski is trotted out as an example of the good kind of integration, as he is a first-generation Polish German, but through his white skin he is able to represent Germany in ways that players such as John Brooks or Fabian Johnson, who played on the 2014 US team, could not.

ANNIE GOH: What about the alternatives to the dominant history of techno? In your talks you mention a few examples of where this historiography might begin—GI discos in the West, break-dancing scenes in the German Democratic Republic, and Eurodance. Can you elaborate on these?

ALEXANDER WEHELIYE: Break dancing is interesting. The East German government sponsored it because it was seen as anti-imperialist.

Over in West Berlin, the GI discos and other clubs that emulated these in their approach to playing Black music (Talk-of-the-Town, NCO-Club, Silverwings, Chic, Labelle, Silver Shadow) or clubs such as Chez Konrad, Sox,

Cha, and Turbine Rosenheim that played R&B and hip-hop and that later introduced house music into the mix, were really central to clubbing in West Berlin during the 1980s. Yet the story that is usually told is that West Berlin in the 1980s was all industrial, rock, or Neue Deutsche Welle, embodied by Einstürzende Neubauten and Nick Cave, or by David Bowie and Brian Eno, who lived there in the late 1970s. It is important to highlight that in many oral histories, people such as Wolle XDP, Kati Schwind, Jonzon, and Thomas Fehlmann, who later became figureheads of Berlin techno, describe their first encounter with music, DJing, and being moved by music through the conduit of Black music. However, at some point they distance themselves from Black music.

Most histories of Berlin techno begin with self-contained acid house parties and exclude how dance music was integrated into Berlin's broader clubbing geography before these parties. My argument asks instead: What if we don't segregate these spheres from each other and don't create such a clear moment of separation between house music, electrofunk, hip-hop, and Eurodance, on the one hand, and techno, on the other—and then link this to the larger question of race and German reunification? They were all part of the same West Berlin world for quite some time. Thus, Black musics such as disco, funk, and R&B are acknowledged as "primitive" resources to be transcended and elevated by white Germans into Berlin techno.

As a result, Blackness must continually be located outside German culture so as to ensure the whiteness of Berlin techno and, by extension, Germanness. Here it is noteworthy to mention that there are no departments for Black studies or similar programs in German universities. Most Black Germans who work in this area teach abroad. While some German scholars of color work in postcolonial studies, Asian-German studies, and Black German studies, often they do so in nonpermanent positions, at marginal institutions, or in activist-oriented fields outside the German university system.

ANNIE GOH: Apart from using music extensively in your scholarly work, from hip-hop and R&B to its popular forms, you have also intricately linked it to technology more broadly, as well as to concepts of the human and posthuman, and the nonhuman. Could you first elaborate on the relationship of race and technology in your work, and comment on the relationship to techno and Berlin techno?

ALEXANDER WEHELIYE: Well, clearly work on race and technology is a massive topic with at least a five-hundred-year history, but I can try to give you the bullet-point version (laughs). If we take writing and literacy as a technology, one of the ways discourses around race have worked in the modern West is that this has always been seen as a sign of civilization. Black culture and non-Western cultures in general, which were oftentimes primarily oral cultures, were positioned as being "uncivilized" as they could not "master" technology. As I covered in my research into sound recording and sound reproduction in the nineteenth century, Western ethnographers often described scenes of natives and Black people running away from record players in colonial contexts as they "perceived the sounds to be real," because they "lacked proper civilized faculties." This is something that continues to play out, where mainstream culture is shocked that Black people and other marginalized communities use and are at the forefront of engaging with mobile technologies or Twitter. I try to counter this in my work by showing how Black cultures have continually innovated modern technologies.

The other part is what we think of as technological. Some machines, if they have been around for a long time, are not considered technological or cutting edge anymore; they aren't high-tech. So the Walkman and the boom box do not appear as technological in the same kind of way as iPhones or laptops. A lot of the innovation that Black culture has participated in around technology has been around sonic technologies. For instance, using the record player not only as a playback device but also as an instrument. Look at dub reggae and hip-hop and disco, and what happened with mixing, scratching, dubbing, and so on, which was intricately related to technology but is not usually considered technological as it wasn't "high-tech."

ANNIE GOH: So, particularly relevant for techno would be dub-techno and its roots in dub reggae and the mixing desk as an instrument as you have written about elsewhere in your work.

ALEXANDER WEHELIYE: Yes, exactly, the mixing desk as an instrument, or the twelve-inch record and the remix, creating sound systems and the idea of mixing records together and so on. Because Detroit techno is so invested in an idea of cutting-edge technology, it is hard to square it with the prevailing Western ideas about Blackness and Black culture as "primitive" and therefore not technologically savvy. Techno is perceived as a white genre in the United States. Whenever I've incorporated the history of techno into my courses, I've had students who were completely astounded that techno originated in Detroit because they conceive of it purely as a white European import.

Sometimes I fantasize about the existence of alternate dimensions that consist only of different dance clubs with each milieu playing one track over and over and over. . . . .

I imagine slipping into one of these parallel universes through the portal of sound, where the sound system is flawlessly calibrated to channel the warmth and complexity of great bass lines, the interplay between the lights and sound takes on synesthetic qualities, the crowd is relaxed and there to dance rather than stand and gawk, and the dance floor is just packed enough to give the impression of losing myself in the crowd but not so much as to require subtly fighting for your spot on the floor (IYKYK). This story explores one of the tracks I hear playing in that imaginary perfect club geography over and over and over. . . . .

Though credited with and celebrated for giving the world the genre of acid house, which completely changed the UK club and youth culture landscape in the later 1980s, the work of DJ Pierre (Nathaniel Pierre Jones) in the 1990s receives far less attention. These recordings, released under his name or more often under different pseudonyms (Photon Inc., Joint Venture, Darkman, etc.), are subsumed under the banner of the microgenre of the Wild Pitch sound, which represents a subcategory of NYC house, which itself is a sibling of Chicago house. The integral components of this sample-heavy Wild Pitch house sound consist of long extended mixes that gradually introduce distinctive sonic elements to create intense euphoric effects when different sounds coalesce at certain points, only to then strip away some of them so that the stacking can begin anew. To call these mixes hypnotic would be simultaneously true and an arrant understatement.[1] Here's how

---

1 DJ Pierre's mixes were usually between seven and ten minutes, but in some cases, such as Joint Venture's "Master Blaster (Turn It Up)" (1992), they clock in at fifteen minutes. Joint Venture, "Master Blaster (Turn It Up)," on *DJ Pierre*, Strictly Rhythm, 1994, CD, https://www.discogs.com/release/26442-DJ-Pierre-DJ -Pierre.

Pierre describes his work: "In the beginning, it might not seem like anything. You don't know what it is. But as you're layering stuff on the track, it starts to tell you a story, it starts to build into something that you can really nod your head to and dance to. By the time you have them all in there, it sounds BIG, like an incredible energy."[2] The DJ Pierre–produced track "Don't Take It Away" was first released under one of his aliases, Audio Clash, as part of the twelve-inch single "Don't Take It Away/Electro Rhythm" on prominent NYC house music label Strictly Rhythm with the serial number SR1255 in 1991. The second track on the A side, "Don't Take It Away (Concept Mix)," made it onto the 1994 CD compilation as the last track of DJ Pierre's ten best Wild Pitch recordings, which was when I purchased a used copy of the CD for $7.99 at the Princeton Record Exchange.[3] I listened to the whole CD countless times but would often press the repeat button when "Don't Take It Away" came on. When I began to digitize all my CDs around 2001 or 2002, I hadn't listened to the DJ Pierre record in a while and was enormously thrilled about the prospect of being able to hear "Don't Take It Away" on my then newly acquired iPod—insert annoying and extremely loud record scratch sound effect here and a very loud aht aht followed by boisterous laughter here. The computer played and encoded all the tracks from the CD except the last, which was, of course, my most beloved. I tried everything: cleaning the CD, using different computers to rip the CD, legal and extralegal download options to acquire the track, all to no avail, which meant that "Don't Take It Away" as a musical object was in many ways lost to me at that point. I rediscovered the track in 2012, in the early days of Spotify's presence in the United States, which is ironic because so much dance music history of the 1980s and 1990s still cannot be found on the big streaming services in 2022, and spent weeks consuming "Don't Take It Away" on repeat. This process of reacquaintance happens every few years, and I'm still in awe of the track's deep spiritual and physical healing powers.

So far, I've offered you details about everything but the music itself, so let me attempt to give you *some* idea of what makes all seven minutes and thirty-two seconds of "Don't Take It Away (Concept Mix)" perfect. The recording commences with what sounds like steam being released from an engine or the launching of a small rocket ship, with the sound getting slightly louder as the sample progresses. This sample will weave in and out of the track for the

2 Matthew, "DJ Pierre Describes Wild Pitch."
3 DJ Pierre, "Don't Take It Away" on *DJ Pierre*, Strictly Rhythm, 1994, CD, https://www.discogs.com/release/26442-DJ-Pierre-DJ-Pierre.

first three minutes and then reemerge intermittently toward the end. Next, the entry of the all-important resonant kickdrum is accompanied almost instantaneously by congas and snares, creating a dialogue between the three distinct drum sounds. After this we encounter the entry of handclaps and beautifully rubbery bass line followed by a brief synth line and the sample of what sounds like a bird but could very well be a pitched-up recording snippet of a human voice that disappears at 2:50 only to rematerialize at the end of the track. Then we have piano stabs and drum rolls so fundamental to house music, very goth-sounding strings taken (I think) from house music group Ten City, and at the 3:54 mark the sample of a BlackFem voice that sings the following lines:

don't take it
don't take it
don't take it awaaaaayyyyyyyyyy
awaaaaaaaayyyyyyyyyyyy
awaaaaaaaaaayyyyyyyyyyyyyyyyyyy

Initially, after being first introduced, the vocal sample and the strings alternate to create tension, and later the producer will modulate the vocals so that at times the "don't" repeats while in other instances "take it" takes center stage rather than the "awaaaaaaaaaaayyyyyyyyyyyyyyyyyy." A few other notable small shifts: around 5:30 the beat drops and comes back in very soon after, and at 6:13 a breakbeat that sounds like the Lyn Collins "Think (About It)" beat popularized by 1980s hip-hop and later indispensable to Baltimore club music enters the scene. After all that, I'm not even sure I've even scratched the surface of what happens on this track given that so much of the alchemy happens in the interaction between the distinctive sounds and frequencies. Although the original sampled vocal snippet is no longer than thirty seconds, it exerts an immense significance in the different ways it flickeringly recurs and transmogrifies throughout the second half of the track, creating a relational tension between opacity and transparency.[4] Of course, once one is familiar with the track, it also shadows the first half through the listener's anticipation of what is to come; in the process the vocal snippet and its variant (re)iterations haunt the Now of the track's seven minutes and thirty-two seconds in toto.

If Pierre's track is a semianonymous, workman-like recording like so many dance music releases now lost to the debris of former micropresents

4 See Glissant, *Poetics of Relation*.

in the past, at least we know he's the track's producer due to databases such as Discogs or WhoSampled, which is much more than can be said about the unspecified BlackFem voice that appears so centrally on "Don't Take It Away." As much as I've tried over the years, I have not been able to identify who sang on the excerpt or what previous recording it was taken from. Given how much cishetero masculinity has been projected onto the history of electronic dance music, expunging practically all vestiges of how R&B and BlackFem voices remain central to the genres that comprise this category, it is imperative to amplify these aspects so that Black queerness and BlackFemness don't become completely lost to the debris history. Thus, it is essential not only to halt and reverse the whitening of techno and other forms of electronic dance music but also to work against the centering of cishet masculinity with the almost exclusive focus on and intense veneration of Detroit techno and the Belleville Three (Juan Atkins, Derrick May, and Kevin Saunderson) at the cost of Black queer and trans DJs and producers (Larry Levan, Frankie Knuckles, and Ron Hardy, to name only the most glaringly obvious examples). The veering from "benign" neglect to downright denigration of singing and vocality in electronic dance music, especially those forms performed by BlackFems across the gender and sexuality spectrum, contributes significantly to both the whitening and cisheterosexualization of these forms of Black music.

The vocals snippet on "Don't Take It Away" stands in for all the other BlackFem vocalists unnamed or named (and even if named usually not credited enough) who have sung lead or background vocals, were sampled, or sang reference tracks that were used on the final recording on techno, disco, house, rock, Eurodance, pop, hip-hop, reggae, and R&B records.[5] As a pushback against the violent ways this creative and affective labor continues to be exploited and disavowed, here is a very partial list of indispensable BlackFem voices that continue to carry so many genres of popular music: Carol Kenyon, Melanie Thornton, Adeva, Norma Jean Wright, Cynthia Johnson, Veda Simpson, Ashanti Shequoiya Douglas, Lori Glori, Chelonis R. Jones, Jewel, Ultra Naté, Kelly Price, Penny Ford, Jocelyn Brown, Alfa Anderson, Yolanda, Lole-

5 See Jarreau, "Black Women Helped Build House Music"; and Rodriguez, "Ghost Voices." For a particularly egregious example of the deeply racialized and gendered vocal theft, see singer Lori Glori's exploitative experience with Austrian DJ Bobo, who sold millions of records across Europe in the 1990s featuring Lori's voice without credit or proper remuneration; see Glori and Farina, "Black Voices—White Producers."

atta Holloway, Paula Brion, Shatasha Williams, Byron Stingily, Paris Grey, Dajae, Kym Mazelle, Eric D. Clark, India, Yazz, Caron Wheeler, Wondress Hutchinson, Kevin Aviance, Shara Nelson, Gaelle Adisson, Juliet Roberts, Christa Robinson, Sabrina Johnston, Tania Evans, *Michel'le*, Blue Raspberry, Luci Martin, Luther Vandross, Kym Sims, Claudia Fontaine, Joi Cardwell, Darryl Pandy, Martha Wash, Vernell "Vee" Sales, Barbara Tucker, Victoria Wilson-James. . . . .

NEW WAVES, SHIFTING TERRAINS

Prince's and David Bowie's Transatlantic Crossovers

When Kanye West claimed in 2013 that his *808s & Heartbreak* was "the first, like, Black new wave album," more than underscoring Kanye's mere lack of knowledge, it highlighted how the mythology of new wave/synthpop's constitutive whiteness, what one critic called "new wave's aggressive whiteness," had projected and enforced its ideological mirage all too well.[1] Despite this tendency, performers such as J*Davey, Toro y Moi, Ebony Bones, Noisettes,

---

1 Caramanica, "Kanye West Talks about His Career." Kanye West, *808s & Heart-break*, Roc-A-Fella Records, CD, https://www.discogs.com/release/1617049
 -Kanye-West-808s-Heartbreak. The phrase "new wave's aggressive whiteness"

Blood Orange, Idle Warship, Santigold, The Black Kids, Solange, and Kenna have all reclaimed the attitudes and sounds of early 1980s new wave and synth-pop for contemporary Black music. Furthermore, though these genres are now not considered to be a part of Black music proper, they were always much more diverse than assumed in hindsight, both in terms of the inclusion of Black musicians and in the way they integrally incorporated Black musical forms. Besides the obvious stature of Grace Jones as one of the most important musicians in new wave and Donna Summer's role as the originator of electronic pop music as we know it today, we could also name Kid Creole and the Coconuts, Thompson Twins, Rip Rig + Panic, Nona Hendryx, Z-Factor, Fun Boy Three, JoBoxers, Big Country, The BusBoys, Haircut 100, The Belle Stars, Culture Club, Romeo Void, Bow Wow, and Savage Progress as non–lily white new wave groups, given that many of these groups included at least one nonwhite member.[2] The list, of course, doesn't include those Black musicians of the early 1980s categorized as R&B, synthesized funk, or Britfunk (The System, Imagination, Linx, Loose Ends, Zapp, etc.) due to the segregated radio landscape in the United States and the racism of musical historiography, even though their sounds were just as synth-heavy and their looks no less beholden to the overuse of black eyeliner and copious amounts of hair gel. This is just to say that there are many more crossovers between new wave/synthpop and Black music than initially meets the ear.

I'm interested in the history of R&B music since the late 1970s, which includes a reevaluation of a genre known in the United States as new wave/synthpop, and referred to in the United Kingdom as new pop or New Romanticism, that sprang up in the wake of punk and postpunk on both sides of the Atlantic, particularly in the historical moment just after disco, and that allowed for the later emergence of different genres across the world, including electro, freestyle, house, and techno, and R&B's central place within these shifting terrains.[3] While synthpop and New Romanticism were not the same, there was much overlap between the two, especially in the United Kingdom; in fact, one might think of the latter as the visual language of the former.

---

   is Robert Christgau's from "Pazz and Jop 1978." See also Cateforis, *Are We Not New Wave?*

2 Apart from Romeo Void and Bow Wow, all these groups featured Black members, and even when they were not lead singers, the Black members significantly shaped both the sonic and visual narratives of these groups. On the broader presence of Black musicians in rock music, see the essays collected in Crazy Horse, *Rip It Up*; and Mahon, *Black Diamond Queens*.

3 See Rimmer, *Like Punk Never Happened*; and Rimmer, *Look*.

Influenced by the androgyny of such glam rock heroes as Roxy Music, David Bowie, and Marc Bolan, the New Romantics pushed back against punk rock's slovenly less-is-more sneering attitudes and fashion by embracing the excesses of British Romanticism crossfaded with the glitter of the disco era. The UK variant of this genre made ample use of then-new synthesizer technologies in order to infiltrate the pop charts and visually highlighted nonnormative gender presentation, especially white androgynous masculinities with Marc Almond of Soft Cell and Boy George of Culture Club as the most striking examples. And though the genre initially espoused the robotic rigidity of Kraftwerk as well as crisp British accents in its vocal and rhythmic stylings, synthpop essentially represented a white British translation of Black American singing styles and musical formations, especially R&B and disco, in much the same way as the Beatles, the Rolling Stones, and Led Zeppelin used the blues as their "source material."[4] Likewise, the omission of Black British R&B groups such as Loose Ends or Imagination from synthpop/New Romanticism despite their many convergences with these genres ensured that the air of whiteness clung to these genres, especially visually.

In other words, while new wave/synthpop was perceived as ostensibly hyperwhite, it was at its core a reformulation of blue-eyed soul for the age of synthesized electronic instrumentation and the MTV era.[5] Prince and David Bowie were integral to the transatlantic formation and circulation of this genre, which is a less controversial statement with regard to Bowie given that he, along with Kraftwerk, is seen as the progenitor of new wave, particularly in his Berlin trilogy of albums.[6] Prince, however, is not very often appreciated as fundamental to new wave or synthpop. Besides emphasizing Prince's and Bowie's various crossovers between Europe and the United States, I will briefly speak about Bowie's role in this archive and then focus on how Prince engaged and reformulated new wave/synthpop as well as some visual tropes associated with New Romanticism in most of his work in the 1980s and how this engagement facilitated his gender and racial provocations in sound and vision.[7]

---

4   See Albiez and Pattie, *Kraftwerk*; Reynolds, *Rip It Up and Start Again*; Pinch and Trocco, *Analog Days*; and Whalley, *Synth Britannia*.

5   On blue-eyed soul, see Brooks, "'This Voice Which Is Not One.'"

6   McCombe, "David Bowie and the Myth of the Berlin Trilogy"; Rüther, *Heroes*; and Seabrook, *Bowie in Berlin*.

7   I also want to resist the narrative that would hold that Bowie's genius stemmed from his chameleonic aptitude for collaboration, where Prince's tightly controlled output depicts him as an individual genius whose collaborators were only fulfilling

Although there's been some critical acknowledgment of the way that white British new wave and synthpop artists incorporated Black musics, little to no consideration exists that takes stock of the manifold ways Black artists such as Prince or Grace Jones actively participated in and shaped these genres. In addition, because the version of David Bowie that is placed as an origin point for new wave/synthpop is the Teutonic Bowie enthralled by the mechanical yet experimental Krautrock rhythms of Neu!, Can, and Cluster and not the Bowie who recorded at Sigma Sound Studios in Philadelphia and collaborated with Black US musicians, for instance, backing vocalists Robin Clark, Ava Cherry, and Luther Vandross as well as guitarist Carlos Alomar and drummer Dennis Davis and called the result *plastic soul*.[8] Later, bassist George Murray was added to the mix, and the three musicians were an integral part of Bowie's discography and live band until 1980 and beyond. In this way, Bowie initiated both the "plastic" blue-eyed soul of the new wave/synthpop era and its reverse crossover with *Young Americans*, especially "Fame," which not only became Bowie's first US mainstream hit but was also successful on the US R&B chart and earned him an invitation to perform the song on *Soul Train* in 1975.[9] Many other white UK new wave/synthpop acts followed in Bowie's footsteps during the second British invasion in the early 1980s; to name only the most obvious example, Soft Cell's "Tainted Love," which was one of the first UK synthpop records to cross over the pond to the United States, was initially recorded by US soul singer Gloria Jones in 1964 and popularized in the UK northern soul scene in the 1970s. We also see and hear in Soft Cell a prototype for British synthpop in the amalgamation of Black music, white queer masculinity, and synthetic pop-funk.

On the other side of the Atlantic, during the early 1980s white US audiences were far more comfortable with white British versions of soul and funk than with African American musicians, yet Black US audiences also

---

his vision; I think that Dez Dickerson and André Cymone were instrumental in helping Prince craft his early 1980s sound on *Dirty Mind* and *Controversy*, as were Lisa Coleman, Sheila E., Wendy Melvoin, and several others for the albums that followed. Prince, *Dirty Mind*, Warner Brothers Records, 1980, LP, https://www .discogs.com/release/3941977-Prince-Dirty-Mind; and Prince, *Controversy*, Warner Brothers Records, 1981, LP, https://www.discogs.com/release/407398-Prince -Controversy.

8 Seymour, *Luther*, 50–65; Famuyide, "David Bowie's Lasting Impact on Black Music"; and Booker, "David Bowie, Race and Black Music."

9 David Bowie, *Young Americans*, RCA Victor, 1975, LP. On reverse crossover, especially during the synthpop era, see George, *Death of Rhythm and Blues*, 158–61.

enthusiastically embraced this new Caucasoid funk. In fact, before its mainstream success via the then-new MTV, British new wave and synthpop was popularized in the urban centers of the United States by Black radio DJs like Frankie Crocker in New York, the Electrifying Mojo in Detroit, or Herb Kent in Chicago. Many white British synthpop groups, their sound already an amalgam of mechanized instruments and singers that emulated Black American musical idioms, collaborated with American R&B producers after they had achieved mainstream success (Scritti Politti with Arif Mardin or The Human League with Jimmy Jam and Terry Lewis, for instance). David Bowie also initiated this trend when he hired Chic's Nile Rodgers to produce *Let's Dance* in 1983, his commercially most successful album.

Prince's crossover success in the 1980s took different paths than those of other Black US artists, especially Michael Jackson and Whitney Houston, due among other things to his continual engagements with and reformulations of new wave and synthpop. While many other inroads into new wave/synthpop territories by more established artists seemed desperate, just like everybody and their cousin's cousin's obligatory disco album did in the late 1970s, or attempted to erase the performers' audible Blackness (hear, for example, Jamie Principle, Cybotron, or better-known Rockwell's and Ready for the World's faux British accents), Prince made these genres his own by taking what he musically wanted and needed from them, yet always bringing it back home to uptown Minneapolis, where everybody, white, Black, Puerto Rican, just a-freakin'. Subsequently, swathed in pink cashmere, traveling over the mountains with stopovers in Erotic City and Glam Slam, finally arriving on the one, a cold early April morning at Paisley Park, always already in your hair and in your heart, Prince turned new wave and synthpop out by infusing and recalibrating them with his own version of funk and R&B. Moreover, during the bulk of the 1980s, Prince as well as his different backing bands, side projects, and numerous protégés/collaborators provided clear and consistent visual performances of new wave (the wardrobe and makeup worn by Prince and his band on the *Dirty Mind* and *Controversy* album covers as well as other promotional materials from this period, including music videos) and New Romanticism (the stylings for the albums, singles, music videos, etc. from 1982's *1999* until the release of *Parade* and the dissolution of The Revolution in 1986) in ways that not many other Black artists did, even if they took on and helped shape these genres' sounds intermittently.[10]

10   Prince, *1999*, Warner Brothers Records, 1982, LP; and Prince and The Revolution, *Parade*, Paisley Park/Warner Brothers Records, 1986, LP.

Clearly, Prince modeled his changing 1980s bands after Sly & the Family Stone's multiracial and heterosocial funk utopia, but it didn't hurt that many synthpop and new wave groups were similarly heterogeneous in their racial and gender makeup, for example, Thompson Twins, Romeo Void, or Rip Rig + Panic. Prince's second feature film, *Under the Cherry Moon* (1986), deftly appropriates and lampoons the idea of old-world European decadence that had been part and parcel of both synthpop and New Romanticism beginning with Bowie's 1970s Thin White Duke persona, especially his role in *The Man Who Fell to Earth*, unsettling the performative whiteness that usually accompanies this mirage by continually highlighting his and costar Jerome Benton's performative Blackness.[11] Prince accomplishes this feat by syncopating the imagined old-world European landscape of the French Riviera with iconography and sounds that conjure 1920's Harlem, and extending the long line of African American expatriates in France, particularly jazz musicians. *Under the Cherry Moon* also recalls the Black male homosocial worlds conjured by Claude McKay in his *Home to Harlem* and *Banjo*, the latter of which is, of course, also set in the south of France. The film's sumptuous black-and-white imagery should also be seen as a precursor for Isaac Julien's 1989 film about the queerness of the Harlem Renaissance, *Looking for Langston*.

Throughout the 1980s Prince embraced visual and sonic modes of androgyny and gender queerness. As with the racial and gender makeup of his bands, Prince drew both on the new wave androgyny of Bowie, Adam Ant, Gary Numan, and Visage and on the long history of Black performances of nonnormative masculinities and femininities by artists such as Little Richard, Rick James, Jackie Shane, Gladys Bentley, P-Funk, Sylvester, and Grace Jones to create something uniquely his own.[12] New wave/synthpop were clearly not the only roots of Prince's journeys in gender messiness; however, their sound and iconography created an opening that allowed Prince to become a global Black crossover superstar while playing with his gender presentation. In the period from *Dirty Mind* to *Sign o' the Times*, Prince also experimented with and altered his voice, initially via "natural" means and then, later, through the aid of technology by pitch-shifting his voice in the

11   This can be seen both in Bowie's and others' fascination with the idea of Weimar Berlin and in early 1980s British synthpop records such as Ultravox's *Vienna*. According to Daphne Brooks, Bowie's Thin White Duke persona traffics in a "performative whiteness that reinstantiates white supremacist pop superstructures." Personal communication with author, August 19, 2018.
12   See Royster, *Sounding Like a No-No.*

recording process, allowing Prince to continuously reframe both his racial and gender identities.[13] More traditional R&B sounds dominated Prince's first two albums, and all the tracks were sung in falsetto, which had a venerable tradition in R&B that includes Smokey Robinson, Ronald Isley, Philip Bailey, Al Green, and Eddie Kendricks, albeit with the proviso that in those early years Prince's falsetto did not enjoy the benefit of being anchored in the performance of cisheteropatriarchal masculinity as with the other male R&B singers. In this way, he was positioned closer to Sylvester James's extravagant and indisputably queer BlackFemness than any of the other Black male singers.

Mirroring the punk-rockish and new wave looks of their album covers, *Dirty Mind* and *Controversy* amalgamate Prince's R&B falsetto and Prince's versioning of the clipped angularity of new wave guitar sounds and rhythms. Then, beginning with *1999*, not only does Prince make synthesizers and drum machines, especially his beloved LinnDrum, the focal point of his band's sound and begin his long-standing lyrical and conceptual focus on changing technological landscapes, but he correspondingly moves away from singing exclusively in falsetto, instead deploying his "natural" register and the deep, seemingly robotic Bowie- and Kraftwerk-inspired vocal inflections that had come to define synthpop since the success of Gary Numan a few years earlier ("Automatic" or "Something in the Water" from *1999* are good examples). In the same way as Bowie's *Young Americans* served as a template for new wave/synthpop, Prince's *1999* sound, along with George Clinton's "Atomic Dog," would come to define much of Black popular music in the 1980s. Prince's falsetto voice does not completely disappear after 1982 (it reappears most prominently on "Kiss" from 1986), sure enough, but he wields it sparingly, and mostly in ad-libs used for specific textural effects rather than being the dominant mode of vocal intonation on his records.

Similarly, Prince continually transmogrified and shuffled among the different registers of his voice on the many partnerships with female musicians—for instance, in the ways Prince deploys the lower registers of his singing as harmonic counterpoints to Sheila E. and his falsetto as an affective accent on "A Love Bizarre" (1985), or on Vanity 6's "If a Girl Answers (Don't Hang Up)," on which he performs Vanity's feminine adversary in a higher speaking voice, or his backing vocals on Martika's "Love . . . Thy Will Be Done."[14] It is

13 Prince, *Sign o' the Times*, Paisley Park/Warner Brothers Records, 1987, LP, https://www.discogs.com/release/123915-Prince-Sign-O-The-Times.

14 Sheila E., "A Love Bizarre," Warner Brothers Records, 1985, single; Vanity 6, "If a Girl Answers (Don't Hang Up)," Warner Brothers Records, 1982; and

highly unusual for masculine voices to take on the supporting role for feminine lead singers, and usually the reverse occurs, as can be heard on numerous white rock singers' deployment of Black female background vocalists,
including David Bowie.[15] Then, beginning with his 1984 Sheila E. collaboration, "Erotic City," Prince begins to technologically manipulate his voice to
a higher register so that for many it sounds more stereotypically "feminine,"
though I would say it sounds neither typically masculine nor feminine, which
is achieved by slowing down the instrumental track of the song, then singing
the vocals in time with the protracted speed, and subsequently speeding both
up to their regular tempo in the final recording.[16] As Prince's longtime engineer Susan Rogers states, "He would sing the whole song at half the tempo in
his normal voice and he'd play guitar parts at half the tempo, and then speed
the machine back up."[17] Thus, Prince played with and manipulated different
aspects of the higher and lower registers of his voice, in both their "natural"
and technologically mediated forms, to challenge the reigning gender norms
in the 1980s popular music landscape.

And, not surprisingly, Prince took this a few steps further by constructing an alter ego for the distorted high-pitched voice, named Camille, by

---

Martika, "Love . . . Thy Will Be Done," Columbia Records, 1991, CD single. On the
gendered power hierarchies embedded in the distinction between lead and background vocals, see Harper, *Are We Not Men?*; and Corbett, *Extended Play.*

15   Stevie Wonder, Sly Stone, and George Clinton had engineered their vocal tracks
in similar ways in the 1970s before Prince. Moreover, Prince frequently made
use of nonlexical vocables (lala, haha, whoo-hoo, etc.) in his falsetto background
vocal harmonizing instead of audible words, on "Forever in My Life," "17 Days,"
the extended version of "I Would Die 4 U," or "Purple Rain," for instance. There
are a few other examples that come to mind in terms of rendering the masculine-
sounding voice as a harmonic backdrop for the lead feminine-sounding voice in a
similar way to Prince, such as Gladys Knight & the Pips, Mariah Carey's long-
term collaboration with singer Trey Lorenz, and Kashif Saleem's backing vocals
on Whitney Houston's 1985 album cut, "Thinking About You." Whitney Houston,
"Thinking About You," on *Whitney Houston*, Arista Records, 1985, LP, https://www
.discogs.com/release/458608-Whitney-Houston-Whitney-Houston.

16   Prince and The Revolution, "Erotic City," on *Let's Go Crazy/Erotic City*, Paisley
Park/Warner Brothers Records, 1984, single, https://www.discogs.com/release
/577951-Prince-And-The-Revolution-Lets-Go-Crazy-Erotic-City.

17   Quoted in Greenman, *Dig If You Will the Picture*, 95. On the history of technologized voices in Black popular music, see track 2.0 in this volume; and on
the relationship between Black culture and sonic technologies more broadly, see
Weheliye, *Phonographies.*

disguising vocalist/dancer Cat Glover's face on the cover of the *Sign 'o' the Times* single as a feminine version of Prince, making it appear as if she were Prince in drag, and using the Camille voice on several tracks on the album of the same name. Prince planned to release an entire album credited completely to Camille, entitled *The Rebirth of the Flesh*, though this did not come pass and most of the Camille songs were incorporated into other projects.[18] Camille has been heard as Prince's uncanny "female" doppelgänger or split personality; some now believe Camille to index nineteenth-century French intersex person Herculine Barbin, due to a vague statement by Prince in a 1997 interview. Though I don't have any quarrels with this interpretation, I do want to note that Prince consistently uses the masculine *he* pronoun when conjuring Camille, for example, in the Lovesexy tour book, or most famously on "If I Was Your Girlfriend":[19]

> If I was your Girlfriend, would you remember
> to tell me all the things you forgot when I was your man?[20]

Rather than conjuring femininity or womanhood, and in line with Lisa Coleman's description of Prince as a "fancy lesbian," Prince's genderplay throughout his career suggests to me a particular performance of BlackFemness, a decidedly exalted and Black queer version of femininity.[21] That is to say, even Prince's performance of masculinity is rooted in and routed through Black-Femness, or as Ekundayo Afolayan remarks, "From his purple suits to press n' curls and high pitched moans, . . . Prince consistently showed us Black femme extravagance."[22] Instead of the performance of femininity per se providing the terrain that queers Camille's and Prince's various other waves of

18 On "Nikes," the first track from his 2016 album *Blonde*, Frank Ocean prominently deploys a voice effect eerily similar to Camille. Frank Ocean, *Blonde*, Boys Don't Cry, 2016, MP3, https://www.discogs.com/release/8932936-Frank-Ocean-Blonde. Much like Prince, Ocean, too, has been negotiating the hegemonic codes of gender and sexuality sonically, lyrically, and visually since declaring in 2013 that he had been in love with another man. On the Black femme, see Gomez, "Fishes in a Pond"; and Keeling, *Witch's Flight*. A fuller discussion of BlackFem can be found on track 8.0 of this volume.

19 Prince, Lovesexy Tour Concert Program.

20 Prince, "If I Was Your Girlfriend," on *Sign "O" The Times*, Paisley Park/Warner Brothers Records, 1987, LP, https://www.discogs.com/release/123915-Prince-Sign -O-The-Times.

21 See Walters, "Revolution Will Be Harmonized."

22 Afolayan, "Whether or Not Prince Knew It, He Was a Disability Icon to Me."

genderfuck, it is already an invocation of an insurgent Black queer femininity aka BlackFemness.[23]

Prince's specific variant of BlackFemness was also in full effect in the 1990s when he scrawled *slave* on his cheek and changed his public name to an icon, which typographically fuses the signs for male (♂) and female (♀) but cannot itself be phonated: ⚧, bringing to life his lyrics from the previous decade:

> I'm not a woman
> I'm not a man
> I am something that you'll never understand?[24]

In closing, I want to echo Alicia Garza's sentiments when she states that Prince in sound, word, and deed asked and embodied, "What will it take for us to live free?"[25] Part of that was Prince's immense proficiency at highlighting and fully embracing the fact that in this world Black people cannot be real; we remain myths, to use Sun Ra's words.[26] This is why Prince was so adept at world-making and situating his creations in our commons, to riff off of Kara Keeling's and Daphne Brooks's comments at the Blackstar Rising and the Purple Reign conference at Yale in January 2017.[27] Nevertheless, we should not forget that Prince, especially after he became a superstar, benefited immensely from and sometimes violently exercised his heterosexuality, for example, when he asked Wendy Melvoin to renounce being a lesbian during his stringent Jehovah's Witness days, and when he so effortlessly embraced his status as an elder musical patriarch in his later years.[28] We should also recall that Black female and openly queer Black performers are rarely

---

23 Going forward, I want to think more deeply about the affective labor of the Black femme voice in Prince's musical oeuvre vis-à-vis gender and race and how the most effective cover versions of his songs have been by women/femme performers like Chaka Khan, Meli'sa Morgan, Stephanie Mills, Mariah Carey, Sinéad O'Connor, Jazmine Sullivan, and Keke Wyatt.

24 Prince and The Revolution, "I Would Die 4 U," Warner Brothers Records, 1984, single, https://www.discogs.com/release/186718-Prince-And-The-Revolution-I -Would-Die-4-U. Prince adopted the ⚧ symbol from 1993 to 2000 during a labor dispute with his record company, Warner Brothers, about the ownership of his recording masters.

25 Garza, "Purple Reigns."

26 John Coney, dir., *Space Is the Place*, Plexifilm, 1974, http://www.imdb.com/title /tt0072195/.

27 Blackstar Rising and the Purple Reign: Celebrating the Legacies of David Bowie and Prince, Yale University, January 25–28, 2017.

28 Walters, "Revolution Will Be Harmonized."

FIGURE 6.1. The author's room, fifth floor, Seelingstrasse 26, 1000 Berlin 19 (ca. January 1985), with the inside sleeve from Prince and the Revolution's *Purple Rain* album cover.

allowed to be iconoclastic geniuses in the way that Prince was. Our heroes are complicated, I guess; after all, David Bowie "flirted" with fascism and made "China Girl" with Iggy Pop in the 1970s.

Coda

I'm still alternatingly irate and despondent that Prince Rogers Nelson no longer dwells in our dimension; because my psyche musta missed the memo on the proper stages of grief, I keep humming:

> How can you just leave me standing
> Alone in a world that's so cold? (So cold).[29]

My first response after Prince's death was complete disbelief: the magical being whose immaculate side-eye I mimetically emulated as a teenager in

---

29 Prince and The Revolution, "When Doves Cry," on *Purple Rain*, Warner Brothers Records, 1984, LP, https://www.discogs.com/release/125874-Prince-And-The -Revolution-Purple-Rain.

FIGURE 6.2. Concert tickets, 1987 and 1986.

cold, gray Berlin simply could not be dead. I learned so many things from Prince, the most important one besides giving proper side-eye being how to wear black eyeliner. I mention the eyeliner and side-eye not in jest or in ironic detachment but, on the contrary, to amplify just how deeply Prince's music and public persona impacted who I was then, who I am, who I be today. The eyeliner and side-eye are indicative of Prince's continual deep mattering in my Blaqueer-ass life; they represent a few of my flesh memories, the traces of musical, affective, and visual glitter that are now and will until the end of my time be part of my physical, emotional, and attitudinal DNA.[30] So I want to

30 Similarly, madison moore writes, "Even . . . until this day, people still yell 'Prince' at me as a homophobic insult. Over the years I started associating the word Prince with faggotry—not Prince's own faggotry but mine. . . . Thank you

FIGURE 6.3. Concert tickets, 1990.

say to him: the rain's been coming down nonstop and particularly hard lately, and all I got is two cigarettes and this broken heart of mine. But I still thank you, because all that was wrong in my world, U made right, and when the world's compassion ceases, still I know that you'll be forever in my life, thank you so much, I wish U love, I wish U heaven.

---

for setting me free. Thank you for helping me accept my identity as a black gay faggot, diamonds, pearls, and all." moore, *Fabulous*, 218.

The playlist features mostly R&B, both mainstream and "indie," though for me the distinction does not exist, and many artists from Chicago (Jeremih, Chief Keef, The GTW, DJ Rashad, Tink, Sicko Mobb, Jean Deaux, and King Deazel) as well as hip-hop, dance music, and a few other genres that embody the spirit of R&B. For example, the vocal cut-up techniques of DJ Rashad's "Rollin" and UK garage-inspired tracks such as PVC's "Our Reason" and Toyboy and Robin's "Jaded" were first heard on dub mixes but also on 1980s R&B songs like Chaka Khan's "My Love Is Alive." Tink embodies the blurred lines between singing and rapping like no one else in 2014, but Chief Keef's "Citgo," Nicki Minaj's/Lil' Wayne's verses on YG's "My N***a," and the deliriously exuberant sounds of King Deazel, Tigga Calore, and Sicko Mobb highlight how fundamental choreographing voices is to hip-hop, too.

Tink's track with Future Brown and Jeremih's collaboration with Shlohmo draw attention to how the worlds of mainstream-ish R&B and off-center dance music are slowly *merging*, albeit in a different way than the many chopped-up Cassie and Brandy samples that have dominated these quarters of the dance music world. However, the two tracks from Tink's *Winter's Dairy* mixtape, Jeremih's "Love Hangover" (produced by Pop & Oak), Fantasia's "Without Me" and Kelly Rowland's "Gone" (both produced by Harmony Samuels), Sevyn Streeter's "nEXT" (produced by Dernst Emile), Courtney Noelle's "Just Fuckn" (produced by John SK McGee), and Miguel's "Party Life" with its postpunk guitar and René & Angela bass line are no less minimalist or futuristic than the former two. The emergence of "indie R&B" as a music-journalistic category continues the long-standing critical neglect of mainstream R&B performers and producers, because critics often equate indie R&B's distance from the mainstream and from what is perceived as stereotypically Black with novelty and innovation.

An earlier version of this interlude was published online in *Cluster Mag: A Magazine of International Popular Culture* in April 2014.

This is why folks can still assume that Aaliyah or Cassie were the first R&B singers to use the restrained, nonmelismatic, and smooth singing style favored by the "indie R&B" set, as if Sam Cooke, Cherrelle, Curtis Mayfield, and Dionne Warwick had not existed. In the early 2013 Twitter flare-up that led to the hashtag #DeepBrandyAlbumCuts, Solange Knowles briefly drew attention to the serious deficiencies in the coverage of contemporary R&B (see figures 13.1, 13.2, and 13.3). Though some bloggers and commentators took Solange's critique seriously, the critical conversation about R&B still lags considerably behind the discussion of hip-hop, to say nothing of indie rock.

Solange's invocation of Brandy Norwood specifically, as opposed to other BlackFem R&B performers, should not go unnoticed here either, given that Brandy is not seen as an innovator by the public at large while she's deemed

FIGURE 13.1. Solange Knowles's Twitter feed, January 5, 2013, 11:39 a.m. Screenshot.

FIGURE 13.2. Solange Knowles's Twitter feed, January 5, 2013, 11:42 a.m. Screenshot.

FIGURE 13.3. Solange Knowles's Twitter feed, January 5, 2013, 12:07 p.m. Screenshot.

the "vocal bible" (i.e., the blueprint for much of contemporary R&B singing) by many BlackFem R&B performers such as Solange, Jill Scott, Jazmine Sullivan, and Kelela.

While hip-hop producers like Mike Will and DJ Mustard get a lot of props, Rodney Jerkins is still seen as bland. I'm not sure how that's possible if you've listened to the vocal arrangements on Brandy's "Angel in Disguise" or Destiny's Child's "Lose My Breath," especially the background vocal ad-libs during the bridges. Going back even further, listen to how Jimmy Jam and Terry Lewis's production alternates between Alexander O'Neal's lead vocals and the two different background vocal arrangements on "The Lovers" (from his 1987 album *Hearsay*, finally available in remastered form) to create sonic tension and drama. One of the most important facets of R&B is the genre's continual tampering with the human voice, in terms of both the performer's vocal acrobatics and the technological manipulation of vocal tracks, ranging from Marvin Gaye and Michael Jackson luminously multitracking their voices, to the use of vocoders and the talk box, to the Auto-Tune stylings of Tink's "Lullaby," Fuse ODG, or Yo Yo Honey Singh's "Brown Rang."

```
<Embed code: >
<iframe width="100%" height="450" scrolling="no"
frameborder="no" src="https://w.soundcloud.com
/player/?url=https%3A//api.soundcloud.com/playlists
/27223035&amp;auto_play=false&amp;hide_related
=false&amp;visual=true"></iframe>
```

Tracklist

King Avriel, "Prelude"

SZA, featuring Chance The Rapper, "Childs Play"

P. Morris, "Affairs"

Kyan, "Shuttle"

Kwabs, "Spirit Fade"

BC Kingdom, "DWN4U/Jeeps"

The GTW, "Calling Cards"

SZA, "Babylon"

Courtney Noelle, featuring Ty Dolla $ign, "Just Fuckn"

Tink, "Money Ova Everything"

Mutya, Keisha & Siobhan, "Lay Down in Swimming Pools" (Kendrick Lamar cover)

Jeremih, "Love Hangover"

Young Fathers, "I Heard"

SZA, "Aftermath"

King Midas Sound, "Meltdown"

Jay Boogie, "6 Speed"

Shlohmo & Jeremih, "Bo Peep (Do U Right)"

Tinashe, featuring ScHoolboy Q, "2 On"

Tink, "Lullaby"

T-Pain, featuring Lil' Wayne, "Can't Believe It"

Chief Keef, "Citgo"

Yo Yo Honey Singh, "Brown Rang"

Sevyn Streeter, "nEXT"

Kelly Rowland, featuring Wiz Khalifa, "Gone"

Fantasia, featuring Kelly Rowland & Missy Elliott, "Without Me"

Rihanna, "Pour It Up"

Shlohmo & Jeremih, "No More"

Blood Orange, "You're Not Good Enough"

Raleigh Ritchie, "A Moor"

Jean Deaux, featuring Sampha, "Find U"

Cooly G, "Come into My Room"

DJ Rashad, "Rollin'"

Future Brown, featuring Tink, "Wanna Party"

YG, featuring Lil' Wayne, Meek Mill, Rich Homie Quan & Nicki Minaj, "My N***a" Remix

Ty Dolla $ign, featuring Joe Moses, "Paranoid"

Tink, "When I'm Lit" ♥ THE GTW REWORK ♥
Sicko Mobb, "Remember Me"
Sage The Gemini, "Red Nose"
TeeFlii, "This D"
Electrik Red, featuring Lil' Wayne, "So Good"
Miguel, "Party Life"
King Deazel, "Crackin"
Sicko Mobb, featuring Heavy, "Fiesta"
Three 6 Mafia, featuring Young Buck, 8Ball, and MJG, "Stay Fly"
Brenmar, featuring Calore, "Payroll"
Trick Daddy, "Take It to Da House"
Destiny's Child, "Lose My Breath"
Shamir, "If It Wasn't True"
PVC, "Our Reason"
Bwana, "Baby Let Me Finish" (Black Orange Juice remix)
Fuse ODG, featuring Wyclef Jean, "Antenna"
D'Banj, "Oliver Twist"
Toyboy & Robin, "Jaded"
Young Thug, "Danny Glover" ("Yasss Thugga" edit)
SBTRKT, featuring Sampha, "Living Like I Do" (Lil Silva mix)

"SOUNDING THAT PRECARIOUS EXISTENCE"

On R&B Music, Technology, and Blackness

Interviewee	Dr. Alexander Ghedi Weheliye
Interviewer	Nehal El-Hadi
Date of interview	May 24, 2018
Length of interview	01:15:54
Location	Phone/Online

NEHAL EL-HADI: I've been really intrigued by your work for a number of years now, and it started off not through academia but through my interest in rap and hip-hop, not so much R&B, but just understanding and writing about music and technology and where both of those meet Blackness. In the past you've described this as a really intimate relationship between Blackness and technology, they're almost inextricable from each other, but somehow we always see them placed as opposite, one can't contain the other. Can you talk a little bit more about that?

[00:01:38]

ALEXANDER WEHELIYE: I think it's clearly very deep and elaborate. However, the easiest way to think about this is that this has its roots in colonialism and slavery and in the assumption that white Europeanness has to somehow be superior to Blackness, and one of the major ways that this has historically progressed is through technology. Particularly through writing technologies initially: literacy, the Bible, and so on, and that has been carried over into other technological realms in that there's still to this day this basic notion and surprise when mainstream society "realizes" just how deeply Black people engage with technology, whether this is Black Twitter or the way that folks on the African continent use different kinds of technologies, mobile banking, for instance, which frequently comes as a shock because there is still this elementary belief that Black people are perhaps outside of Western civilization. This is built on not only the presumed white, western intellectual superiority but its embodiment in technology.

NEHAL EL-HADI: Yes. I had pulled out a passage from a book called *Singing the Classical, Voicing the Modern*, by Amanda Weidman, and I had pulled it up in response to your work, but there's a point in here that she makes, and it's an introduction to a track where she starts off with:

> Music lives a curiously double life. It is associated with the technical—the musicological terminology of notes and intervals, the acoustic terminology of frequencies and amplitudes—and with the sentimental—meaning, emotion, and a sense of the ineffable. In fact, the coexistence of these discourses and their essential incommensurability seem somehow constitutive of "music" as we know it. On one side, to paraphrase Raghava Menon, is the meaningful: message, memory, murmur; on the other side, the mathematical: arithmetic, fractions, and time intervals. The way in which these discourses are pitted against one another reflects a mode of thinking about music that is, I would argue, peculiar to modernity and, indeed, to a particular postcolonial predicament. . . ."Voice" and "oral tradition" have in the twentieth century become more than merely descriptive. Rather, they are

A shorter version of this interview was published online in *The Puritan*, no. 42 (Summer 2018) http://puritan-magazine.com/sounding-that -precarious-existence-on-rb-music-technology-and-blackness/#top.

loaded terms in a discourse about authenticity that derives its urgency from the perceived onslaught of technologies of recording and electric sound reproduction.[1]

So this idea that this conversation about music, technology, race is really a discussion about postcolonialism.

[00:05:11]

ALEXANDER WEHELIYE: I wouldn't only say postcolonialism, since slavery clearly also played into this, but I definitely think that a large part of it is an inheritance from colonialism not only as a historical practice but as a set of ideas and beliefs that were necessary in order for European colonialism to happen over such an extended historical period in the modern era: Europeans have to feel utterly superior to non-European populations. And another way that this also plays out, which was initially one of the main reasons that I wanted to think about Black music and technology to counteract the assumption that Black music was in one way or another "natural," particularly, the Black singing voice, the Black-Fem singing voice.[2] That it is not about training, practice, instrument, artistry, or labor but that somehow, when a Black person, particularly when a BlackFem person, opens their mouths to sing, these transcendent and guttural notes just come gushing out, as if Aretha Franklin had not sung in her father's church for so many years before she even recorded and had that extensive training. There's a lot going on there, not only in terms of technology as hardware but also specifically about the human voice, the BlackFem voice as a technology. There's resistance to that because it is perceived to be something that happens naturally.

NEHAL EL-HADI: Yes, definitely. Just building on that as well, if we start from Blackness is intertwined with technology, how does this change our location in understanding both Blackness and technology?

[00:07:59]

ALEXANDER WEHELIYE: I think it depends on (a) what we're pursuing and (b) what kinds of technologies we're talking about. To me, what is really important is, as a result of Black culture so frequently being perceived as antitechnological, oftentimes there's not a precise lan-

---

1   Weidman, *Singing the Classical, Voicing the Modern*, 245.
2   I take my definition of BlackFem from Chelsea Frazier. For a fuller elaboration, see track 8.0 in this volume.

guage about describing phenomena like the BlackFem singing voice. So we might have certain descriptors for R&B singing voices such as *soulful, melismatic, churchy,* and so on, but there's very little in terms of specific lexicons for what different Black singing styles entail. And I'm not talking about this only at the level of breathing and breath exercises, breath control, but really in terms of the larger picture of what these voices are able to do in relationship to other voices and also in relationship to technological apparatuses: microphones, recording studios, samples, software (Pro Tools or Auto-Tune, for example), other instruments, and so on, even on the live stage. So, to me, it's more about trying to understand more accurately the artistry of singing within the field of R&B music as a set of mutable and embodied cultural practices. And a lot of that is thinking about technology both in the sense of recording studios, live venues, MP3s, but also in relationship to the concrete practices of singing, the labor that's exerted through the voice, and the performative dimensions of that work. The point is never to say, "Oh, you know, we Black people are technological too" (laughs), because to me that neglects how Black cultures engage with technology differently for a number of complicated sociohistorical reasons. Sometimes it's about limitations and pushing against those, such as turning the record player into an instrument in the early days of hip-hop, or even before that, in Jamaican sound system culture. It was necessary to use turntables in the South Bronx in the 1970s because music education programs were destroyed, and other instruments were not available, but it's never only that. So much of Black cultural practices oftentimes push against the limit of white mainstream definitions and intended uses of technology and continually innovate without automatically looking back nostalgically. You see this incessant drive for transformation in sampling and in the R&B singing voice. For example, once the kind of melismatic singing of an Aretha Franklin and later Whitney Houston becomes popularized and available for other populations, as it did in the 2000s, Black singers move in other directions. That is also tied to the fact that the Black church, particularly the Black Pentecostal church, is not the primary training ground for Black musicians anymore, not for people who play traditional instruments nor for singers. And it is at least partially a response against the existence of Celine Dion, Christina Aguilera, and later Adele, and all the white singers on *American Idol*, who perform these types of singing styles that were considered unmistakably Black in earlier moments.

So Black performers begin experimenting with other modes of singing and vocalization.

NEHAL EL-HADI: So how did you get to this point, and not your intellectual history, because you document that really well, but what has it been that brought you here?

[00:13:27]

ALEXANDER WEHELIYE: R&B music is the music that I've listened to the most in my lifetime, that I have the deepest affective relationship with. I remember there were a few years in the late 1980s and early 1990s, where I still listened to R&B, but it wasn't my main listening, and then I remember hearing Mary J. Blige's "Real Love" coming out of what seemed like every car in New York and New Jersey. And thinking, oh wow, I need to go out and buy that album, and that made me reengage with R&B. Even though it hadn't completely disappeared from my life, I didn't seek out R&B that often in that period of my life. And growing up in 1980s West Germany, R&B was something that I needed to seek out, it wasn't something that was readily available to me, because there was no, I mean I think it's similar in Canada, there was no format radio that exclusively played Black music.

NEHAL EL-HADI: I didn't come here until 2000, I was in England.

ALEXANDER WEHELIYE: Yeah, correct. But the same thing in England. Now you have the legalized pirate radio that plays dance music, grime, and things like that, but back in the day it was the BBC, and only the BBC. That was it. And there were the big artists: Whitney Houston, Michael Jackson, Lionel Richie, Prince, and Janet Jackson, and a few other exceptions that were readily available through radio and MTV, but overall, beyond that, I had to seek out Black music in 1980s Germany. This included listening to special radio shows on the Armed Forces Network, going to clubs that played Black music, having friends tape records for me because nonmainstream Black artists' import-only releases were expensive and not easily available in Germany. And then later MTV and other music video channels, waiting for the soul shows to come on and taping videos off that with friends, all these kinds of things that had to be done in order to engage with R&B music. I also didn't really know all that much about the lives or public personas of the Black performers because there was also no culture around Black music in 1980s West Germany. In the United States, for instance, you had *Ebony*, *Essence*, and Black teen magazines that wrote articles about DeBarge or other prominent R&B artists in the 1980s. Remembering that moment with Mary J. Blige, and there were a few others as well where I really thought, oh, I should really go back to this because I think I was sort of pooh-poohing R&B music for a little moment. Hip-hop seemed to be much more exciting. But one of the things I also realized retrospectively is that I listened to hip-hop from an R&B perspective, meaning that the wordplay, "the bars," and all that stuff, while nice, to me it's much more about the quality of the rappers' voices and their intonation. So the newer generation, sometimes referred to as the *mumble rapper generation*, doesn't really bother me. I mean, they disturb me in specific instances, because I don't like their music, but the sheer existence of these rappers doesn't irk me like some other hip-hop listeners of my generation, because a lot of the stuff that's happening in hip-hop now is really interesting precisely in terms of the voice. Thinking about someone like Young Thug or even Drake, who has a vocal coach, and a number of other artists that have been able to combine vocalizing with rapping, I really enjoy that. But I also recognized, for example, I love A Tribe Called Quest because of the interplay of Q-Tip's and Phife's voices. I like their music too, but it's not necessarily about the lyrics themselves but how they presented them and their vocal delivery.

[00:19:35]

NEHAL EL-HADI: When you were saying that, I was just thinking back to Myka 9 from Freestyle Fellowship, and he rapped, but he also scatted and sang . . .

ALEXANDER WEHELIYE: Yesssss! That was a really great moment, right? And Pharcyde as well. That moment in California just after the explosion of gangsta rap, Del the Funky Homosapien, Digital Underground (RIP Shock G), etc., it was all very melodic, and it really laid the groundwork for a lot of the things that are happening in hip-hop now.

[00:20:32]

NEHAL EL-HADI: You also had people like Nate Dogg, who were hip-hop. I wouldn't describe him as R&B at all, he was pure hip-hop, but then he had this beautiful voice.

ALEXANDER WEHELIYE: I think even N.W.A. or Above the Law before that. De La Soul and N.W.A. were actually the two groups that really got me into hip-hop (laughs). Because I liked hip-hop before, but I wasn't like . . .

NEHAL EL-HADI: Just so you know, you've totally dated yourself right now.

ALEXANDER WEHELIYE: It's fine. I mean, before that I did love the Grandmaster Flash, Sugarhill Gang, Kurtis Blow moment, but not the mid-1980s Eric B. and & Rakim sound, I can appreciate it intellectually, but it was just really dry. Those James Brown drums, I'm like, um . . . nope (laughs). But with both De La Soul and NWA, there was more of the P-Funk influence and this intense melodicism. I remember someone putting "Express Yourself" by NWA on a cassette tape for me, and without knowing who the artist was, I was like, damn! There was one more thing that I forgot to say earlier about how I got here in terms of the R&B. When I wrote "'Feenin'" all those years ago in 2001 and I felt that there was barely enough academic or journalistic writing on R&B, and I had been hoping that someone would write a great book about R&B, which has not happened in the interim. There's still so little critical literature about R&B music since the 1980s when compared to jazz, the blues, or hip-hop. It's been something I've worked on intermittently over the years, but I didn't initially conceive of it as a book. Then I thought maybe it's not a bad thing to make this into a book because I do feel so passionately about it and have thought so much about it.

NEHAL EL-HADI: The title "Feenin," I've said this before, I was never big into R&B, but what drew me in was if there was any R&B group that I could allow, it was Jodeci. Because they were also extremely hip-hop.

ALEXANDER WEHELIYE: I mean, I love Jodeci, but it was more Mary J. Blige for me because her earliest records were based on samples that I knew from hip-hop, and then following Mary from *What's the 411* to *My Life*, such an amazing album, which was so steeped in R&B history yet also a deeply hip-hop-infused album in terms of how it used samples from the history of R&B. So much happened in R&B as a genre in the 1990s. Initially, I started thinking about the project as R&B versus hip-hop, but at this point in time it's really hard to think about hip-hop without thinking about R&B and vice versa, because they've basically become one.

NEHAL EL-HADI: Hip-hop is now everywhere too. It's very, I don't know.

[00:24:52]

ALEXANDER WEHELIYE: What becomes interesting is why and how certain things are classified as R&B and certain things as hip-hop. That's where I want to push back a little bit: on the almost complete engulfment of R&B by hip-hop. It's also because of the shifts in the music industry, R&B music as a genre has been hit the hardest by the dominance of streaming, particularly BlackFem performers. In terms of how the music industry is currently operating, I would find it hard to imagine for there to be an SWV, an Xscape, a TLC, or a Mary J. Blige, and all the other names of that moment in the 1990s where R&B literally becomes the cultural dominant moving toward the late 1990s with Missy and Timbaland also pushing the boundary between hip-hop and R&B. Besides SZA there hasn't really been a major breakthrough for a BlackFem R&B artist in the past few years. What I wanted to say about Nate Dogg, of course hip-hop became mainstream in the 1990s through R&B. Through using not only Nate Dogg but particularly now-unknown female hook singers, Michel'le being one of the more well-known ones, but there were so many others. There were so many different hook singers, Kelly Price and Faith Evans, on the Bad Boy songs, for example. On the West Coast, it was similar; there were two or three women such as Nanci Fletcher who did all of the hooks and the vocal arrangements on the hip-hop records, which then took over the mainstream.

NEHAL EL-HADI: Like Jewel on the West Coast?

[00:28:04]

ALEXANDER WEHELIYE: Yes, Jewel was another one. She even pursued a solo career but did not gain prominence in the way that Kelly Price and Faith Evans did. In order for hip-hop to become mainstream, it had to have this symbiosis with R&B. Particularly on the hooks sung by these BlackFem R&B performers, and then when Auto-Tune rolled around in the late 1990s, it became possible and a lot cheaper for male hip-hop performers to manipulate their own voices instead of hiring women session singers. And then Auto-Tune actually freed folks up to experiment with their voices, particularly the masculine folks. Even though they might not use Auto-Tune audibly in this day and age, I don't think we would have the iLoveMakonnen, Drake, Kanye, Future, Doja Cat, Gunna, Lil Nas X, Coi Leray, all these folks continually deploying their voices in new and interesting ways, whether it's technologically manipulated or not. So I think it is definitely *that* . . . And of course, there are the samples too, in the early days, vocal R&B samples were important to hip-hop.

[00:30:03]

NEHAL EL-HADI: Going back to "'Feenin,'" what was also very intriguing to me about the way that you thought was what geographies you considered. Some of them were a little more obvious, like the domestic sphere and the sonic zone, but then you also have the Black voice as a site, the phonograph and other sound technologies as a site, sonic topographies as a site. And I was like, this is a really interesting way to think about space and place, and I'd love to hear you talk more about it.

[00:30:36]

ALEXANDER WEHELIYE: I'm trying to think how the best to formulate the terms of what I'm thinking about. Let me come at this from a slightly different direction. While a lot of this is specific to the United States and to a certain extent to the North American continent—and it's been interesting to see how Canadian R&B artists get folded into the R&B genre in that usually they don't mark themselves as being different from US performers, Tamia, Glenn Lewis, dvsn, or Melanie Fiona, for example, in the same way that hip-hop artists like Drake do. Also, there's always been other traditions of R&B singing, if you look at the history of British R&B music, the kind of melismatic, grainy, and throaty singing embodied by folks such as Jennifer Holliday or Aretha Franklin in the United States has never been dominant there because of the strong reggae influence there, which generally favors more smooth, nonmelismatic voices, has been really prominent. That's one way to kind of think about the geographic specificity of all these things, right? I should also say that even in the United States Aretha, Gladys, and Patti coexisted with Dionne, Diana, and Roberta. We could also think about how the singing voice plays out in non-English-speaking music, in a genre like bachata, and how that is becoming incorporated into hip-hop and R&B. In addition, even though folks in US hip-hop and R&B have largely left behind Auto-Tune as something that you can hear— it's still used in every single studio to correct "mistakes" (laughs). But as a desired, audible effect. There are few exceptions of course, such as Future, but, in general, Auto-Tune is not being utilized in the same way as during the heyday of T-Pain. But on the other hand, it is hugely influential in global pop music. Whether it's in K-pop or various forms of pop music on the African continent like Afrobeats, which is performed primarily between London, Ghana, and Nigeria. Auto-Tune is also prominent in Tanzanian pop music and in pop music in the Middle East. And what seems interesting to me there is that Auto-Tune was a kind of moment where the singing voice was democratized around the globe, particularly for non-English-speaking performers, not from North America. While frequently disparaged, Auto-Tune really opened up the space for folks from the African continent to also be considered soulful. In the same way that disco production techniques did for pop performers around the world in the 1970s.

To me, Auto-Tune represents a digital form of melisma, it's another way of treating the voice and adding all these denotive layers to the singing voice, and it is not throwaway, or nonartistry. So that's been interesting. And of course, R&B music in general has not received the same critical attention as other forms of Black music because it is primarily concerned with what we believe to be the domestic sphere and interpersonal relationships that are not considered political. That's why in some of my talks I use Amaal Nuux's (a Somali Canadian singer-songwriter based in Toronto) phrase "Scream my name like a protest" because I thought it was a really nice way to think about what it means to have intimacy—very, very broadly defined—whether it's sex, sensuality, or something else, in relationship to what's going on in the streets. That you can't really have one without the other. Because people joke about things like "side-chick anthems" in R&B music, they deride it as a genre instead of imagining how these types of songs also imagine romantic relationships beyond traditional monogamous heterosexual coupledom.

Of course, there are R&B songs in which BlackFem performers sing about their partners being incarcerated, and listeners become exposed to the affective dimensions of the prison-industrial complex. You get a very, very different way in which these larger quote/unquote social-political-economic forces operate and constitute what is considered to be domestic space in that they're always in relationship to one another. When I started doing talks about R&B, there were a couple of times when people asked, Well, what makes all of this political? Initially I refused to answer the question because I thought it was beside the point. Of course, R&B is political! And finally, I condensed my thoughts and started to say that R&B music gives us the soundtrack to Black everyday life under slow genocidal conditions. I think that that is, to me, what still makes R&B an important genre beyond my and others' mere enjoyment of the music, the artistry, the wit and humor, the sexiness, and the emotions. How do we have interiorities, interpersonal relationships, and so on in environments where, to paraphrase Audre Lorde, we're not supposed to exist. Not meant to survive but also not exist. Period. And to me sounding that precarious existence is where contemporary R&B really shines.

NEHAL EL-HADI: I had read somewhere where you had said that, and that shifted my relationship to R&B because now I see it on a scalar level of the things that I was interested in. That it was a zooming in, and when you pulled out, you were still dealing with the same world that other forms of music were dealing with. And it's not even on a level of being explicit or not, but it was a zooming in, it was a different scale. And that particular quote of yours shifted how I listened to music.

[00:38:49]

ALEXANDER WEHELIYE: One of the main things that I was also thinking about is trying to be specific about the way that R&B singing has changed. Even though it's never a complete shift, and one of the things that is really important for me to highlight is that there have always been R&B singers that were not these powerhouse—I'm running out of adjectives—grainy-voiced, melismatic, "sanging" singers. And that's the common complaint lodged against contemporary singers like Frank Ocean and SZA being "vibe" singers and not "sanging-ass" singers. People say there's no conviction, there's no drama in contemporary R&B in the way that you got in Whitney Houston, in earlier periods of Mariah Carey, or Kelly Price. The way that I read that is not necessarily as a retreat but that the way that folks such as Frank Ocean, Solange, Kelela, and even to a certain extent Mariah Carey in her later career or Jazmine Sullivan, who both have powerhouse voices but often deploy their softer, quieter registers, use the layering and multitracking of their voices is to highlight BlackFem interiority. It's not projecting the melisma outward but going inward and giving us an idea of—clearly, I'm not saying that this is a one-to-one representation of the performer's interiority—a vocal staging of interiority. Contemporary R&B singing and vocalization projects interiority outward by using different facets of the R&B singing voice, the multitracking, but also oftentimes highlighting the micropolitical dimensions of interpersonal interactions, histories, structures, and so on. And I feel that particularly with Frank Ocean—not surprisingly, this is very gendered, too, given that he gets to occupy the space of an experimental auteur in ways that Jazmine Sullivan or Toni Braxton does not—who has been able to create an observational mode of R&B music and singing. On *Blonde* and *Endless* (both 2016) and his recordings since then, you get an idea of a person living their everyday life, but Trayvon Martin and the other killings of Black folks by the police do not disappear, they continue to shape the world of Ocean's narrators. But the records also feature intimate, quotidian moments such as Ocean driving from New Orleans to LA, meeting a potential love interest in a gay bar, or a recording of his brother and a voicemail message from his friend's mother, which creates a nonlinear stream-of-consciousness mode of R&B. Ocean wants to not call his music R&B anymore because he finds that limiting, but I would want to insist that it is still R&B, and that there's nothing limiting about this genre, especially given that most contemporary forms of popular music are based on R&B. I think that there are a lot of things that R&B can still give us, but, in general, the labor of what R&B offers gets severely devalued. Because for a lot of people R&B music has become functional music for certain types of intimate situations but carries no significance beyond those. It's not automatically music that you play in your car loudly, it's not necessarily the music that you hear in the clubs, so for a lot of folks R&B becomes music to have sex to. There's nothing wrong with that, of course, but I think that the genre accomplishes a lot of other important things beyond soundtracking bedroom acrobatics, and those are not appreciated in the same way. To put it more crudely, while hip-hop, despite its immense mainstream success, is frequently imagined as oppositional and therefore political, the same assumption does not hold for R&B in the contemporary moment. And it's been interesting to see that the few moments in which R&B music has been explicitly "political," has addressed Black Lives Matter and other forms of Black protest, none of them really work, either politically or aesthetically. In earlier moments there was a song by Black Men United in the 1990s, "Freedom" from the *Panther* soundtrack (1995), and it was like the "We Are the World" model, every R&B performer was on there. I think the Black Men United song was called "We Will Know."

NEHAL EL-HADI: "U Will Know." I just googled it.

ALEXANDER WEHELIYE: Was it on a soundtrack?

NEHAL EL-HADI: Yeah, *Jason's Lyric* (1994).

ALEXANDER WEHELIYE: Yes! It's got everyone on it.

NEHAL EL-HADI: Oh my god, it's got everybody in 1994. Aaron Hall, Al B. Sure!, Boyz II Men, D'Angelo wrote it, El DeBarge, Keith Sweat, Lenny Kravitz played guitar on it. Okay.

[00:45:10]

ALEXANDER WEHELIYE: And there was the *Panther* soundtrack, which I think also came out around the same time. A large group of female R&B singers, including Aaliyah, Mary J. Blige, En Vogue, Meshell Ndegeocello, TLC, Queen Latifah, Vanessa Williams, SWV, and Brownstone, covered Joi Gilliam's song "Freedom." Moments like that existed in previous eras, which seemed to me more organic, whereas the contemporary R&B records such as Usher's "Chains" (2015) that are designed as overtly political often fall flat. Some more effective endeavors include Blood Orange's song "Sandra's Smile" (2016), which is about Sandra Bland but is more oblique and poetic than it is explicit.[3] Though clearly it's about Sandra Bland, the song does not directly depict how Bland died at the hands of the police. I remember that it was really jarring to put together all these images of Bland smiling in relationship to not only her dying but the violent way she died, and the video of it circulating online at the time. Thus, Blood Orange uses the genre of R&B to highlight the way that BlackFem bodies are affected by state violence in a way that not even Beyoncé incorporates. After all, it's the mothers of the slain young Black men who are featured in the visuals for *Lemonade* and not mothers and the grandmothers of the slain Black female persons, whether it's cis or trans women/girls. And in that sense, "Sandra's Smile" did a lot more work than a more tra-

---

3 Blood Orange, "Sandra's Smile," on *Freetown Sound*, Domino Records, 2016, CD, https://www.discogs.com/Blood-Orange-Freetown-Sound/release/8912995.

ditional we're-gonna-storm-the-barricades type of protest song about stopping police violence could have accomplished.

Recently R&B has become the cornerstone of every genre of music even more so than it always has been, for instance, in white female pop singers like Ariana Grande, Taylor Swift, Adele, or Demi Lovato, all of whom draw heavily on R&B singing styles but do not perform in or affiliate with R&B as a genre. So it's not that R&B disappeared per se but that it has re-disappeared as a genre of its own while being ingested by all these other genres, including country music and pop music. However, that also means that particularly for BlackFem R&B performers, there has not been nearly as much space for them at the moment because listeners can basically get everything, at least sonically, from other places. At least in the United States there used to be an entire ecosystem for Black music, particularly R&B, consisting of radio stations, record stores, and particular kinds of music festivals such as Essence Fest. In part as a result of the way that Billboard has restructured the tabulation of its charts since 2012, and because streaming effectively excluded genre-specific institutions and allowed Billboard to determine what counts as hip-hop, R&B, or country. Whereas previously songs had to be played on Black radio in the United States in order for them to appear on the Black music charts. Being hit the hardest by the restructured tabulation of the Billboard charts, because there is no longer the ecosystem to nourish artists and their craft, R&B music has all but disappeared as its own genre. This is one of the reasons most of the BlackFem R&B performers who have risen to prominence since the early 2000s have done so through reality shows: Keyshia Cole, K. Michelle, Jennifer Hudson, Fantasia, and Tamar Braxton, veritably every single one. Moreover, BlackFem performers from earlier generations can often only maintain relevance by participating in reality shows, even those who were such commercial behemoths as Mariah Carey or Toni Braxton, for instance. And then there was the *R&B Divas* franchise, on which Kelly Price, Dawn Robinson, Faith Evans, and a number of other BlackFem musicians appeared. That has been interesting but also limiting in terms of what is possible for BlackFem performers. Reality shows provide R&B singers with the drama and narrative arc seemingly necessary to appeal to present-day audiences. However, because BlackFem R&B singing is not perceived as art or as labor, these reality shows often violently erase the differences between the singer's biography/persona and the content of their songs in much the same way R&B biopics like *The Tempta-tions, The Jacksons: An American Family,* or *What's Love Got to Do with It* do.

NEHAL EL-HADI: That is really fascinating. In your interview with Marginalia, you talk about R&B moving from being the musical repre-sentation of authentic Blackness to its antithesis in the 1980s and after. Can you explain that a little bit, especially in light of what you were just saying about Meghan Trainor and Adele?

[00:52:59]

ALEXANDER WEHELIYE: I mean that happened in the 1950s and 1960s, you had your Elvis, Pat Boone, the Beatles, the Rolling Stones, right? All of them whitewashing Black music in different ways. This is something that has been there, but it has never been to the point where it actually erased Black R&B performers. It just used to be seg-regated, that R&B singers performed in what was known here in the United States as the *chitlin circuit,* and they were played on Black radio, but they didn't necessarily cross over to the pop mainstream. If you look at the 1960s and 1970s, the music that people feel spoke to the political climate then was R&B music. Aretha Franklin's "Respect," Sam Cooke's "A Change Is Gonna Come," James Brown's "I'm Black and I'm Proud," and then even in the 1970s with Curtis Mayfield, Marvin Gaye, Stevie Wonder, et cetera, were not always explicitly political in their lyrics. And what happens in the 1980s is that, in the aftermath of disco and the widespread white heterosexual backlash against the mainstream success of this genre (especially the prominence of Black-Fem singers such as Donna Summer, Sylvester, or Gloria Gaynor) in the United States, R&B leaves the pop charts, which is something that people generally write out of the history of R&B music. Disco was up-tempo R&B music. Other things went into it, too, of course, but disco was primarily based on R&B, and in the backlash against disco at the end of the 1970s, Black music goes underground, most clearly in the rebirth of disco as house music, or at the very least leaves the US mainstream. And then the 1980s gives you the remarkable crossover success of Whitney, Prince, Michael and Janet Jackson. But a lot of the other artists that really defined R&B in the 1980s rarely crossed over to the pop charts. If you look at someone like Luther Vandross, he, for most of his career, tried to cross over to the pop charts, which didn't really happen for him until fairly late in his career with a very saccharine song. Beyond that, in the 1980s R&B was not mainstream music, and that changed in the 1990s. If you think about how Michael Jackson, his record company, how hard they had to fight for representation on MTV in 1983, right? It's hard to imagine now that Michael Jackson could not be played on MTV in the early 1980s. Granted, he was not the superstar that he later became, but how? How? But that's how things were. What happens in the 1980s is that R&B becomes very aspirational, meaning that it becomes the sound of the burgeoning (and extremely precarious) Black middle class. That's the moment when quiet storm emerges as a R&B subgenre and radio format geared toward Black middle-class audiences. This is the moment when you get Anita Baker, Freddie Jackson, or Sade, which is when R&B becomes feminized, queered, and associated with middle-class aspirationalism, and then hip-hop comes along, and it's all aggressive and "masculine," it's about "Fuck the Police" and not "Let's Get It On" or "Caught Up in the Rapture of Love." I'm making the point very starkly, because there's a lot of layers there, but I do think that it really boils down to that. And then what you see with Mary J. Blige and Jodeci is the way they embrace not only the hip-hop sound but also the look and the attitude. Early in her career Mary J. Blige, diametrically opposed to earlier R&B performers, refused to smile for pictures. You have that late 1980s moment of new jack swing where hip-hop and R&B grew together, but that was really different. The multicolored clothes, the dancing, was part of the MC Hammer moment. And then in the 1990s the way R&B takes on hip-hop was really different. None of these things, to be clear, are value judgments on my part. I love new jack swing, but I also love Jodeci and Mary J. Blige, but I do think that it sends a different kind of signal, and that's how R&B reestablished itself by, to a certain extent, remaking itself in the face of hip-hop but also masculinizing itself, and making itself more "urban" and "street." If you look at Mary J. Blige's or SWV's early videos, they're not about interior spaces; they're about the street and wearing street clothing rather than sequined gowns. A few years later, Mariah Carey would really take hip-hop/R&B fusion into the pop charts through her megahits, like "Breakdown," "Fantasy," but even the earlier "Dream Lover," which is based on a well-known hip-hop sample. That's where R&B music had to go in order for it to be recognized as being something authentically Black again. And then that disappeared, and now we're in this moment where, again, a lot of people are definitely more invested in how Kendrick Lamar represents Blackness than how SZA represents Blackness. Beyoncé's output might be the exception here. To me Beyoncé is clearly in dialogue with R&B and comes from that tradition, but she's not beholden to the same laws as other BlackFem R&B performers, whether it's Tamar Braxton, K. Michelle, or even SZA. But she operates in a different kind of space. She transcends the genre, so to speak. And we could think about "Formation" as a more explicitly political response to politics, but even that is fairly oblique. It's also the visuals, it's the videos, and it's also her performance at the Super Bowl that make the political stakes clear, not necessarily the lyrics on their own.

NEHAL EL-HADI: I would consider that a hip-hop track, even who was involved in writing and producing it, and how she uses her voice.

[01:02:09]

ALEXANDER WEHELIYE: Precisely, I often use "Formation" to show how there's so little actual singing on that track and to highlight how many different styles of vocalization there are in contemporary R&B. I think at the end of the day what it really comes down to is that the masculine performers get classified as hip-hop, whereas the female and fem performers get classified as R&B, as is the case with "Formation."

NEHAL EL-HADI: There's a gendering there.

ALEXANDER WEHELIYE: That's the thing about Beyoncé. Beyoncé is also a great rapper. Other R&B performers—SZA, Brandy, and Kehlani—are also a really amazing rappers. Kehlani, like Frank Ocean, one more R&B singer that can rap quite well, is also very open about her queerness. The point being that male performers such as Drake, ILoveMakonnen, Young Thug, Roddy Ricch, Gunna, or Lil Uzi Vert get labeled as hip-hop despite the prevalence of vocalizing and singing on their records, whereas BlackFem artists with similar vocal profiles are placed in R&B.

NEHAL EL-HADI: A lot of the R&B singers, Erykah Badu, Angie Stone, they were all rappers.

ALEXANDER WEHELIYE: Yes. One thing I wanted to say because you mentioned Erykah Badu. The whole neo-soul movement in the 1990s was a genre created by a record company. Kedar Massenburg generated that category to market Erykah Badu, because he didn't feel there was any kind of ready-made slot for her. It was then used as a way to reassert a certain kind of authentic Blackness within R&B music that emphasized traditional musicianship and used the term *soul* as opposed to R&B to conjure previous forms of authenticity and Blackness. That neo-soul moment, not necessarily in terms of the musicians themselves, but in terms of the marketing and the way that people picked up on it: "We're not going to do this hip-hop thing anymore," even though, ironically, they were all deeply influenced by hip-hop, "and it's going to be real soulful singers and live instruments, and not this throwaway commercial stuff."

NEHAL EL-HADI: It becomes about genre as a marketing label rather than a set of practices?

[01:05:41]

ALEXANDER WEHELIYE: Mary J. Blige's 1994 album, *My Life*, was not tagged as neo-soul, not even retroactively, even though it is steeped in older soul traditions. Nor was Meshell Ndegeocello included in that category although she was one of the first artists to release what would later be known as a neo-soul record with *Plantation Lullabies* (1993). And she also did do the hip-hop thing on her first album as well, with R&B, but she didn't get included because she was not part of that particular moment with D'Angelo, Jill Scott, Erykah Badu, Maxwell, J Dilla, and The Roots worlds.

NEHAL EL-HADI: I do have one last question about your work in general. Having read a lot of your writing over the years, there's something archival about your work. It's not just presenting ideas; you're also documenting what doesn't get documented. Is that intentional?

[01:07:13]

ALEXANDER WEHELIYE: I definitely think that that's one of the pillars of my engagement with contemporary popular culture, to document those often-fleeting cultural moments. Also, one has a different type of access to culture in the Now by living with and through them. Not that that makes it automatically more immediate. There're so many different ways in which you could take that. For instance, it would be really difficult for me to reconstruct what happened in 1921 when the first blues was recorded. I don't know what it felt like to hear those sounds in that moment. Whereas with contemporary music, because I'm surrounded by it, for example, hearing it coming out of a passing car, as a soundtrack to a TV show, etc., there are instances where I stop and say, Oh wow, how did we get here, and what does this mean? It is definitely about documenting in very specific ways, which is important since so many cultural objects disappear, despite and because of the "unlimited" capacities for digital storage. So much music can still not be streamed on mainstream platforms, and with the exception of *Keyshia Cole: The Way It Is* and *Braxton Family Values*, none of the reality shows that feature BlackFem R&B performers are available to stream or on DVD. Researching contemporary R&B allows for an extreme form of zooming in that is easier—at least for me—to achieve when living through that historical era. There are historians that clearly can reconstruct epochs from archival sources, but to me it's always been really important to bear witness to what happens in my particular time. And, for instance, track 3.0 in this volume, which initially began as a section that I cut from "'Feenin'" (2002), which I started revisiting around 2010, because there had been so many new developments in mobile technology in the interim. That enabled me to analyze the two different historical moments side by side since I witnessed firsthand how the relationship between R&B music and mobile technologies transformed so radically: how the cell phones were being deployed in R&B in the late 1990s and early 2000s, and then how mobile technologies completely saturated the genre by the late 2000s. Of course, now, in 2018, so many of these phenomena have completely disappeared. Like ringtones are gone. (laughs) I actually still have the same ringtone that I made in 2010.

NEHAL EL-HADI: What is it?

[01:12:16]

ALEXANDER WEHELIYE: It's DJ Mujava—"Township Funk (Ikonika's Nexus-6 mix)" from 2009, and I chose it because it sounds like an analog phone ring. I don't have ringtones for anything else beyond my phone, but back then people bought musical ringtones in droves—they were hailed as saving the ailing music industry—there was software to make ringtones from your own MP3s, there were all these different ways in which music and mobile tech were symbiotic, which has completely shifted. Clearly, in the streaming era, music and mobile devices are still closely linked but not in the same way as in the brief heyday of musical ringtones. It was particularly critical for me to pay attention and to bear witness to how the ringtone moment affected R&B music. But also be aware of the previous history, given that songs about telephone (mis)communication in R&B and other forms of pop music existed since the 1960s (e.g., Aretha Franklin's "Call Me" or New Edition's "Mr. Telephone Man"), and there will probably be songs about these machines even after telephones have vanished, when we communicate via chips implanted in our head. Because phones have a very particular function and because they've endured for so long, so much meaning and affect is attached to them. In pop music, especially R&B, phones come to represent the joys and frustrations of interpersonal communication, there's just so much there in terms of missed connections, longing, hearing the voices of loved ones and so on. Currently, there's probably no more devastating indicator of the failure of interpersonal communication than being left on "read" when someone doesn't respond to your text message/iMessage; there's so much affect bundled up within how we technologically interact. I've always felt that you hear those pleasures and disappointments most audibly in R&B music, and that allows us to make sense of those technologies differently. Instead of emphasizing the mechanical hardware, R&B music reveals and amplifies the emotional and social operating systems of communication technologies.

NEHAL EL-HADI: That is a great place to wrap it up beautifully.

ALEXANDER WEHELIYE: Thank you.

"SCREAM MY NAME LIKE A PROTEST"

R&B Music as BlackFem Technology of Humanity
in the Age of #Blacklivesmatter

The prominence of #BlackLivesMatter and the broader upsurge of the Movement for Black Lives over the past years has pressured Black art and music to take on more explicitly politicized stances in order to address the continued disregard for Black life by state and nonstate institutions in the United States and in many other parts of the world. Not surprisingly, this politicization has most often taken the path of highlighting how the violences of white supremacy affect cisgender and heterosexual Black male persons in the public sphere. Given that R&B music focuses on Black everyday livingness, interiority, care, vulnerability, and interpersonal relationships from female/fem perspectives, the genre spotlights the "minor" aspects of the genocidal conditions and the different forms of generalized trauma ensuing from these conditions that mark the continued existence of Black life in the Western world. Thus, rather than hearing R&B as a retreat from the political, as occurs too often, this track investigates how R&B music by artists such as Jazmine Sullivan, Tiffany Gouché, We Are King, Solange, Sampha, SZA, Durand Bernarr, Amaal Nuux, Blood Orange, Kehlani, Mhysa, Kelela, Dawn Richard, and Frank Ocean have deployed this genre to center BlackFem-defined interpersonal intimacy, interiority, care, and healing. Contemporary R&B music offers important Black political imaginaries beyond the cishetero masculinist precincts of the traditionally "political," which echoes the holistic Black/queer feminist-inspired activism and organizing associated with Black Lives Matter.

Two quotes from Ethiopian American BlackFem R&B singer Kelela illustrate this problematic:

> "I was mad I didn't write anything that addressed what I'm talking about 90% of the day. I had a problem with the fact I didn't do that, it took me a while to get there."
>
> On the flipside, an artificially constructed song on the importance of #blacklivesmatter or the discussion of privilege would be hollow, immediately obvious—so why sweat it? "Right," she says. "I sat in that shitty feeling for months until it clicked: that actually there's nothing I can make that wouldn't be imbued with my experience as a black woman."[1]

After finishing the album *Take Me Apart*, however, she had a moment of worry—none of the songs blatantly reference her Blackness. Kelela was frustrated for a bit, but she soon realized that all that she bears is informed by that slice of herself. "It's a very black thing to be tender and vulnerable on a track. And I didn't really process that until a little bit later. It's silly to even think that there's only one way that we can express our identity."[2]

These statements by queer Ethiopian American R&B singer Kelela on the eve of the release of her debut album in 2017 highlight the vexed status of R&B music as a sign for Blackness, especially for BlackFem performers, in

---

This chapter was previously published in *The Comet—150 Years W. E. B. Du Bois: Afrofuturism 2.0*, edited by Natasha A. Kelly, 135–57 (Berlin: Orlanda Verlag, 2020).

1 Iqbal, "Kelela."
2 Starling, "Kelela Is Ready for You Now."

the contemporary moment, because pro-Black politics or wokeness is defined in such narrow terms and is usually thought to reside only in the lyrics of in Black popular music but not its sounds. Taking into consideration how the sound of R&B creates different modalities of the political renders it "silly to even think that there's only one way that we can express our identity," as Kelela herself states. But it is precisely the idea that Black identity and politics can only be articulated in one particular masculinist way that deems R&B music apolitical. Rather, Kelela brings to the fore the many ways that Black life is always already political, saying, "There's nothing I can make that wouldn't be imbued with my experience as a black woman." Nevertheless, I would also like to ask: How do the sonic tapestries and vocal calisthenics of modern R&B generate sounding sanctuaries of BlackFemness that function as provisionary political shelters, as relational restorative processes, from the traumatic storms of anti-Blackness, misogynoir, transphobia, and homophobia?

In order to better understand why Kelela felt the need to justify her neglect of explicit declarations of very specific variants of politicized Blackness, it's necessary to briefly survey R&B's history, especially its complex relationship to hip-hop. Although contemporary manifestations of R&B have imported certain masculinist tendencies from hip-hop, it still remains a BlackFem genre. While hip-hop performs Black "masculine" modes of address, R&B stages more "fem" versions of Black subjectivity and life, particularly love and sex stories without hip-hop's hardened outer shield. Moreover, R&B is the only musical category in which Black female and fem performers dominate. Modern R&B is also the popular musical field most concerned with interpersonal relationships, and while it is considered a particularly Black genre due to the racial identity of most of its performers and its fan base of Black women and Black queer men, obvious sociopolitical overtones remain a rarity.

This tendency to circumvent strictly political manifest content and the genre's "femness" might explain the absence of any sustained critical discourse about R&B (particularly when juxtaposed with the overflowing archive of hip-hop criticism), or discussions that do not reduce this genre to mere musical mirrors of Black freedom movements. According to Daphne Brooks, "Cultural critics have largely overlooked contemporary R&B—and particularly Black women's R&B—in favor of a critical privileging of other forms. Viewed as the most politically salient popular music form, hip hop is often perceived as the genre most worthy of cultural critique and political actualization. Black women's popular desire is thus depoliticized and disregarded for its reflections on domestic and socioeconomic politics and sexual fulfillment."[3]

Besides the critical orphaning of R&B music in the wake of hip-hop, Brooks's argument draws attention to the active depoliticization of the genre and its thematics, especially Black women's desire, once hip-hop comes on the scene in the 1980s. Rather than contribute to the depoliticizing of R&B music, I'm trying to understand how the BlackFem singing voice in R&B music, as a technology of Black humanity and a major site for a motley conglomerate of affective labor, has transformed over the past thirty-five years and how this interfaces with broader political currents in Black life.

Beyond its sheer beauty, which is "both sensual and abstract," R&B music functions as the soundtrack to Black everyday life under slow genocidal conditions by continually highlighting, in text and sound, the existence of Black interiorities, interpersonal relationships, vulnerability, lust, care, longing, desperation, and so on, in environments where, to paraphrase Audre Lorde, we are not supposed to exist.[4] Not only not meant to survive but also to not exist. Contemporary R&B really shines when sounding out that precarious existence through layered and polyvalent harmonies. In addition, one of the most important facets of R&B is the genre's continual tampering with the human voice, in terms of both the performer's vocal acrobatics and the technological manipulation of vocal tracks, ranging from Aretha Franklin and Mariah Carey brilliantly multitracking their voices to the extensive use of the vocoder, the talk box, and Auto-Tune. This reveals the materiality of the Black singing voice, its labor, which is usually naturalized because it springs from Black flesh, rendering the BlackFem singing voice and the interiorities it performs as a technology of humanity—technology defined in this context as the harnessing of scientific knowledge to the concrete aspirations of Black life. My aim is to understand more accurately the artistry and politics within the field of R&B music as a set of mutable and embodied cultural styles, as BlackFem technologies of humanity, which involves thinking about technology both in the sense of microphones, recording studios, live venues, MP3s, software, but also in relationship to the physiological practices of singing, the labor that's exerted, and the elaborate performative dimensions of that work.

As Farah Griffin remarks, "Let me clarify what I mean by the black woman's voice. . . . I do not mean the voice that comes out every time any black woman anywhere opens her mouth to sing. Nor do I want to imply that there is

3   Brooks, "'It's Not Right but It's Okay,'" 38.
4   Christian, "Race for Theory," 52.

something in the structure of the black diaphragm, neck, throat, and tongue, teeth, or mouth that contributes to a certain vocalization. No, I don't mean a black voice as markedly different as skin color or texture of hair. Instead I am talking of a cultural style. A particularly New World style with roots in West Africa."[5] We might understand the particular cultural styles of contemporary R&B singing as a form of "Black feminist surrogation," which Daphne Brooks describes as "an embodied cultural act that articulates Black women's distinct forms of palpable sociopolitical loss and grief as well as spirited dissent and dissonance."[6] In the era we inhabit, this loss and grief is embodied not only in the very real threat of being killed, incarcerated, and/or detained but also in the generalized trauma resulting from the endless medial circulation of Black folks dying and being violated. In *Blackness and Value: Seeing Double*, Lindon Barrett maintains that the Black voice serves as a significant symbol of value within African American culture.[7] In this sense, the Black singing voice resituates the authority of Man as the emblem for the human, instead providing through sonorous materiality and cultural style BlackFem surrogation or BlackFem technologies of humanity.

Barrett's distinction is important because in the wake of hip-hop's rise to prominence, the vocal mechanics of rapping, in contradistinction to singing, place it closer to speech and therefore to the masculine abstraction of the *signing* voice. Consequently, hip-hop becomes associated with public, politicized Blackness, while R&B comes to be heard as apolitical and functional "baby-making music," or the soundtrack to other resolutely "private" bedroom exploits. In the present, Black singing appears as "softer" and less assertive than rapping, which has now become the standard against which Black musical political expressivity is measured. To be clear, rapping is, of course, not reducible to pure speech and meaning making, especially since post-2010 hip-hop has all but erased any steadfast distinctions between singing and rapping in the post-Auto-Tune vocalizations of artists such as Future, Drake, Dej Loaf, Young Thug, Doja Cat, ILoveMakonnen, Roddy Ricch, Lil Uzi Vert, and so on. The point, however, is that contemporary R&B singing is not accorded the same reverence as these hip-hop-based vocal machina-

5 Griffin, "When Malindy Sings," 105–6. According to Nina Eidsheim, "The voice is composed of a collection of bodily organs involved in the production of sound, the acoustical conditions in which it is emitted and sensed, and the style and technique involved in its lifetime of training, what Farah Jasmine Griffin calls 'cultural style.'" Eidsheim, *Race of Sound*, 10.

6 Brooks, "'All That You Can't Leave Behind,'" 183.

7 For a more detailed consideration of Barrett's work, see track 2.0 in this volume.

tions and that by making singing and other nonrapping vocalizations the genre's new norm, hip-hop has essentially ingested and almost wholly displaced the art and labor of R&B singing both commercially and artistically. We can also hear this displacement in the frequent sampling of BlackFem R&B performers' vocal snatches by both male rappers and R&B singers, such as Bryson Tiller's use of Mariah Carey and Janet Jackson; Tory Lanez's deployment of Brownstone; Kanye West's extensive sampling and interpolation of Nina Simone's, Aretha Franklin's, Lauryn Hill's, and Chaka Khan's singing; and, last but not least, Drake's utilization of Aaliyah, Destiny's Child, Whitney Houston, and Anita Baker. This sampling is different from having female R&B singers deliver hooks, which was how hip-hop became a mainstream juggernaut in the 1990s, since male performers wield disembodied recorded BlackFem voices in order for these to undertake the affective labor that the masculine-identified voice seemingly cannot.

As Richard Iton remarks about R&B's status post-hip-hop, "Hip-hop logically, then, became linked with the preservation of masculine privilege, youth, heterosexuality, lower-income status. . . . Rhythm and blues would be seen as the locus for the formation of feminine identities, articulation of a [B]lack bourgeois sensibility."[8] And I would add that R&B has also become the space for the sonic articulation of queerness and BlackFemness. While much of this is the consequence of "mere" economics—it is cheaper for R&B singers to multitrack one voice instead of paying several group members to sing harmonies; it is less expensive for rappers to sing their own hooks instead of paying an R&B singer to do so—it also highlights the continued devaluation of R&B music as an art form, especially BlackFem creative and affective labor. Where is the appreciation for BlackFem R&B singers' sounding of the spirited labor of love and pain? I'm interested here in both the alternate modalities of the political offered by contemporary R&B music and the affective labor carried out by the BlackFem singing voice as a prime location for the productivity of the Black somatic.

I take my definition of BlackFem from Black/queer ecofeminist scholar Chelsea Frazier, who delineates this term thus:

> The purpose of using the term Black-fem . . . (as opposed to "Black woman" or "Black female," which appears much more frequently in the Black feminist intellectual tradition) is two-fold. First, it is meant to describe a variety of "affectable" Black subjectivities forged through the

8 Iton, *In Search of the Black Fantastic*, 154.

connective tissue of White, cis-heterocapitalist colonial logics. Second, the term is meant to mark the liminal spaces between the distinct (and not to be conflated) categories of Black woman, Black female, and Black (queer) femme. . . . This language critiques the assumed central subject of Black feminism—the Black (heteronormative, heterosexual, and/or homonormative) woman. Furthermore, Black-fem marks and considers the intricacies of a broader range of feminine subjectivities with which Black feminism—as a political/ecological project—must be concerned.[9]

It is precisely these "intricacies of a broader range of feminine subjectivities" as they intersect with trans and cis, nonbinary and binary, queer and hetero, female persons and male persons—among many other factors that Frazier lays out so beautifully—that I am interested in pursuing further through the aural and cultural lenses of R&B music. It is my contention that R&B music is a prime location for the public articulation and performance of an extensive archive of different forms of BlackFemness.

As a set of Black/queer identities enfleshed in different ways by both Black female and male persons as well as by a Black/queer feminist analytical concept, BlackFemness differs from Black femininity, Black womanhood, and the Black feminine because it is not defined by white cisheteropatriarchy, yet it cannot be completely disentangled from this category. Thus, BlackFem should not be construed exclusively as a singular identity but more accurately, following Frazier and others, as a critical approach, an analytic in a similar vein to the way Barbara Smith thinks about Black (lesbian) feminist analyses in her pathbreaking 1977 essay "Toward a Black Feminist Criticism," in which she reads and claims Toni Morrison's *Sula* as a lesbian text without the explicit presence of recognizably lesbian acts or identities in the novel. Analogously, I'm after a set of approaches that is not ineludibly contingent on the mimetic depiction of BlackFem persons in cultural texts; though, clearly, this doesn't mean that representations of persons on the BlackFem spectrum of a variety of genders are not important. Rather, we do well to follow Kara Keeling's lead and to imagine how the BlackFem "offers a glimpse into the range of mechanisms whereby transformations within and alternatives to existing organizations of life might be affected. . . . We apprehend the [B]lack femme as a figure that exists on the edge of the visible and the invisible, serving as a

---

9 Frazier, "Thinking Red, Wounds, and Fungi in Wangechi Mutu's EcoArt," 173.

portal through which present (im)possibilities might appear."[10] At the perilous interstices where audibility/inaudibility, imperceptibility/perceptibility, reverberate with and against each other, a BlackFem analytic unlocks the portal to a vestibular geography of different modalities of beautiful Black/queer livingness and healing. My questions: Can we conceive of BlackFemness as a series of world-shattering forms of Black/queer femininity? How can we fashion strategies/approaches/methods that would unearth and accentuate the BlackFemness of cultural texts? How do we understand the embodiment and/or performance of BlackFemness by male persons in relationship to the violence this often engenders without neglecting the privileges of maleness (not masculinity)? What would it mean to center BlackFemness rather than continuing and deepening its disregard, a disrespect often based on the ap/expropriation of BlackFem affective, physical, cultural, intellectual, and reproductive labor, in the academy and beyond? We should also note that affective labor is not merely gendered but feminized and not performed exclusively by cis women, which brings it into the purview of BlackFemness.

The performance of affective labor can be perceived most clearly in the parasitic relationship between contemporary BlackFem R&B performers and reality television. While entertainers are expected to maintain active social media presences to bring their lives closer to fans, both newer artists such as Fantasia, Jennifer Hudson, K. Michelle, and Keyshia Cole but also BlackFem R&B singers from earlier periods maintaining their careers, like Toni Braxton, SWV, Kelly Price, and Keke Wyatt, for instance, could not exist in the music industry without the narrative scaffolding of reality TV; as Michael Arceneaux shows, "It's allowed Black female singers in particular to have the sort of three-dimensional representation their labels could never provide for them."[11] These shows provide R&B singers with the drama and narrative arc seemingly necessary to appeal to present-day audiences.

According to Black gender studies scholar Brittnay Proctor's dazzling consideration of Patrice Rushen and the affective labor demanded of Black women singers:

> The [B]lack woman musician, like the [B]lack woman domestic, would become the receptacle for the production of feelings and emotions. . . . The voice of the [B]lack woman musician creates affections that cohere around the feelings and emotional capacity of others. Conflating [B]lack

10 Keeling, *Witch's Flight*, 1, 9.
11 Arceneaux, "How Reality TV Saved the R&B Star."

women's use of voice in performance with [B]lack women's natural performance of emotions, [B]lack women musicians have been trapped in the liminal understandings of what constitutes authentic [B]lack performance. The valorization of "tragedy" and "hopeless agony" is a byproduct of these trappings. Consequently, [B]lack women's intentions to feel and render their affectability sonically always run the risk of being used to maintain [B]lack women's subjection.[12]

"Conflating [B]lack women's use of voice in performance with [B]lack women's natural performance of emotions" on reality shows such as *R&B Divas*, BlackFem singers are tasked with bringing numerous stereotypes to life, often by being asked to exploit their previous experiences of violent and/or sexual trauma as well as their encounters with sex work. As a result, BlackFem subjection must be maintained as a necessary precondition for these artists' continued subsistence in the music industry. A few years ago, for instance, ex–Destiny's Child member LaTavia Roberson's labor on *R&B Divas Atlanta*, while not as "spectacular" as the violence experienced by K. Michelle or Keke Wyatt, was necessarily purely affective because she had lost her voice and thus could not sing or perform due to anxiety and depression. Rather than offering help, the show maximized the drama of Roberson's mental health issues by centering the season on her will-she-or-won't-she-sing story line. In general, these shows at least make a nominal effort at pretending to care about the music, the art these singers produce, and not only the drama and melodrama BlackFems can perform, which was clearly not the case here.[13] In this sense, Roberson's necessary refusal of the somatic work of singing is rearticulated and expropriated through the exploitative dramatization of the affective labor entailed by her inability to sing. In the absence of the pretense of music, only the performance and exploitation of Roberson's mental issues for a national TV audience remains. Overall, certain branches of reality TV would be unthinkable without BlackFem affective labor.

---

12 Proctor, "'Shout It Out,'" 4.

13 According to Racquel Gates, the structural scaffolding of reality shows such as *Love & Hip Hop* or *R&B Divas* works very hard to obscure both the labor and the cultural work that BlackFem performers contribute to these shows; she writes, "When shows like *Love & Hip Hop* largely erase their cast members' work and labor in order to highlight the melodramatic story lines instead, these women must find innovative ways to make their labor visible." Gates, *Double Negative*, 164.

However, because BlackFem R&B singing is not perceived as artful or indeed as labor, these reality shows often violently erase the differences between the singer's biography/persona and the content of their songs in much the same way as R&B biopics like *The Temptations, The Jacksons: An American Family,* or *What's Love Got to Do with It*. Nonetheless, these shows not only serve as career launchpads or boosters for a wide variety of Black-Fem R&B musicians but also focus on and bring to life the many nonstate violences perpetrated against BlackFem persons in ways seldom seen on either the small or the silver screen until very recently, in the same vein as R&B songs about intimate forms of violence, whether it's Kelly Rowland's "Dirty Laundry," Jazmine Sullivan's "Call Me Guilty," or Aaliyah's "Never No More," to name only a few examples. The problem, then, is not that these violences as well as joys and forms of sociality are represented or that these shows are enjoyed by R&B fans but that they come to wholly define the performers' personality/persona and their art beyond the reality-show tenure.

Jazmine Sullivan's marvelous 2015 album, *Reality Show,* undertakes the care work of humanizing, enfleshing the stock BlackFem figures that populate reality TV. On each song on the album, Sullivan takes on a different persona from this cosmos—most poignantly on "Mascara," which amplifies the many forms of labor that go into producing BlackFem use value in a reality television—and social media–saturated world.[14] The song's chorus maintains:

> I never leave the house without makeup on
> I keep mascara in my pocket if I'm running to the market
> 'Cause you never know who's watching you
> So I got to stay on.

BlackFemness appears as a recurring cycle of techniques that require vigilance, constant negotiation, and upkeep, which while generating worth are disparaged by the cisheteronormative world we inhabit. "Mascara" takes on the form of the character Sullivan portrays responding to her detractors, both imagined and real, as representatives of the devaluation of BlackFem labor, especially those forms of work, work, work associated with physical appearance and beauty that are deemed useless, frivolous, excessive, and not as labor at all. She responds to the haters thus:

14 Jazmine Sullivan, "Mascara," on *Reality Show,* RCA Records, 2015, CD, https://www.discogs.com/Jazmine-Sullivan-Reality-Show/release/6549750.

No, I ain't got a job, but so what?
I don't need it when I'm getting everything that I want
It's a small price to pay when you're living this good.

Of course, the narrator does, in fact, have an occupation, which is creating and conforming to traditional ideals of feminine beauty, for which she
is remunerated with a high standard of living. This verse concludes with the
following queries:

Don't I deserve to be privileged?
Don't I deserve to get the very best?

Why are these questions even necessary, because clearly she is worthy of
the best of the best and all the privilege even before she beats her face for a
simple grocery store run?

Sullivan adds to the complexity of BlackFem affective labor by centering
and sounding the labor of a specific kind of BlackFemness and also noticeably
marking the distinction between art and artist in the song so that it doesn't
"conflat[e] [B]lack women's use of voice in performance with [B]lack women's
natural performance of emotions," to echo Proctor. In order to accomplish
this, Sullivan wields her formidable powers of storytelling as a lyricist and
deploys different dimensions of her vocal instrument. In fact, Sullivan's first
hit, "Bust Your Windows," was heard as purely autobiographical, and perhaps
the *Reality Show* album is a response to this conflation of singer and song,
which represents the flip side of the assumption that BlackFem performers
do not write their own songs or are not involved in the production in any
way, that is, do not contribute in any substantive way to the material and
corporeal modes of production beyond "mere" singing.

Besides clearly differentiating her autobiography from the personalities
on *Reality Show* in the lyrical content of the songs, Sullivan uses distinctive registers of her vocal instrument to give texture to the diverse array of
characters she depicts on the album. On "Mascara" Sullivan utilizes at least
three different vocal registers and intonations that alternatingly indicate the
main figure defiantly responding to her detractors, her pacifyingly comfort-
ing herself, and her gently pleading for acceptance from the audience, for
instance, when she sings "Don't I deserve to be privileged?" Though this
versatility of her instrument is part of Sullivan's politico-musical genius, in
another way it represents an additional manifestation of the extraction of
BlackFem labor, because Sullivan is forced to develop so many techniques

in word and sound to create a sonic rift between herself as a person and the persona she is portraying on this particular track. More simply, as a BlackFem performer, Sullivan is forced to expend vast amounts of affective labor in order to establish the "artness" of her music, which, sadly, also makes for great art.

The extensive arsenal of multivocality, experimental harmonizing, and juxtaposition of different singing styles exhibited by Sullivan and others highlights how contemporary R&B has largely jettisoned the melismatic pyrotechnics that had defined the genre from the 1980s onward and that had found its apex in the overuse and deracination of melisma on *American Idol*. Of course, this is not a complete shift but nevertheless a move away from melisma as the defining characteristic of both R&B singing and the BlackFem singing voice. As a result, instead of doubling down on what had distinguished R&B from hip-hop, that R&B performers could properly sing and not just vocalize, the genre has taken a different path. That is, once the affective labor of BlackFem melismatic singing becomes deracinated and also decoupled from the practices of Black American churches (Celine Dion, Adele, etc.), Black artists, BlackFem ones in particular, devise alternative modalities of performing affect, interiority, and, of course, Blackness, which include the double-time singing pioneered by Mariah Carey on "Breakdown," the creative use of Auto-Tune, and the move toward creating oceans or sheets of harmony through the creative multitracking of BlackFem R&B singers' different vocal tracks.[15]

Overall, I argue that the use of singing and speaking voices in these ways creates different kinds of BlackFem sonic intimacies and also eschews the performance of the type of affective labor usually expected of BlackFem R&B singers, as we saw earlier with reality shows. Besides the juxtaposition of a wide variety of singing styles, vocal registers, samples, and so on, in the past few years R&B has been defined by an increased emphasis on harmonic, almost ambient, vibe-oriented singing, something akin to dub reggae techniques but for the BlackFem singing voice. Mariah (no middle name) Carey, Janet (Damita Jo) Jackson, and Brandy (Rayana Norwood) pioneered these performances within R&B by creating harmonically intersecting sheets of

15 Mariah Carey, featuring Bone Thugs-n-Harmony, "Breakdown," Columbia Records, 1997, single, https://www.discogs.com/Mariah-Carey-Featuring-Bone-Thugs-N -Harmony-Breakdown/master/138726. In the United Kingdom, because local R&B was created through the fusion with reggae music, melismatic singing was never the preferred mode of R&B singing. See L. Palmer, "'Men Cry Too.'"

vocalization that artfully blend the higher and lower registers as well as different textures of their vocal instruments.

When Carey began her career in the early 1990s, she mostly deployed the higher registers of her voice, including the whistle tone her artistry is frequently reduced to, while at the same time collaborating with singer Trey Lorenz, whose deeper, masc-sounding voice served as a harmonic backdrop for the lead fem expressing voice, which is highly unusual in any genre of pop music, where fem-sounding voices are almost always asked to play supporting roles to masc ones.[16] Carey increasingly sought out collaborations with rappers including Ol' Dirty Bastard, Busta Rhymes, Bone Thugs-n-Harmony, and Da Brat that provided counterparts to the higher registers of her vocalizing, and then, beginning with tracks such as 1997's "Breakdown" and "Fourth of July," Carey by and large uses the lower registers of her own voice instead of relying exclusively on male singers or rappers to create this effect of harmonically overlapping planes of vocalization that combine the higher and lower registers of Carey's vocal instrument.

Analogously, Janet Jackson's "Love Will Never Do (Without You)" (1989) rotates between her higher, fem-sounding and lower, masc-sounding voices in a seamless fashion.[17] There are a few other examples of contemporary R&B musicians using their voices in similar ways, especially when it involves queer desire, as in the case of masculine-presenting Black/queer singer Tiffany Gouché switching the registers of her beguiling voice to entice her potential female lovers or Majid Jordan's singer deploying his androgynous falsetto to tell his original heartthrob:

I can't take making love to anyone but you
You make my body erupt
I can't take waking up to anyone but you.[18]

16 I use *masc* in a similar fashion to *fem* in order to amplify the nonessential, performative aspects of the Black singing voice and also to route the analysis of masculinity through a Black/queer lens.

17 Janet Jackson, "Love Will Never Do (Without You)," A&M Records, 1989, CD single, https://www.discogs.com/Janet-Jackson-Love-Will-Never-Do-Without-You/master/92696. We can hear precursors of this vocal alternating even earlier in Jackson's 1986 collaborations with Jimmy Jam and Terry Lewis, on "Nasty" or "Control," for instance, where Jackson switches back and forth between a clipped form of rhythmic vocalization in the verses and choruses but wields more melodic and upper registers of her voice during the bridges.

18 Majid Jordan, "OG Heartthrob," on *The Space Between*, OVO Sound, 2017, MP3, https://www.discogs.com/Majid-Jordan-The-Space-Between/release/15955897.

We could even go back to the way Ruth Pointer shifts from her alto to an even lower register on "Automatic" (1984) to intimate the robotic response she has to her love object. Of course, queerness and same-sex desire in R&B are nothing new if you consider Carl Bean's "I Was Born This Way," The Miracles' "Ain't No One Straight in LA," Barbara Mason's "Another Man," and the response by Tout Sweet, "Another Man Is Twice as Nice" (see track 10.0), SZA saying on "Love Galore" that she's dated a few ladies (see track 0.0), or the oeuvres of Meshell Ndegeocello, Rachid, Kehlani, Moses Sumney, TheeSatisfaction, Serpentwithfeet, Janelle Monáe, Rahsaan Patterson, Syd, MNEK, Amanda Perez, Tevin Campbell, Sylvester, Durand Bernarr, and Jackie Shane, among others, all openly queer/trans performers who to varying degrees address sexual identities and same-sex lovers in their lyrics.

In addition, Jackson's *The Velvet Rope* (1997), with its underscoring of quiet interiority, queerness, depression, sexual abuse and trauma, bondage, vulnerability, the AIDS crisis, and so on, especially coming from such a superstar, most definitely broadened the horizon of what was possible within R&B both lyrically and vocally, while also serving as a template for later artists such as Kelela. Released the same year as *The Velvet Rope*, Mariah Carey's *Butterfly* (1997) also saw another BlackFem superstar experiment with her vocal styles and turn inward lyrically by, albeit obliquely, addressing the abuse Carey had undergone during her marriage to Tommy Mottola, who was not only twice her age but also the head of her record company. Another precursor to contemporary R&B singing styles and the enactment of vulnerable interiorities, which was released during the same twelve-month span as Jackson's and Carey's albums, appears in the watery imaginary and dub-inspired immersive R&B of Maxwell's album *Embrya* (1998), which explicitly embraces BlackFemness in the form of a watery, embryonic world of love and sensuality.[19] Besides these three albums, that year also saw the release of Brandy's *Never Say Never* (1998), which, while not thematically drinking from the same fountain as the other three, nevertheless serves as a model for the type of nonmelismatic R&B singing that has now become the norm in the genre. The shift from the externalized grandeur of melisma to the overlapping, concentric circles of harmonic folds suggests BlackFem forms of affective labor—in line with Kelela's comments about the politics of Black vulnerability at the beginning of this track—that turn inward rather than outward to perform interiority and vulnerability rather than unmitigated

19 Maxwell's album partakes in what Jared Richardson refers to as the "Black queer aquatic." See Richardson, "Black Organs and Optics."

strength and resilience: R&B becomes the repository for BlackFem vulnerability by undertaking the labor of sounding a wide variety of interiorities and intimacies that are necessary for the existence of the "properly political," especially in the present moment. They suggest BlackFem technologies of humanity that emphasize care and healing.

On his 2016 albums, *Endless* and *Blonde*, Frank Ocean presents so many different vocal inflections, techniques, and technological modifications, ranging from not-quite-everyday speech to quasi rapping, to sampling, to several different forms of R&B singing styles, to what sounds like classic Broadway show tunes, that listeners can veritably feel his quest create new musical languages through the aural prism of R&B while also attempting to leave behind the strictures of hegemonic masculinity.[20] And while my description might render Ocean's work as an almost random, unappealing grab bag of styles and approaches, it succeeds because the results sound both unmistakably like Frank Ocean and incontrovertibly Black via the conduit of R&B as a BlackFem technology of humanity. Instead of heightened drama and ostentatious, sweeping emotions, Ocean gives us stream-of-consciousness, conversational reminiscences, pop culture references, and quotidian observational R&B. This can be heard beautifully, on *Endless* in the sequencing from "U-N-I-T-Y," wherein he switches from an almost-rapping rhythmic intonation to traditional R&B singing, which then gives way to a sample of legendary Black drag queen and ballroom culture originator Crystal LaBeija from the 1967 documentary *The Queen*.[21] The LaBeija sample is followed by the song "Comme des Garçons," which sounds akin to a lilting, lopsided show tune.

We can hear the vulnerability in the intricately imbricated strata of choruses on Kelela's declaration to a lover that, though long powerless in the face of their seductive charms and after many stops and starts, she has finally had "Enough." Instead of using loudness and aggression in her vocal performance, Kelela sonically signals her vulnerability through restrained softness, and the intensity doesn't come from strength of volume but from how the different vocal tracks gently but audibly augment and interrupt each other, creating a soothing and immersive but not frictionless bath of sound. Another prominent example of this trend, though perhaps not as personal and idiosyncratic,

20 Frank Ocean, *Blonde*, Boys Don't Cry, 2016, CD; and Frank Ocean, *Endless*, Boys Don't Cry, 2016, MP3, https://www.discogs.com/Frank-Ocean-Endless/master /1077026.

21 On LaBeija's act of Afro-fabulation in this film, see Nyong'o, *Afro-Fabulations*, 1–5.

is Rihanna's 2016 album, *Anti*, or the way SZA uses samples of her mother and grandmother doling out advice throughout her 2017 album *Ctrl* to highlight the BlackFem traditions of knowledge and care she draws on in her songs. On the whole, I argue that the use of singing and speaking voices in these ways creates different kinds of BlackFem sonic intimacies and vulnerabilities, while at the same time eschewing the performance of the type of hyperemotive and over-the-top affective labor usually expected of BlackFem R&B singers.

I want to now draw on a few examples from the archive of contemporary R&B that explicitly address the violent precarity of Black lives and the resulting experience of trauma. The first is a song by Toronto-based Somali Canadian singer Amaal Nuux, who forms a part of, on the one hand, the long history of Black Canadian R&B artists that includes Tamia, Bass is Base, Deborah Cox, The Weeknd, Melanie Fiona, Miquel Brown, Glenn Lewis, PartyNextDoor, Divine Brown, Denise Katrina Matthews aka Vanity of Vanity 6, and Salome Bey, and, on the other hand, current Somali-Canadian hip-hop and indie artists like Cold Specks, Robin Banks, and Layla Hendryx who deftly negotiate between and betwixt gendered variants of Canadianness, Blackness, and diasporic Somaliness in their music and public personas. Amaal's closest international analogue might be Cherrie, the tremendously successful Swedish Somali R&B singer, whose music is presented in her native Swedish language but still sounds distinctly R&B and unmistakably Black.

In Amaal Nuux's 2017 single "Scream," the brilliant fusion of the political and the intimate, the bedroom is rendered uncomplicated by virtue of not being the streets on which Black people are wantonly killed by state and non-state agents and on which Black people protest the fundamental disregard for Black life. For Nuux BlackFem intimacy cannot be separated from what goes on in public and is in and of itself a form protest and healing:

Everywhere but here is complicated
But right now it's simple in my mind
Bed sheets on your skin my focus is isolated
Let's lock this door from the inside
Nobody gon' tell me what to do when it comes to you
Scream my name
Like a protest
Like a protest
I wanna hear you say my name.[22]

22 Amaal Nuux, "Scream," Public Records/Universal Music Canada, 2017, MP3.

In fact, besides bedsheets, skin, and locking the door from the inside, there's not much description of the affects and sensations associated with intimacy (scream my name like a protest, my kind of statement, rattling cages, etc.). In stark contrast to many other invocations of "Black Love" in R&B and beyond, which portray cisheterosexual coupling among "respectable" Black folks as a politics of uplift in and of itself, Amaal presents an unusual discourse in which these sensual acts are positioned in direct relation to the street protests via the conduit of analogy. Just as immersion in music has been shown to contribute to neurological and psychic healing and repair, especially in the aftermath of trauma, here the anger and hurt about having to protest for the mattering of Black lives is rechanneled through the agency afforded by "Nobody gon' tell me what to do when it comes to you." An agency in the "private" sphere that is perhaps compounded by the dangers associated with street protests for young Black Muslim women such as Nuux in Toronto and other places. Amaal has also spoken about how challenging it has been for her, coming from a religious background, to publicly sing about sex, lust, and intimacy.[23]

The chorus of the song itself makes this continuum palpable, because Nuux's insistence that her lover say her name echoes numerous R&B songs that employ this particular trope, the most well known being Destiny's Child's "Say My Name," but additionally in the post–Black Lives Matter political climate conjures also the hashtag #SayHerName and associated forms of activism that specifically address the many ways Black female persons are affected by state violence, which is rendered invisible by the still very much present focus on cishet Black male persons.[24] Thus, Nuux's song brings the street to the bedroom while at same time draping the purportedly private and apolitical boudoir linens all over the street signs in your neighborhood so that the rally not only serves to draw attention to the killing of specific Black persons and to demand abolishing police brutality, the police, and all carceral apparatuses attached to it but is also about transfiguring the avenue and the bedroom into a series of possibilities for a different world. We should also never underestimate how much the immersion in music contributes to neurological healing and repair, especially in the aftermath of trauma.[25]

23 Rayner, "Toronto's Somali Muslim R&B Singer Amaal."
24 Destiny's Child, "Say My Name," Columbia Records, 2000, CD single, https://www.discogs.com/Destinys-Child-Say-My-Name/release/1440586.
25 Sacks, *Musicophilia*; Levitin, *This Is Your Brain on Music*; and Patel, *Music, Language, and the Brain*.

Amaal's 2019 video "Later," based on her personal experience, is largely set on a FEAT bus, taking women and children from Toronto to visit their incarcerated loved ones in prison in Kingston, Ontario.[26] In fact, during the final frames Amaal dedicates the video to this program that provides services for the loved ones of those incarcerated. Along the way we witness a moment of elation and intimacy in a gas station bathroom, where the women change into nicer clothes, refresh their makeup, and dance. This continues on the bus during the last leg of their journey when the women continue to help each other get ready.[27] As with "Scream," Amaal refuses to disentangle the personal and the structural by stressing how carceral systems shape and curtail her romantic relationship but also provide the basis for BlackFem pleasure and intimacy with the other women on the bus, signaling possibilities in which Blackness is not completely engulfed by the necrocarcerality. Both the song and music video for Blood Orange's (Devonté Hynes) "Sandra's Smile" (2015) offer a decidedly BlackFem perspective on the mattering of Black lives, with the song lyrics commemorating victim of police killing Sandra Bland, who in death smiles on almost every image available of her on the internet, and Sybrina Fulton, Trayvon Martin's mother, whose words are referenced in the following lines:

I mean, why should she forgive?
Do we lose you if we don't?[28]

26 Amaal Nuux, "Later," on *Black Dove*, Public Records/Universal Music Canada, 2019, MP3; see the YouTube video, accessed February 15, 2023, https://www .youtube.com/watch?v=OmHftkSAQEw.
27 About the video Amaal writes:

My latest video [for 'Later'] is the one that I am most proud of. It's the most real because it's about a situation that I actually went through, and it's telling that story in the most raw way. It's about me being in a relationship with somebody who was incarcerated, and I was being the loving girl, visiting him every single weekend. There was a bus—only one in Canada—that's dedicated to taking children and women to go see their loved ones. It's a true story, and the bus that I would take, we were able to contact [the company] and have them involved. It's dedicated to them and the work they've done.

Taylor, "Amaal Nuux Is the Toronto R&B Artist You Need to Know."
28 Blood Orange, "Sandra's Smile," on *Freetown Sound*, Domino Records, 2016, CD, https://www.discogs.com/Blood-Orange-Freetown-Sound/release/8912995; see also the YouTube video, accessed February 15, 2023, https://www.youtube.com /watch?v=GLPsk89aUKw.

Hynes does not so much scream Sandra Bland's name like a protest as tenderly croon her name and affectionately conjure her smile. Like Kelela, neither Hynes nor Amaal deploys stereotypically masculine aggressive styles of address but rather mellifluous, delicate forms of singing and vocalization in their quest to chant down Babylon, which is important to understanding these BlackFem instantiations of political analysis and modes of resistance and the shifting landscapes of contemporary R&B vocal styles more broadly.

To fully understand contemporary R&B singing is to bear witness to another's wound, which leads to an encounter with one's own trauma. Hynes views, listens to, and channels Sandra Bland's and Sybrina Fulton's injuries, which index the particular perilous status of BlackFem lives in the present, putting these in relation to his own precarity. The black-and-white video shines a spotlight on the reclamation of the street despite the dangers this harbors for BlackFem persons but also conjures the significance of communal rhythmic vocalization in the Movement for Black Lives and in earlier Black freedom movements. As forms of "marronage theorizing" about trauma, which are "less about keeping time or score and more about inculcating meanings into life," to use Joy James's phrasing, Amaal and Hynes offer intersubjective qua relational witnessing of trauma and rhythmically chanted retorts to the repeated and generalized traumatization so as to contribute to the mundane, quotidian survival and healing of BlackFem persons on the street and in the bedroom.[29]

Much of my thinking about these questions was inspired not only by the R&B music I've been discussing but also by a final student project for one of my courses in the fall of 2017. We had read June Jordan, Audre Lorde, and Alice Walker, among many others, and had in-depth discussions about which parts of one's personality, cultural background, home language, affective and bodily demeanors, and so on have to be brutally suppressed in order to exist within "elite" university spaces. Informed by Harriet's Apothecary in Brooklyn, whose tagline is "Resistance Recipes: Black Resilience in the Face of Bullshit," on the last day of the term the students collectively transformed the classroom into a Black/queer healing space, which consisted of seven different stations spread across the room that included diary writing, beauty, painting, photography, DJing, basketball, and jewelry making, representing each individual student's particular modality for healing. Additionally, there was dancing, food, laughter, decorations, special lighting, a twerking contest, a spirited performance of SZA's "Supermodel" by one of the students, and an awkward yet joyful impromptu communal improvisatory composition of a

29 J. James, "Political Trauma," 349, 352.

song. The "outside" world and the killing of Black folks, of course, did not vanish during those ninety minutes, nor did the seemingly less violent acts perpetrated in the academy under the guise of standards, professionalization, collegiality, scholarly rigor, disciplinarity, publication metrics, and so on. Nevertheless, restorative and ameliorative forms of healing and knowledge production transpired and materialized in that transient space, which puts it in line with contemporary Black/queer and Black feminist activism's attunement to interiority, care, mental health, restorative justice, and healing as integral parts of political action but also as imperative for enabling scholarly work and existing in university structures.

I should note that my invocation of healing is never tidy, discrete, or complete but a series of ongoing, often opaque and fragmentary, deeply relational processes that most likely do not have end points. Current R&B music exemplifies an important part of repairing and rewiring neurological pathways and physiological triggers in the face of ongoing and sustained low-level and high-level trauma. Among many other things, the temporary Black/queer healing terrain the students created and the BlackFem technologies of humanity in contemporary R&B music teach me daily to remain vigilant about the deep and constitutive entanglements between the interpersonal, affective, interior, and intimate, on the one hand, and the capital *P* political and knowledge production, on the other, while also not forgetting that change, thought, an-archic formations, and insurgency begin in one's immediate surrounding, whether this is the bedroom, the street, the classroom, the prison, the faculty lounge, or the subway car.

Similarly, the BlackFem technologies of humanity in contemporary R&B music amplify restorative and ameliorative forms of healing and knowledge production, putting them in line with contemporary Black/queer and Black feminist activism's attunement to interiority, care, mental health, restorative justice, and healing as integral parts of the political. They also, to summon Kara Keeling again, provide "a [BlackFem] portal through which present (im)possibilities might appear," that emotionally charged aperture defined by the unfathomable depth of expertly engineered overlapping vocal tracks that make it impossible to differentiate between "I can't breathe" and "waiting to exhale," because they tenderly but unyieldingly purr the following hymn:

Shoop, Shoop, Shoop. Shoop be doop, shoop, shoop.[30]

30 Whitney Houston, "Exhale (Shoop Shoop)," Arista Records, 1995, CD, https://www
    .discogs.com/Whitney-Houston-Exhale-Shoop-Shoop/release/1623575.

It wasn't until fairly late into putting together this volume that I realized that tracks 2.0, 3.0, and 9.0 were not intimately linked only in their content, because I had forgotten or, much more likely, repressed the contextual connective tissue that lurks in the shadows of how these pieces manifest on the page.

SCENE 1: I presented an early version of what became track 3.0 circa 2010 to a working group session closed to the public that consisted of about ten scholars from different disciplines working on different aspects of the voice. The assembled academics included one person who had been in the audience in the spring of 2000 when I publicly lectured about what would later become my essay "'Feenin'" (and here track 2.0) for the first and only time. During the Q&A after my presentation at the 2010 working group meeting, with no forewarning, the scholar who had attended my talk in the spring of 2000 played snippets of a recording of my voice that he had made without my consent during my just-concluded lecture. As if that itself were not intrusive enough, he had also used the then-trendy Songify app by Smule to distort and "songify" sections of my talk so that the recording sounded like I was singing my ideas through Auto-Tune.[1] And, yes, of course, he *was*, just as, naturally, I was the only Black person there. To be frank, I really struggle to remember very much of what transpired after the incident, except being in a state of shock and going into deep disassociation mode. *Microaggression* seems quaint when it clashes with the violence of the furtive recording and the public playing of my distorted and "songified" sentences sans either my previous knowledge or prior permission, especially if you add to this the obdurate quietness that greeted this act, with none of the other folks there addressing the proverbial elephant in the room, and the fact that this person and I were expected to occupy the same space for the next day and a half.

1 Wikipedia, s.v. "Songify the News," March 27, 2022, https://en.wikipedia.org/wiki /Songify_the_News.

As if to corroborate just how deeply Auto-Tune suffused the US cultural imaginary around 2010, the Songify app by Smule became all the rage via the YouTube show *Auto-Tune the News*, especially the "Bed Intruder Song," featuring Black gay man Antoine Dodson, who had become a viral sensation through a newscast of him speaking about the attempted sexual assault on his sister, Kelly Dodson, on a local Huntsville, Alabama, news station in 2010.[2] Dodson's exalted BlackFemness became meme fodder for various social media networks and was featured extensively on *Auto-Tune the News*, which then led to the creation of the Billboard-charting "Bed Intruder Song" in collaboration with the white musicians the Gregory Brothers.[3] Though set in motion by a violent event—the testimony about the invasion of his home and the attempted rape of his sister, Kelly Dodson—virtually all of the viral memes focused on Antoine Dodson, while also "comically" deriding his BlackFem, southern, working-class mannerisms and speech patterns. While I would have enthusiastically celebrated many other scenarios that placed me in proximity to Antoine Dodson, auto-tuned or not, the use of the Songify app by the colleague was far from innocuous given the racialized and gendered baggage the then fairly fresh technologies (Songify and Auto-Tune) had already amassed. *No technology is neutral!*[4]

SCENE 2: Cut to December 2016, when Katherine McKittrick and I were presenting papers at the same academic gathering; although we had known each other for quite some time, this was where we first spoke about a potential collaboration. The writerly cooperation between the two of us materialized very quickly and over the course of the first half of 2017 transmuted into what is now track 9.0. Katherine and I began work on the piece in January 2017 and after much diligent labor on both of our parts submitted the final manuscript in August of that year. At this 2016 conference, someone mentioned that the professor who had taped and songified me without my knowledge or consent in 2010 had just taken up the position of dean of the humanities at the university where the event was being held. The person revealed this information without any prior knowledge of what had happened in 2010; they were simply speaking in passing about the new dean at their institution. I had long forgotten about this incident and don't recollect

<hr>

2 Antoine Dodson and The Gregory Brothers, *Bed Intruder Song*, Gregory Residence, 2010, MP3, https://www.discogs.com/release/5831667-Antoine-Dodson
   -The-Gregory-Brothers-Bed-Intruder-Song.
3 See Peoples, "Forgotten Kelly Dodson."
4 Brand, *No Language Is Neutral*.

relaying this information to anyone after it occurred, but hearing the name of the professor-turned-dean quickly brought back the anger I had felt in 2010. Dearest of readers, if you're anticipating a broader thematic climax or a big splashy crescendo with a succinct teleological end point, I'm terribly sorry to disappoint: instead, as so often, there's simply living on, living with. What happened at that scholarly gathering in 2010 seemed crueler and more invasive precisely because of my strong love for both Auto-Tune and Antoine Dodson. In the end, this story, my story, should not be reduced to a mere aggressive faux pas committed by the professor-turned-dean but construed as an index of the broader academic structures we labor under, which are often coercive, expropriative, and exploitative and which almost always work in not-so-subtly racialized, gendered, and sexualized ways; it's just that these assemblages don't always reveal themselves so unambiguously. Seeing that so much of *Feenin* is devotedly steeped in the praxes of collaboration and dialogue in the form of responses, interviews, and coauthorship, the "Songify incident" underscores the exact obverse of this cooperative spirit and its attendant methodologies based on other ways of thinking, interacting, conversating, and collaborating.[5] And, yes, I still harbor strong affirmative feelings for and ideas about both Antoine Dodson and the audible use of Auto-Tune in Black music.

5   On nonexpropriative and cooperative methodologies as constitutive of Black studies, see McKittrick, *Dear Science and Other Stories.*

TRACK 9.0

808S AND HEARTBREAK

Alexander Ghedi Weheliye and Katherine McKittrick

In an article about the Roland TR-808, discontinued by Roland in 1984, Kurt Werner, Jonathan Abel, and Julius Smith III write that the drum machine was "considered somewhat of a flop—despite significant voice design innovations, disappointing sales and a lukewarm critical reception seemed

This chapter was first published online in *Propter Nos* 2, no. 1 (Fall 2017), https://trueleappress.files.wordpress.com/2017/10/propter-nos-2-12.pdf.

Heading source: "This Is Why You and I and We Dance. We'll Go Out to the Floor" is from Kanye West, "Paranoid," on *808s and Heartbreak*, Roc-A-Fella Records, 2008, CD, https://www.discogs.com/release/1617049-Kanye-West-808s-Heartbreak.

clear indicators that digitally-sampled drum machines were the future."[1] Centralizing an analysis of the circuits, subcircuits, and software of the Roland TR-808, the authors suggest that since its discontinuation there has been an inability to digitally replicate the analog sounds of the Roland TR-808. The authors take the machine apart, break it up, and think about inabilities, noting that misinformation and misconceptions about the sound, the beats, the bass of the original 808s has led to the inability to emulate it.[2] They find remnants of Ace Tone's 1964 R1 Rhythm Ace. They write, "A bass drum note is produced when the μPD650C-085 CPU applies a common trigger and (logic high) instrument data to the trigger logic."[3] They pay close attention to the circuit behavior of the 808. They emulate.

The authors dive into the mechanical circuitry and deep beats and bass of the Roland TR-808 drum machine but say little about its significance for the musical, sonic, and textural sciences that are imagined alongside the unit. We thus consider the insights developed in "A Physically-Informed, Circuit-Bendable, Digital Model of the Roland TR-808 Bass Drum Circuit" and overlay them with the mathematics of Black life, in order to think through the mechanics of emulation with and outside of itself. This is especially meaningful since a "lack of interest drove second-hand prices [for the TR-808] down and made it an attractive source of beats for techno and hip-hop producers."[4] Emulation, in this sense, honors Black creative labor and invention, the boom-bap-blonk-clap of 808s, as diasporic literacy, yet also understands this work as a series of inaccurate repetitions that disclose the awful, the hurtful, and the intrusive.[5] Emulations, like 808s, are injuriously loving. We situate the 808s as one of many enunciations of Black studies,

---

1   K. Werner, Abel, and Smith, "Physically-Informed, Circuit-Bendable, Digital Model." On April 1, 2017, in the midst of the writing of this piece, Ikutaro Kakehashi, founder of the Roland Corporation and Ace Electronic Industries, died. Kakehashi developed the Roland TR-808, the Roland CR-78, MIDI (Musical Instrument Digital Interface), and many other instrument technologies, including the R1 Rhythm Ace, which, in part, underlies the TR-808.

2   K. Werner, Abel, and Smith, "Physically-Informed, Circuit-Bendable, Digital Model," 1.

3   K. Werner, Abel, and Smith, "Physically-Informed, Circuit-Bendable, Digital Model," 2.

4   K. Werner, Abel, and Smith, "Physically-Informed, Circuit-Bendable, Digital Model," 1.

5   Clark, "Developing Diaspora Literacy."

as heavy waves and vibrations that intersect with and interrupt Black life discursively and physiologically, as heartbreak. Heartbreak captures, at least a little, those injuriously loving emulations of what it means to be Black and human within the context of white supremacy. Heartbreak works with and in excess of the bio-mythological heart, the hollow muscular organ and its narratives of affectively variegated tenderness and loss. Heartbreak represents the reverberating echoes of our collective plantocratic historical pasts in the present. Heartbreak elucidates how the violence of racial capitalism inaccurately reproduces Black life. Heartbreak bursts apart. Heartbreak is feeling outside of oneself. Heartbreak is the demand to feel outside of one's individuated self. Heart/////break cannot be recuperated. Heartbreak fails the heartbroken. Heartbreak waits. It sounds. It envelops us like the thumping bass of the TR-808. Heartbreak cannot be repaired or resisted. It emulates but defies emulation.

Boom

Before house and techno musics, before hip-hop, before Miami bass, before electro, I hear and feel R&B group Blaque's 1999 song "808."[6] Before getting to the song's historical significance, I want to emphasize how the track's music and lyrics amplify the pleasure and joy of feeling the thump of the 808 machine, of sensing its meta/physical reverberations around and through the flesh:

'Cause I'll be goin' boom like an 808
Be makin' circles like a figure 8
You know it feels good from head to toe
Now hold on to me baby here we go
You'll be goin' boom baby boom baby boom
And I'll be goin' ooh baby ooh baby ooh
(check it out)

Blaque's song encodes the flesh memory of the innumerable hours I've spent listening to music made with the TR-808 in clubs, in living rooms, on headphones while walking, hearing/feeling the 808s boom from passing cars, and so on, and the sheer enjoyment derived from it in a way that is difficult to cordon off into words on the page. Blaque's song achieves this feat by

6 Blaque, "808," Columbia Records, 1999, CD maxi-single, https://www.discogs.com /release/6214917-Blaque-808.

analizing the fleshy neural feelings set off by the boom of the 808, because "it feels good from head to toe," and the internal neuro-viscous reward system derived from love and sex. By conjuring the power of Blaque's superlative skills at moving their audience, the song also imagines a different kind of physical sensation:

See what I believe is
We was granted the power
What's that? Power, wha . . .
Ha, the power to make you dance
Like this

Like this? Like what, though? Like . . . wo? Like a Sssshhhh?[7]

Love and sex are always knotted to broken hearts, because the throb of feeling good, from dome to foot, has a painful musicological history. The heart (muscle) and its narratives of loss and tenderness—tender losses—move to, stop with, pause on, slide across the boom of racial-sexual violence. Heartbreak, then, is always already part of the 808's Black circuitry, boomingly amplifying joy and pain, sunshine and rain.[8] The thump, the boom, creates shivering circuits of pleasure laced with damage, loss, sorrow.

"808" was written by Robert Sylvester Kelly, who preyed on young Black girls from Chicago's South Side and secretly married his protégé Aaliyah Dana Haughton when she was a teenager. The members of Blaque were very young when this song was released, the youngest member only sixteen. While Kelly appears in the music video for "808," it is not clear how much interaction occurred between him and the members of Blaque. The bitter irony of Kelly's predatory ways is that as an artist, he has been extremely adept at writing songs from "female perspectives"—for example, his duet with Sparkle, "Be Careful"; Nivea's "Laundromat"; several songs for the Chang-

7 Kelly Rowland, featuring Eve, "Like This," Columbia Records, 2007, CD single, https://www.discogs.com/Kelly-Rowland-Featuring-Eve-Like-This/release /4750638; Mýa, "My Love Is Like . . . Wo," A&M Records, 2003, CD single, https:// www.discogs.com/Mýa-My-Love-Is-Like-Wo/release/3837497; and Somethin' for the People, featuring Trina & Tamara, "My Love Is the Shhh!," Warner Brothers Records, 1997, CD single, https://www.discogs.com/Somethin-For-The-People -Featuring-Trina-Tamara-My-Love-Is-The-Shhh/release/636617.
8 Maze, featuring Frankie Beverly, "Joy & Pain," Capitol Records, 1981, single, https://www.discogs.com/Maze-Featuring-Frankie-Beverly-Joy-Pain/release /1206998.

ing Faces; or his own "When a Woman's Fed Up."[9] How does being a sexual predator who referred to himself as the pied piper of R&B correlate with Kelly's adeptness for writing songs for Black women performers?[10] Rather than thinking that this cross-gender grokking is something that supersedes or mitigates Kelly's predation, we want to insist that this tendency contributes to his continued violation and sexual assault of numerous Black women and girls. It is tantamount to not shushing the many different forms of violation in this context, since they represent the structural conditions of possibility for sexual violence but also remain significant in their own "right," even while they are too often drowned out by the focus on the physical aspects of violence, sexual and otherwise. What structures and repertoires must be in place in order for acts of sexual violence to occur, and what acts of violation (of trust, of corporeal boundaries, of confidence, and so on) precede physical/sexual violence?[11] What modes of violation follow the brutalizations, for instance, when family members and friends refuse to believe victims, or when state apparatuses vilify and criminalize survivors? Where do broken hearts go? They probably cannot find their way home.[12] "For Black girls, home is both refuge and where your most intimate betrayals happen. You cannot turn off that setting. It is the dining room at your family's house, served with a side of your uncle's famous ribs. Home is where they love you until you're a ho."[13]

Kelly's musical ability for cross-gender identification feeds into and cannot be disentangled from his predatory actions. It is not per chance that Kelly would often prey on young girls after Lena Mae McLin's gospel choir classes at Kenwood Academy in Chicago, his alma mater, playing the role of musical

9   Sparkle's niece was one of the first girls to accuse Kelly of sexual abuse, and Sparkle later testified against Kelly during his 2008 trial on child pornography charges.
10   Kelly's recorded output contains just as many, if not more, misogynist entries, for instance, "Feeling on Yo Booty" or "Feels Like You're Ready." On R. Kelly as pied piper and the pied piper legend, see Heath, "Why R. Kelly Calls Himself 'the Pied Piper of R&B.'"
11   Beth Richie shows how intimate households, communities, and the state often work in concert to create a "violence matrix," which consists of "physical assaults against women," different forms of "sexual aggression," and emotional exploitation. Richie, *Arrested Justice*, 132–33.
12   Whitney Houston, "Where Do Broken Hearts Go," Arista Records, 1988, single, https://www.discogs.com/Whitney-Houston-Where-Do-Broken-Hearts-Go/release/12416260.
13   Cottom, "How We Make Black Girls Grow Up Too Fast." See also DeRogatis, "Parents Told Police Their Daughter Is Being Held."

mentor in order to gain favor and groom his victims.[14] This raises the general question we are uncomfortably left with: In what ways do desire, sexuality, violence, and ungendering coexist in (Black) life and in relationship to the TR-808? Kelly's oeuvre also includes several cuts besides "808" that deploy machinery and technology within the context of love and sexuality ("You Remind Me of a Jeep," "Ignition," etc.) that extend the tradition of sex machines or feeling computer blue, because there must be something wrong with the machinery.[15] Considering that Kelly, like many other Black celebrities, claims that he himself was a victim of sexual violence, are there ways to think about racism as being engulfed by not only increased "group-differentiated vulnerabilities to premature death" but also the extreme susceptibility to many different forms of sexual violence and violation?[16] Perhaps not being able to elude sexual violence is the ghost in the machine of this particular version of kinship, to emulate Saidiya Hartman's memorable aphorism.[17]

What if the kind of heartbreak Kelly violently enacted cannot be resisted or repaired? What if it just settles in, awful, hurtful, and intrusive? Receding at certain moments, like the driving away of a car with an elaborate booming system, only to abruptly reappear at the most inopportune situations, its reverberations shaking you up to the core when you least expect it. What do we do with that? Can the 808s and the mechanics of the deep boom signal—at least in a small way—something else? This is sexual violence writ large. This is violence that is purposefully enacted within the context of long-standing intelligible plantocratic logics, where multiple affective and structural registers of Black love are always dragged through and into and across the sexual trauma of racial capitalism. I don't want this. We don't want this. Can the 808s and the mechanics of the deep boom signal something else without losing the messed-up vicious stagnancy of the predation (or the sinister twin practice of forgetting and/or excusing the violence in the name of either art/ musical genius or racial solidarity)? Perhaps this is where we learn, at least momentarily, that Black life and love are not something you can have but

14 Hopper, "Read the 'Stomach-Churning' Sexual Assault Accusations."
15 Prince and The Revolution, "Computer Blue," on *Purple Rain*, Warner Brothers Records, 1984, LP, https://www.discogs.com/release/125874-Prince-And-The -Revolution-Purple-Rain.
16 Heath, "Confessions of R. Kelly"; and Gilmore, "Race and Globalization," 261. See also Richie, *Arrested Justice*.
17 "Slaves were the ghosts in the machine of kinship." Hartman, *Lose Your Mother*, 139.

something you do and can never get.[18] Perhaps that which is awful and hurtful and intrusive, as unresisted heartbreak, should stand alone (un-flee-able), in plain sight and as negative affect, with the difficult knowledge that the act of naming violence does not engender the kind of reparation sexual violence requires, particularly if we take into account the countless acts of violation that precede, accompany, and follow sexual violence. Thus, predation represents a brutality in itself, unrepaired, intelligibly negative, and with a booming soundtrack—even in the unspeakability . . . like a ssshhh. How do we, who watch this and narrate this and hear this and live this, come to terms with the irreparable? Coming to terms with the unrecoupable means, above all else, having to exist with it and necessarily going on living. What cannot not be possessed does not follow the laws of redemption; instead, it lingers as living in and with the afterlife of the TR-808's sonorous echo. Living in and with. Something you do and can never possess.

Blaque have stated that their name is an acronym for *Believing in Life and Achieving a Quest for Unity in Everything.* Blaque member Natina Reed was killed when a car hit her as she was crossing the street on October 26, 2012.[19] In addition, the group was mentored by Lisa "Left Eye" Lopes, who was tragically killed in a car accident in 2002 and who had set her boyfriend's Atlanta mansion on fire in 1994 after a violent dispute, which had its basis in Lopes's heartbreak.[20] Is it possible to believe in (Black) life when surrounded by death and violence? Blaque are now also signifiers for the disappearance of R&B singing groups, or the last great flowering of R&B singing groups at the turn of the millennium (Destiny's Child, 3LW, 702, B2K, 112, and more—many with abbreviated band names wherein the numbers signify a particular history, place, or identity). While much of this is the consequence of "simple" economics—it is cheaper for R&B singers to multitrack one voice instead of paying several group members to sing harmonies; it is less expensive for rappers sing their own hooks through Auto-Tune rather than paying an R&B singer to do so—it also highlights the continued devaluation of R&B music

---

18 McKittrick, "Fantastic/Still/Life," 28. En Vogue, "My Lovin' (You're Never Gonna Get It)," on *Funky Divas*, EastWest Records, 1992, CD, http://www.discogs.com/En-Vogue-Funky-Divas/release/8869669.
19 Dinh, "Blaque's Natina Reed Killed."
20 Madden, "Lisa 'Left Eye' Lopes Burns Down Andre Rison's Mansion."

as an art form, especially Black women's creative and affective labor, which are so central to this genre. Where is the appreciation for Black women R&B singers' sounding of the strenuous labor of both love and heartbreak?[21] How does the Black female voice carry out the care work of Black women's labor, which cannot be recognized as such, as Saidiya Hartman argues? Where is the love for that something *you* do?[22]

The importation of the TR-808 sound into Black musical cultures is often attributed to Afrika Bambaataa's "Planet Rock" (1982), which replays and emulates two different Kraftwerk tracks ("Numbers" and "Trans-Europe Express").[23] In 2016 several men came forward to state that Bambaataa had sexually molested them when they were as young as thirteen.[24] All of the men told of difficult family circumstances when they were young boys and declared that Bambaataa had taken on a parental role in their lives and served as their mentor before he began to sexually abuse them for extended periods of time. The narrative of these survivors becomes part of the computing that structures the boom of the TR-808s; desire and pleasure are qualified by the significant yet variable expression of sexual violence/violation as and with technology. Names are fading . . . Aaliyah, the unnamed young girls from Chicago's South Side, Bambaataa's awful and injurious sonic boom, and the unlisted and untenderness.

Rewind and come again, re-rewind. Marvin Gaye's 1982 "Sexual Healing" was one of first songs that featured the TR-808 drum machine.[25] It was also Gaye's last hit before he was shot by his father, with whom he had a contentious relationship, with a gun that he had given to his father as a present in 1984.

21   "It scares me to feel this way." Tina Turner, "What's Love Got to Do With It?" on *Private Dancer*, Capitol Records, 1984, LP, https://www.discogs.com/release /3709972-Tina-Turner-Private-Dancer.

22   Hartman, "Belly of the World." Roberta Flack and Donny Hathaway, "Where Is the Love," Atlantic Records, 1972, single, https://www.discogs.com/Roberta-Flack-Donny -Hathaway-Where-Is-The-Love-Mood/release/8548745. In her 1978 essay that carries the same title as this song, June Jordan writes, "As a Black feminist, I must ask myself: *Where is the love?* How is my own lifework serving to end these tyrannies, these cor- rosions of sacred possibility?" Jordan, *Civil Wars*, 146.

23   Afrika Bambaataa and The Soul Sonic Force, "Planet Rock," Tommy Boy Records, 1982, CD single, http://www.discogs.com/Afrika-Bambaataa-The-Soul-Sonic-Force -Music-By-Planet-Patrol-Planet-Rock/release/2047.

24   Rys, "Afrika Bambaataa Sexual Abuse Allegations."

25   Marvin Gaye, "Sexual Healing," CBS Records, 1982, single, http://www.discogs.com /Marvin-Gaye-Sexual-Healing/release/584968.

"My father," Marvin told David Ritz in Europe in 1982 during a discussion of "Sexual Healing,"

> likes to wear women's clothing. As you well know, that doesn't mean he's homosexual. In fact, my father was always known as a ladies' man. He simply likes to dress up. What he does in private, I really don't know—nor do I care to know. You met him at a time when he was relatively cool about it. There have been other periods when his hair was very long and curled under, and when he seemed quite adamant in showing the world the girlish side of himself. That may have been to further embarrass me. I find the situation all the more difficult because, to tell you the truth, I have the same fascination with women's clothes. In my case, that has nothing to do with any attraction for men. Sexually, men don't interest me. But seeing myself as a woman is something that intrigues me. It's also something I fear. I indulge myself only at the most discreet and intimate moments. Afterward, I must bear the guilt and shame for weeks. After all, indulgence of the flesh is wicked, no matter what your kick. The hot stuff is lethal. I've never been able to stay away from the hot stuff.[26]

Gaye was heartbroken for most of his life, in part due to his father's visible ungendering, so much so that he added an *e* to his last name. The extreme physical violence meted out to him by Marvin Pentz Gay Sr. resulted in Gaye suffering from extreme anxiety and stage fright and also in Gaye extending the abuse in different forms to the relationship with his much younger second wife, Jan Gaye.[27]

Perhaps 808s soundtrack Black studies and provide a technology, or boom, of Blackness that organizes itself through heartbreak—actuating both heart muscles and a kind of ongoing hurtful tenderness ingrained in the flesh. With this, 808s provide aural glimpses and moments of heartbreak that cannot be forgotten—they are plain in sight, harmfully—and situate sexual violence as a terrain that demands a response that is not invested in prior injured states.[28] Responses and alternatives to injury are awful and difficult and forever; they emerge as song, story, grooving, crying, fight, jumping, quietness, laughing, poem. And more. Always more. This is living, necessarily living, and finding our way through earlier modes of heartbreaking damage

26 Ritz, *Divided Soul*, 18. See also Walcott, "Black Men in Frocks."
27 See J. Gaye and Ritz, *After the Dance*.
28 Georgis, *Better Story*.

that comprise the mattering of Black life, though not exclusively so. Where is the love?

Shhhh

808s are one way to think about Black life as an invitation to listen. The book *Phonographies: Grooves in Sonic Afro-Modernity* provides a way to imagine how technology—most crudely, machines—is an enunciation of Black life. The book uses sonics, or flows, to delineate this enunciation of life within the context of racial violence and modernity. These ideas also emerge in relation to vocoders, drum kits, LinnDrums, 808s, clap machines, and other Virtual Studio Technologies (VSTs). How do these sounds, vibrations, and machines offer us a genre of being human that does not begin with objecthood? Heart///// break. What do 808s *do to* us? And how do mechanics-machines refuse Black humanity (the logics of the Middle Passage and plantation slavery did and continue to roboticize Black people) while demanding that objectification cannot/ should not define Black life (I can never be your robot)?[29] These questions are not exactly new, of course—there is a really long and comprehensive list of scholars who think about the mechanization, objectification, and commodification of Black and other marginalized people and long-standing resistances to practices of dehumanization. But the sounds and vibrations can also engender "flesh memory"—and this overlaps with but is very different from what M. NourbeSe Philip calls *bodymemory*, right?—which interrupts the objectification-resistance dualism by asking how sound or vibrations, the 808s and the clap machines, are not simply extrahuman devices or technological appendages that refine or degrade humanness as cyborg.[30] Instead, the 808s narrate life, Black life. So, the VSTs—the sounds and beats and grooves they make—are not outside us or of us, but praxis. The story—the stories told above—cannot be told without the deep boom, clap, unspeakable yet audible heartbreak. Like a sssshhh—eviscerated, ear-piercing silence.

Avoiding a linear-Afro-future-posthumanist territory—by giving technology as purely embodied by machines too much clout—how do we talk or write or think about loving, desperately, the unspeakability of music and the loudness of heartbreak? The 808s are not the answer, but they might help us sort this through. With this, we must refuse disciplinary and epistemological

29 Kanye West, "RoboCop," on *808s and Heartbreak*, Roc-A-Fella Records, 2008, CD, https://www.discogs.com/release/1617049-Kanye-West-808s-Heartbreak.

30 Philip, "Dis Place." See also McKittrick, *Demonic Grounds*, 46–52.

bifurcations (the tendency to analytically separate the sciences, for example, from poetics), to study autopoeisis and self-replicating systems, and to think about the mechanics of Blackness outside corporeal Black politics, where our broken flesh or our degraded bodies are either liberatory devices *or* signifiers of anti-Blackness. Heartbreak. So, to rephrase: What do 808s do to us, physiologically, psychically, poetically? In what ways do the 808s contribute to the mattering forces of Black life?

Jumping

Sylvia Wynter. Her first use of the term *the science of the word* appears (I think) in her 2001 essay "Towards the Sociogenic Principle: Fanon, Identity, the Puzzle of Conscious Experience, and What It Is Like to Be Black."[31] In this essay Wynter thinks through how Frantz Fanon's understanding of selfhood disrupts a teleologically biocentric, and fundamentally anti-Black, understanding of the human, and how his writings open up the entangled workings of physiology and narrative. While Wynter explores these entanglements in most of her writings after 1984—she writes, often, that humans are hybrid beings, simultaneously bios and mythois—"Towards the Sociogenic Principle" offers a sustained discussion of the ways in which practices of racism and anti-Blackness are narratively connected to the physiological and neurobiological sciences. This is to say that the larger symbolic belief system (what we might call our Eurocentric origin stories or cosmogonies, whether theological or Darwinian or both) of which anti-Blackness is a part is constitutive of, not separate from, the naturally scientific (what we might call flesh and blood and brain) aspects of humanness. We *reflexly* experience the knowledge system we are part of. Remember, too, this belief system is lawlikely instituted: how we know our selves and each other, how we *believe in*, how we reflexly respond to the world around us, functions to stably reproduce the existing order; we navigate that order as though it is natural and outside of ourselves and outside our story-making abilities . . . but it is *we* who make the world what it is, it is *we* who *believe in, desperately* (and thus naturalize), the prevailing biocentric belief system.[32] However, this world-making only occurs within and against the constraints of our current biocentric order.

31 See also Fanon, *Black Skin, White Masks*; Césaire, *Discourse on Colonialism*; and Césaire, "Poetry and Knowledge."
32 See Wynter, "Re-enchantment of Humanism."

The entanglements Wynter explores do not situate the human on a bio-centric frame (which is one of natural selection wherein some people are more evolved than others, some people are more human than others, some people are closer to humanity than others; where the sciences are neutral, and stories and poetics are not neutral, and so on). In Wynter's formulation of the human, an extension of and mashing up of Aimé Césaire and Frantz Fanon, we are biologic storytellers. We did not, to give an obvious example, evolve from prelinguistic to linguistic beings; humans have *always been* sto-rytellers. In the long conversation in *On Being Human as Praxis*, she thinks about this in relation to the markings in Blombos Cave—clearly written 77,000-year-old linguistic communications scribed by humans.[33] The con-ceptual leap Wynter offers calls into question our entire order of being: the crude and long-standing commitment to the biocentric belief system that naturalizes Black people as unevolved and less-than-human is totally un-done if humans are not absolutely sutured to an evolutionary apes-to-Aryan system of knowledge. Heart////break. The science of the word thus under-lines two overlapping analytics: the deep connections between narrative and neurobiology and physiology (reflexly); the disruption of biocentric systems of knowledge (we are not what they say we are).

Working with Wynter's conceptualization of the science of the word, 808s and other music inventions and reinventions evidence and enunciate Black life. The practice of loving, desperately, the unspeakability of music is found, in part, in our neurobiological and physiological and intellectual response to that music and music makers. Our neurobiological and physiological and intellec-tual response to the deep boom, clap, blip, which is untracked and everywhere and seeping into us and emanating outward and beckoning friendships and starting fights and teaching and storying and moving and keeping a beat (off-beat) and heartbreak. The science of the word imagines a different beginning from which to think through Black music and technologies as well as other analytical questions. It is a total refusal of objecthood (as our Black origin story, as our archive, as our future, more heartbreak, "the suffocating reifica-tion," Fanon wrote) and therefore provides a pathway to imagine Black life as human cosmogony:

> I feel my soul as vast as the world, truly a soul as deep as the deepest
> of rivers; my chest has the power to expand to infinity. I was made
> to give and they prescribe for me the humility of the cripple. When I

33 Wynter and McKittrick, "Unparalleled Catastrophe for Our Species?"

opened my eyes yesterday I saw the sky in total revulsion. I tried to get up but eviscerated silence surged toward me with paralyzed wings. Not responsible for my acts, at the crossroads between Nothingness and Infinity, I began to weep.[34]

Wreckage

It has been argued that music shapes and moves and repairs our neurosystem.[35] With music, memory and language and words are built and rebuilt.[36] With music, neurons are strengthened and reattached. With music. I have

---

34 Fanon, *Black Skin, White Masks*, 119; the phrase "suffocating reification" is found on p. 89.

35 Sacks, *Musicophilia*; Levitin, *This Is Your Brain on Music*; and Patel, *Music, Language, and the Brain*.

36 This is in contradistinction to dysgraphia (the inability to write due to brain damage or disorder, deployed by Christina Sharpe) and aphasia (a communication disorder that results from damage to the parts of the brain that contain language, deployed by Frank B. Wilderson III). Here, I think, Sylvia Wynter's science of the word is especially helpful. In my understanding, dysgraphia and aphasia are mobilized by Sharpe and Wilderson as "literary" or "theoretical" terms that help them think about anti-Blackness and other forms of oppression. These terms help the authors tease out how some people cannot *see or write or imagine* Black humanity. These terms are *applied to* our existing biocentric system. These terms help the authors make sense of Black dehumanization. These terms help the authors work out how when some folks see Black, they can only enunciate it in relation to hegemonic white supremacist normative conceptions of humanity. Yet both terms, dysgraphia and aphasia, carry the heavy clinical weight that is paired with learning disabilities, autism spectrum disorders, and other neuroatypicalities. In addition to the taxing weight laid on those who are cast, in these scholarly works, as neurologically damaged and imperfect (disabled)—a move that refuses human-impairment as an alternative form of humanity—I want to suggest that if they were informed in any way by Wynter's framework they would have (perhaps) shied away from deploying-and-emptying these terms. *Or, alternatively and definitely more interestingly*, the authors may have understood these terms as *simultaneously* clinical-narrative. One cannot discount the clinical underpinnings of these terms—no matter how hard one tries! So, what is at stake, for (Black and non-Black) neuroatypical and nonneurotypical people, for (Black and non-Black) people with learning disabilities, for neurotypical (Black and non-Black) people when brain dysfunction, symbolically, explains racism or anti-Blackness or the inability to "see" or "read" Black "correctly"? What happens when "illness" or "disorder" explains why we, or why they, hate? How are race and disability—impairment as the

argued elsewhere, working with Wynter's "Black Metamorphosis," that the connections and wires and threads, between music and self and environment and others, not only conceptually subvert plantocratic and white supremacist (market) systems but also provide a way to track Black life as livingness (and thus outside narratives of dysselection).[37] More specifically, music, music making, music sharing, music dancing, music jumping, music singing—the act of loving music deeply, the act of feeling and loving music intensely—is one way Black communities physiologically and neurobiologically navigate racist worlds. I do not think there is specificity of or to Black neurobiologies

---

embodiment of Blackness or impairment as projection of anti-Blackness—being analytically mobilized to understand racial violence? And how do we grapple with the unsettling numbers, the math, the accumulations, the reams of paper that read: Black folks with impairments are more likely to be incarcerated, murdered by police, and so on? What of the story of violence resulting in brain damage, communication disorder, the inability to write? What Wynter taught me (Katherine) is that the bifurcation of science and poetics is a kind of disciplined brutality. I have spent a lot of time thinking about how the willful separation of the literary and the scientific does the work of colonial positivism—suggesting, explicitly, that there are kinds and types of discreet knowledge while also hiving off ways of knowing and being. So, dysgraphia and aphasia can *never* be simply symbolic or metaphoric or literary. They are deeply clinical, and they are lived, too, as *clinically poetic* narratives within our prevailing system of knowledge that despises difference. If we trust Wynter's formulation of bios-mythois (and I, Katherine, do)—it means these terms are *always* bios-mythois. Just as the 808s cannot be dislodged from that awful violence and be rendered "pure technology" and without history, the clinical-medical-neurological-and-*poetic* contours of impairment and neuroatypicality-nonneurotypicality cannot be dislodged from dysgraphia-aphasia. If this (a metaphorically impaired humanity) informs the analytical frame then, theoretically, it risks reflexly reproducing a dehumanizing law-like logic wherein ability and neurotypicality *actualize* what it means to be totally and fully human. This not only legitimizes biocentric corporeal categories in hierarchical terms, it also fails to imagine relational struggles across a range of corporeal and racial identifications. Singularity is required and Man-as-human restfully and stably reproduces itself at the apex of this formulation. With this, the trope of the "disorder"—which is being mobilized as a way to understand, say, racism or anti-Blackness or scripts that degrade Blackness—is locked into a biocentric frame, with disability, neuroatypicality, illegibility, in fact, inadvertently positioning the authors of the symbolic-literary dysgraphia-aphasia as normally and normatively able, typical, legible, nondisordered! Sharpe, *In the Wake*; and Wilderson, "Vengeance of Vertigo." See also Wynter and McKittrick, "Unparalleled Catastrophe for Our Species?"

37 Wynter, "Black Metamorphosis"; and McKittrick, "Rebellion/Invention/Groove."

and physiologies. I am not suggesting that. But I do think that the conditions of being Black—the experience and living memory of the abyss, to borrow from Édouard Glissant—has opened up attachments to musical narratives-genealogies-sounds that we should pay attention to.[38] For me, this is a radical reinvention of the self and our embodied knowledge! It is humanizing. So, if music shapes and moves and repairs our brains and bones and blood and nerves, if the boom of the TR-808 breaks our heart and jumps and moves us as we love music deeply and intensely, is this not a kind of neurophysiological resistance, refusal, or fugitivity within the praxis of Black life, at least fleetingly? What do we learn from and about each other in these moments of heartbreak and love? What do we pass on, what do we keep to ourselves, in order to practice Black livingness in a world that refuses Black life? How do we tell each other this feeling might be or is forever? *Do* we tell each other heartbreak might be forever? Is pain forever?[39] How do we share fugitivity and waywardness?

With all of this in mind what we want to notice is not *solely* the consequences of violence—the fucked-up predatory acts and stunningly quiet (as I see it) wreckage of violation experienced by those violated. The consequences and wreckage matter, deeply. But we must also ask ourselves, at the same time, without throwing that wreckage in the bin, under what conditions does human life become victim-wreckage and, as well, how do we tell this story by centralizing the ways in which our present system of knowledge rewards—physiologically! socially!—violation? What is it about our colonial plantocratic system of knowledge that enacts violation as an articulation of Black masculinity (not Black men, Black masculinity), and how does this interface with Black masculinity's ungendering in relation to white supremacy? And how, in this wreckage that is, in fact, Black life, do we find enunciations of humanity and the unmet promises of freedom? Heartbreak is not, then, a signifier of racial oppression or love lost. It is not a noun. Heartbreak is an aesthetic-physiological practice. It is sorrow song. It untangles that violence; it does not describe violence for profit. Because in order even to begin to do justice to this physio-aesthetic praxis, to Black life, it must exceed and unsettle the accumulative logic of cisheteropatriarchal racial capitalism.

We have to ask ourselves: How do we want to know this—sexual violence, racist sexual violence—differently and in a way that does not replicate the

---

38 Glissant, *Poetics of Relation*.
39 "No pain is forever." Rihanna, featuring Young Jeezy, "Hard," on *Rated R*, Def Jam Recordings, 2009, CD, https://www.discogs.com/Rihanna-Rated-R/release/4975541.

violence? This is what I want to get to. This is very hard for me. I don't know. I still feel the alibis piling up. How do we tell the story outside of the splash of sexual violence (and thus anti-Blackness), since summoning the violence encountered by Black folks is so often bullied into doing the psychic, physiological, and affective dirty work for white supremacy? Whenever there is some type of crisis around "intimate" violences in particular, Black folks are summoned as ciphers through which that labor is accomplished without it having to affect the actual structures of white supremacy. Instead of confronting the many violences, sexual and otherwise, white men *and* women committed against Black female persons ("high crimes against the flesh," Spillers calls it in "Mama's Baby, Papa's Maybe"), the broken and torn Black person, lynched, stands in as representative-knowable-enclosed-locked-down violence. Rather than reproducing the violence or accumulatively enumerating it, we seek to "tell a story about degraded matter and dishonored life that doesn't delight and titillate, but instead ventures toward another mode of writing," other modes of being, other modes of living in and living with.[40] Living on.

We Don't Have Much of a Relationship Now

Robyn Rihanna Fenty embodies a number of admirable qualities as a performer and public figure; however, none are as "savage" and awe-inspiring as the way she navigated the public scrutiny after Chris Brown brutalized her within an inch of her life in 2009 and the photos of her badly bruised and swollen face and body were leaked to TMZ by the Los Angeles Police Department.[41] Fenty was twenty-one at the time. She shouldn't have had to do this. Like a shhhh: eviscerated silence. Fenty refused again and again to become the proper and respectable poster child for victims of intimate partner violence, even though she was continually vilified as a "crazy Island woman" and confronted with her violated past and the images thereof as incontrovertible proof. In other words, the mainstream media demanded that she publicly provide the affective labor of being a violated Black woman by performing victimhood in very specific ways that would vilify Brown; she did neither. Fenty's broken face and her broken heart—violence and violation → violation as violence, and vice versa—did not drive the invasive media queries and

40 Hartman, "Venus in Two Acts," 7.
41 Much of our thought on Fenty was inspired by Bierria, "'Where Them Bloggers At?'"; Fleetwood, "Case of Rihanna"; H. Black, *Dark Pool Party*; and H. Black, "'I Feel Like Everything Shouldn't Exist.'"

publicity. Rather, as we know and as is so often the case, her (awful, hurtful) story of violence served as an occasion to discuss the larger problem of intimate partner violence, and, of course, to prove the pathology of Black folks and Black life. Violation.

Fenty has, instead, addressed the thorny complexities of the imbrication of sexuality and violence through her music and music videos ("Man Down," "S&M," "Love on the Brain," and "Bitch Better Have My Money" are only the most prominent). Retrospectively, Fenty said the following about her relationship with Brown after she was violently violated:

> [I thought] maybe I'm one of those people built to handle shit like this. Maybe I'm the person who's almost the guardian angel to this person, to be there when they're not strong enough, when they're not understanding the world, when they just need someone to encourage them in a positive way and say the right thing. [I thought I could change him,] a hundred percent. I was very protective of him. I felt that people didn't understand him. Even after . . . But you know, you realize after a while that in that situation you're the enemy. You want the best for them, but if you remind them of their failures, or if you remind them of bad moments in their life, or even if you say I'm willing to put up with something, they think less of you—because they know you don't deserve what they're going to give. And if you put up with it, maybe you are agreeing that you [deserve] this, and that's when I finally had to say, "Uh-oh, I was stupid thinking I was built for this." Sometimes you just have to walk away. [Now,] I don't hate him. I will care about him until the day I die. We're not friends, but it's not like we're enemies. We don't have much of a relationship now.[42]

Slowly jumping from believing that she was "one of those people built to handle shit like this" to realizing that she "was stupid thinking [she] was built for this," Fenty refuses being (and thus cannot be) conscripted into the long-standing narrative of the Black-superwoman-machine, who feels no pain, who does all the care work, who labors on behalf of everyone except herself. Instead, she implicitly states, "I can never be your robot." She sits with and lives on and with the heartbreak, moving on but never completely leaving the scene. Sorry. At this time, we are no longer accepting repair jobs. Heart/////break. Over the years Fenty has emphasized both her own heartbreak and her heartbreak over the way Brown, someone she loved, was

42 Bailey, "Rihanna Talks Chris Brown."

rendered monstrous by the mainstream media. Her insights and struggles are meaningful, especially considering how white men—the Afflecks and the Polanskis and the rest—who exhibit similar violent behavior in a range of their heterosexual relationships are seldom treated the same way. Bringin' on the heartbreak, I repeat softly under my breath: she shouldn't have had to do this, she really shouldn't . . . Are you ready to be heartbroken?[43]

In 2010 there was a huge poster in the halls of my department at Queen's University. The huge poster was of Fenty's broken face. After seeing the poster the first time, I did not return to it; Fenty remained in my pathway, but I did not look at the poster or read the text that narrated and explained her brokenness. Other posters about "gender studies," such as indigenous activism, fat shaming, and queer cultures, as well as Muslim women and feminism, accompanied the Fenty poster. The posters were part of a big class project wherein, from my understanding, the students pick a topic related to the course, highlight important images and ideas about that topic, and place all this information on a huge poster. My knowledge of poster assignments and projects comes from the discipline of geography. The Association of American Geographers has poster guidelines that the posters in the hallway, in my view, emulated: posters make a unified, coherent statement; materials, both textual and visual, should be of professional quality and be clearly legible from a distance of four feet; text should be limited to brief statements; graphic materials will be displayed on a 4 × 8-foot poster board (landscape oriented only).[44] The only poster that depicted Black women featured Fenty's damaged, bashed-in face. Fenty's encasing and entombment in the hallway poster serve as synecdoches of these broader currents, since her public image is wedded to violence and violation, we and she are not allowed to forget, there's no reprieve from this ongoing heartbreak. What gets lost in the shuffle is the labor of heartbreak that the poster and Fenty are forced to perform, all without her consent.[45]

43 Mariah Carey, "Bringin' On the Heartbreak," on *Charmbracelet*, Island Records, 2002, CD, https://www.discogs.com/Mariah-Carey-Charmbracelet/release/666818; and Lloyd Cole and the Commotions, "Are You Ready to Be Heartbroken?," on *Rattlesnakes*, Polydor Records, 1984, LP, https://www.discogs.com/Lloyd-Cole-And-The-Commotions-Rattlesnakes/release/441936.

44 Association of American Geographers, 2022 annual meeting session guidelines, https://aag-annualmeeting.secure-platform.com/a/page/sessions/session-guidelines (accessed March 6, 2023).

45 Similarly, in 2014, a surveillance video of Janay Rice being brutally beaten by her husband, football player Ray Rice, in an elevator was made public by TMZ and circulated widely on social media.

As quiet as it's kept, we continue living, regardless of whether we found love in hopeful place or not, intensely feeling the thumping boom of heartbreak (flesh encasing that hollow organ, un-flee-ing. Jump.).

The chorus of Fenty's "We Found Love" repeats the following line over and over: "We found love in a hopeless place."[46] The bass drum does not appear until one minute and eight seconds—zeros, ones, and eights—into the song, and its booming entry is preceded by a crescendo of cascading keyboards as well as a drum roll, so central to house music. All these factors combined generate intense sonic tension so that the arrival of the bass drum registers as both like relief and like punishment. In this way, the structure of "We Found Love" approximates finding love: the flowing discharge of endorphins and resulting euphoria but also evokes the violence of being thumped by the beat in a hopeless place. Heart/////break. Add to this Fenty's voice, which remains almost impassive, displaying a "cool affect" that sounds like it is resisting the booming rush of the song structure/instrumentation. It is as if Fenty's vocalizing is physically/physiologically refusing the unacknowledged care work demanded from the Black female voice in popular music. The track's music video features scenes from a volatile heterosexual intimate relationship in which the lovers are portrayed by Fenty and a model/actor (Dudley O'Shaughnessy, who has an uncanny resemblance to Chris Brown). In addition to the unmistakable timbre of Fenty's voice, the alarm bells, the central keyboard riff—which resembles a siren—and the stark contrast between Fenty's vocals and music on this track amplify the joy and the heartbreak of living, continuing to exist and subsist. I was always struck by the following line: "Feel the heartbeat in my mind." Does this mean that the neurological system emulates, synthesizes, the beat of the heart, the thump of the bass?[47] Is it a heartbeat of pleasure (we found love; living) or the throb of pain (hopeless place, fear, trauma)? Most likely it's both, mixed and engineered at different volumes and

46 Rihanna, featuring Calvin Harris, "We Found Love," Def Jam Recordings, 2011, CD single, https://www.discogs.com/Rihanna-Feat-Calvin-Harris-We-Found-Love /release/3177028.

47 See The Artist (Formerly Known as Prince), "Sex in the Summer," on *Emancipation*, NPG Records, 1996, CD, https://www.discogs.com/The-Artist-Formerly -Known-As-Prince-Emancipation/release/1158522. Several scientists and theorists have postulated not only that humans can discern lower frequencies better than high ones but that this is partially a consequence of fetuses hearing the lower frequencies of the mother's heartbeat and of her voice in utero, which is crucial for early neural development. See Hove et al., "Superior Time Perception for Lower Musical Pitch."

intensities, depending on the time of day, not overcoming but surviving, living with, breathing in, subsisting through. Boom, like an 808.

Rachel Kaadzi Ghansah has observed how young Black female fans of Beyoncé relate to Fenty in the aftermath of the visible violence she experienced. She writes:

> I'm not certain they really hate Rihanna, or find joy in her hurt—instead I think what they really hate is that Rihanna knows firsthand, like so many women and girls, and perhaps like so many of them, that being violently hit by a man doesn't ever feel like a kiss. It feels the opposite. It is a humiliation that is impossible to forget. So what I think the Hive hates about Rihanna is that there is no fun, no fantasy in that kind of knowledge of womanhood, just a reflection of the real but all-too-often silent life they too must wade through as young women of color in America.[48]

These reactions to Fenty underscore yet another layer, dimension, facet, of the labor demanded of her: transcending, overcoming violence, violation, and heartbreak. The way Fenty was treated in the aftermath of her brutal violation—Chris Brown's assault, the leaking of the photos by the police, and the way she was treated by the media—forms a part of ungendering, given that Black women are thought to be inured to pain, deserving of violence, and thus not qualified for protection in the same way as white women. As Beth Richie writes: "Black women in vulnerable positions within disadvantaged communities fall so far from the gaze that is now sympathetic to some women who experience violence that they have virtually no right to safety, protections, or redress when they are victimized. At best, they are relegated to the status of undeserving. More often, those Black women with the least privilege, who live in the most dangerous situations, are criminalized instead of being protected or supported."[49] But care work is still violently expected, injuriously demanded. There is a beautiful and heartbreaking part in the 2014 film *Girlhood* (*Bande de filles*) that centers around Fenty's song "Diamonds"

48 Ghansah, "How Sweet It Is to Be Loved by You."
49 Richie, *Arrested Justice*, 21–22. Similarly, Bierria remarks, "Black women who are victims of violence are not simply accused of bringing it upon themselves, they are dis-positioned as its perpetrator. . . . Seemingly, when Black women are violated, their experiences of it and testimonies of resilience and resistance are vulnerable to politics that define their actions as instigating the violence." Bierria, "'Where Them Bloggers At?,'" 106.

that highlights the joy and pain of Black livingness.[50] While much of the film adopts an anthropological lens on the Black life of French teenage girls residing on the outskirts of Paris, this scene imagines a momentary and clearly limited instant of free livingness. With her new friends Lady, Adiatou, and Fily, the film's protagonist, Marieme, rents a hotel room in Paris so that they can escape for a night the strictures of anti-Black racism, misogynoir(e), family, work, and school that govern their lives. At one point during the evening, Lady, Adiatou, and Fily begin listening, dancing, and lip-syncing to Fenty's song, while Marieme sits on the bed and watches them. Marieme then joins the other three girls as they all joyously dance, embrace each other, and mime the words:

> Shine bright like a diamond
> Shining bright like a diamond
> We're beautiful like diamonds in the sky.[51]

The scene is bathed in gorgeous blue light, which serves to heighten the boom and rush of pleasure of the moment, and to visually distinguish it from the heartbreak of the characters' everyday lives, the specters of violence and violation. Finally, as the song and scene move toward an ending, viewers hear not only Fenty's voice on the soundtrack but Lady, Adiatou, Marieme, and Fily singing along with the song's English-language lyrics with audible French accents: "Feel the warmth, we'll never die, we're like diamonds in the sky." Living on.

LinnDrums

Prince did not like Roland TR-808 drum machines. He preferred LinnDrum machines.

"Flesh memory" can be linked to and interfaced with M. NourbeSe Philip's "bodymemory." The flesh, though, does something different than the body

---

50 Sciamma, *Girlhood*. Though I'm not sure whether this is apocryphal or not, Fenty was supposedly so enamored with this scene that she did not charge a licensing fee for the film's use of "Diamonds" in its entirety, as is customary. This is complicated by the fact that the director of the film is a white French woman, Céline Sciamma. I raise this primarily to bring into focus the labor requested of Fenty in this context.

51 Rihanna, "Diamonds," Def Jam Recordings, 2012, CD single, https://www.discogs.com/Rihanna-Diamonds/release/4001175.

conceptually: it marks the specificity of Black human life in its entanglements with the various forms of matter. Hortense Spillers distinguishes between body and flesh, and, initially, for Spillers, the flesh was primarily the
space of objecthood and the abject.[52] In *Habeas Viscus: Racializing Assemblages, Biopolitics, and Black Feminist Theories of the Human* and Spillers's
writings published since "Mama's Baby," the flesh emerges not as a utopian
zone or even an exclusively positive one but as a realm of possibility, she calls
it *empathy*, for Black life that is not beholden to inclusion into the category
of the Man-as-human (to use Sylvia Wynter's phrasing). So while the body
remains an elusive mirage, an unattainable abstraction for those situated in
the shadows of freedom, the flesh offers a liminal domain not beholden to
inclusion in discourses and institutions designed to kill us. The flesh rescued
the TR-808 from obsolescence.

One way to understand Black culture's relationship to technology is
through the way that especially Black music/sound humanizes by enfleshing supposedly discrete, abstract, rigid, inhuman machines by making them
usable in heretofore nonexistent modalities, whether this is the turntable, the
player piano, or the 808.[53] Take the way that Brandy intonates the 808 on this
particular, never officially released track that she recorded with Timbaland in
2011:

> You hear me from a block away, I still got getaway
> Baby can you hear me now, can you hear me now?
> Baby can you hear me now, can you hear me now?[54]

Not one of the many internet lyric sites provides transcriptions of Brandy's
rhythmic harmonic ad-libs: eeightt-ohh-eeightt—eeightt-eeightt, sung in her
unmistakable husky tone and reoccurring for the duration of the song; they
only archive the alphabetic words. Clearly, this is not the science of the word
as imagined by Wynter's elaboration of Césaire—but it does allow us to
think about the mechanics of voice and how Brandy's "eeightt-ohh-eeightt—
eeightt-eeightt" parallels and is purposed for nonlinguistic beats. The tone of
Brandy's voice and her intonation are fundamental to how the song works,

52 Spillers, "Mama's Baby, Papa's Maybe."
53 This is really different from the idea of the cyborg, which is, for both of us, a
    figure that extends the colonial project precisely because it seeks to dislodge
    itself from the flesh and denies practices of Black and non-Black servitude, even
    if sutured to these enfleshments and embodied racial economies in abstract
    refusal.
54 Timbaland, featuring Brandy, "808," no label, 2011, MP3.

how it achieves its effects in the flesh. It is also fundamental to shifting the signification of the machine and envisioning what the machine can and cannot do. Emulating the sensation of the TR-808, Brandy's vocal apparatus, like Blaque's, undertakes the care work of humanizing the technology. This can be likened to, but does not twin, how modern mobile technologies become and are incorporated into humanness via their use in Black popular music.[55] Jayson Greene's commentary seems to willfully misunderstand Fenty's use of Bajan Creole while also pointing to her singing voice (known as "Rihanna Voice") as technology: "Rihanna Voice has become an industry-wide idea, *a creative property* like the Korg synth or LinnDrum, that the quick-working line cooks of the pop industry daub *onto tracks like hot sauce from squeeze bottle*."[56] Comparing "Rihanna Voice" to using hot sauce feeds too easily into the "crazy Island woman" trope mentioned previously. Calling up other condiments in this context—soy sauce, mayonnaise, whatever—would be a wisecrack; these are inventions only ingested, seemingly, by non-Black people. The hot sauce squeeze bottle so perfectly recalls that crude Fanonian moment (good eatin', zone of nonbeing) by refusing Fanonian subtleties (upsurge, *we are not*, actually, zones of nonbeing!). There are, too, altogether different registers of analogy available by imagining the use of "Rihanna Voice" as adding flecks of gold or glitter to the mix, for instance . . . or grasping for but not reaching a kind of shimmering poetics. Shine bright like a diamond. In addition, besides conjuring histories of Black enslavement, the description of "Rihanna Voice" as a "creative property" in the vein of LinnDrums and Korg synthesizers disregards that the latter technologies are ownable and owned objects from which the Linn Electronics and Korg corporations derive substantial pecuniary profit whereas Fenty does not. Boom like an 808. Here, too, we take Black women's creative imagining of space—the beat, intention of Brandy's eeightt-ohh-eightt and "Rihanna Voice"—to undo the supposedly empty and/or inhuman Black geographies of sound.[57]

55 See track 3.0 in this volume.
56 Greene, "Is Rihanna the Most Influential Pop Singer" (emphases added). While Fenty has spoken about feeling the need to "tone down" using the inflections of her mother tongue, Bajan Creole, in both her singing and speech, it bears mentioning that she has consistently recorded songs ("Dem Haters," "Man Down," etc.), beginning with her 2005 debut single "Pon de Replay," that have deployed Bajan Creole (and other Afro-Caribbean intonations). Fenty has also collaborated with Caribbean artists such as Dwane Husbands and Vybz Kartel.
57 McKittrick, *Demonic Grounds*, 121–41.

In this way, both spheres facilitate the imagining of the flesh or Black life "as cosmogony."

$$(\text{human} + \text{machines} + \text{human heart}) \times \text{rhythm} \leftrightarrow \text{technology}$$

Heartbreak

Spreading fast and there's no cure (and there's no cure)
No need to run from heartache (It's gonna get ya)
It's gonna get you, get you for sure
(Everybody, everybody sing it, yeah)
—New Edition, "N.E. Heartbreak" (1988)

Openness and messiness and incompleteness are a pleasure, especially when theorized alongside the inflexible and thick category of race, but it is awful and painful to live open and undone. I had an exchange with two Black poets about two very different things. And these exchanges made me think about the many ideas I have gathered to learn about race and theorize about race and live as racialized, in day-to-day (scholarly and nonscholarly) contexts. These terms. I remember them mostly from graduate school. They were sometimes coveted, sometimes rejected. But they all sought to "destabilize" race and/or Blackness. It goes something like this: race is fluid and third space and liminal, and Blackness is fragmented and unfinished and on the threshold, and race is hybrid-on-the-border-messy, and Black is fractured, incomplete, flexible. And I thought: it is painful and harmful to live like that, isn't it? It hurts to live always undone and unfinished. It is heartbreaking. It is heartbreaking even when the impossibility is joyful, or you catch a glimpse of a life outside that inflexible weight.

Afro-Scottish poet and novelist Jackie Kay writes about this perpetual state of destabilized unbelonging in a poem from her 1993 collection, *Other Lovers*, entitled "In My Country." A video of Kay reading this and another poem provide context, wherein Kay, who was adopted in the 1950s by white Scottish parents, narrates several stories of white people relaying to her that being Black and being Scottish are a contradiction. For instance, a white woman asking her mother, "Is that your daughter?" and demanding to know from Kay, "Where do you come from?"[58] As a Black person in Scotland, Kay is an interloper, always already undone and unfinished:

58 Robertson-Pearce, "Jackie Kay."

a woman passed round me
in a slow watchful circle,
as if I were a superstition;
or the worst dregs of her imagination,
so when she finally spoke
her words spliced into bars
of an old wheel. A segment of air.
Where do you come from?
"Here," I said, "Here. These parts."[59]

My former graduate student Kara Melton calls this "moving through." She explores Black mobility as a kind of constrained possibility with "moving through" underscoring the physical *cost* of navigating the geographies of racism and anti-Blackness.[60] What is the physiological cost? Is the claim to or of "these parts" possible for Black people? What other geographic options are there? No return. Heartbreak.[61]

Eeightt

The flesh is struggle for me. Why is that? Spillers gave us the flesh newly. The flesh in her well-known and well-cited important essay, "Mama's Baby," is an undoing of the captive (enslaved) body. Reading that essay, I remember thinking, unlike the body, flesh "does" something outside of captivity, outside the terms of plantocratic commodification. This is memory work for me, as I have only recently read work on Spillers, rather

Spillers and Wynter are very different in terms of their modes of thought, how they think and write; though they both do love long complexly interlaced sentences. What first connected their oeuvres for me were their considerations of Black studies, which for very different reasons departed from most, if not all, other analyses of this antidisciplinary "field."[62] Both thinkers are acutely attuned to the histories of Black studies in the university, and Spill-

---

59 Kay, *Other Lovers*, 24.
60 Melton, "'A Kind of Logic, a Kind of Dominant Logic.'"
61 McKittrick, "Worn Out." See also Brand, *Map to the Door of No Return*.
62 Spillers, "*Crisis of the Negro Intellectual*"; and Wynter, "On How We Mistook the Map for the Territory."

than Spillers herself (perhaps I am a heretic for not returning, just as I am a heretic for not adoring James Baldwin—who I respect but do not adore). Of course, you explore the work of flesh and enfleshment deeply in *Habeas*. I am not afraid to share that I struggled with this book; it was difficult for me to teach, to be very specific, and I had some difficulty connecting Wynter to Spillers (my confession is that perhaps my overinvestment in the former has displaced the latter). That aside, I keep thinking about the flesh that encases the body and, as well, what is at stake in understanding the body and flesh as, analytically and theoretically, connectedly disconnected. I guess I worry about privileging the flesh. When I read Wynter on flesh, I connect it to ritual and rites—gendered storytelling practices that reify humanity in genre-specific terms. So the flesh is marked by knowledge, yet it is not, in its entirety, knowledge itself. Instead, Wynter asks (me) how flesh has been folded into prevailing systems of knowledge (enunciating Spillers's inventions) as it elicits a purely biocentric system as the fiction through which a new worldview must be engendered. The flesh, then, tells a story, but it must not be *the* story. I want

ers's question about the status and scope of the object of study in Black studies was answered for me by Wynter's insistence on making the human—both the countless different forms of heart/////break caused by Man and the coeval existence of other genres of the human in Black life—the focal point of Black thinking and action. This is why I started my discussion of Wynter and Spillers in *Habeas Viscus* with their theorizations of Black studies rather than other parts of their theoretical apparatuses. Wynter's discussion of the flesh is not the same as Spillers's, and my reading of the flesh departs from both their interpretations, even as it builds on them. More specially, the flesh exemplifies, for me, the science of the word, because of its invocation of biology and the foundational mythologies of the Abrahamic religions, specifically their enmeshment in the annals of colonialism and thus in sociogenic inscriptions of particular modes of humanness. Wynter writes about it in terms of the bifurcation between the fallen flesh and redeemed spirit that initially marks the difference between the celibate clergy "as the embodiment of the Spirit" and the noncelibate laity "as the embodiment of the Fallen Flesh" during the European Middle

more praxis, and I am uncertain the flesh can provide that praxis outside of the biocentric codes that render it so richly meaningful. I have come to despise the body, as an analytical site—and I am repeatedly disappointed and terrified because it is always present in my refusal. I do not think the flesh and the body are the same, but I keep seeing bodies thrown everywhere, all over the page, without anything in them, not even eyes or throats or muscles or blood or bones, just empty bags of flesh. No hearts! Heartless! Too many times analyses of the body, the Black body, replicate that singular Fanonian crisis (look, look, look! look at Blackness! look! LOOK!) without using the lens he begins *Black Skin* with (our genetic and social development are shaped by prevailing systems of knowledge, beside ontogeny and phylogeny stands sociogeny, Black-skin-white-masks, there is no singularity). This is why your discussion of intonation matters to me, a lot—because intonation is not just the enunciation

Ages.[63] Later this master code transmutes into "reason/sensuality, rationality/irrationality in the reoccupied place of the matrix code of Redeemed Spirit/Fallen Flesh . . . , thus creating "the new 'idea of order' on whose basis the coloniality of being, enacted by the dynamics of the relation between Man—overrepresented as the generic, ostensibly supracultural human—and its subjugated Human Others (i.e., Indians and Negroes), . . . was to be brought into existence as the foundational basis of modernity."[64] For Spillers the divergence between body and flesh represents "the central [distinction] between captive and liberated subject-positions" in the aftermath of the Middle Passage and plantation slavery in the Americas.[65] She also adds the dimension of ungendering to the concept of the flesh, writing, "This materialized scene of unprotected female flesh—of female flesh 'ungendered'—offers a praxis and a theory; text for living and for dying."[66] Finally, "the flesh" moves us away from debates about "dehumanization" and all

63   Wynter, "Unsettling the Coloniality," 278.
64   Wynter, "Unsettling the Coloniality," 287–88.
65   Spillers, "Mama's Baby, Papa's Maybe," 206.
66   Spillers, "Mama's Baby, Papa's Maybe," 208. While Spillers highlights the specificity of the ungendering of Black women here, in a different part of the essay she refers to the "ungendering and defacing project of African persons." Spillers, "Mama's Baby Papa's Maybe," 214.

and performance of "look!"; intonation ("look!") is reflexly felt (heartbreak) (which is not exactly *affect*, is it, but can be studied as such?). Fanon centers the biologic without privileging it as the only way to be or know or live Black. Reading him with Wynter allows us to notice how he does something really fantastic with the social production of race precisely because he does not lean on biology (skin) to wholly understand Blackness, but rather understands sociogeny as constituting and thus relational to the *biological story of our skin*. This, for me, provides a different way of thinking about race and Blackness, because the body in itself, by itself (heartless), *cannot* sustain Fanon's and Wynter's nuanced worldviews. We can thus demand a different humanity that is already here, relational to *but not of* the prevailing biocentric order . . . Black life is the praxis of refusing such an order. Heart-full and heartbroken. Look! Blap. Squonk.

the insufferable body blah-blah-blah in academic discourse. The flesh is not merely inert violated matter, but praxis incarnate. In several writings Wynter uses flesh in this way, describing hybrid bios-mythois humanness as theory made flesh, for instance, when she writes, "The positive verbal meanings attributed to their respective modes of kind are alchemically transformed into living flesh, as its members all reflexly subjectively experience themselves, in the mimetically desirable, because opiate-rewarded, placebo terms of that mode of symbolic life prescribed by the storytelling code."[67] For me the term *flesh* conjures mattering movements in Black that resolutely defy the purely biocentric, precisely because of its complicated histories. At the same time, flesh provides openings for different formings and matterings beyond both Man and to some extent the human. My work continues to center the ungendered flesh of Black life as praxis. Living in, living with. Boom.

67   Wynter and McKittrick, "Unparalleled Catastrophe for Our Species?," 34. Variations of this phrase also appear in the following essays: Wynter, "Africa, the West and the Analogy of Culture"; Wynter, "'Genital Mutilation' or 'Symbolic Birth?'"; Wynter, *Human Being as Noun*?; Wynter, "Pope Must Have Been Drunk"; and Wynter, "Rethinking 'Aesthetics.'"

Maybe one way to think race or Blackness is that it functions by making the biologic reflexly real in the domain of social production: Blackness enfleshes social production; Black life socializes the biologic outside the terms of dysselection. Trying to make it real but compared to what?[68]

So we are talking about relationality, and how extrahuman devices and intense narratives of love allow us to notice what is beautifully human about those who have never been free. This sense of being, in relation to technologies—including technologies that are bound up in unpleasant stories, like the TR-808—adds a layer to what we know about Black humanity. What we know, really well, is dehumanizing objecthood and innovative resistance and the complex navigation of the structural, gendered, colonial, plantocratic workings of racial capitalism. What extrahuman devices and narratives expose is an analytical pathway that is in articulation with Black humanity; that is, a lens or a framework or a worldview that is cognizant of but does not seek results or answers that are beholden to either oppression or resistance. Put slightly differently, these extrahuman devices and narratives expose *navigation* without dwelling on its oppression-resistance poles; they expose what kind of mechanisms and schemas and sounds and instruments (musical and not) help make this world navigable for those who are, in most instances, disciplined and surveyed and always imagined as static-in-place (look!). These extrahuman devices are succor. Mark Campbell discusses these kinds of possibilities through his work on turntables and mixtapes.[69] He argues, really beautifully, how the found objects and technologies that inform and enhance Black cultural production and music making provide us with new ways of narrating humanity. This account does not split the 808s from the performer; it does not deny the disappointing and repurposed and sometimes awful and brutal history of 808s; it does not focus on the empty "body" that is manipulating or repurposing or playing the 808s. Instead, this narration of humanity understands these moments, people, histories, beats, disappointments, as coinstituting each other, which, in turn, reframes Blackness outside existing calcified and superfluous and normative white supremacist guidelines (measured vis-à-vis Man-as-human). With this, we have to ask, How is the navigation made, and how does the navigation feel? How does the succor offer relief or joy or sadness or heartbreak or anger or the

68 Roberta Flack, "Compared to What?," on *First Take*, Atlantic Records, 1969, LP, https://www.discogs.com/Roberta-Flack-First-Take/release/758676.
69 Campbell, "Everything's Connected."

intensely beautiful, physiologically? This is, for me, a mathematics of Black humanity that already is; or the arithmetic of Black life that will have been.

We gon keep it bumpin while the 808 is jumpin.[70]

Wicked Mathematics

You + me's not just arithmetic
it's wicked mathematics
the combinations we could do
would make your maths look like A B C
—Nicolette, "Wicked Mathematics" (1992)

In some ways we are splitting and overlapping racial processes (enfleshment and navigation) in order to work out how extrahuman technologies figure into Black life and humanity. I have been working with mathematics and other number systems to try and think through these kinds of tensions and analytical difficulties. Mathematics is, for me, an unfamiliar system of knowledge. I am not a mathematician, but I am curious about how practices of categorization are not always, for the unfree, equated with knowable classificatory systems that capture and seal off their abjection. Mathematics underwrites multiple strands of Cartesian logics and positivism, and, in terms of time and place, the practice of slavery is situated firmly amid European empiricism, various kinds of human and nonhuman data collection, and matters of fact. In many ways, mathematics enumerates commodification and dispossession through accounting and making Black fact. As noted above, the economy of Black objecthood is long studied and theorized. My question is, How do we think outside that system, if only transitorily, to draw attention to Black life? How has the practice of counting numbers—not even mathematics per se—fooled us into replicating Black objecthood by rewarding (academic and otherwise) systems of accumulation? Here we can stack up a whole bunch of numbers: Middle Passage ledgers, the lashes and the cotton bales, counted the uncountable Black trans-sex-worker deaths, the ten or sixty or seven men and boys shot in the back in March 2014, the seven thousand, in 1998, women with broken faces, the red records. Why are we only noticing those accounts that cannot bear Black life (the ledger)? We must, of course. We must unforget these numbers. But we also know, for example, that the field of

70 Kelis, featuring Too $hort, "Bossy," Virgin Records, 2005, CD, http://www.discogs.com/Kelis-Featuring-Too-hort-Bossy/release/1939897.

mathematics is vast (algebra, calculus, geometry, logic, computation, graph theory, chaos theory, statistics, and much more), so why attach Black history and Black experience and Black bodies and Black flesh only to a plantocratic accounting system that denies these other ways of knowing numbers? This is not, then, about refuting mathematics; it is about imagining Black life from the perspective of struggle. For me, the science of the word uses and dwells on that accounting system as a way to explode knowable mathematical solutions (noticing the hugeness of this system of knowledge and numbers, infinities and pi, the irresolvable), insisting that the word (poetics, narrative) is implicit to how we count what we count (we are responsible for, we make and adore, the accounts and the accounting). At the same time, the science of the word interrupts that system by noticing how sometimes it cannot capture other ways of poetic relational knowing; the science of the word thus seeks out the ways Black people have understood themselves in numerical and mathematical ways that are not so easily sutured to plantocratic and colonial accounting systems.[71] Black life and love are not something you can have, but something you do and can never get. This returns me to the 808s or the LinnDrum machines or eeightt-ohh-eeightt/eeightt-eeightt: here are mathematics—measured and unmeasured bam, drop, eeightt—that reveal a new or different register of Black life (I hope!): that, perhaps, is wicked mathematics.

Wicked mathematics. Trying to calculate the incalculable, that which cannot be captured by or in the sociogenic code of Man but which discloses and creates human life as Black life. Ida B. Wells-Barnett, W. E. B. Du Bois, and Sun Ra come to mind in terms of "wicked mathematics," since they all use mathematics, numbers, calculations, tabulations, charts, tables with and against the master-codes of Man. Of course, on the other side stand slave ship registers, or schoolteacher's ledger in Toni Morrison's *Beloved*, which lists in different columns the animal and human characteristics of the enslaved.[72] And numbers are different from mathematics, but they coconstitute one another to make meaning, to tell the story, to bend or calcify how we know the world. Du Bois and Wells-Barnett both deployed numbers to show how Black life in the late nineteenth-century United States was constituted by economic, political, sexual, and physical violence. In her

<hr>

71 This also points to mathematics that are not fully sutured to colonial accounting systems—African fractals or "anumeric" cultures, for example—which points to other ways of knowing. See Vuolo, "What Happens When a Language Has No Numbers?"; and Sol, "Hidden Figure."
72 T. Morrison, *Beloved*.

autobiography Wells-Barnett states that she uses "the statistics of lynching [to] prove that according to the charges given, not one-third of the men and women lynched are charged with assaults on white women, and brand that statement as a falsehood invented by the lynchers to justify acts of cruelty and outrage."[73] While we've now come to realize the futility of this particular numbers game, which is why there's still the need to show that Black lives matter via the incessant cumulative enumeration of Black deaths, there is an inventiveness and enfleshed livingness to Wells-Barnett's and Du Bois's mathematics.[74]

Outside biocentric ledgers and coloniality, there is also the long tradition of playing the numbers in Afro-diasporic and other communities (Italian lotto, policy, bolita, playing the bug, and so on). In *The Philadelphia Negro*, Du Bois writes, "Gambling goes on almost openly in the slum sections and occasions, perhaps, more quarreling and crime than any other single cause." He then goes on to quote at length an article from the *Public Ledger*: "Hundreds of poor people every day place upon the infatuating lottery money that had better be spent for food and clothing. They actually deny themselves the necessaries of life to gamble away their meagre income with small chance of getting any return. . . . Many children go hungry and with insufficient clothing as a result of policy playing. . . . The policy evil is, to my mind, the very worst that exists in our large cities as affecting the poorer classes of people."[75]

Clearly, these numbers perturb Du Bois, but he also states in another context, "History writes itself in figures and diagrams," for which one needs numbers, for sure. Such a shame Du Bois could not see the history being written in the numeric playing of the bug. Or is playing the bug in the system, the conjuring of other a-systems, maybe they're eeightt-ohh-eeightt—eeightt-eeightt wedged between Black life as world-mattering and Black life as world-(de)forming? Racial capitalism draws a line between sorting and

73 Wells-Barnett, *Crusade for Justice*, 136.
74 Du Bois, "Program for a Sociological Society." "A software bug is an error, flaw or fault in the design, development, or operation of computer software that causes it to produce an incorrect or unexpected result, or to behave in unintended ways." Wikipedia, s.v. "Software Bug," last edited on January 4, 2023, https://en.wikipedia .org/wiki/Software_bug.
75 Quoted in Du Bois, *Philadelphia Negro*, 265.

playing, accounting and gambling, the (ledger) books and the (scoreboard) books. The numbers are inhabited; mathematics provides a method that determines the outcome. Heart/////Break.

Cardiomyopathy

Something's jumpin' in your Shirt.
—Lisa Marie with Malcolm McLaren & The Bootzilla Orchestra, "Something's Jumpin' in Your Shirt" (1989)

I read somewhere that you can die from heartbreak. You can die of a broken heart. Heartbreak can lead to depression, mental health struggles, and heart disease just as they can and do often produce irreparable heart////break. The American Heart Association calls this "broken heart syndrome."[76]

Broken heart syndrome can lead to severe, short-term heart muscle failure. Broken heart syndrome is usually treatable. The most common signs and symptoms of broken heart syndrome are chest pain and shortness of breath. You can experience these things even if you have no history of heart disease. In broken heart syndrome, a part of your heart temporarily enlarges and doesn't pump well, while the rest of your heart functions normally or with even more forceful contractions.

I have always known we could die from a broken heart. We may not go the way of all flesh, by and through and because of heartbreak. We may just die a little—those moments when our heart doesn't pump well, the shortness of breath, the constricted, stifling circuits of chest pain. I have realized, too, I cannot sufficiently work through contradictory workings of love and anticipatory loss, and so I get stuck, mid-heartbreak. My heart keeps breaking, over and over, every single day. I can only explain the feeling as cold air being shot through my upper chest. Freezing cold air moving through my chest, day after day. It is not simply sorrow. It opens up, too, with possibilities. Last summer I woke up in the middle of the night with excruciating pains in my chest. My first thought was: heart attack (family history, predisposition, stress, and alla that) rather than heart/////break, because the purely physical is more readily available as a diagnosis in a biocentric world. The throbbing aches got worse

76 American Heart Association, "Is Broken Heart Syndrome Real?" See also Carey et al., "Increased Risk of Acute Cardiovascular Events."

whenever I tried to lie down. I waited to call the doctor's office until the morning, because I didn't want to wake my sleeping daughters and subject them to the potential heartbreak of having to worry about the health of their parent at such a young age. After many hours of agony and speculation via numerous medical websites, my physician confirmed to me that I was afflicted with an acute case of heartburn. Since heartburn is not a direct result of that particular hollow muscle, it was always a mystery to me why it was called that in English. As a consequence of experiencing its painful boom so intensely in and around my heart, I finally understood viscerally why this condition was named *heartburn* and how it differed from yet may be related to heart////break.

Can I get another take?

I wasn't being honest in the last paragraph, taking an easy way out and not truly resting with heart////break. My full armor was still on; it's dazzling and beautiful.[77] My heartburn was related to heart///break. It has been almost ten years now: Lawyers. Department of Children and Family Services. Police. Doctors. Custody evaluators. Therapists. More lawyers. At some point I am forced to justify to Them why my experience of sexual violation/violence and my queerness do not make me an unfit parent . . . Eviscerated silence. Boom. Heart////break.

This why I write and speak about ungendering/Black queerness and sexual violence/violation in detached, hushed scholarly tonalities—armor on, decked out in those gorgeously abstract gold fronts, like a shhh—while knowing that I do so because they mark the core of who I am. There I is, living in, living with.[78] I try to strip off the armor slowly, carefully, but it's difficult. The armor has merged with my "natural" body, blanketing my flesh, enshrining my psyche, encasing that hollow muscle. Fuck a cyborg, though, really. Boom . . . Like What?

Sitting on an airplane, I pause watching *Moonlight* for what must be the tenth time; it reduces me to not just tears but abject bawling face and all the emotions associated with it.[79] As opposed to Mary J., I can't even pre-

77 Dawn Richard, *Armor On*, Our Dawn Entertainment, Cheartbreaker Music Group, 2012, MP3, https://www.discogs.com/Dawn-Richard-Armor-On/release/3599447.

78 The Notorious B.I.G., "One More Chance (Remix)," Bad Boy/Arista, 1995, CD single, https://www.discogs.com/release/1087336-Notorious-BIG-One-More-Chance.

79 B. Jenkins, *Moonlight*.

tend that I'm not gon cry.[80] Granted, I sob at many things: everything from Black Ink Crew, to Hortense Spillers's sentences, to the worst manipulative Disney movies; and I still haven't been able to listen to Prince's "Conditions of the Heart" or "Sometimes It Snows in April" since his passing in 2016. Simply thinking about these songs brings tears to my eyes. Still. And while I have many intellectual reservations about Barry Jenkins's film and its reception, my critical shield washes away with blubbering, messy tears whenever I enter the world of this film. Undone every time, *Moonlight* hits me like the full weight of twenty 808s; boooooom; heart////break. The film shatters my heart, for myself, for all sensitive femme/feminine Black boys and splinters at a world so intent on violently destroying our too-muchness, on paralyzing our wings, brutally overseeing how our softness congeals into a tough, protective veneer. Where do you go when your being is too much for this world? Where? Where is our love?

Though supremely frustrated that we do not see an adult version of the Chiron played so brilliantly by Ashton Sanders in the second part of the film's triptych, I understand why the Trevante Rhodes's Chiron in the third part must so fiercely don his thick sheath of masculinity. For some of us, it's not protuberant triceps and gold-plated grills but intricate theoretical vernaculars, themselves extensions of necessary-for-survival-street-corner-verbal-dexterities, tumbling out of our mouths and dripping from our fingers, that are supposed enshrine us like intellectual superpowers. Still the same function. We were never meant to survive into adulthood, at least not as sensitive femme/feminine Black boys. How do you inhabit a universe where you can't even be imagined utopically (like a grown Chiron portrayed by Ashton Sanders), let alone tenderly, lovingly?

So I began to weep for myself and all the Black boys like me, reflexly recollecting palpably, physically, physiologically, what it felt like, what it still sometimes feels like, to spend hours assembling and wedging into your armor just to walk down the block, or to simply enter a room full of strangers, because something between Infinity and Nothingness might pop off, sometimes a word, other times a look or a slight bodily movement. I inspect my armor again, now roughly four decades old, sensing that it has become a little too tight, a bit itchy, ripped there, chipped here, and worn out all over. Living in, living with . . . heart/////break, possibilities, openings.

80   Mary J. Blige, "Not Gon' Cry," on *Waiting to Exhale (Original Soundtrack Album)*, Arista Records, 1995, CD, http://www.discogs.com/Various-Waiting-To-Exhale -Original-Soundtrack-Album/master/78487.

"This Is Why You and I and We Dance. We'll Go Out to the Floor"

Loving intensely and then monumental loss. Loving quietly, consistently and then booming hurt. We can also go the way of the flesh. We can die from a broken heart. This is terrifying, particularly if understood in relation to the heartbreaking history that underlies TR-808s. 808s break hearts. Boom. Jump. Succor. This is part of what we want to understand and patiently learn. The long histories of racial violence, the looming and real violations, the heart and the 808s, the mathematics and the flesh, the science of the word— these are sites that may not ordinarily be understood or thought together, but when they are, they reveal Black life and Black livingness as shifting locations enfleshed by the arteries of enduringly heartbreaking and joyful routes and roots. The hollow muscular organ filled up.

WAYWARD SHUDDERING,

BEAUTIFUL TREMORS

(AGW's Quiet Storm Remix)

Sui generis just like Hartman's previous two books, *Wayward Lives, Beautiful Experiments: Intimate Histories of Social Upheaval* gives so much; it is errant para-historiography, social survey animated by countless reckless acts of self-expenditure, ornate lexicon of foreshadowed delinquency, resonant photograph of biographies that could have been, architectural digest of the lives of the poor and infamous, forensic probe into non-yet-existent criminal deeds of extravagant insubordination, sexological manual gone AWOL in the glittery fringes of a dress impulsively discarded in the hallway, baroque grammar book on the many uses of the double descriptive, treatise on the luxuriously recalcitrant splendor of survival, and, above all, song, lots of songs—and some other sounds too. Songs, murmurs, chords, shouts, ululations in the minor key of "radical thought in deed," often intoned by "bull daggers, aesthetical Negroes, lady lovers, pansies, and anarchists," and if you listen very attentively, you'll hear them mellifluously intoning the refrain: "Young black women were radical thinkers who tirelessly imagined other ways to live and never failed to consider how the world might be otherwise."[1] I am not sure I can do justice to all that Hartman's words, sounds, smells, colors, and ideas make possible in their focus on the obscured chorine rather than the showgirl diva at the center of the stage and in their invitation to imagine knotty, lacerating, lustrous, fissured, tender, violent, and layered Black socialities, but I want to riff and linger on a few of these here.

Between, below, adjacent to, and beside the sometimes totalizing narratives found in certain strands of Black studies, Hartman tenderly, lovingly, and exactingly imagines, re-creates, draws, charts, and sounds out the "beautiful anarchy" (87) of the "third revolution of Black intimate life" (59) that occurred in the newly urban centers of Philadelphia and New York from the end of the nineteenth century until 1930 and that followed the earlier upheavals on "the slave ship and the plantation" (59). While there's certainly no necessity to shout, it sure feels good when they "scream [your] name like a protest," sending tremors of pleasure and shudders of anxiety down the spine in chorus, because "intimate life unfolds in the streets," transforming "eros into a communal luxury" (229).[2]

"No need to scream, only to listen, permitting everything she felt to pour out—the aspiration, the love, the girl broken in two, the grief" (236). "Everywhere but here is complicated."[3] Can you say my name? "Say my name, say my name."[4] Can you say her name? Can you say their name? What is

The subtitle of this chapter is a reference to the quiet storm radio format pioneered in the 1970s at Howard University's WHUR Radio in Washington, DC, by Black queer DJ Melvin Lindsey, who died of AIDS-related complications in 1992. See E. Black, "Tribute to Melvin Lindsey"; Gibson, Patron, and Wilkins, "Quiet Storm"; and Harvey, "Quiet Storm."

1 Hartman, *Wayward Lives, Beautiful Experiments*, 60, 61, 34, 8 (hereafter cited parenthetically in the text).
2 "Scream [your] name like a protest" is from Amaal Nuux, "Scream," Public Records/Universal Music Canada, 2017, MP3.
3 Nuux, "Scream."
4 Destiny's Child, "Say My Name," Columbia Records, 2000, CD, https://www.discogs.com/Destinys-Child-Say-My-Name/release/1440586. See also track 8.0 in this volume.

"the form adequate to conveying the story of these unknown and anony-mous radicals"?[5] Can you make out the hope, the sorrow, and the care in the nonexistent maternal ballad: "Do bana cobe, gene, gene me?"[6] Like a pro-test, Hartman's narratives "exceed the words, the verses" (346), knowing as little as our mamas what the ballad's words may signify but grasping very well how all the things "secreted, harbored deep inside are felt and exclaimed" (346). What. . . . If? All the things . . ."Ben d' nu - li, nu - li, nu - Ii, nu - Ii, ben d' le."[7] All the things . . . Damn![8]

Wayward Lives reminds me on every page why, like Samuel Delany, I, too, am "a sentence lover . . . , forever delighted, then delighted all over, at the things sentences can trip and trick you into saying, into seeing. I'm astonished—just plain tickled!—at the sharp turns and tiny *tremors* they can whip your thoughts across. I'm entranced by their lollop and flow, their prickles and points."[9] Hartman's book overflows with beautifully heartbreaking—or is it heartbreakingly gorgeous?—sentences, this time not defined by heartrend-ing shrieks but by the "lollop and flow" of defiant whispers, unruly and un-finished songs, loving hisses, high-pitched moaning, and too-loud humming, unharshly alerting us to the "tumult, vulgar collectivism and anarchy" (4) encased in "the fierce urgency of the now" (24). That said, in addition to the terrible beauty of the conglomerate of words that constitute the build-ing blocks of this tempestuously chanting book, I am left with one word, *chorine*, entranced and tickled by all the things it is, all the things it could be, just all the things, especially its analogous existence to the function of background vocals as multiplicatory harmonic beds for the lead vocals in R&B music. I shudder in delight at its meaning and at how Hartman weaves it throughout *Wayward Lives*, engendering the chorine as method, but am also deeply transfixed by its sound, the shapes it forces the roof of my mouth, my larynx, my tongue, and my lips to create, enunciating *chorine* over and over again in my head, trying to work it into everyday conversation and laboring to concoct an adjectival version of this word that reverberates through the air just right. So far, I have conjured the following candidates: *chorinesque, chorine-like, chorinific, chorinal, chorinous, chorinic, choriniful*, . . . All the things. Beyond the tumultuous thrill incited by the term's sonic resonance,

5 Hartman, "On Working with Archives."
6 See Du Bois, *Souls of Black Folk*, 254. See also Moten, "Uplift and Criminality."
7 Du Bois, *Souls of Black Folk*, 254.
8 Spillers, "'All the Things You Could Be by Now.'"
9 Delany, Gregory, and McCaffery, "Semiology of Silence," 134 (emphasis mine).

the word so fittingly describes Hartman's transcendent chorinal modalities of thinking, writing, and envisaging throughout this text, in which she slowly recoils from "the great man or the tragic hero" (348), in favor of a universe in which "untranslatable songs and seeming nonsense make good the promise of revolution" (348).

> Don't you know
> They're talkin' 'bout a revolution
> It sounds like a whisper
> Don't you know?[10]

Take, for instance, Hartman's restaging of W. E. B. Du Bois's sociological work from the turn of the twentieth century, particularly his groundbreaking 1899 study, *The Philadelphia Negro*, which required him to take up residence in that city's Seventh Ward for a year. Rather than simply dismissing Du Bois's deep victorio-patriarchal disquiets about the putative sensual immorality and criminality of young Black women, Hartman remixes Willie D. (Willie is what Du Bois's mama called him) in a chorinic style, taking his authoritatively Prussian lead vocals, filtering them through circles and layers of echo and delay, while also setting them atop a bass line so thunderously deep as to be deemed indelicate if not altogether vulgar and adding a plethora of harmonic vocal tracks inaudible in Du Bois's original mix to amplify the "drama hiding behind the statistics and skewed gender ratios" (91).[11] The overlapping sheets of vocal harmonies in Hartman's chorinal mix ring out an open enclosure at the tumultuous crossroads of "the Girl problem and the Negro problem" (20), and if you are skilled at eavesdropping, you might hear the vertiginous sounds of the words "riot, rush, tremble, flight, and strike" (109) being uttered ASMR-style by the folks on the corner of Seventh and Lombard, whether they're coming from their place of employment, on their way to their job, or simply working the street. After all, everybody in the "beautiful anarchy" (87) of this street symphony is "on the way to some place better than this" (87).[12] Was the choir rehearsing in the basement of that

10 Tracy Chapman, "Talkin' Bout a Revolution," on *Tracy Chapman*, Elektra Records, 1988, LP, https://www.discogs.com/Tracy-Chapman-Tracy-Chapman/release /7242971.

11 For a different consideration of Du Bois's use of numbers, see Weheliye, "Diagrammatics as Physiognomy"; and track 9.0 in this volume.

12 Monica, *Street Symphony*, Arista Records, 1999, CD https://www.discogs.com /Monica-Street-Symphony/release/2502766. The acronym ASMR stands for autonomous sensory meridian response.

building down the block on Lombard singing "Loverboy c'mon and take me / Only you know how to make me / Shudder with anticipation," *or* were they reciting "Were you there when they crucified my Lord? (Oh, sometimes it causes me to tremble)."[13] I can't quite tell; does it matter what or who causes you to tremble or shudder, where and how you find wayward paths to the "vulgar pleasures, the glitter and shine" (117), so long as they are harbingers of "wild hope and the gift of chance" (120)?

In *Wayward Lives* Willie Du Bois, the enfleshed chorine, shudders in disgust and shame but also trembles with the palpably anticipatory pleasure of experiencing "only everything that he feared" (119). How did Du Bois respond to "the stories he collected each day in his interviews"? (104). When did the disembodied social scientist "yield to the heartbreak of cold facts"? (96). How did he survive "eight hundred thirty-five hours of hope and despair"? (104).[14] In what ways did Du Bois's vexed relationship to his own sexuality shape his moral code when confronting the "tumult, vulgar collectivism, and anarchy" (4) in the Seventh Ward? Would *dear Du Bois* ever come to the realization that "experiments with conjugality" (102) and "flexible and elastic [modalities of] kinship were not a 'plantation holdover,' but resources of Black survival, practices that documented the generosity and mutuality of the poor"? (91).[15] Along with Willie and some unnamed residents of the Seventh Ward, the dramatis personae of Hartman's Philadelphia chorus features among others Du Bois's wife, Nina Du Bois; Mamie and James Shepherd; Mary Riley; the wealthy white social reformers Hannah Fox and Helen Parrish; and Fanny Fisher, all in their own ways trying to live free, striving for an "improvisation with the terms of social existence" (228), yet their interests, desires, circumstances, and dreams often brutally clashing against each other.

13 Mariah Carey, "Loverboy," Virgin Records, 2001, CD single, https://www.discogs .com/Mariah-Loverboy/release/156712; and Bayard Rustin, "Were You There (When They Crucified My Lord)," on *Bayard Rustin Sings Twelve Spirituals on the Life of Christ*, Fellowship Records, 1952, LP, https://www.discogs.com/Bayard -Rustin-Bayard-Rustin-Sings-Twelve-Spirituals-On-The-Life-Of-Christ/release /2903614.

14 Du Bois spent 835 hours interviewing Seventh Ward residents.

15 As Hartman notes about Du Bois's experience in Philadelphia, "By outward appearances he remained a dispassionate observer. His gentlemanly comportment and reserved New England manner—even his friends called him *dear Du Bois*—was off-putting, and it exaggerated the gulf between him and ordinary black folks" (104). Moreover, Du Bois's mother referred to him as Willie. See Lewis, *W. E. B. Du Bois*.

Hartman's exacting yet sympathetic rendering does not displace Du Bois or his ideas and methods as much as lead him to get "lost in the company of minor figures" (345) so he can "fall in step with the chorus" (348), and readers can discover him anew. Maybe William Edward Burkhardt shudders just a tiny bit, maybe he trembles violently, who knows. What we can say with certainty after reading *Wayward Lives* is that back on the corner of Lombard and Seventh as a retort to Du Bois's social scientific but still somewhat reckless eyeballing, the two "young women locked arms, turned away and continued their stroll" (119); they resumed to "delight in rumor and created scandal by embellishing [the queer parlor drama (150)] of he said and she said until the truth was no longer possible to discern" (95).

Remember when you said, "She's got the papers, but I've got the man," and later, when you saw them holding hands on Market Street, it turned out "another man was lovin yours too," and his too-much-sugar-in-the-tank behind then had the nerve to say, "Another man is twice as nice."[16] Well, do I have some news for you, girl:

16 Barbara Mason, "She's Got the Papers (But I Got the Man)," WMOT Records, 1981, single, https://www.discogs.com/Barbara-Mason-Shes-Got-The-Papers-But-I-Got -The-Man/release/5941854. Mason's record was a response to Richard "Dimples" Fields, featuring Betty Wright, "She's Got Papers on Me," CBS Records, 1981, single, https://www.discogs.com/Richard-Dimples-Fields-Shes-Got-Papers-On -Me/release/1165516. Dimples's record also engendered another response by Jean Knight & Premium, "You Got the Papers (But I Got the Man)," Cotillion Records, 1981, single, https://www.discogs.com/Jean-Knight-Premium-You-Got-The-Papers -But-I-Got-The-Man-Anything-You-Can-Do-I-Can-Do-As-Well-As-You/release /3116335. Mason followed up "She's Got the Papers (But I Got the Man)" three years later with "Another Man" (about her man's male lover), which precipitated an answer record from the perspective of the male lover, Tout Sweet's "Another Man Is Twice as Nice." Listen to Barbara Mason, "Another Man," West End Records, 1983, single, https://www.discogs.com/Barbara-Mason-Another-Man/release/79903; and Tout Sweet, "Another Man Is Twice as Nice," Buzz Records, 1983, single. Both Hartman and Mason mention specific streets in Philadelphia, as did Du Bois, of course. Here's the relevant verse about Market Street from Mason's song:

And I passed him on the steps one day
And he was switching more than I was
And I even caught him holding hands
Walking right down Market Street
We all know what Market Street is
He was so desirable
And this's gonna be such a waste.

You, me and he
What we gonna do, baby
You, me and he
What we gonna do, baby?[17]

Carol Cooper locates the Tout Sweet record in networks of what she terms "cryptoheterosexuality" in Black NYC nightlife of the 1980s. After attending a ball at Tracks, where the contestants' performance of masculine "realness" is too real, prompting the MC to tell everyone: "This category is for butch queens only! If you are straight, you cannot walk! I repeat, this category is for faggots who are queer, not faggots who are straight!" Cooper remembers the Midtown club Down Under:

> a popular after-work hangout for black white-collar workers, there to unwind and maybe see the occasional transvestite track performance. It, along with the Silver Shadow, Leviticus, Pegasus, Le Martinique, and other long-vanished disco bars, catered to a broad cross section of single urban professionals, most with omnivorous tastes in music, intoxicants, and pleasure. One of the most popular songs played there was recorded in answer to the infamous novelty hit by Barbara Mason, 'Another Man.' This new version, by someone under the pseudonym Toot Suite, was sung in the persona of the gentleman who had first shared, then stolen, Barbara's man away. In places where the difference between 'faggots who are queer and faggots who are straight' is merely a matter of interpretation, the crude honesty of that song always put everyone in a more candid frame of mind. If you weren't particularly thinking about sex, it forced the issue. If you were considering going home with some charming new acquaintance, it held focus your powers of discrimination. And if you were only into the music for music's sake, it provided a memorable chuckle.

Cooper, Pop Culture Considered as an Uphill Bicycle Race, 254.

17 Mtume, "You, Me and He (Polygamy Mix)," Epic Records, 1984, single, https://www.discogs.com/Mtume-You-Me-And-He/release/1522089. Hartman's book is in dialogue with the long history of R&B songs about nonmonogamous relationships, whether these are desired by all the participants or not. In the contemporary moment, these songs are often referred to as "side-chick" anthems and include such classics as Shirley Murdock's "As We Lay," SZA's "The Weekend," Whitney Houston's "Saving All My Love for You," or Xscape's "My Little Secret." I was particularly interested in the Mason, Sweet, and Mtume tracks because they center the plight of the "side dude," and in Mason's and Sweet's cases their lover has/is a male paramour. For an extended history of the shadowy male figure always waiting in the wings of heterosexual coupling in Black folklore and music, see Hanchard, "Jody."

Before I can explore "the ache of what might be" (30) to figure out what we gonna do, baby, another errantly untranslatable maternal melody of loss, one that could not be vocalized by the mothers and grandmothers but only the daughters, rings from a chorale across the breach of the Atlantic: "The girls are singing about those taken from Gwolu and sold into slavery in the Americas. They are singing about the diaspora. Here it was—my song, the song of the lost tribe. I closed my eyes and I listened."[18] I, too, close my eyes. I shudder, I tremble, because "to fall in step with the chorus is to do more than shake your ass and hum the melody, or repeat the few lines of the bit part handed over like a gift from the historian. . . . [S]he eludes the law and transforms the terms of the possible" (349).

No need to scream, only to listen, permitting everything she felt to pour out—the aspiration, the love, the girl broken in two, the grief. (236)

18 Hartman, Lose Your Mother, 166–67.

DISCOGRAPHY

Advanced Chemistry. *Fremd im eigenen Land.* MZEE Records, 1992, CD single. https://www.discogs.com/release/1080189-Advanced-Chemistry-Fremd-Im-Eigenen-Land.

Afrika Bambaataa & Soulsonic Force. "Planet Rock." Tommy Boy Records, 1982, CD single. http://www.discogs.com/Afrika-Bambaataa-The-Soul-Sonic-Force-Music-By-Planet-Patrol-Planet-Rock/release/2047.

The Artful Dodger. *Rewind: The Sound of UK Garage.* London/Sire Records, 2001, CD. https://www.discogs.com/release/112146-The-Artful-Dodger-Rewind-The-Sound-Of-UK-Garage.

The Artist (Formerly Known as Prince). "Sex in the Summer." On *Emancipation.* NPG Records, 1996. https://www.discogs.com/The-Artist-Formerly-Known-As-Prince-Emancipation/release/1158522.

Badu, Erykah. *But You Caint Use My Phone.* Motown Records, 2015, MP3. https://www.discogs.com/Erykah-Badu-But-You-Caint-Use-My-Phone/master/1057379.

Blaque. "808." Trackmasters/Columbia Records, 1999, CD single. http://www.discogs.com/Blaque-808/release/539643.

Blige, Mary J. *My Life.* Uptown/MCA Records, 1994, CD. https://www.discogs.com/master/78734-Mary-J-Blige-My-Life.

Blige, Mary J. "Not Gon' Cry." On *Waiting to Exhale (Original Soundtrack Album).* Arista Records, 1995, CD. http://www.discogs.com/Various-Waiting-To-Exhale-Original-Soundtrack-Album/master/78487.

Blige, Mary J. *What's the 411?* Uptown/MCA Records, 1992, CD. https://www.discogs.com/master/78837-Mary-J-Blige-Whats-The-411.

Blood Orange. "Sandra's Smile." On *Freetown Sound.* Domino Records, 2016, MP3. https://www.discogs.com/Blood-Orange-Freetown-Sound/release/8912995.

Bowie, David. *Scary Monsters.* RCA Victor, 1980, LP. https://www.discogs.com/release/423056-David-Bowie-Scary-Monsters.

Bowie, David. *Young Americans.* RCA Victor, 1975, LP. https://www.discogs.com/release/3864735-David-Bowie-Young-Americans.

Brothers Keepers. "Adriano (Letzte Warnung)." Nitty Gritty Music (Warner Brothers), 2001, CD. single. https://www.discogs.com/release/504374-Brothers-Keepers-Adriano-Letzte-Warnung.

Carey, Mariah. "Bringin' On the Heartbreak." On *Charmbracelet*. Island Records, 2002, CD. https://www.discogs.com/Mariah-Carey-Charmbracelet/release /666818.

Carey, Mariah. "Loverboy." Virgin Records, 2001, CD single. https://www.discogs .com/Mariah-Loverboy/release/156712.

Carey, Mariah, featuring Bone Thugs-n-Harmony. "Breakdown." Columbia Records, 1997, single. https://www.discogs.com/Mariah-Carey-Featuring-Bone -Thugs-N-Harmony-Breakdown/master/138726.

Chapman, Tracy. "Talkin' Bout a Revolution." On *Tracy Chapman*. Elektra Records, 1988, LP. https://www.discogs.com/Tracy-Chapman-Tracy-Chapman /release/7242971.

Cher. *Believe*. Warner Records, 1998, CD. https://www.discogs.com/master/69286 -Cher-Believe.

Lloyd Cole and The Commotions. "Are You Ready to Be Heartbroken?" On *Rattlesnakes*. Polydor Records, 1984, LP. https://www.discogs.com/Lloyd-Cole-And -The-Commotions-Rattlesnakes/release/441936.

Daft Punk. *Discovery*. Virgin Records, 2001, CD. https://www.discogs.com/master /26647-Daft-Punk-Discovery.

D'Angelo. *Voodoo*. Virgin Records, 2000, CD. https://www.discogs.com/DAngelo -Voodoo/release/15906733.

Destiny's Child. "Bug-A-Boo." On *The Writing's on the Wall*. SONY Music, 1999, CD. https://www.discogs.com/release/2863169-Destinys-Child-The-Writings -On-The-Wall.

Destiny's Child. "Say My Name." Columbia Records, 2000, CD single. https://www .discogs.com/Destinys-Child-Say-My-Name/release/1440586.

DJ Pierre. "Don't Take It Away." On *DJ Pierre*. Strictly Rhythm, 1994, CD. https:// www.discogs.com/release/26442-DJ-Pierre-DJ-Pierre.

Drake. "Hotline Bling." Cash Money Records, 2015, MP3. https://www.discogs.com /release/7312552-Drake-Hotline-Bling.

Sheila E. "A Love Bizarre." Warner Brothers Records, 1985, single. https://www .discogs.com/release/361375-Sheila-E-A-Love-Bizarre.

Elliot, Missy Misdemeanor, and 702. "Beep Me 911." Elektra Records, 1997, CD single. https://www.discogs.com/master/49367-Missy-Misdemeanor-Elliott -Featuring-702-And-Magoo-Beep-Me-911.

En Vogue. "My Lovin' (You're Never Gonna Get It)." On *Funky Divas*. EastWest Records, 1992, CD. http://www.discogs.com/En-Vogue-Funky-Divas/release/8869669.

EPMD. "You Gots to Chill." Fresh Records, 1986, single. https://www.discogs.com /EPMD-You-Gots-To-Chill/release/60290.

Fields, Richard. "Dimples," featuring Betty Wright. "She's Got Papers on Me." CBS Records, 1981, single. https://www.discogs.com/Richard-Dimples-Fields-Shes -Got-Papers-On-Me/release/1165516.

The Firm. "Phone Tap." On *The Firm: The Album*. Aftermath/Interscope Records, 1997, CD. https://www.discogs.com/release/24998164-The-Firm-The-Album.

Flack, Roberta. "Compared to What?" On *First Take*. Atlantic Records, 1969, LP. https://www.discogs.com/Roberta-Flack-First-Take/release/758676.

Flack, Roberta, and Donny Hathaway. "Be Real Black for Me." Atlantic Records, 1971, single. https://www.discogs.com/Roberta-Flack-Donny-Hathaway-Youve-Lost-That-Lovin-Feelin-Be-Real-Black-For-Me/release/2236719.

Flack, Roberta, and Donny Hathaway. "Where Is the Love." Atlantic Records, 1972, single. https://www.discogs.com/Roberta-Flack-Donny-Hathaway-Where-Is-The-Love-Mood/release/8548745.

Gaye, Marvin. "Sexual Healing." CBS Records, 1982, single. http://www.discogs.com/Marvin-Gaye-Sexual-Healing/release/584968.

Ginuwine. "Same Ol' G." Blackground/SONY Music, 1999, CD single. https://www.discogs.com/master/341397-Ginuwine-Same-Ol-G.

Ginuwine. "2 Way." On *The Life*. Sony Music, 2001, CD. http://www.discogs.com/Ginuwine-The-Life/master/258621.

Ginuwine and Aaliyah. "Final Warning." On *100% Ginuwine*, Blackground/SONY Music, 1999, CD. https://www.discogs.com/release/227125-Ginuwine-100-Ginuwine.

Glashaus. "Eine Hymne für mein Volk." On *Glashaus II (Jah Sound System)*. Pelham Power Productions, 2002, CD. https://www.discogs.com/release/845834-Glashaus-Glashaus-II-Jah-Sound-System.

Glashaus. "Erhalte meine Liebe." On *Drei*. Pelham Power Productions, 2005, CD. https://www.discogs.com/release/845825-Glashaus-Drei.

Glashaus. "Nal." On *Glashaus II (Jah Sound System)*. Pelham Power Productions, 2002, CD. https://www.discogs.com/release/845834-Glashaus-Glashaus-II-Jah-Sound-System.

Glashaus. "Prelude zu Bald." On *Glashaus II (Jah Sound System)*. Pelham Power Productions, 2002, CD. https://www.discogs.com/release/845834-Glashaus-Glashaus-II-Jah-Sound-System.

Glashaus. "Spuren im Sand. "On *Glashaus II (Jah Sound System)*. Pelham Power Productions, 2002, CD. https://www.discogs.com/release/845834-Glashaus-Glashaus-II-Jah-Sound-System.

Hancock, Herbie. *Sunlight*. CBS Records, 1978, LP. https://www.discogs.com/release/527548-Herbie-Hancock-Sunlight.

Houston, Whitney. "Exhale (Shoop Shoop)." Arista Records, 1995, CD single. https://www.discogs.com/Whitney-Houston-Exhale-Shoop-Shoop/release/1623575.

Houston, Whitney. "Thinking About You." On *Whitney Houston*. Arista Records, 1985, LP. https://www.discogs.com/release/458608-Whitney-Houston-Whitney-Houston.

Houston, Whitney. "Where Do Broken Hearts Go." Arista Records, 1988, single. https://www.discogs.com/Whitney-Houston-Where-Do-Broken-Hearts-Go/release/12416260.

Jackson, Janet. "Love Will Never Do (Without You)." A&M Records, 1989, CD single. https://www.discogs.com/Janet-Jackson-Love-Will-Never-Do-Without-You/master/92696.

Jamelia. "Call Me." Rhythm Series, 2000, CD single. http://www.discogs.com/Jamelia-Call-Me/release/1108420.

Jay-Z. "I Just Wanna Love U (Give It 2 Me)." Roc-A-Fella Records, 2000, CD single. http://www.discogs.com/Jay-Z-I-Just-Wanna-Love-U-Give-It-2-Me/release /781701.

Jodeci. "Feenin." On *Diary of a Mad Band*. Uptown/MCA Records, 1993, CD. https://www.discogs.com/Jodeci-Diary-Of-A-Mad-Band/release/251832.

Kandi. "Hey Kandi." On *Hey Kandi*. Columbia Records, 2000, CD. http://www .discogs.com/Kandi-Hey-Kandi/master/175988.

K-Ci and Jo Jo. "Crazy." MCA Records, 2001, CD single. https://www.discogs.com /release/6157721-K-Ci-JoJo-Crazy.

Kelis, featuring Too $hort. "Bossy." Virgin Records, 2005, CD single. http://www .discogs.com/Kelis-Featuring-Too-hort-Bossy/release/1939897.

Khan, Chaka, featuring Melle Mel. "I Feel for You." Warner Brothers Records, 1984, single. https://www.discogs.com/release/517013-Chaka-Khan-I-Feel-For -You.

Knight, Gladys, & the Pips. "Hero." On *Visions*. CBS Records, 1983, LP. https:// www.discogs.com/release/1590822-Gladys-Knight-The-Pips-Visions.

Knight, Jean, & Premium. "You Got the Papers (But I Got the Man)." Cotillion Records, 1981, single. https://www.discogs.com/Jean-Knight-Premium-You-Got-The -Papers-But-I-Got-The-Man-Anything-You-Can-Do-I-Can-Do-As-Well-As-You /release/3116335.

Kraftwerk. *The Mix*. Elektra/Warner Brothers Records, 1991, CD. https://www .discogs.com/master/42218-Kraftwerk-The-Mix.

LB. *Pop Artificielle*. Shadow Records, 2000, CD. https://www.discogs.com/master /30371-LB-Pop-Artificielle.

Lil Tjay, featuring 6LACK. "Calling My Phone." Columbia Records, 2021, MP3. https://www.discogs.com/Lil-Tjay-Ft-6LACK-Calling-My-Phone/release /17601781.

Lisa Marie, with Malcolm McLaren and The Bootzilla Orchestra. "Something's Jumpin' in Your Shirt." Epic Records, 1989, single. https://www.discogs.com/Lisa -Marie-With-Malcolm-McLaren-The-Bootzilla-Orchestra-Somethings-Jumpin -In-Your-Shirt/release/141198.

Madonna. "Music." Maverick/Sire Records, 2000, CD single. https://www.discogs .com/release/74025-Madonna-Music.

Majid Jordan. "OG Heartthrob." On *The Space Between*. OVO Sound, 2017, MP3. https://www.discogs.com/Majid-Jordan-The-Space-Between/release/15955897.

Martika. "Love . . . Thy Will Be Done." Columbia Records, 1991, CD single. https:// www.discogs.com/release/505837-Martika-LoveThy-Will-Be-Done.

Mason, Barbara. "Another Man." West End Records, 1983, single. https://www .discogs.com/Barbara-Mason-Another-Man/release/79903.

Mason, Barbara. "She's Got the Papers (But I Got the Man)." WMOT Records, 1981, single. https://www.discogs.com/Barbara-Mason-Shes-Got-The-Papers-But-I -Got-The-Man/release/5941854.

Maxwell. "Submerge." On *Embrya*. Columbia/SONY Music, 1998, CD. https://www .discogs.com/master/153997-Maxwell-Embrya.

Maze, featuring Frankie Beverly. "Joy & Pain." Capitol Records, 1981, single. https://www.discogs.com/Maze-Featuring-Frankie-Beverly-Joy-Pain/release/1206998.

Monica. "Blackberry." On *Still Standing*. J Records, 2010, CD. http://www.discogs.com/Monica-Still-Standing/release/2279141.

Monica. *Street Symphony*. Arista Records, 1999, CD. https://www.discogs.com/Monica-Street-Symphony/release/2502766.

Mtume. "You, Me and He (Polygamy Mix)." Epic Records, 1984, single. https://www.discogs.com/Mtume-You-Me-And-He/release/1522089.

Mýa. "My Love Is Like . . . Wo." A&M Records, 2003, CD single. https://www.discogs.com/Mýa-My-Love-Is-Like-Wo/release/3837497.

Naidoo, Xavier. *Nicht von dieser Welt*. Pelham Power Productions, 1998, CD. https://www.discogs.com/release/529138-Xavier-Naidoo-Nicht-Von-Dieser-Welt.

Naidoo, Xavier. "Seine Strassen." 3P (Sony BMG), 2000, CD single. https://www.discogs.com/release/2169657-Xavier-Naidoo-Seine-Strassen.

New Edition. "N.E. Heartbreak." On *Heart Break*. MCA Records, 1988, LP. https://www.discogs.com/New-Edition-Heart-Break/release/1562508.

Nicolette. "Wicked Mathematics." Shut Up and Dance Records, 1992, single. http://www.discogs.com/Nicolette-Wicked-Mathematics/release/160361.

The Notorious B.I.G. "One More Chance (Remix)." Bad Boy/Arista, 1995, CD single. https://www.discogs.com/release/1087336-Notorious-BIG-One-More-Chance.

Nuux, Amaal. "Later." On *Black Dove*. Public Records/Universal Music Canada, 2019, MP3.

Nuux, Amaal. "Scream." Public Records/Universal Music Canada, 2017, MP3.

Ocean, Frank. *Blonde*. Boys Don't Cry, 2016, CD. https://www.discogs.com/release/8932936-Frank-Ocean-Blonde.

Ocean, Frank. *Endless*. Boys Don't Cry, 2016, MP3. https://www.discogs.com/Frank-Ocean-Endless/master/1077026.

Polo G. "Rapstar." Columbia Records, 2021, MP3. https://www.discogs.com/Polo-G-Rapstar/release/18220837.

Prince. *Controversy*. Warner Brothers Records, 1981, LP. https://www.discogs.com/release/407398-Prince-Controversy.

Prince. *Dirty Mind*. Warner Brothers Records, 1980, LP. https://www.discogs.com/release/3941977-Prince-Dirty-Mind.

Prince. *1999*. Warner Brothers Records, 1982, LP. https://www.discogs.com/release/125881-Prince-1999.

Prince. *Sign o' the Times*. Paisley Park/Warner Brothers Records, 1987, LP. https://www.discogs.com/release/123915-Prince-Sign-O-The-Times.

Prince and The Revolution. "Computer Blue." On *Purple Rain*. Warner Brothers Records, 1984, LP. https://www.discogs.com/release/125874-Prince-And-The-Revolution-Purple-Rain.

Prince and The Revolution. "Erotic City." On *Let's Go Crazy/Erotic City*. Paisley Park/Warner Brothers Records, 1984, single. https://www.discogs.com/release/577951-Prince-And-The-Revolution-Lets-Go-Crazy-Erotic-City.

Prince and The Revolution. "I Would Die 4 u." Warner Brothers Records, 1984, single. https://www.discogs.com/release/186718-Prince-And-The-Revolution-I-Would-Die-4-U.

Prince and The Revolution. *Parade*. Paisley Park/Warner Brothers Records, 1986, LP. https://www.discogs.com/release/125869-Prince-And-The-Revolution-Parade.

Prince and The Revolution. "When Doves Cry." On *Purple Rain*. Warner Brothers Records, 1984, LP. https://www.discogs.com/release/125874-Prince-And-The-Revolution-Purple-Rain.

Richard, Dawn. *Armor On*. Our Dawn Entertainment, Chartbreaker Music Group, 2012, MP3. https://www.discogs.com/Dawn-Richard-Armor-On/release/3599447.

Rihanna. "Diamonds." Def Jam Recordings, 2012, CD single. https://www.discogs.com/Rihanna-Diamonds/release/4001175.

Rihanna, featuring Calvin Harris. "We Found Love." Def Jam Recordings, 2011, CD single. https://www.discogs.com/Rihanna-Feat-Calvin-Harris-We-Found-Love/release/3177028.

Rihanna, featuring Young Jeezy. "Hard." On *Rated R*. Def Jam Recordings, 2009, CD. https://www.discogs.com/Rihanna-Rated-R/release/4975541.

Rowland, Kelly, featuring Eve. "Like This." Columbia Records, 2007, CD single. https://www.discogs.com/Kelly-Rowland-Featuring-Eve-Like-This/release/4750638.

Rule, Ja, et al. "Put It on Me." Murder Inc./Def Jam Records, 2000, CD single. https://www.discogs.com/master/104665-Ja-Rule-Featuring-Lil-Mo-Vita-Put-It-On-Me.

Rustin, Bayard. "Were You There (When They Crucified My Lord)." On *Bayard Rustin Sings Twelve Spirituals on the Life of Christ*. Fellowship Records, 1952, LP. https://www.discogs.com/Bayard-Rustin-Bayard-Rustin-Sings-Twelve-Spirituals-On-The-Life-Of-Christ/release/2903614.

702. "You Don't Know." Motown Records, 1991, CD single. https://www.discogs.com/release/1258668–702-You-Dont-Know.

Shalamar. *Heartbreak*. Solar Records, 1984, LP. https://www.discogs.com/Shalamar-Heartbreak/release/1431870.

Sisters Keepers. "Liebe und Verstand." Nitty Gritty Music (Warner Brothers), 2001, CD single.

Somethin' for the People, featuring Trina & Tamara. "My Love Is the Shhh!" Warner Brothers Records, 1997, CD single. https://www.discogs.com/Somethin-For-The-People-Featuring-Trina-Tamara-My-Love-Is-The-Shhh/release/636617.

Songz, Trey. "LOL :-)." Atlantic Recording Corporation, 2009, CD single. http://www.discogs.com/Trey-Songz-LOL—The-Remixes/release/2044187.

Soul, Aaron. *Ring, Ring, Ring*. Def Soul, 2001, CD single. https://www.discogs.com/release/2290917-Aaron-Soul-Ring-Ring-Ring.

Street Jams: Electric Funk, Parts 1 and 2. Rhino Records, 1992, CD. https://www.discogs.com/release/184399-Various-Street-Jams-Electric-Funk-Parts-1–4.

Sullivan, Jazmine. "Mascara." On *Reality Show*. RCA Records, 2015, CD. https://www.discogs.com/Jazmine-Sullivan-Reality-Show/release/6549750.

Super Collider. *Head On*. Loaded Records, 1999, CD. https://www.discogs.com
/master/43892-Super_Collider-Head-On.

SWV. *Release Some Tension*. RCA/BMG Records, 1997, CD. https://www.discogs
.com/master/78404-SWV-Release-Some-Tension.

SZA. "Good Days." Top Dawg Entertainment, 2020, MP3. https://www.discogs
.com/release/16639632-SZA-Good-Days.

SZA. "Love Galore." On *Ctrl*. Top Dawg Entertainment, 2017, MP3. https://www
.discogs.com/release/10416609-SZA-Ctrl.

Timbaland, featuring Brandy. "808." No label, 2011, MP3.

Tout Sweet. "Another Man Is Twice as Nice." Buzz Records, 1983, single. https://
www.discogs.com/Tout-Sweet-Another-Man-Is-Twice-As-Nice/release/366342.

Turner, Tina. "What's Love Got to Do With It?" On *Private Dancer*. Capitol Records,
1984, LP. https://www.discogs.com/release/3709972-Tina-Turner-Private-Dancer.

Vanity 6. "If a Girl Answers (Don't Hang Up)." On *Vanity 6*. Warner Brothers Records, 1982, LP. https://www.discogs.com/release/560291-Vanity-6-Vanity-6.

Warwick, Dionne. "Heartbreaker." Arista Records, 1982, single. https://www
.discogs.com/Dionne-Warwick-Heartbreaker/release/378860.

Watley, Jody, featuring Eric B. & Rakim. "Friends." MCA Records, 1989, single.
https://www.discogs.com/master/131097-Jody-Watley-With-Eric-B-Rakim
-Friends.

West, Kanye Omari. *808s & Heartbreak*. Roc-A-Fella Records, 2008, CD. https://
www.discogs.com/release/1617049-Kanye-West-808s-Heartbreak.

Young Money, featuring Nicki Minaj. "Looking A**." On *Rise of an Empire*. Cash
Money Records, 2014, MP3. https://www.discogs.com/Young-Money-Rise-Of
-An-Empire/release/5742091.

Zapp. "Computer Love." Warner Brothers Records, 1985, single. https://www
.discogs.com/Zapp-Computer-Love/release/561605.

Zapp. "It Doesn't Really Matter." On *The New Zapp IV U*. Warner Brothers Records,
1985, LP. https://www.discogs.com/master/9474-Zapp-The-New-Zapp-IV-U.

Zapp. "Radio People." On *The New Zapp IV U*. Warner Brothers Records, 1985, LP.
https://www.discogs.com/master/9474-Zapp-The-New-Zapp-IV-U.

Zapp and Roger. "I Want to Be Your Man." Reprise Records, 1993, single. https://
www.discogs.com/Roger-I-Want-To-Be-Your-Man/release/508205.

FILMOGRAPHY

Akomfrah, John, dir. *The Last Angel of History*. London: Icarus Films, 1995.

Beadle-Blair, Rikki, dir. *Metrosexuality*. London: BBC, 1999. DVD.

Cokes, Anthony. *Mikrohaus, or the Black Atlantic?* Video, 2006–2008. Vimeo,
uploaded February 25, 2013. https://vimeo.com/60528438.

Coney, John, dir. *Space Is the Place*. New York: Plexifilm, 1974.

Contreras, Felix. "Young Latinos, Blacks Answer Call of Mobile Devices." NPR,
December 1, 2009. https://www.npr.org/2009/12/01/120852934/young-latinos
-blacks-answer-call-of-mobile-devices#commentBlock.

Glori, Lori, and Sarah Farina. "Black Voices—White Producers: Gespräch mit Lori Glori and Sarah Farina." Deutsches Museum für Schwarze Unterhaltung und Black Music, livestreamed December 16, 2020. https://www.youtube.com/watch ?v=GNpHF5KuROE.

Jenkins, Barry. *Moonlight*. Vancouver: Lionsgate, 2016. DVD.

Julien, Isaac, dir. *Looking for Langston*. London: Sankofa Film and Video, 1989. DVD.

Mack, Tim, and Michael John Warren. *Drake: Better Than Good Enough*. MTV, June 23, 2010. Documentary.

Prince, dir. *Under the Cherry Moon*. Los Angeles: Warner Brothers, 1986. DVD.

Robertson-Pearce, Pamela. "Jackie Kay." From *In Person: 30 Poets*, filmed by Pamela Robertson-Pearce, edited by Neil Astley (Hexham, UK: Bloodaxe Books, 2008). YouTube, uploaded May 25, 2009. https://www.youtube.com/watch?v =HiEyuJTyAlI.

Sciamma, Céline, dir. *Girlhood (Bande de filles)*. France: Strand Releasing, 2014. DVD.

Sextro, Maren, and Holger Wick, dirs. *We Call It Techno!* Berlin: Sense Music, 2008. DVD.

Whalley, Benjamin, dir. *Synth Britannia*. London: BBC Four, 2009. Documentary.

BIBLIOGRAPHY

Adams, Anne V. "The Souls of Black Volk: Contradiction? Oxymoron?" In *Not So Plain as Black and White: Afro-German Culture and History, 1890–2000*, edited by Patricia Mazón and Reinhild Steingröver, 209–32. Rochester, NY: University of Rochester Press, 2005.

Afolayan, Ekundayo. "Whether or Not Prince Knew It, He Was a Disability Icon to Me." *Black Girl Dangerous* (blog), April 22, 2016. https://www.bgdblog.org/2016 /04/whether-or-not-prince-knew-it/.

Agamben, Giorgio. *Means without End: Notes on Politics*. Translated by Cesare Cesarino and Vincenzo Binetti. Minneapolis: University of Minnesota Press, 2000.

Albiez, Sean, and David Pattie, eds. *Kraftwerk: Music Non-stop*. New York: Continuum, 2010.

Allen, Jafari S. *There's a Disco Ball between Us: A Theory of Black Gay Life*. Durham, NC: Duke University Press, 2021.

Althusser, Louis. "Marxism and Humanism." In *For Marx*, translated by Ben Brewster, 221–47. New York: Verso, 1990.

American Heart Association. "Is Broken Heart Syndrome Real?" Last reviewed May 4, 2022. https://www.heart.org/en/health-topics/cardiomyopathy/what-is -cardiomyopathy-in-adults/is-broken-heart-syndrome-real.

Araujo, Luiz. "History of Pagers and Beepers." *LafaCity.Info*, accessed July 12, 2010. http://lafacity.info/index.php/cell-phones-history/3-history-of-pagers-and -beepers.

Arceneaux, Michael. "How Reality TV Saved the R&B Star." *Vibe*, May 28, 2014. https://www.vibe.com/2014/05/opinion-how-reality-tv-saved-rb-singers.

Awkward, Michael. *Soul Covers: Rhythm and Blues Remakes and the Struggle for Artistic Identity (Aretha Franklin, Al Green, Phoebe Snow)*. Durham, NC: Duke University Press, 2007.

Ayim, May, Katharina Oguntoye, and Dagmar Schultz. *Showing Our Colors: Afro-German Women Speak Out*. 1986. Amherst: University of Massachusetts Press, 1992.

Badmington, Neil. *Readers in Cultural Criticism: Posthumanism*. New York: Palgrave, 2000.

Bailey, Alyssa. "Rihanna Talks Chris Brown, Staying Single, and Why She's Not Having Casual Sex." *ELLE*, October 2015. http://www.elle.com/culture/celebrities/news/a31010/rihanna-vanity-fair-november-interview/.

Balibar, Étienne. "The Nation Form: History and Ideology." In *Race, Nation, Class: Ambiguous Identities*, edited by Immanuel Maurice Wallerstein and Étienne Balibar, 86–106. London: Verso, 1991.

Balibar, Étienne. "Racism as Universalism." In *Masses, Classes, Ideas: Studies on Politics and Philosophy before and after Marx*, translated by James Swenson, 215–28. New York: Routledge, 1994.

Banks, Adam J. *Digital Griots: African American Rhetoric in a Multimedia Age*. Carbondale: Southern Illinois University Press, 2011.

Baraka, Amiri. *Blues People: Negro Music in White America*. Edinburgh: Payback Press, 1995.

Barrett, Lindon. *Blackness and Value: Seeing Double*. New York: Cambridge University Press, 1999.

Bat. "What Is Hypersoul?" Hyperdub, accessed June 27, 2014. https://hyperdub.net/softwar/hypersoul.cfm.

Bax, Daniel, and Joshua Aikins. "Wir sind stolz, Deutsche zu sein." *taz*, December 7, 2001. https://taz.de/Wir-sind-stolz-Deutsche-zu-sein/!1137009/.

Beers, David. "Irony Is Dead! Long Live Irony!" *Salon*, September 25, 2001. http://www.salon.com/life/feature/2001/09/25/irony_lives/print.html.

Bell, David, and Barbara Kennedy, eds. *The Cybercultures Reader*. London: Routledge, 2000.

Benjamin, Ruha. *Race after Technology: Abolitionist Tools for the New Jim Code*. New York: John Wiley, 2019.

Benjamin, Walter. *Gesammelte Schriften*. Edited by Rolf Tiedemann and Hermann Schweppenhäuser. Frankfurt: Suhrkamp, 1972.

Benjamin, Walter. "Der Sürrealismus: Die letzte Momentaufnahme der europäischen Intelligenz." In *Gesammelte Schriften*, edited by Rolf Tiedemann and Hermann Schweppenhäuser, 2:295–310. Frankfurt: Suhrkamp, 1972.

Benjamin, Walter. "Über den Begriff der Geschichte." In *Gesammelte Schriften*, edited by Rolf Tiedemann and Hermann Schweppenhäuser, 1.2:691–704. Frankfurt: Suhrkamp, 1972.

Bierria, Alisa. "'Where Them Bloggers At?': Reflections on Rihanna, Accountability, and Survivor Subjectivity." *Social Justice* 37, no. 4 (122) (2011): 101–25.

Black, Eric M. "A Tribute to Melvin Lindsey and the Original Quiet Storm." eb-4prez, February 14, 2018. https://eb4prez.wixsite.com/eb4prez/single-post/2018/02/14/a-tribute-to-melvin-lindsey-the-original-quiet-storm.

Black, Hannah. *Dark Pool Party*. Los Angeles: Dominica, 2016.

Black, Hannah. "'I Feel Like Everything Shouldn't Exist': An Interview with Hannah Black." Interview by Chris Randle. *Hazlitt*, August 23, 2016. http://hazlitt.net/feature/i-feel-everything-shouldnt-exist-interview-hannah-black.

Black Digerati. "I Use My T-Mobile Sidekick to Get Online More Than My Computer!" *Black Web 2.0*, September 4, 2009. http://www.blackweb20.com/2009/09/04/i-use-my-t-mobile-sidekick-to-get-online-more-than-my-computer/ (accessed July 12, 2010).

Booker, Bobbi. "David Bowie, Race and Black Music." *Philadelphia Tribune*, January 15, 2016. https://www.phillytrib.com/entertainment/david-bowie-race-and-black-music/article_65c4180c-5a59-5e3b-a7bc-17ce58a27ee8.html.

Boyce Davies, Carole, and Elaine Savory Fido, eds. *Out of the Kumbla: Caribbean Women and Literature*. Trenton, NJ: Africa World Press, 1990.

Brand, Dionne. *A Map to the Door of No Return: Notes on Belonging*. New York: Doubleday, 2002.

Brand, Dionne. *No Language Is Neutral*. Toronto: McClelland and Stewart, 1998.

Braun, Christoph. "Oh Herr, Alles wird Dein! Im Land der Pop-Propheten." Accessed July 12, 2010. http://www.fluter.de/look/article.tpl?IdLanguage=5&IdPublication=2&NrIssue=20&NrSection=12&NrArticle=2140.

Brock, André, Jr. *Distributed Blackness: African American Cybercultures*. New York: New York University Press, 2020.

Brody, Jennifer DeVere. *Punctuation: Art, Politics, and Play*. Durham, NC: Duke University Press, 2008.

Brooks, Daphne A. "'All That You Can't Leave Behind': Black Female Soul Singing and the Politics of Surrogation in the Age of Catastrophe." *Meridians: Feminism, Race, Transnationalism* 8, no. 1 (2007): 180–204.

Brooks, Daphne A. "'It's Not Right but It's Okay': Black Women's R&B and the House That Terry McMillan Built." *Souls* 5, no. 1 (2003): 32–45.

Brooks, Daphne A. *Liner Notes for the Revolution: The Intellectual Life of Black Feminist Sound*. Cambridge, MA: Harvard University Press, 2021.

Brooks, Daphne A. "'Sister, Can You Line It Out?': Zora Neale Hurston and the Sound of Angular Black Womanhood." *Amerikastudien/American Studies* 55, no. 4 (2010): 617–27.

Brooks, Daphne A. "'This Voice Which Is Not One': Amy Winehouse Sings the Ballad of Sonic Blue(s)Face Culture." *Women and Performance* 20, no. 1 (2010): 37–60. https://doi.org/10.1080/07407701003589337.

Brown, Jacqueline Nassy. "Black Liverpool, Black America, and the Gendering of Diasporic Space." *Cultural Anthropology* 13, no. 3 (1998): 291–325.

Brown, Jacqueline Nassy. *Dropping Anchor, Setting Sail*. Princeton, NJ: Princeton University Press, 2005.

Brown, Jayna. "Buzz and Rumble: Global Pop Music and Utopian Impulse." *Social Text* 28, no. 1 (102) (2010): 125–46.

Brustein, Joshua. "Mobile Web Use and the Digital Divide." *Bits* (blog), *New York Times*, July 7, 2010. http://bits.blogs.nytimes.com/2010/07/07/increased-mobile-web-use-and-the-digital-divide/.

Bull, Michael. *Sound Moves: iPod Culture and Urban Experience*. New York: Routledge, 2007.

Butler, Judith. *Antigone's Claim: Kinship between Life and Death*. New York: Columbia University Press, 2000.

Campbell, Mark V. "Everything's Connected: A Relationality Remix, a Praxis." *CLR James Journal* 20, nos. 1–2 (2014): 97–114.

Campt, Tina M. *A Black Gaze: Artists Changing How We See*. Cambridge, MA: MIT Press, 2021.

Campt, Tina M. *Other Germans: Black Germans and the Politics of Race, Gender, and Memory in the Third Reich*. Ann Arbor: University of Michigan Press, 2005.

Caramanica, Jon. "Kanye West Talks about His Career and Album 'Yeezus.'" *New York Times*, June 11, 2013. https://www.nytimes.com/2013/06/16/arts/music/kanye-west-talks-about-his-career-and-album-yeezus.html.

Carby, Hazel V. *Imperial Intimacies: A Tale of Two Islands*. London: Verso, 2019.

Carey, Iain M., Stephen DeWilde, Tess Harris, Christina R. Victor, and Derek G. Cook. "Increased Risk of Acute Cardiovascular Events after Partner Bereavement: A Matched Cohort Study." *JAMA Internal Medicine* 174, no. 4 (2014): 598–605.

Cateforis, Theodore. *Are We Not New Wave? Modern Pop at the Turn of the 1980s*. Ann Arbor: University of Michigan Press, 2011.

Century, Douglas. "A World Divided into Two-Way-Pager Camps." *New York Times*, January 14, 2001. https://www.nytimes.com/2001/01/14/style/noticed-a-world-divided-into-two-way-pager-camps.html.

Césaire, Aimé. *Discourse on Colonialism*. 1955. Translated by Joan Pinkham. New York: Monthly Review Press, 1972.

Césaire, Aimé. "Poetry and Knowledge." 1946. In *Refusal of the Shadow: Surrealism and the Caribbean*, edited by Krzysztof Fijałkowski and Michael Richardson, 134–46. London: Verso, 1996.

Christgau, Robert. "Pazz and Jop 1978: New Wave Hegemony and the Bebop Question." *Village Voice*, January 1979. https://www.robertchristgau.com/xg/pnj/pj78.php.

Christian, Barbara. "The Race for Theory." *Cultural Critique* 6 (1987): 51–63.

Chude-Sokei, Louis. "When Echoes Return: Roots, Diaspora and Possible Africas (a Eulogy)." *Transition* 104 (2011): 76–92.

Clark, Vèvè A. "Developing Diaspora Literacy: Allusion in Maryse Conde's *Heremakhonon*." In *Out of the Kumbla: Caribbean Women and Literature*, edited by Carole Boyce Davies and Elaine Savory Fido, 303–20. Trenton, NJ: Africa World Press, 1990.

Clay, Andreana. "Like an Old Soul Record: Black Feminism, Queer Sexuality, and the Hip-Hop Generation." *Meridians: Feminism, Race, Transnationalism* 8, no. 1 (2007): 53–73.

Clifford, Stephanie. "For BlackBerry, Obama's Devotion Is Priceless." *New York Times*, January 8, 2009. http://www.nytimes.com/2009/01/09/business/media /09blackberry.html.

Coleman, Beth. "Sound Effects: Tricia Rose Interviews Beth Coleman." In *Technicolor: Race, Technology, and Everyday Life*, edited by Alondra Nelson and Thuy Linh N. Tu, with Alicia Headlam Hines, 142–53. New York: New York University Press, 2001.

Connor, Steven. "The Modern Auditory I." In *Rewriting the Self: Histories from the Renaissance to the Present*, edited by Roy Porter, 203–23. London: Routledge, 1997.

Cooper, Carol. *Pop Culture Considered as an Uphill Bicycle Race: Selected Critical Essays (1979–2001)*. New York: Nega Fulo Books, 2006.

Corbett, John. *Extended Play: Sounding Off from John Cage to Dr. Funkenstein.* Durham, NC: Duke University Press, 1994.

Cottom, Tressie McMillan. "How We Make Black Girls Grow Up Too Fast." *New York Times*, July 29, 2017. https://www.nytimes.com/2017/07/29/opinion/sunday /how-we-make-Black-girls-grow-up-too-fast.html.

Crazy Horse, Kandia, ed. *Rip It Up: The Black Experience in Rock 'n' Roll.* New York: Macmillan, 2004.

Crenshaw, Kimberlé. "Mapping the Margins: Intersectionality, Identity Politics, and Violence against Women of Color." *Stanford Law Review* 43, no. 6 (1991): 1241–99.

Cruz, Jon. *Culture on the Margins: The Black Spiritual and the Rise of American Cultural Interpretation.* Princeton, NJ: Princeton University Press, 1999.

Crystal, David. *Language and the Internet.* New York: Cambridge University Press, 2006.

Crystal, David. *Txtng: The Gr8 Db8.* New York: Oxford University Press, 2008.

Cushing, Ellen. "Late-Stage Pandemic Is Messing with Your Brain." *Atlantic*, March 8, 2021. https://www.theatlantic.com/health/archive/2021/03/what -pandemic-doing-our-brains/618221/.

Dash, Anil. "Cats Can Has Grammar." *Anil Dash* (blog), April 23, 2007. http:// dashes.com/anil/2007/04/cats-can-has-gr.html.

Delany, Samuel R., Sinda Gregory, and Larry McCaffery. "The Semiology of Silence." *Science Fiction Studies* 14, no. 2 (1987): 134–64.

Deleuze, Gilles. *Francis Bacon: The Logic of Sensation.* 1981. Translated by Daniel W. Smith. Minneapolis: University of Minnesota Press, 2003.

Deleuze, Gilles, and Félix Guattari. *Anti-Oedipus: Capitalism and Schizophrenia.* 1972. Translated by Robert Hurley, Mark Seem, and Helen R. Lane. Minneapolis: University of Minnesota Press, 1983.

Deleuze, Gilles, and Félix Guattari. *Kafka: Toward a Minor Literature.* 1975. Translated by Dana Polan. Minneapolis: University of Minnesota Press, 1986.

Deleuze, Gilles, and Félix Guattari. *A Thousand Plateaus: Capitalism and Schizophrenia.* 1980. Translated by Brian Massumi. Minneapolis: University of Minnesota Press, 1987.

Denk, Felix, and Sven von Thülen. *Der Klang der Familie: Berlin, Techno and the Fall of the Wall*. Chicago: Books on Demand, 2014.

DeRogatis, Jim. "Parents Told Police Their Daughter Is Being Held against Her Will in R. Kelly's 'Cult.'" *BuzzFeed*, July 17, 2017. https://www.buzzfeed.com /jimderogatis/parents-told-police-r-kelly-is-keeping-women-in-a-cult.

Derrida, Jacques. "The Ends of Man." In *Margins of Philosophy*, translated by Alan Bass, 109–36. Chicago: University of Chicago Press, 1982.

Derrida, Jacques. "White Mythology: Metaphor in the Text of Philosophy." In *Margins of Philosophy*, translated by Alan Bass, 207–71. Chicago: University of Chicago Press, 1982.

Dery, Mark. "Black to the Future: Interviews with Samuel R. Delany, Greg Tate, and Tricia Rose." In *Flame Wars: The Discourse of Cyberculture*, edited by Mark Dery, 179–222. Durham, NC: Duke University Press, 1994.

Diedrichsen, Diedrich, ed. *Loving the Alien: Science Fiction, Diaspora, Multikultur*. Berlin: ID Verlag, 1998.

Dinh, James. "Blaque's Natina Reed Killed in Car Accident at Age 32." *MTV*, October 27, 2012. https://www.mtv.com/news/hk4lzw/natina-reed-blaque-dead.

Dixon, Melvin. "I'll Be Somewhere Listening for My Name." *Callaloo* 23, no. 1 (2000): 80–83.

Dozier, Ayanna. *Janet Jackson's "The Velvet Rope."* New York: Bloomsbury, 2020.

Dredge, Stuart. "5m Song Sales Milestone for Tap Revenge Games." *Mobile Entertainment News*, June 4, 2010. http://www.mobile-ent.biz/news/37390/5m-song -sales-milestone-for-Tap-Tap-Revenge-games (accessed July 12, 2010).

Du Bois, W. E. B. *The Autobiography of W. E. B. DuBois: A Soliloquy on Viewing My Life from the Last Decade of Its First Century*. New York: International Publishers, 1968.

Du Bois, W. E. B. *The Philadelphia Negro: A Social Study*. Philadelphia: Publications of the University of Pennsylvania, 1899.

Du Bois, W. E. B. "A Program for a Sociological Society (Speech to the First Sociological Club, Atlanta University, Atlanta, Georgia)." Microfilm edition of the W. E. B. Du Bois Papers, Reel 80, 1897. Manuscript Division, University of Massachusetts at Amherst.

Du Bois, W. E. B. *The Souls of Black Folk*. 1903. Edited by Donald B. Gibson. New York: Penguin Classics, 1996.

Dudley, Homer. "Homer Dudley's Speech Synthesizer." Accessed September 19, 2010. http://www.obsolete.com/120_years/ machines/vocoder).

du Gay, Paul, Stuart Hall, Linda James, Hugh Mackay, and Keith Negus. *Doing Cultural Studies: The Story of the Sony Walkman*. London: Open University Press, 1997.

Edwards, Brent Hayes. "The Taste of the Archive." *Callaloo* 35, no. 4 (2012): 944–72.

Edwards, Brent Hayes. "The Uses of Diaspora." *Social Text* 19, no. 1 (2001): 45–73.

Eidsheim, Nina Sun. *The Race of Sound: Listening, Timbre, and Vocality in African American Music*. Durham, NC: Duke University Press, 2018.

Ellison, Treva Carrie. "Black Femme Praxis and the Promise of Black Gender." *Black Scholar* 49, no. 1 (2019): 6–16.

Elshtain, Jean Bethke. *Public Man, Private Woman: Women in Social and Political Thought*. Princeton, NJ: Princeton University Press, 1993.

El-Tayeb, Fatima. "'If You Cannot Pronounce My Name, You Can Just Call Me Pride': Afro-German Activism, Gender, and Hip Hop." *Gender and History* 15, no. 3 (2003): 459–85.

Eshun, Kodwo. *More Brilliant Than the Sun: Adventures in Sonic Fiction*. London: Quartet Books, 1998.

Everett, Anna. "Digitextuality and Click Theory: Theses on Convergence Media in the Digital Age." In *New Media: Theories and Practices of Digitextuality*, edited by Anna Everett and John Thornton Caldwell, 3–28. New York: Routledge, 2003.

Famuyide, Kazeem. "David Bowie's Lasting Impact on Black Music." *Stashed*, January 11, 2016. http://thestashed.com/2016/01/11/david-bowies-lasting-impact-on-black-music/ (accessed December 21, 2018).

Fanon, Frantz. *Black Skin, White Masks*. 1952. Translated by Richard Philcox. New York: Grove, 2008.

Fanon, Frantz. *The Wretched of the Earth*. Translated by Constance Farrington. New York: Grove, 1991.

Fleetwood, Nicole R. "The Case of Rihanna: Erotic Violence and Black Female Desire." *African American Review* 45, no. 3 (2012): 419–35.

Fortunati, Leopoldina. "Is Body-to-Body Communication Still the Prototype?" *Information Society* 21, no. 1 (2005): 53–61.

Fortunati, Leopoldina. "The Mobile Phone: Towards New Categories and Social Relations." *Information, Communication and Society* 5, no. 4 (2002): 513–28.

Foster, Thomas. "The Souls of Cyber-Folk." In *Cyberspace Textuality: Computer Technology and Literary Theory*, edited by Marie-Laure Ryan, 137–63. Bloomington: Indiana University Press, 1999.

Foucault, Michel. *The Order of Things: An Archaeology of the Human Sciences*. New York: Vintage, 1973.

Frazier, Chelsea M. "Thinking Red, Wounds, and Fungi in Wangechi Mutu's Eco-Art." In *Ecologies, Agents, Terrains*, edited by Christopher P. Heuer and Rebecca Zorach, 167–94. New Haven, CT: Yale University Press, 2018.

Fuentes, Marisa J. *Dispossessed Lives: Enslaved Women, Violence, and the Archive*. Philadelphia: University of Pennsylvania Press, 2016.

Fuentes, Marisa J. "Genres of History and the Practice of Loss." *Small Axe: A Caribbean Journal of Criticism* 25, no. 1 (2021): 167–74.

Gallon, Kim. "Making a Case for the Black Digital Humanities." In *Debates in the Digital Humanities 2016*, edited by Matthew K. Gold and Lauren F. Klein, 42–49. Minneapolis: University of Minnesota Press, 2016..

Garza, Alicia. "Purple Reigns: A Black Lives Matter Tribute to Prince." Black Lives Matter, April 2016. http://prince.blacklivesmatter.com/prince-rogers-nelson-by-alicia-garza/ (accessed December 21, 2018).

Gates, Racquel J. *Double Negative: The Black Image and Popular Culture*. Durham, NC: Duke University Press, 2018.

Gaye, Jan, and David Ritz. *After the Dance: My Life with Marvin Gaye*. New York: Harper Collins, 2015.

George, Nelson. *The Death of Rhythm and Blues*. New York: Penguin, 1988.

Georgis, Dina. *The Better Story: Queer Affects from the Middle East*. Albany: State University of New York Press, 2013.

Ghansah, Rachel Kaadzi. "How Sweet It Is to Be Loved by You: The BeyHive." *NPR: The Record*, March 17, 2014. http://www.npr.org/sections/therecord/2014/03/17 /258155902/how-sweet-it-is-to-be-loved-by-you-the-beyhive.

Gibson, Teneille, Mariela Patron, and Tracee Wilkins. "Quiet Storm: Melodies, Moods and Mixes of Melvin Lindsey." *NBC4 Washington*, November 24, 2021. https://www.nbcwashington.com/news/local/quiet-storm-melodies-moods -mixes-of-melvin-lindsey/2884692/.

Gilbert, Jeremy, and Ewan Pearson. *Discographies: Dance Music, Culture and the Politics of Sound*. London: Routledge, 1999.

Gilmore, Ruth Wilson. "Race and Globalization." In *Geographies of Global Change: Remapping the World*, edited by Ronald John Johnston, Peter J. Taylor, and Michael J. Watts, 261–74. 2nd ed. Malden, MA: Blackwell, 2002.

Gilroy, Paul. *Against Race: Imagining Politics beyond the Color Line*. Cambridge, MA: Harvard University Press, 2002.

Gilroy, Paul. "Analogues of Mourning, Mourning the Analogue." In *Stars Don't Stand Still in the Sky: Music and Myth*, edited by Karen Kelly and Evelyn Mc-Donnell, 261–71. New York: New York University Press, 1999.

Gilroy, Paul. *The Black Atlantic: Modernity and Double Consciousness*. Cambridge, MA: Harvard University Press, 1993.

Gitelman, Lisa. *Scripts, Grooves, and Writing Machines: Representing Technology in the Edison Era*. Stanford, CA: Stanford University Press, 1999.

Glissant, Édouard. *Poetics of Relation*. 1990. Translated by Betsy Wing. Ann Arbor: University of Michigan Press, 1997.

Goggin, Gerard. *Cell Phone Culture: Mobile Technology in Everyday Life*. London: Routledge, 2006.

Goggin, Gerard. *Global Mobile Media*. London: Routledge, 2011.

Gomez, Jewelle. "Fishes in a Pond: An Interview with Jewelle Gomez." In *Femme: Feminists, Lesbians, and Bad Girls*, edited by Laura Harris and Elizabeth Crocker, 145–60. New York: Routledge, 1997.

Goodman, Steve. *Sonic Warfare: Sound, Affect, and the Ecology of Fear*. Cambridge, MA: MIT Press, 2010.

Gopinath, Sumanth. "Ringtones, or the Auditory Logic of Globalization." *First Monday* 10, no. 12 (2005). https://firstmonday.org/ojs/index.php/fm/article /download/1295/1215?inline=1.

Gracyk, Theodore. *Rhythm and Noise: The Aesthetics of Rock*. Durham, NC: Duke University Press, 1996.

Green, Nicola. "On the Move: Technology, Mobility, and the Mediation of Social Time and Space." *Information Society* 18, no. 4 (2002): 281–92.

Green, Richard C., and Monique Guillory. "Question of a 'Soulful Style': Interview with Paul Gilroy." In *Soul: Black Power, Politics, and Pleasure*, edited by Monique Guillory and Richard C. Green, 250–65. New York: New York University Press, 1998.

Greene, Jayson. "Is Rihanna the Most Influential Pop Singer of the Past Decade?" *Pitchfork*, April 5, 2017. https://pitchfork.com/features/overtones/10052-is -rihanna-the-most-influential-pop-singer-of-the-past-decade/.

Greene-Hayes, Ahmad. "'Queering' African American Religious History." *Religion Compass* 13, no. 7 (2019): e12319. https://doi.org/10.1111/rec3.12319.

Greenman, Ben. *Dig if You Will the Picture: Funk, Sex, God, and Genius in the Music of Prince*. New York: Henry Holt, 2017.

Griffin, Farah Jasmine. "When Malindy Sings: A Meditation on Black Women's Vocality." In *Uptown Conversation: The New Jazz Studies*, edited by Robert G. O'Meally, Brent Hayes Edwards, and Farah Jasmine Griffin, 102–25. New York: Columbia University Press, 2004.

Grose, Jessica. "Why Your Brain Feels Broken." *New York Times*, February 24, 2021. https://www.nytimes.com/2021/02/24/parenting/quarantine-brain-memory.html.

Halberstam, Judith, and Ira Livingston, eds. *Posthuman Bodies*. Bloomington: Indiana University Press, 1995.

Haley, Sarah. "Intimate Historical Practice." *Journal of African American History* 106, no. 1 (2021): 104–8. https://doi.org/10.1086/712011.

Haley, Sarah. *No Mercy Here: Gender, Punishment, and the Making of Jim Crow Modernity*. Chapel Hill: University of North Carolina Press, 2016.

Hall, Stuart. "When Was 'the Post-colonial'? Thinking at the Limit." In *The Post-colonial Question: Common Skies, Divided Horizons*, edited by Iain Chambers and Lidia Curti, 242–60. London: Routledge, 1996.

Hanchard, Michael. "Jody." *Critical Inquiry* 24, no. 2 (1998): 473–97.

Hancox, Dan. "On the Buses: Sodcasting and Mobile Music Culture." *Dan Hancox: A Miasma of Lunatic Alibis* (blog), October 23, 2009. http://dan-hancox .blogspot.com/2009/10/on-buses-sodcasting-and-mobile-music.html.

Hanson, Michael. "I'm a Brotha' but Sometimes I Don't Feel Black." In *Afrogeeks: Beyond the Digital Divide*, edited by Anna Everett and Amber Wallace, 13–27. Irvine: Center for Black Studies Research, 2007.

Haraway, Donna. "A Cyborg Manifesto: Science, Technology, and Socialist Feminism in the 1980s." In *Simians, Cyborgs, and Women: The Reinvention of Nature*, 149–82. New York: Routledge, 1991.

Haraway, Donna. "Ecce Homo, Ain't (Ar'n't) I a Woman, and Inappropriate/d Others: The Human in a Post-humanist Landscape." In *Feminists Theorize the Political*, edited by Judith Butler and Joan W. Scott, 86–100. New York: Routledge, 1992.

Hardt, Michael, and Antonio Negri. *Multitude: War and Democracy in the Age of Empire*. New York: Penguin, 2004.

Harper, Phillip Brian. *Are We Not Men? Masculine Anxiety and the Problem of African-American Identity*. New York: Oxford University Press, 1998.

Harris, Cheryl. "Whiteness as Property." *Harvard Law Review* 106, no. 8 (1993): 1707–91.

Hartman, Saidiya V. "The Belly of the World: A Note on Black Women's Labors." *Souls* 18, no. 1 (2016): 166–73.

Hartman, Saidiya V. *Lose Your Mother: A Journey along the Atlantic Slave Route.* New York: Farrar, Straus and Giroux, 2007.

Hartman, Saidiya V. "On Working with Archives: An Interview with Writer Saidiya Hartman." Interview by Thora Siemsen. *Creative Independent*, April 18, 2018. https://thecreativeindependent.com/people/saidiya-hartman-on-working -with-archives/.

Hartman, Saidiya V. *Scenes of Subjection: Terror, Slavery, and Self-Making in Nineteenth-Century America.* New York: Oxford University Press, 1997.

Hartman, Saidiya V. "Venus in Two Acts." *Small Axe: A Caribbean Journal of Criticism* 12, no. 2 (26) (2008): 1–14.

Hartman, Saidiya V. *Wayward Lives, Beautiful Experiments: Intimate Histories of Social Upheaval.* New York: W. W. Norton, 2019.

Harvey, Eric. "The Quiet Storm." *Pitchfork*, May 15, 2012. https://pitchfork.com /features/underscore/8822-the-quiet-storm/.

Hauser, Kasper. *Obama's BlackBerry.* New York: Little, Brown, 2009.

Hayles, N. Katherine. *How We Became Posthuman: Virtual Bodies in Cybernetics, Literature, and Informatics.* Chicago: University of Chicago Press, 1999.

Heath, Chris. "The Confessions of R. Kelly." GQ, January 20, 2016. http://www.gq .com/story/r-kelly-confessions.

Heath, Chris. "Why R. Kelly Calls Himself 'the Pied Piper of R&B.'" GQ, February 3, 2016. http://www.gq.com/story/why-r-kelly-calls-himself-pied-piper.

Heckman, Davin. "'Do You Know the Importance of a Skypager?': Telecommunications, African Americans, and Popular Culture." In *The Cell Phone Reader: Essays in Social Transformation*, edited by Anandam Kavoori and Noah Arceneaux, 173–86. New York: Peter Lang, 2006.

Henriques, Julian. *Sonic Bodies: Reggae Sound Systems, Performance Techniques, and Ways of Knowing.* London: Continuum, 2011.

Henry, Paget. *Caliban's Reason: Introducing Afro-Caribbean Philosophy.* New York: Routledge, 2000.

Hill, Edwin C. *Black Soundscapes, White Stages: The Meaning of Francophone Sound in the Black Atlantic.* Baltimore, MD: Johns Hopkins University Press, 2013.

Hine, Darlene Clark, Trica Danielle Keaton, and Stephen Small, eds. *Black Europe and the African Diaspora.* Urbana: University of Illinois Press, 2009.

Hines, Alicia Headlam, Alondra Nelson, and Thuy Linh N. Tu. "Introduction: Hidden Circuits." In *Technicolor: Race, Technology, and Everyday Life*, edited by Alondra Nelson and Thuy Linh N. Tu, with Alicia Headlam Hines, 1–12. New York: New York University Press, 2000.

Hirshey, Gerri. *Nowhere to Run: The Story of Soul Music.* New York: Da Capo, 1994.

Hopper, Jessica. "Read the 'Stomach-Churning' Sexual Assault Accusations against R. Kelly in Full." *Village Voice*, December 16, 2013. http://www.villagevoice.com /music/read-the-stomach-churning-sexual-assault-accusations-against-r-kelly -in-full-6637412.

Hove, Michael J., Céline Marie, Ian C. Bruce, and Laurel J. Trainor. "Superior Time Perception for Lower Musical Pitch Explains Why Bass-Ranged Instruments

Lay Down Musical Rhythms." *Proceedings of the National Academy of Sciences* 111, no. 28 (2014): 10383–88. https://doi.org/10.1073/pnas.1402039111.

International Telecommunication Union. *Measuring the Information Society*. ICT Development Index 2011. International Telecommunication Union (Geneva), 2011. https://www.itu.int/net/pressoffice/backgrounders/general/pdf/5.pdf.

Iqbal, Nosheen. "Kelela: 'I Know Deep Down I'm a Star.'" *Guardian*, October 28, 2017. http://www.theguardian.com/music/2017/oct/28/kelela-know-deep-down -star-singer-r-and-b.

Iton, Richard. *In Search of the Black Fantastic: Politics and Popular Culture in the Post–Civil Rights Era*. New York: Oxford University Press, 2008.

Jackson, Lauren Michele. *White Negroes: When Cornrows Were in Vogue . . . and Other Thoughts on Cultural Appropriation*. Boston: Beacon, 2019.

Jaji, Tsitsi Ella. *Africa in Stereo: Modernism, Music, and Pan-African Solidarity*. New York: Oxford University Press, 2014.

James, C. L. R. (Cyril Lionel Robert). "Black Studies and the Contemporary Student" (1969). In *The C. L. R. James Reader*, edited by Anna Grimshaw, 390–404. Malden, MA: Blackwell, 1992.

James, Joy. "Political Trauma." In *The Bloomsbury Handbook of 21st-Century Feminist Theory*, edited by Robin Truth Goodman, 345–54. New York: Bloomsbury, 2019.

Jarreau, Renee. "Black Women Helped Build House Music. Their Credit Is Often Left off Records." *ZORA*, July 10, 2020. https://zora.medium.com/black-women -helped-build-house-music-their-credit-is-often-left-off-records-8fc505300bd1.

Jenkins, Henry. *Convergence Culture: Where Old and New Media Collide*. New York: New York University Press, 2006.

Johnson, Jessica Marie. *Wicked Flesh: Black Women, Intimacy, and Freedom in the Atlantic World*. Philadelphia: University of Pennsylvania Press, 2020.

Johnson, Lynne D. "Sorry Jay-Z Auto Tune Isn't Dead, T-Pain Has an iPhone App to Spread It to the Masses." *Fast Company*, September 4, 2009. http://www .fastcompany.com/blog/lynne-d-johnson/digital-media-diva/sorry-jay-z-auto -tune-isnt-dead-t-pain-has-iphone-app-spread.

Jones, Meta DuEwa. *The Muse Is Music: Jazz Poetry from the Harlem Renaissance to Spoken Word*. Urbana: University of Illinois Press, 2011.

Jones, Steven G. *Virtual Culture: Identity and Communication in Cybersociety*. Thousand Oaks, CA: Sage, 1997.

Jordan, June. *Civil Wars*. Boston: Beacon, 1981.

Jordan, June. *Some of Us Did Not Die: New and Selected Essays of June Jordan*. New York: Basic/Civitas, 2002.

Judy, Ronald A. T. "Untimely Intellectuals and the University." *boundary 2* 27, no. 1 (2000): 121–33.

Katz, James Everett, ed. *Handbook of Mobile Communication Studies*. Cambridge, MA: MIT Press, 2008.

Katz, James Everett, and Mark A. Aakhus. *Perpetual Contact: Mobile Communication, Private Talk, Public Performance*. New York: Cambridge University Press, 2002.

Kay, Jackie. *Other Lovers*. Hexham, UK: Bloodaxe Books, 1993.

Keeling, Kara. "Electric Feel." *Cultural Studies* 28, no. 1 (2014): 49–83. https://doi
.org/10.1080/09502386.2013.779735.

Keeling, Kara. "Looking for M—Queer Temporality, Black Political Possibility, and
Poetry from the Future." *GLQ: A Journal of Lesbian and Gay Studies* 15, no. 4
(2009): 565–82.

Keeling, Kara. *The Witch's Flight: The Cinematic, the Black Femme, and the Image
of Common Sense*. Durham, NC: Duke University Press, 2007.

Keeling, Kara, and Josh Kun. "Introduction: Listening to American Studies."
American Quarterly 63, no. 3 (2011): 445–59.

Kelley, Emma Dunham. *Four Girls at Cottage City*. 1895. New York: Oxford University Press, 1988.

Kelley, Robin D. G. *Yo' Mama's Disfunktional! Fighting the Culture Wars in Urban
America*. Boston: Beacon, 1998.

King, Jason. "Any Love: Silence, Theft, and Rumor in the Work of Luther Vandross." *Callaloo* 23, no. 1 (2000): 422–47.

King, Jason. "The Sound of Velvet Melting: The Power of 'Vibe' in the Music of
Roberta Flack." In *Listen Again: A Momentary History of Pop Music*, edited by
Eric Weisbard, 172–99. Durham, NC: Duke University Press, 2007.

King, Tiffany Lethabo. *The Black Shoals: Offshore Formations of Black and Native
Studies*. Durham, NC: Duke University Press, 2019.

Kittler, Friedrich. *Discourse Networks, 1800/1900*. Translated by Michael Metteer
and Chris Cullen. Stanford, CA: Stanford University Press, 1990.

Kittler, Friedrich. *Gramophone, Film, Typewriter*. Translated by Geoffrey Winthrop-
Young and Michael Wutz. Stanford, CA: Stanford University Press, 1999.

Kolko, Beth E., Lisa Nakamura, and Gilbert B. Rodman, eds. *Race in Cyberspace*.
New York: Routledge, 2000.

Kronengold, Charles. "Exchange Theories in Disco, New Wave, and Album-
Oriented Rock." *Criticism* 50, no. 1 (2008): 43–82.

Laclau, Ernesto. *On Populist Reason*. London: Verso, 2005.

Lang, Michael. "Young Blacks and Latinos Are Labeled the 'Hyerusers' of Mobile
Devices." *Noire Digerati—the Future Face of Technology*, November 30, 2009.
http://www.noiredigerati.com/articles/2009/11/30/young-blacks-and-latinos
-are-labeled-the-hyerusers-of-mobile.html (accessed July 12, 2010).

Larsen, Nella. *"Quicksand" and "Passing."* Edited by Deborah E. McDowell. New
Brunswick, NJ: Rutgers University Press, 1986.

Lastra, James. *Sound Technology and the American Cinema: Perception, Representation, Modernity*. New York: Columbia University Press, 2000.

Lauré al-Samarai, Nicola. "History, Theory, Experience: Aspects of Diaspora in
Black German Feminist Thought." Paper presented at the conference Challeng-
ing Europe: Black European Studies in the 21st Century, Johannes Gutenberg
University, Mainz, Germany, October 23, 2005.

Lefebvre, Henri. *Rhythmanalysis: Space, Time and Everyday Life*. Translated by
Stuart Elden and Gerald Moore. New York: Continuum, 2004.

Levinson, Paul. *The Soft Edge: A Natural History and Future of the Information
Revolution*. New York: Routledge, 1997.

Levitin, David J. *This Is Your Brain on Music: The Science of a Human Obsession.* New York: Plume, 2007.

Lewis, David Levering. *W. E. B. Du Bois: Biography of a Race, 1868–1919.* New York: Henry Holt, 1994.

Licoppe, Christian. "The Mobile Phone's Ring." In *Handbook of Mobile Communication Studies,* edited by James Katz, 139–52. Cambridge, MA: MIT Press, 2008.

Lindsey, Treva B. "If You Look in My Life: Love, Hip-Hop Soul, and Contemporary African American Womanhood." *African American Review* 46, no. 1 (2013): 87–99.

Ling, Rich, and Scott W. Campbell. *The Reconstruction of Space and Time: Mobile Communication Practices.* New York: Transaction, 2009.

Lipsitz, George. *The Possessive Investment in Whiteness: How White People Profit from Identity Politics.* Philadelphia: Temple University Press, 1998.

Lockard, Joe. "Virtual Whiteness and Narrative Diversity." *Undercurrent,* no. 4 (1994). http://darkwing.uoregon.edu/~ucurrent/uc4/4-lockard.html.

Lowe, Lisa. "Other Humanities." Talk presented at the Humanities Institute, State University of New York, Stony Brook, March 28, 2000.

Macharia, Keguro. *Frottage: Frictions of Intimacy across the Black Diaspora.* New York: New York University Press, 2019.

Macpherson, Crawford Brough. *The Political Theory of Possessive Individualism: Hobbes to Locke.* Oxford: Clarendon Press, 1962.

Madden, Sidney. "Today in Hip-Hop: Lisa 'Left Eye' Lopes Burns Down Andre Rison's Mansion." *XXL Mag,* June 9, 2015. http://www.xxlmag.com/news/2015/06/today-hip-hop-lisa-left-eye-lopes-burns-andre-risons-mansion/.

Mahon, Maureen. *Black Diamond Queens: African American Women and Rock and Roll.* Durham, NC: Duke University Press, 2020.

Marshall, Wayne. "Mobile Music and Treble Culture." *Wayne and Wax* (blog), September 1, 2009. http://wayneandwax.com/?p=2332.

Massumi, Brian. *Parables for the Virtual: Movement, Affect, Sensation.* Durham, NC: Duke University Press, 2002.

Matthew, Terry. "DJ Pierre Describes Wild Pitch—and Some Straight Talk about Acid House." *5 Magazine,* May 3, 2013. https://5mag.net/features/dj-pierre-wild-pitch-acid-house-origin/.

May, Harvey, and Greg Hearn. "The Mobile Phone as Media." *International Journal of Cultural Studies* 8, no. 2 (2005): 195–211.

McCombe, John. "David Bowie and the Myth of the Berlin Trilogy: Tearing Down Musical Walls in the 1970s." *Journal of Popular Culture* 50, no. 5 (2017): 949–67. https://doi.org/10.1111/jpcu.12604.

McDowell, Deborah E. *The Changing Same: Black Women's Literature, Criticism, and Theory.* Bloomington: Indiana University Press, 1995.

McKittrick, Katherine. *Dear Science and Other Stories.* Durham, NC: Duke University Press, 2021.

McKittrick, Katherine. *Demonic Grounds: Black Women and the Cartographies of Struggle.* Minneapolis: University of Minnesota Press, 2006.

McKittrick, Katherine. "Fantastic/Still/Life: On Richard Iton (a Working Paper)." *Contemporary Political Theory* 14, no. 4 (2015): 24–32.

McKittrick, Katherine. "Mathematics Black Life." *Black Scholar* 44, no. 2 (2014): 16–28.

McKittrick, Katherine. "Rebellion/Invention/Groove." *Small Axe: A Caribbean Journal of Criticism* 20, no. 1 (49) (2016): 79–91.

McKittrick, Katherine. "Worn Out." *Southeastern Geographer* 57, no. 1 (2017): 96–100.

Meintjes, Louise. *Sound of Africa! Making Music Zulu in a South African Studio.* Durham, NC: Duke University Press, 2003.

Melton, Kara. "'A Kind of Logic, a Kind of Dominant Logic': Navigating Colonialism, Honoring Black Mobility, and Thinking on Moving Through." Master's thesis, Queen's University, 2016. https://qspace.library.queensu.ca/handle/1974/14599.

Mickle, Tripp. "Farewell to the iPod." *New York Times*, May 10, 2022. https://www.nytimes.com/2022/05/10/technology/apple-ipod-phasing-out.html.

Moody, Nekesa Mumbi. "Rappers Aim for Ringtones." *News and Observer*, November 2, 2007. http://www.newsobserver.com/105/story/757666.html.

moore, madison. "DARK ROOM: Sleaze and the Queer Archive." *Contemporary Theatre Review* 31, no. 1–2 (2021): 191–96. https://doi.org/10.1080/10486801.2021.1878510.

moore, madison. *Fabulous: The Rise of the Beautiful Eccentric.* New Haven, CT: Yale University Press, 2018.

Moraga, Cherríe, and Gloria Anzaldúa, eds. *This Bridge Called My Back: Writings by Radical Women of Color.* 2nd ed. Albany, NY: Kitchen Table: Women of Color Press, 1983.

Morrison, Gary. "Vocoders and Vocoder-Derivatives with *SuperCollider*." Accessed April 12, 2006. http://www.lonestar.texas.net/~mr88cet/VocodingWebDemo/VocoderDemo.html.

Morrison, Matthew D. "Race, Blacksound, and the (Re)Making of Musicological Discourse." *Journal of the American Musicological Society* 72, no. 3 (2019): 781–823.

Morrison, Toni. *Beloved.* New York: Plume, 1987.

Morrison, Toni. *Sula.* New York: Plume, 1973.

Morton, David. *Off the Record: The Technology of Sound Recording in America.* New Brunswick, NJ: Rutgers University Press, 2000.

Moten, Fred. *In the Break: The Aesthetics of the Black Radical Tradition.* Minneapolis: University of Minnesota Press, 2003.

Moten, Fred. "Uplift and Criminality." In *Stolen Life*, 115–39. Durham, NC: Duke University Press, 2018.

"Multimedia Communications *Research Laboratory*." Bell Labs, Accessed April 28, 2001. http://www. bell-labs.com/org/1133/heritage/ Synthesis/.

Nancy, Jean-Luc. *Being Singular Plural.* Translated by Robert Richardson and Anne O'Byrne. Stanford, CA: Stanford University Press, 2000.

Neal, Mark Anthony. *Black Ephemera: The Crisis and Challenge of the Musical Archive*. New York: New York University Press, 2022.

Neal, Mark Anthony. *Songs in the Key of Black Life: A Rhythm and Blues Nation*. New York: Routledge, 2014.

Neal, Mark Anthony. *Soul Babies: Black Popular Culture and the Post-soul Aesthetic*. New York: Routledge, 2002.

Niemczyk, Ralf, and Sebastian Zabel. "Freie Abfahrt für freie Bürger." *Spex* (January 1992): 57–60.

Noble, Safiya Umoja. *Algorithms of Oppression: How Search Engines Reinforce Racism*. New York: New York University Press, 2018.

Nyong'o, Tavia. *Afro-Fabulations: The Queer Drama of Black Life*. New York: New York University Press, 2018.

Nyong'o, Tavia. "Afro-Philo-Sonic Fictions: Black Sound Studies after the Millennium." *Small Axe: A Caribbean Journal of Criticism* 18, no. 2 (44) (2014): 173–79.

Nyong'o, Tavia. "I Feel Love: Disco and Its Discontents." *Criticism* 50, no. 1 (2008): 101–12.

Nyong'o, Tavia. "'I've Got You under My Skin': Queer Assemblages, Lyrical Nostalgia and the African Diaspora." *Performance Research* 12, no. 3 (2007): 42–54.

Nyong'o, Tavia. "Unburdening Representation." *Black Scholar* 44, no. 2 (2014): 70–80.

Opitz, May "Aufbruch." In *Farbe bekennen: Afro-deutsche Frauen auf den Spuren ihrer Geschichte*, edited by Katharina Oguntoye, May Opitz, and Dagmar Schultz, 202–7. Berlin: Orlanda Frauenverlag, 1986.

Palmer, Lisa Amanda. "'Men Cry Too': Black Masculinities and Feminisation of Lovers Rock in the UK." In *Black Popular Music in Britain since 1945*, edited by Jon Stratton and Nabeel Zuberi, 115–30. New York: Routledge, 2016.

Palmer, Tyrone S. "'What Feels More Than Feeling?': Theorizing the Unthinkability of Black Affect." *Critical Ethnic Studies* 3, no. 2 (2017): 31–56.

Patel, Aniruddh D. *Music, Language, and the Brain*. New York: Oxford University Press, 2010.

Patterson, Robert J. *Destructive Desires: Rhythm and Blues Culture and the Politics of Racial Equality*. New Brunswick, NJ: Rutgers University Press, 2019.

Pearson, Keith Ansell. *Viroid Life: Perspectives on Nietzsche and the Transhuman Condition*. New York: Routledge, 1997.

Peoples, Gabriel A. "The Forgotten Kelly Dodson: Viral Performance and the Interplay of Excess and Erasure." *Women and Performance: A Journal of Feminist Theory* 30, no. 2 (2020): 170–94. https://doi.org/10.1080/0740770X.2020.1869412.

Philip, Marlene NourbeSe. "Dis Place: The Space Between." In *Feminist Measures: Soundings in Poetry and Theory*, edited by Lynn Keller and Cristanne Miller, 287–316. Ann Arbor: University of Michigan Press, 1994.

Phillips, Yoh. "'It's Just a Family Record': The Making of SZA's 'Good Days' as Told by Its Producers." *Billboard*, February 4, 2021. https://www.billboard.com/articles/columns/hip-hop/9521355/sza-good-days-producers-interview/.

Pierre, Jemima. *The Predicament of Blackness: Postcolonial Ghana and the Politics of Race*. Chicago: University of Chicago Press, 2012.

Pinch, Trevor, and Frank Trocco. *Analog Days: The Invention and Impact of the Moog Synthesizer*. Cambridge, MA: Harvard University Press, 2004.

Plant, Sadie. *On the Mobile: The Effects of Mobile Telephones on Social and Individual Life*. Schaumburg, IL: Motorola, 2001. http://catalog.hathitrust.org/api /volumes/oclc/251509801.html.

Plant, Sadie. *Zeroes and Ones: Digital Women and the New Technoculture*. New York: Doubleday, 1997.

Powell, Elliott H. "Addict(ive) Sex: Toward an Intersectional Approach to Truth Hurts' 'Addictive' and Afro-South Asian Hip Hop and R&B." In *Popular Music and the Politics of Hope: Queer and Feminist Interventions*, edited by Susan Fast and Craig Jennex, 173–86. New York: Routledge, 2019.

Powell, Elliott H. "Funking Our Way to Freedom." GLQ: *A Journal of Lesbian and Gay Studies* 24, no. 2 (2018): 387–90.

Prince. Lovesexy Tour Concert Program. 1988. https://www.amazon.com/PRINCE -Lovesexy-Concert-Program-Programme/dp/B073Q9MGZG.

Proctor, Brittnay L. *Minnie Riperton's Come to My Garden*. New York: Bloomsbury Academic, 2022.

Proctor, Brittnay L. "'Shout It Out': Patrice Rushen as Polyphonist and the Sounding of Black Women's Affectability and Genius." *Journal of Popular Music Studies* 29, no. 4 (2017): 1–11.

Radano, Ronald. "Denoting Difference: The Writing of Slave Spirituals." *Critical Inquiry* 22, no. 1 (1996): 506–44.

Radano, Ronald. *Lying Up a Nation: Race and Black Music*. Chicago: University of Chicago Press, 2003.

Ramsey, Guthrie P. *Race Music: Black Cultures from Bebop to Hip-Hop*. Berkeley: University of California Press, 2003.

Rayner, Ben. "Toronto's Somali Muslim R&B Singer Amaal on Embracing Songs about 'Sexuality and Intimacy.'" *Toronto Star*, July 19, 2019. https://www.thestar .com/entertainment/music/2019/07/19/torontos-somali-muslim-rb-singer -amaal-on-embracing-songs-about-sexuality-and-intimacy.html.

Reardon, Marguerite. "Americans Text More Than They Talk." CNET, September 22, 2008. https://www.cnet.com/tech/mobile/americans-text-more-than-they-talk/.

Reed, Ishmael. *Flight to Canada*. New York: Simon and Schuster, 1976.

Reynolds, Simon. "Feminine Pressure: 2-Step Garage (the Director's Cut, plus Footnotes)." *Energy Flash* (blog), January 10, 2009. http://energyflashbysimonreynolds .blogspot.com/2009/01/footnotes-to-feminine-pressure-2step.html.

Reynolds, Simon. *Rip It Up and Start Again: Postpunk, 1978–1984*. New York: Penguin, 2006.

Rheingold, Howard. *Smart Mobs: The Next Social Revolution*. New York: Basic Books, 2003.

Richardson, Jared. "Black Organs and Optics: Gazing at Viscera in the Work of Doreen Garner." *Women and Performance: A Journal of Feminist Theory* 27, no. 1 (2017): 81–95.

Richie, Beth. *Arrested Justice: Black Women, Violence, and America's Prison Nation*. New York: New York University Press, 2012.

Rimmer, Dave. *Like Punk Never Happened: Culture Club and the New Pop*. London: Faber and Faber, 1985.

Rimmer, Dave. *The Look: New Romantics*. London: Omnibus, 2003.

"Ringmasters Chart Debuts." *Billboard Magazine* (December 2006): 8.

Ritz, David. *Divided Soul: The Life of Marvin Gaye*. New York: McGraw-Hill, 1985.

Rodriguez, Krystal. "Ghost Voices: The Women of House Music." TIDAL *Magazine*, March 18, 2019. https://tidal.com/magazine/article/women-of-house -music/1–54410.

Rose, Tricia. *Black Noise: Rap Music and Black Culture in Contemporary America*. Hanover, NH: University Press of New England, 1994.

Royster, Francesca T. *Sounding Like a No-No: Queer Sounds and Eccentric Acts in the Post-soul Era*. Ann Arbor: University of Michigan Press, 2013.

Rüther, Tobias. *Heroes: David Bowie and Berlin*. London: Reaktion Books, 2014.

Rys, Dan. "Afrika Bambaataa Sexual Abuse Allegations: What's Been Said, Disputed and What's Next." *Billboard Magazine*, May 10, 2016. http://www.billboard.com/ articles/columns/hip-hop/7364592/afrika-bambaataa-abuse-allegations.

Sacks, Oliver. *Musicophilia: Tales of Music and the Brain*. Vintage, 2007.

Sage, Simon. "Study: BlackBerry Adds 15 Hours to Work Week." *Intomobile.com*, August 24, 2009. http://www.intomobile.com/2009/08/24/study-blackberry -adds-15-hours-to-work-week/.

Sanneh, Kelefa. "Responding to Rap, R&B Is Reborn." *New York Times*, April 8, 2001. https://www.nytimes.com/2001/04/08/arts/music-responding-to-rap-r-b -is-reborn.html.

Schiffer, Michael Brian. *The Portable Radio in American Life*. Tucson: University of Arizona Press, 1991.

Schröder, Matthias. *God Is a DJ: Gespräche mit Popmusikern über Religion*. Neukirchen-Vluyn, Germany: Aussaat Verlag, 2000.

Scott, David. "Preface: Is Postcolonial Art Contemporary?" *Small Axe: A Caribbean Journal of Criticism* 24, no. 1 (2020): vii–x.

Scott, David. "The Untimely Experience of the Contemporary." *Small Axe: A Caribbean Journal of Criticism* 24, no. 2 (2020): vii–x.

Seabrook, Thomas Jerome. *Bowie in Berlin: A New Career in a New Town*. London: Jawbone Press, 2008.

Sedgwick, Eve Kosofsky. *Between Men: English Literature and Male Homosocial Desire*. New York: Columbia University Press, 1985.

Seymour, Craig. *Luther: The Life and Longing of Luther Vandross*. New York: Harper Collins, 2004.

Seymour, Craig. "The Producers." *Vibe Magazine* (May 2001): 123.

Sharpe, Christina. *In the Wake: On Blackness and Being*. Durham, NC: Duke University Press, 2016.

Smith, Barbara, ed. *Home Girls: A Black Feminist Anthology*. Albany, NY: Kitchen Table—Women of Color Press, 1983.

Smith, Barbara. "Toward a Black Feminist Criticism." *The Radical Teacher*, no. 7 (1978): 20–27.

Smith, Danyel. *Shine Bright: A Very Personal History of Black Women in Pop*. New York: Random House, 2022.

Smythe, S. A. "What Is to Be Done? A Foreword, After." *Forum for Modern Language Studies* 57, no. 2 (2021): 264–67.

Sol, Misty. "Hidden Figure: A Meditation on Genius and the African Origin of Math." Philadelphia Printworks, February 26, 2017. https://philadelphiaprintworks .com/blogs/zine/hidden-figure-a-meditation-on-genius-and-the-african-origin-of -math.

Spillers, Hortense J. "'All the Things You Could Be by Now, If Sigmund Freud's Wife Was Your Mother': Psychoanalysis and Race." 1996. In *Black, White, and in Color: Essays on American Literature and Culture*, 376–427. Chicago: University of Chicago Press, 2003.

Spillers, Hortense J. "*The Crisis of the Negro Intellectual*: A Post-date." 1994. In *Black, White, and in Color: Essays on American Literature and Culture*, 428–70. Chicago: University of Chicago Press, 2003.

Spillers, Hortense J. "The Idea of Black Culture." *CR: The New Centennial Review* 6, no. 3 (2006): 7–28. https://doi.org/10.1353/ncr.2007.0022.

Spillers, Hortense J. "Mama's Baby, Papa's Maybe: An American Grammar Book." 1987. In *Black, White, and in Color: Essays on American Literature and Culture*, 203–29. Chicago: University of Chicago Press, 2003.

Spillers, Hortense J., Saidiya Hartman, Farah Jasmine Griffin, Shelly Eversley, and Jennifer L. Morgan. "'Whatcha Gonna Do?': Revisiting 'Mama's Baby, Papa's Maybe: An American Grammar Book': A Conversation with Hortense Spillers, Saidiya Hartman, Farah Jasmine Griffin, Shelly Eversley, and Jennifer L. Morgan." *Women's Studies Quarterly* 35, nos. 1–2 (2007): 299–309.

Spivak, Gayatri. *Outside in the Teaching Machine*. New York: Routledge, 1993.

Stadler, Gustavus, ed. "The Politics of Recorded Sound." Special issue, *Social Text* 28, no. 1 (102) (2010): 87.

Starling, Lakin. "Kelela Is Ready for You Now." *The FADER*, October 10, 2017. http:// www.thefader.com/2017/10/03/kelela-cover-story-take-me-apart-interview.

Steenson, Molly, and Jonathan Donner. "Beyond the Personal and Private: Modes of Mobile Phone Sharing in Urban India." In *The Reconstruction of Space and Time: Mobile Communication Practices*, edited by Rich Ling and Scott W. Campbell, 231–50. New Brunswick, NJ: Transaction, 2009.

Stephens, Michelle Ann. "Disarticulating Black Internationalisms: West Indian Radicals and the Practice of Diaspora." *Small Axe: A Caribbean Journal of Criticism* 9, no. 17 (2005): 100–111.

Tagliamonte, Sali, and Derek Denis. "Linguistic Ruin? Lol! Instant Messaging and Teen Language." *American Speech* 83, no. 1 (2008): 3–34.

Tal, Kali. "Duppies in the Machine, or, 'Anybody Know Where I Can Buy a Copy of the UPNORTH-OUTWEST GEECHEE JIBARA QUIK MAGIC TRANCE MANUAL FOR TECHNOLOGICALLY STRESSED THIRD WORLD PEOPLE?'" Kali Tal, June 30, 1998. https://www.kalital.com/Texts/Articles/Duppies.html.

Tal, Kali. "The Unbearable Whiteness of Being: African American Critical Theory and Cyberculture." *WIRED Magazine*, October 1996, 36–52.

Taussig, Michael. *Mimesis and Alterity: A Particular History of the Senses*. New York: Routledge, 1993.

Taylor, Jodi. "Amaal Nuux Is the Toronto R&B Artist You Need to Know." *Coveteur: Inside Closets, Fashion, Beauty, Health, and Travel*, July 12, 2019. https://coveteur.com/2019/07/12/amaal-nuux-talks-new-ep-black-dove/.

Thomas, Sheree, ed. *Dark Matter: A Century of Speculative Fiction from the African Diaspora*. New York: Warner Books, 2000.

Towns, Armond R. *On Black Media Philosophy*. Oakland: University of California Press, 2022.

Townsend, Corey. "SZA Sang in Italicized Times New Roman, While Ella Mai Made Thugs Sway at 2018's BET Experience." *The Root*, June 23, 2018. https://www.theroot.com/sza-sang-in-italicized-times-new-romans-while-ella-mai-1827075899.

Tyrangiel, Josh. "Auto-Tune: Why Pop Music Sounds Perfect." *Time*, February 5, 2009. http://www.time.com/time/magazine/article/0,9171,1877372,00.html.

Ulaby, Neda. "OMG: IM Slang Is Invading Everyday English." *NPR*, February 18, 2006. http://www.npr.org/templates/story/story.php?storyId=5221618.

Urry, John. *Mobilities*. Malden, MA: Polity, 2007.

Valdés, Vanessa K. "The Afterlives of Arturo Alfonso Schomburg." *Small Axe: A Caribbean Journal of Criticism* 24, no. 1 (2020): 142–51.

Veal, Michael E. *Dub: Soundscapes and Shattered Songs in Jamaican Reggae*. Middletown, CT: Wesleyan University Press, 2007.

"Vocoder." Accessed June 19, 2001. http://www.Riteh.hr/~markb/who/jmbg/vocoders/vocoder.htm.

Vuolo, Mike. "What Happens When a Language Has No Numbers?" *Slate*, October 16, 2013. http://www.slate.com/blogs/lexicon_valley/2013/10/16/piraha_cognitive_anumeracy_in_a_language_without_numbers.html.

Walcott, Rinaldo. "Black Men in Frocks: Sexing Race in a Gay Ghetto (Toronto)." In *Claiming Space: Racialization in Canadian Cities*, edited by Cheryl Teelucksingh, 121–34. Waterloo, ON: Wilfred Laurier University Press, 2006.

Waligora-Davis, Nicole. *Sanctuary: African Americans and Empire*. New York: Oxford University Press, 2011.

Walters, Barry. "The Revolution Will Be Harmonized." *Out Magazine*, April 2009. http://www.out.com/entertainment/2009/04/16/revolution-will-be-harmonized.

Ward, Brian. *Just My Soul Responding: Rhythm and Blues, Black Consciousness, and Race Relations*. Berkeley: University of California Press, 1998.

Watkins, S. Craig. *The Young and the Digital: What the Migration to Social-Network Sites, Games, and Anytime, Anywhere Media Means for Our Future*. Boston: Beacon, 2009.

Weheliye, Alexander G. "Diagrammatics as Physiognomy: W. E. B. Du Bois's Graphic Modernities." *CR: The New Centennial Review* 15, no. 2 (2015): 23–58.

Weheliye, Alexander G. *Habeas Viscus: Racializing Assemblages, Biopolitics, and Black Feminist Theories of the Human*. Durham, NC: Duke University Press, 2014.

Weheliye, Alexander G. "'Ich will mich nicht ausgrenzen': Alexander G. Weheliye im Gespräch mit dem HipHop-Pionier Moses Pelham." Heinrich Böll Stiftung:

Migration—Integration—Diversity, 2005. http://www.migration-boell.de/ (accessed July 11, 2009).

Weheliye, Alexander G. "In the Mix: Hearing the Souls of Black Folks." *Amerikastudien/American Studies* 45, no. 4 (2000): 535–54.

Weheliye, Alexander G. "Introduction: Black Studies and Black Life." In "States of Black Studies." Special issue, *Black Scholar* 44, no. 2 (Summer 2014): 5–10.

Weheliye, Alexander G. "Keepin' It (Un)Real: Perusing the Boundaries of Hip-Hop Culture." *CR: The New Centennial Review* 1, no. 2 (2001): 287–306.

Weheliye, Alexander G. *Phonographies: Grooves in Sonic Afro-Modernity*. Durham, NC: Duke University Press, 2005.

Weidman, Amanda J. *Singing the Classical, Voicing the Modern: The Postcolonial Politics of Music in South India*. Durham, NC: Duke University Press, 2006.

Wells-Barnett, Ida B. *Crusade for Justice: The Autobiography of Ida B. Wells*. Chicago: University of Chicago Press, 1972.

Werner, Craig Hansen. *A Change Is Gonna Come: Music, Race, and the Soul of America*. Ann Arbor: University of Michigan Press, 2006.

Werner, Kurt James, Jonathan S. Abel, and Julius O. Smith III. "A Physically-Informed, Circuit-Bendable, Digital Model of the Roland TR-808 Bass Drum Circuit." In *Proceedings of the 17th International Conference on Digital Audio Effects, Erlangen, Germany, September 1–5, 2014*, 1–8. Erlangen: International Audio Laboratories Erlangen, 2014.

White, Simone. *Dear Angel of Death*. New York: Ugly Duckling Presse, 2018.

Wilderson, Frank B., III. "The Vengeance of Vertigo: Aphasia and Abjection in the Political Trials of Black Insurgents." *InTensions* 5 (2011): 1–41. https://intensions.journals.yorku.ca/index.php/intensions/article/view/37360/1817.

Winkler, Thomas. "Deutscher Pop entdeckt religiöse Inhalte." Goethe Institute, October 2003. http://www.goethe.de/ges/rel/thm/de61704.htm (accessed April 23, 2005).

Wohlfahrtsausschüsse, ed. *Etwas besseres als die Nation: Materialien zur Abwehr des gegenrevolutionären Übels*. Berlin: Edition ID-Archiv, 1994.

"Wolfgang von Kempelen's and Subsequent Speaking Machines." Accessed February 19, 2001. http://www.ling.su.se/ staff/hartmut/kemplne.htm.

Wollrad, Eske. *Weißsein im Widerspruch: Feministische Perspektiven auf Rassismus, Kultur und Religion*. Bremen, Germany: Ulrike Helmer, 2005.

Womack, Autumn. *The Matter of Black Living: The Aesthetic Experiment of Racial Data, 1880–1930*. Chicago: University of Chicago Press, 2022.

Woods, Scott. "Will You Scrub Me Tomorrow." *Village Voice*, December 12, 2000. https://www.villagevoice.com/2000/12/12/will-you-scrub-me-tomorrow/.

Wortham, Jenna. "Mobile Internet Use Shrinks Digital Divide." *Bits* (blog), *New York Times*, July 22, 2009. http://bits.blogs.nytimes.com/2009/07/22/mobile-internet-use-shrinks-digital-divide/.

Wynter, Sylvia. "Africa, the West and the Analogy of Culture: The Cinematic Text after Man." In *Symbolic Narratives/African Cinema: Audiences, Theory and the Moving Image*, edited by June Givanni, 25–76. London: BFI, 2000.

Wynter, Sylvia. "Beyond the Word of Man: Glissant and the New Discourse of the Antilles." *World Literature Today* 63, no. 4 (1989): 637–48. https://doi.org/10.2307/40145557.

Wynter, Sylvia. "Black Metamorphosis: New Natives in a New World." Unpublished manuscript. 1970.

Wynter, Sylvia. "Columbus, the Ocean Blue, and Fables That Stir the Mind: To Reinvent the Study of Letters." In *Poetics of the Americas: Race, Founding, and Textuality*, edited by Bianard Cowan and Jefferson Humphries, 141–202. Baton Rouge: Louisiana State University Press, 1997.

Wynter, Sylvia. "'Genital Mutilation' or 'Symbolic Birth?' Female Circumcision, Lost Origins, and the Aculturalism of Feminist/Western Thought." *Case Western Reserve Law Review* 47, no. 2 (1997): 501–52.

Wynter, Sylvia. "Human Being as Noun? Or *Being Human* as Praxis: Towards the Autopoetic Turn/Overturn: A Manifesto." 2007. http://readingfanon.blogspot.com/2014/10/sylvia-wynter-human-being-as-noun-or.html.

Wynter, Sylvia. "On Disenchanting Discourse: 'Minority' Literary Criticism and Beyond." In *The Nature and Context of Minority Discourse*, edited by Abdul JanMohamed and David Lloyd, 432–69. New York: Oxford University Press, 1990.

Wynter, Sylvia. "On How We Mistook the Map for the Territory and Reimprisoned Ourselves in Our Unbearable Wrongness of Being, of Désêtre: Black Studies toward the Human Project." In *Not Only the Master's Tools: African-American Studies in Theory and Practice*, edited by Lewis Ricardo Gordon and Jane Anna Gordon, 107–69. Boulder, CO: Paradigm, 2006.

Wynter, Sylvia. "The Pope Must Have Been Drunk, The King of Castile a Madman: Culture as Actuality, and the Caribbean Rethinking Modernity." In *The Reordering of Culture: Latin America, the Caribbean and Canada in the Hood*, edited by Alvina Ruprecht and Cecilia Taiana, 17–41. Montreal: McGill-Queen's Press, 1995.

Wynter, Sylvia. "The Re-enchantment of Humanism: An Interview with Sylvia Wynter." Interview by David Scott. *Small Axe: A Caribbean Journal of Criticism* 4, no. 2 (2000): 119–207.

Wynter, Sylvia. "Rethinking 'Aesthetics': Notes Towards a Deciphering Practice." *Ex-Iles: Essays on Caribbean Cinema*, edited by Mbye B. Cham, 237–79. Trenton, NJ: Africa World Press, 1992

Wynter, Sylvia. "Towards the Sociogenic Principle: Fanon, Identity, the Puzzle of Conscious Experience, and What It Is Like to Be 'Black.'" In *National Identities and Sociopolitical Changes in Latin America*, edited by Mercedes F. Durán-Cogan and Antonio Gómez-Moriana, 30–66. New York: Routledge, 2001.

Wynter, Sylvia. "Unsettling the Coloniality of Being/Power/Truth/Freedom: Towards the Human, after Man, Its Overrepresentation—an Argument." CR: *The New Centennial Review* 3, no. 3 (2003): 257–337.

Wynter, Sylvia, and Katherine McKittrick. "Unparalleled Catastrophe for Our Species? Or, to Give Humanness a Different Future: Conversations." In *Sylvia Wynter: On Being Human as Praxis*, edited by Katherine McKittrick, 9–89. Durham, NC: Duke University Press, 2015.

Young, Hershini Bhana. *Illegible Will: Coercive Spectacles of Labor in South Africa and the Diaspora*. Durham, NC: Duke University Press, 2017.

Ziegbe, Mawuse. "Drake Reveals Songwriting Process in 'Better Than Good Enough' Documentary." *MTV*, June 21, 2010. http://www.mtv.com/news/articles/1642017/20100621/drake.jhtml (accessed December 8, 2011).

Page locators in *italics* indicate figures.

period, 131; denial of everyday institutional racism, 130–32; lack of Black
culture in 1980s, 162–63; neo-Nazis, 107,
130–31; political parties' stance toward
pogroms, 123–24; post–World War II
narratives, 122; reunification, 121–22, 133;
reunification, violence against nonwhite
people in era of, 18, 122–23, 129–30; Third
Reich, 102, 106–7; Turkish Germans,
110n18; university system, 109–10n16, 133;
Volk, and Nazism, 106–7. *See also* Berlin
Ghansah, Rachel Kaadzi, 220
GI discos, 132–33
Gilbert, Jeremy, 63, 64, 81–82
Gilroy, Paul, 29, 59n60, 102
Ginuwine, 56, 61, 84–85
Girlhood (Bande de filles) (film), 220–21
Gladys Knight & the Pips, 3n6, 147n15
glam rock, 142
Glashaus, 110–20
Glissant, Édouard, 84, 96, 215
Glori, Lori, 138
Glover, Cat, 148
Goggin, Gerard, 92n45
Goh, Annie, 121–34
"Good Days" (SZA), 13
Gopinath, Sumanth, 86n26
Gouché, Tiffany, 190
Gracyk, Theodore, 56
grand piano, transformation of, 120
Green, Nicola, 95
Griffin, Farah, 181–82
Guattari, Félix, 69–71
Gucci Mane, 88

Haas, Martin, 110
*Habeas Viscus: Racializing Assemblages,
Biopolitics, and Black Feminist Theories
of the Human* (Weheliye), 24–25, 35, 36,
222, 226
Hall, Stuart, 24n1, 27
Hanchard, Michael, 59n60
Hancock, Herbie, 64, 64n74
Haraway, Donna, 45n19, 54n47
Hardt, Michael, 105n7
Hardy, Ron, 138
Harlem, 145
"harmonic bed," 56n52, 239

Harriet's Apothecary (Brooklyn), 196
Hartman, Saidiya, 7–8, 11, 21, 44, 208,
237–43; chorinal modalities in, 238–41
Haughton, Aaliyah Dana. *See* Aaliyah
Hayles, N. Katherine, 38–47, 50–51, 60,
61, 73–74
Head On (Super_Collider), 64n74
healing, 196–97; neurosystem, music's effect
on, 212–15
heartbreak: armor for, 234–35; of Black
life, 20–21; and Black livingness, 214–15,
220–21; Blackness as undone and unfinished, 224–25; broken heart syndrome,
233, 236; disability/disorder, mobilized to
understand race, 213–14n36; and emulation, 202–3; forgetting/excusing/silencing
of violent incidents, 205, 209, 215–16,
220; heart////break, 20–22, 226, 233–35;
heartburn, 234; of interpersonal violence,
208–9, 216–21; intonation, 227–28;
responses and alternatives to, 209–10;
tragedies, 207; trauma of sexual violence,
204–8; and ungendering, 206, 209, 220,
227n66, 234. *See also* affective labor of
BlackFem voices; trauma
Hegemann, Dimitri, 127
hegemonic western formations, 33,
38, 42–43
hegemony, attributed to African America,
103n2, 104
Henriques, Julian, 23, 25
Herero and Nama peoples, 131
"Hero" (Gladys Knight & the Pips), 3n6
Hershey, Barbara, 3
"Hey Kandi" (Kandi), 82–83
Hill, Lauryn, 58n58
Hilton, Paris, 92n44, 92n45
hip-hop, 4; Afro-German, 107–9, 110n18,
112–13; choreographing voices as fundamental to, 153; engulfment of R&B by,
164–65, 182–83, 189; female masculinity
look, 109; gangsta rap, 163; gendered
voices in, 79–80, 173, 180, 182–83; guest
raps, 57, 58n57; hook singers, 58n57, 165,
183, 207; influence on instrumental and
studio production, and singing styles,
57–58; as "masculine" genre, 79, 182;
mumble rapper generation, 163;